CHURCH AND STATE IN THE CITY

CHURCH AND STATE IN THE CITY

*Catholics and Politics
in Twentieth-Century San Francisco*

William Issel

TEMPLE UNIVERSITY PRESS
Philadelphia

TEMPLE UNIVERSITY PRESS
Philadelphia, Pennsylvania 19122
www.temple.edu/tempress

Publication of this volume was aided by grants from the History Department of San Francisco State University and the Friends of the Archives of the Archdiocese of San Francisco.

Library of Congress Cataloging-in-Publication Data

Issel, William.
    Church and state in the city : Catholics and politics in twentieth-century San Francisco / William Issel.
        p.   cm. — (Urban life, landscape, and policy)
    Includes bibliographical references and index.
    ISBN 978-1-4399-0991-1 (cloth : alk. paper)
    ISBN 978-1-4399-0992-8 (paper : alk. paper)
    ISBN 978-1-4399-0993-5 (ebook)
    1. Catholics—Political activity—California—San Francisco—History—20th century.
2. Church and state—California—San Francisco—History—20th century.   3. Religious pluralism—California—San Francisco—History—20th century.   4. Public interest—California—San Francisco—History—20th century.   5. Political culture—California—San Francisco—History—20th century.   6. San Francisco (Calif.)—Politics and government—20th century.   7. San Francisco (Calif.)—Religious life and customs.
8. San Francisco (Calif.)—Social conditions—20th century.   9. San Francisco (Calif.)—Social policy.   I. Title.

    F869.S39C347 2013
    306.209794'61—dc23

                                                            2012015150

♾ The paper used in this publication meets the requirements of the American National Standard for Information Sciences—Permanence of Paper for Printed Library Materials, ANSI Z39.48-1992

Printed in the United States of America

2 4 6 8 9 7 5 3 1

Contents

Illustrations follow page 118

ACKNOWLEDGMENTS

A mong the many people I want to thank, David Selvin and Robert W. Cherny stand out. On a blustery February day in 1993, I drove across the bridge from San Francisco to the Berkeley hills for an interview with David Selvin, a retired labor journalist and historian. I had recently co-written a book with Cherny about politics, power, and urban development in San Francisco from the Civil War to 1932 and had started oral history interviews for a sequel that would take the story up to the 1990s. Selvin had been an eyewitness to the San Francisco general strike in 1934 and was writing his book *A Terrible Anger,* a work that many today consider to be the single best treatment of the topic.* I asked him to give me his recollections of the role of the various nongovernmental interest groups during the strike. He began his reply by saying that it would be difficult to exaggerate the importance of the role played by the Catholic Church. He claimed that this was generally true in San Francisco throughout the first half of the twentieth century. In early 1941, Selvin went to work for the anti–Nazi Bund Jewish Survey Committee; his charge was to set up a new civil rights group in the city, the Bay Area Council against Discrimination. When he presented his outline proposal for the project to his boss, Eugene Block, Block read it over and asked, "Have you talked to Franklin Street about this?" It turns out that this particular phrase, with its reference to the chancery office located behind St. Mary's Cathedral, was widely used at the time by San Franciscans doing work related to social and economic policy. Given the

---

*David F. Selvin, *A Terrible Anger: The 1934 Waterfront and General Strikes in San Francisco* (Detroit: Wayne State University Press, 1996).

influence and power of the church in the city, they wanted to get the nod from "Franklin Street" before going public with their projects.

My interview with Selvin and subsequent discussions with Cherny convinced me that the existing narrative of San Francisco history required a thorough reconsideration. Thanks to the generous cooperation of Jeffrey M. Burns, director of the Chancery Archives of the Archdiocese of San Francisco, I expanded my previous research into the role of Catholics in the labor movement and immersed myself in the archival records of the church and other institutions. I discovered that the Catholic Church and Catholic laypeople—in complex relations with business, labor, and city officials—had played key roles in shaping politics and public policy. This book is the product of that research. It describes how, from the early 1890s through the 1970s, Catholic faith–based politics shaped the language and the outcome of debates over how to define the common good and how to implement the public interest in San Francisco.

In addition to my debt to Selvin and Cherny for their quintessential contributions to this book, I am indebted to the many scholars who have discussed San Francisco politics with me, graciously shared information, replied to queries, and critiqued my research on San Francisco since I presented my paper on Catholic critics of capitalism at the Urban Change and Conflict conference organized by the University of London's Centre for Environmental Studies in 1977. Since then, a growing number of urban studies scholars have addressed the role of Catholics and other religious communities in the political cultures of American cities. Their work has contributed to an urban studies literature that is informed by contemporary thinking about the relationship between urban politics and the American constitutional order, as well as grounded in evidence about religion, class dynamics, ethno-racial differences, gender, and sexuality. The extensive references to these scholars in my endnotes makes clear my indebtedness to the rich literature they have produced and that has helped to clarify my thinking about San Francisco and its place in the national urban community.

Special thanks go to Carl Abbott, Christopher Agee, Edward Dyanand Asregadoo, Steven Avella, Martin Benjamin, Barbara Berglund, Shana Bernstein, Allan Bérubé, Rodger Birt, Graeme Bowman, Gray Brechin, Albert S. Broussard, Kenneth Burt, Andrew Canepa, Rose Marie Cleese, Catherine Collomp, Carlos B. Cordova, Carol Cuenod, Peter D'Agostino, Wilhelm Damberg, David Dalin, Philip J. Davies, Mike Davis, Richard DeLeon, John P. Diggins, Roy Domenico, Philip J. Dreyfus, Philip J. Ethington, Robert A. Fung, Daniel P. Gonzales, Archie Green, Richard Gribble, Chester Hartman, Michael J. Heale, Ava Kahn, Michael Kazin, Anne Klejment, Him Mark Lai, Kevin Leonard, Roger W. Lotchin, Stefano Luconi, Glenna Matthews, Michael McCone, Martin

Meeker, Eric Monkkonen, Kevin J. Mullen, Meredith Akemi Oda, Clay Mansfield O'Dell, Eva Jefferson Paterson, Matteo Pretelli, Jerry Roberts, Hadley R. Roff, Lisa Rubens, Gail Rubin, Reuel Schiller, Harvey Schwartz, Stephen Schwartz, Jules Tygiel, Richard Walker, Charles Wollenberg, and Alexander von Hoffman. I also thank Martin Benjamin, Jeffrey M. Burns, Robert W. Cherny, Bertram M. Gordon, Mary Claire Heffron, James Grusky Issel, Marjorie P. Lasky, Zane L. Miller, Zeese Papanikolas, David Stradling, and the two anonymous readers for Temple University Press for reading and commenting on all or parts of the manuscript.

I am also indebted to San Francisco State University, both for its support of my research and for the opportunity it provided to work with stimulating colleagues and students. There are too many students whose interest, questions, and research papers have made my studies of San Francisco a genuinely collaborative effort for me to thank all of them by name, but several deserve special thanks for assisting in the research and writing of this book and for giving me permission to incorporate some of their work into the book. Marie Bolton, James Collins, Benjamin R. Crittenden, Michael Kelly, George Malachowski, Giovanna Palombo, John J. Rosen, Max Silverman, Rachel Tamar Van, and Mary Anne Wold helped with archival research and interviews. Chapter 11 contains material from John Rosen's extraordinary research reports on the mayoral elections of 1967 and 1971; he and Stuart McElderry also contributed to Chapter 9. Chapter 8 contains material researched by John Baranski, Eric Fure-Slocum, and Max Silverman for their master's theses and doctoral dissertations. Chapter 10 contains material researched by Robert Vallas.

This book could not have been written without the assistance of Jeffrey M. Burns, director of the Chancery Archives of the Archdiocese of San Francisco; Susan Goldstein, Pat Akre, Christina Moretta, and their colleagues at the San Francisco History Center of the San Francisco Public Library; Susan Sherwood and Catherine Powell of the Northern California Labor Archives and Research Center at San Francisco State University; Helene Whitson, special collections director at San Francisco State University; and Linda Wobbe, archivist of the College of St. Mary's of California. Thanks are also due to the librarians and staff of the Amistad Research Center at Tulane University; the Moorland-Spingarn Research Center, Howard University, Washington, D.C.; the Anne Rand Research Library of the International Longshore and Warehouse Union; the Baker Library of the Harvard Business School; the Bancroft Library and the Doe Library at the University of California, Berkeley; the California State Archives; the Library of Congress; the National Archives in San Bruno, California, Suitland, Maryland, and Washington, D.C.; and the Southern California Library for Social Studies and Research.

I also thank Zane Miller for suggesting that I consider publishing my book in his Temple University Press series and acknowledge the friendly and professional assistance of the outstanding Temple team: Mick Gusinde-Duffy, Charles Ault, Lynne Frost, Susan Deeks, and Gary Kramer; in addition, I thank indexer Linda Hallinger. Finally, I thank my wife, Dr. Mary Claire Heffron, and my children and grandchildren for their love and support.

Since I began archival research and interviews for this book more than two decades ago, I have published some of my research findings in articles and other books: "'Citizens outside the Government': Business and Urban Policy in San Francisco and Los Angeles, 1890–1932" *Pacific Historical Review* 57 (May 1988): 117–145; "Business Power and Political Culture in San Francisco, 1900–1940," *Journal of Urban History* 16 (November 1989): 52–77; "'Land Values, Human Values, and the Preservation of the City's Treasured Appearance': Environmentalism, Politics, and the San Francisco Freeway Revolt," *Pacific Historical Review* 68 (November 1999): 611–646; "New Deal and Wartime Origins of San Francisco's Postwar Political Culture: The Case of Growth Politics and Policy," in *The Way We Really Were: The Golden State in the Second Great War,* edited by Roger W. Lotchin (Urbana: University of Illinois Press, 2000), 68–92; "Jews and Catholics against Prejudice," in *California Jews,* edited by Ava F. Kahn and Marc Dollinger (Hanover, N.H.: Brandeis University Press, 2003), 123–134; "'The Catholic Internationale': Mayor Joseph Alioto's Urban Liberalism and San Francisco Catholicism," *U.S. Catholic Historian* 22 (Spring 2004): 99–120; "Catholics and the Campaign for Racial Justice in San Francisco from Pearl Harbor to Proposition 14," *American Catholic Studies* 119 (Fall 2008): 21–43; "Faith-Based Activism in American Cities: The Case of the San Francisco Catholic Action Cadre," *Journal of Church and State* 50 (Summer 2008): 519–540; and *"For Both Cross and Flag": Catholic Action, Anti-Catholicism, and National Security Politics in World War II San Francisco* (Philadelphia: Temple University Press, 2010). I thank the publishers of these works for permission to reprint some material from them, as well as the editors and readers for comments on the original manuscripts. Responsibility for any errors or omissions that may have escaped my attention is mine alone.

INTRODUCTION

City of Contests

Many myths populate the conventional wisdom about American cities, but one of the most tenacious is the notion that San Francisco has always been the nation's "Left Coast" city: a decidedly un-American carnival of secular humanism featuring warring tribes of radicals thumbing their noses at tradition and authority while onlookers adopt a devil-may-care tolerance for whomever turns up no matter what they do. The myth developed from a kernel of truth, the reality that from Gold Rush days, to the Dot Com Boom, to the Great Recession, San Francisco has attracted more than its share of rebels and bohemians whose adventures and escapades fit the mythic profile. But to imagine the San Francisco story as primarily a narrative of the libertine lifestyles and noisy antics of its more rebellious residents writ large is to lose sight of the city's actual history: one that is both more complicated and closer to the American mainstream. Perhaps the most glaring omission in the construct of mythical San Francisco is its erasure of religion in the city's history, including hard fought contests among faith-based religious reformers, libertarian-oriented capitalists, and secular socialists and communists that have marked the city's public life.

The streets of twentieth-century San Francisco rang with the sound of these contests. Residents clashed over who should be included in the definition of "the public," which members of the public should have a say in determining the priorities of life in the city, and how the common good, the public interest, should be defined and implemented. The city's history has featured conservative Christians as well as irreligious radicals, laissez-faire capitalists as well as revolutionary socialists, white supremacists as well as racial liberals, not to mention those whose worldviews have defied simplistic labels. This latter group, for instance, includes the Roman Catholic nuns who were fierce critics of unfettered capitalism and fought for the rights of men and women in the workplace, while at the same time opposing feminism and birth control.

These contests have shaped the city's twentieth-century history and contributed to its contemporary reputation as a place where participation in the political process for defining the common good is open to all residents, irrespective of class, ethnicity, color, creed, gender, sexual orientation, or disability. The purpose of this book is to reconsider San Francisco history, over nearly a century, while taking into account the role of Catholic faith-based activism. The book develops a two-part argument. First, San Francisco politics beginning in the 1890s was directly influenced by the deliberate attempts of the Catholic Church and devout Catholic men and women to influence the terms of debate about the common good and to shape public policy according to their faith-based values. Second, Catholics found themselves in conflict with laissez-faire capitalists, secular liberals, and anti-Catholic socialists and communists. These secular aspirants for political influence were just as determined as their religious rivals to shape the city's public philosophy and its public policies. Despite their sometimes irreconcilable differences, laissez-faire capitalists, anticapitalist socialists and communists, and secular liberals envisioned the good society as one built on a foundation of individual rights and freedom of choice unencumbered by traditions of faith and clerical authority. This put them on a collision course with the church and with those politically active Catholics for whom God-given duties and obligations that individuals owed to one another should set limits to individual freedom and constrain the content of government policies in a city named for St. Francis.[1]

The contests that resulted from the competition among these rival constituencies were highly complex affairs; after all, the city housed others besides Catholics; Catholics did not think with one mind and behave as a political bloc; and religious faith did not always trump other sources of political thought and action among Catholics. The complexities only increased as the great events of the twentieth century impinged on the city, as its population increased in size and ethno-racial and cultural diversity, and as San Franciscans pursued their local political agendas in the context of national and international developments from the 1890s through the 1970s.[2] Like that of many American big cities in the twentieth century, especially major international port cities, San Francisco's experience was marked above all by social diversity and by robust social movements and efforts at political reform. San Francisco was not—no city can be said to be—typical, but its economic role as a regional, national, and international business center, its cultural role as a favored destination for migrants and immigrants, and its political role as a site for policy innovation all qualify it to be a significant, and distinctive, American study site.[3]

The roots of the long debate over defining the common good in San Francisco can be found in late-nineteenth-century contests between capital and labor, contests that also involved the Catholic Church and Catholic laypeople. A newly organized business front decided that business priorities were equivalent to the community interest and that capitalists were best equipped to shape the city's future. These determined businessmen found themselves in a struggle with residents, many of them inspired by Catholic social theory, who were sympathetic to the claims of white working-class men for equity in the workplace and equality in the councils of government. From 1901 to the 1930s, despite an aggressive anti-union movement and robust hostility to socialism and anarchism, sympathy for the rights of white working-class men attracted support among a broad spectrum of community leaders and ordinary voters. However, few challenged white supremacy and the restricted gender roles that limited women to the domestic realm and to public roles associated with the health, education, and welfare of children. During the New Deal years, from 1933 to roughly 1941, the city's culture and politics were invigorated by the reorientation of national discourse on behalf of expanded legal rights for organized labor and a by a distinctive local Catholic activism in public life. During World War II and into the Cold War years of the 1960s, a San Francisco version of mid-twentieth-century post–New Deal liberalism was challenged and then reformulated.

By the late 1960s, events and social changes external to the city and dramatic population changes during and after World War II, including a decline in the Catholic population of the city and changes in Catholicism itself, combined to cause a diminishing of the Catholic influence in San Francisco public life. A distinctive era of San Francisco history was coming to an end—an era that witnessed high degrees of influence of the Catholic notions that the common good derived from and must operate within the bounds of a God-given moral order, that individual rights must be balanced with duties and obligations given by Catholic tradition and values, and that local government should ensure that public policies are partial to and compatible with the specific content of Catholic Christian moral values. Since the 1960s, in San Francisco as in the United States generally, American political culture has increasingly privileged individual rights and freedom of choice unbounded by faith traditions, along with government neutrality vis-à-vis the values of particular religious moral traditions and the preferences of faith-based interest groups.[4]

My purpose in this book is to present an analytical narrative of a series of contests over defining the public interest that demonstrate the central role of Catholicism, in complex relations with capitalism and with other social and institutional interests, in shaping the city's public life. With regard to capitalism, San Francisco's experience provides a dramatic illustration of the assertion that "it is impossible to exaggerate the role of business in developing great cities in America."[5] Capitalists and business organizations found themselves embroiled in continual contests with the political left (including the Communist Party), organized labor, and the Catholic Church. Individual businessmen and business organizations were key players in the political processes used to initiate, implement, and monitor government policies; because city policy emerged from decisions of federal, state, and local governments, business concerned itself with all three levels of the political system. During the 1890s, businessmen created economic institutions designed to articulate their policy interests with efficiency and effectiveness. During the Progressive era and the 1920s, they used these new organizations, as well as political action groups and informal personal networks, to create governing coalitions and guide day-to-day urban decision making in ways that would accommodate business priorities. Businessmen and their organizations, often in league with members of the professions, were also key players in the origin and development of city planning.[6]

Never a monolithic political bloc, businessmen and their organizations bargained and competed with rivals while accommodating to internal differences. They rose above these divisions often enough to create an effective partnership with public officials. They served in elected and appointed positions themselves, and they worked as unofficial advisers to municipal officeholders; they played quasi-public roles in the routine operation of municipal agencies; they assisted research bureaus in contract work with city governments; and they assumed leadership roles in the establishment and management of municipal reform organizations and of large-scale urban infrastructure projects. Divisions among businessmen and their need to work in ways that required cooperation and compromise did not stand in the way of political success, and after World War II the political process became exceedingly complicated due to the rising power of organized labor. But no other community interest groups rivaled business in its ability to influence the debate about the public interest during the first half of the twentieth century, and business power remained formidable thereafter.

The power, privilege, and prestige of business did not mean that religion, specifically Catholicism, existed only on the margins. In San Francisco and nationwide, the relationship between religion and politics during the nineteenth century and the first half of the twentieth century was significantly different from today. It is, of course, true that the concept of separation of church and state has been a central principle of American life since the Bill of Rights became part of the U.S. Constitution in 1791. Congress could not make Catholicism or any other religion the official faith of the country, nor could the federal government interfere with individual decisions about what faith to practice (or not). But before the 1940s, constitutional interpretation and federal policy allowed religious activists in cities and states considerable latitude when it came to bringing their faith-based values into the public sphere where government policy was debated.[7] The large number of Catholics in the San Francisco population, where they predominated in the blue-collar workforce and in business, government, and the professions, was a distinctive feature of San Francisco society. Not all Catholics practiced their religion, but a sizeable number of devout Catholics brought their faith-based convictions to bear in the public realm, as well as in their private lives, in ways that marked the city's political culture as it developed after the 1890s. Catholic San Franciscans believed that it would be a hollow democracy indeed if antireligious and non-religious people were allowed to shape the public interest according to their beliefs, but Catholics were prohibited from doing so.[8]

Retelling the story of twentieth-century San Francisco with Catholicism at the center—in its relationships with business, labor, other interests groups, and city government—benefits the ongoing project among historians of urban America that aims to make the story of our big cities more evidence-based, more attentive to social diversity, and hence more sophisticated.[9] It has the added advantage of fostering serious consideration of one of the most important transnational challengers of both capitalism and Catholicism during the twentieth century: socialism, especially the Communist Party variant. Socialism played an important role in urban politics beginning in the 1880s. The Communist Party aspired to be a force in the nation's cultural and political life starting in the 1920s, the decade in which the status and power of organized business reached a new high, and developed even further during the 1930s, when the reputation of business sank to a new low but the political power of the Catholic Church grew to its highest point thus far.[10] Contests to define the public interest took on a distinctive character in San Francisco because of the particular way that the local capitalist, Catholic, secular liberal, and socialist and communist struggles over power, privilege, and prestige were fought out, in the context of national and international events, from the 1890s to the end of the 1970s.

Church and State in the City begins in the 1890s and continues with chapters arranged generally in chronological order, but it is meant to be neither a decade-by-decade chronicle nor a comprehensive political history of the city. The purpose is to stimulate debate about the contours of San Francisco history and to contribute to rethinking the role of religion in American urban history, not to present a definitive account. The book, moreover, is frankly revisionist in challenging the notion that the history of urban politics and policy can be best understood as the unfolding of a coherent, progressive, secular modernization of urban political culture. Each chapter explores particular contests, selected because of their importance to city residents at specific moments in urban political development, the analysis of which provides insight into the complex and dynamic combination of change and continuity that marked the city's history at every point of the twentieth century. The individual chapters have also been written so that readers will find each a coherent stand-alone historical analysis. Readers who wish a sense of the cumulative impact of the events included in the book will want to read it from beginning to end. Taken as a whole, the book offers a new interpretation, or reconsideration, of San Francisco's history during the twentieth century.

1

"THE TRUE INTERESTS OF A CITY"

The Public Interest in a Divided City

On January 7, 1897, James Duval Phelan, the newly inaugurated mayor of San Francisco, walked into the office of the Merchants Association and asked its secretary "to prepare a list of names from which the Committee of 100 might be selected."[1] Three days before his visit, Phelan had promised to bring the city into the twentieth century with "a more scientific and satisfactory charter"—a new framework for municipal government that would be drafted by a committee of citizen volunteers and ratified by the electorate. Phelan turned to the Merchants Association for volunteers because he believed its members were especially qualified to set the future priorities and policies for the eighth-largest city in the nation. Phelan and his like-minded colleagues regarded themselves as prophets of modernity and progress and referred to their proposals as "Progressive."[2]

The political process that eventually produced a new city charter in 1898 began a war of words as San Franciscans involved themselves in the national debate over the proper role of business and labor in community affairs, as well as in a series of conflicts over the meaning of social categories of gender, ethnicity, race, and religion, in defining the public interest. The contests between business and several competing claimants seeking to represent labor would especially define the city's public life during this period. American Federation of Labor (AFL) unionists demanded a voice in public policy as well as in job-related matters; socialists and other leftists (many of whom belonged to AFL unions) claimed they best represented the community and pushed for fundamental changes in the economy and institutions of government. Women's rights advocates rejected the cultural assumption of women's inferiority, and supporters of women's suffrage demanded the right to vote and hold public office. Once they achieved that right, they challenged the tradition that restricted women's public roles to health care, education, and welfare. Catholic Church clerics and lay Catholic activists demanded a role for their faith-based moral principles in the setting of San Francisco's priorities. Numerous Catholic businessmen, salaried professionals, and wage workers took the church's emerging doctrines on social justice to heart and rejected both revolutionary socialism and laissez-faire capitalism. These Catholic activists insisted on a moral economy and worked to limit unilateral business power.[3]

Catholic support for economic reform did not translate into advocacy of social and cultural reform. Catholics, with few exceptions, also defended traditional hierarchical racialist definitions of gender, family, and community, thereby complicating the picture considerably. Among the Irish, German, and Italian Catholic residents, most men (and women) accepted ethno-religious traditions that specified inequality between the sexes as a feature of a God-given natural order that did not detract from the dignity and worth of women.[4] These traditionalist opponents of feminist conceptions of women's rights also supported policies to maintain white supremacy. Phelan, for instance, was a leader in campaign to keep out Chinese, Japanese, and other immigrants from Asia.[5]

A banker and cosmopolitan connoisseur of the arts, Phelan brought a genuine sense of noblesse oblige to his public activities as mayor, charter reformer, anticorruption crusader, U.S. senator, and cultural entrepreneur. He aspired to oversee San Francisco's transformation into "The New San Francisco," a Pacific Coast metropolis famous as a world-class destination.[6] And like other business owners in the city who sought to create a "reawakening of the independent spirit of Pioneer days," Phelan believed that civic wisdom in a democracy was more likely to be found among the male offspring of cultured capitalists of European descent than among other city residents, especially those from non-European backgrounds, who toiled for wages or filled their hours with domestic work. His leading role in organizing the Merchants Association in 1894 put Phelan in the company of a number of businessmen reformers who turned to organized political effort during the 1890s with an enthusiasm that resembled religious revivalism. In 1892, these men, who were in their twenties and thirties, created the California League of Progress; they believed that "since the future was theirs, they were entitled, or even compelled, to take a hand in shaping it to their best advantage." Frederick J. Koster assumed the presidency of the group in 1896, at age twenty-eight, and led a successful campaign for a bond issue by the State of California that paid for a new trans-bay ferry boat depot.[7]

The Ferry Building opened for business in 1898, the same year that Phelan, then thirty-five, congratulated San Franciscans on the passage of their new city charter. The charter provided for public ownership of utilities (and the new bureaucracies that would operate the proposed water, power, and transit companies); civil-service protection for city employees; minimum wage and maximum hour provisions for city employees; provision for initiatives and referendums on the city ballot; and a variety of measures that strengthened the power of the mayor and weakened the powers of the Board of Supervisors (city council). The Ferry Building's 235 foot high tower made it an imposing structure that still defines the downtown skyline adjacent to the waterfront, and the new city charter defined the powers of local government for thirty years. Both of these projects went forward after receiving majority votes by the (male) electorate, but it was businessmen outside the government who initiated the projects, defined them as necessary for the city's progress, and sold them to the voters as beneficial to the public interest. When confronted with opposition from other elements of the community, many business leaders—but not all—were willing to make changes in their original plans, and they successfully defused opposition and achieved success. Business power thus occupied a central place in the politics of defining the public interest beginning in the 1890s, a discourse and practice friendly to government and private sector cooperation in economic development and the reform of institutions of government, ambivalent about labor unions, and hostile to racial and gender equality. Business power was synonymous with the Chamber of Commerce. Founded in 1849, the chamber had long been a permanent fixture in city affairs when bankers like Phelan and downtown retailers organized the Merchants Association in 1894. For the next seventeen years, the two business groups worked in tandem. Then, in 1911, the chamber, Merchants Association, and two additional organizations—the Downtown Association and the Board of Trade—merged to create a powerful single voice representing San Francisco business.[8]

Phelan, Koster, and their colleagues who founded the new chamber intended it to be far more than a single-purpose booster organization or merely one of many community organizations in San Francisco. Koster expressed the new chamber's spirit in his inaugural address as president: "I have said that the Chamber of Commerce is not of a class or for a class; and yet we are in a sense a class—a class upon whom it is fair to lay great burden of responsibility, responsibility for the development of fairness, because where that does not exist the community cannot thrive; responsibility toward causing the community to properly protect investments within its bounds."[9] The chamber made itself a partner with the San Francisco city government, and it seized the same role with the California state government and with the federal government. Officially nonpartisan, the chamber prided itself on its role in providing information to voters during local and state elections. Unabashedly bullish on "The City," the chamber established a public advertising program designed to attract investment capital and tourist dollars. Relentless in its pragmatism, the chamber also developed close political relationships with rival organizations in the Bay Area, southern California, and the Pacific Northwest. San Francisco activists then organized the California State Chamber of Commerce, using the new institutionalized relationships to conduct both competition and cooperation in ways that were meant to protect the long-term common interests of all parties.[10]

Koster's references to the need for community affairs to be conducted with fairness and the importance of protecting business investments communicated his and his fellow businessmen's attitude toward both local government officials and labor unions. From their point of view, municipal government required continuous and systematic oversight because its elected officials were too beholden to the voters. And the voters were too often members of, or sympathetic with, labor unions that represented the interests only of their members, not the interests of the community as a whole. These convictions led the chamber to create two affiliate organizations: a Bureau of Governmental Research in 1916 that would monitor the operations of municipal government and then, five years later, an Industrial Association that would oversee labor relations. The bureau carried out activities similar to its counterparts in cities across the nation: "to study public business, cooperate with officials and specifically work for economy and efficiency in municipal affairs." The Chamber of Commerce provided startup costs and helped pay the bills. The Industrial Association was similar to other "American Plan" organizations created to limit the success of the growing labor movement in calling for "Industrial Freedom." The employers would not deny workers the freedom to join unions; nor would they surrender their own freedom from any obligation to hire only union members or to bargain with unions over wages, hours, and working conditions.[11]

Organized business quickly moved to shape events that it often neither initiated nor desired. Taking the offensive, it worked to shape the future of the Bay Area by means of both formal and informal political activities. At the same time, it defensively adjusted to challenges posed by urban rivals, as well as to changes in national and international business conditions. San Francisco's livelihood derived primarily from commercial and financial activities, and its gradual loss of its predominant role in the Pacific Basin after the 1890s generated a nervous concern among its business leaders about the city's future. Because these San Franciscans invested both in and beyond the city, they led the way in promoting statewide business unity by creating the California State Chamber of Commerce.[12]

In San Francisco itself, their overlapping membership on the boards of the Chamber of Commerce, Bureau of Governmental Research, and Industrial Association made the leaders of these groups a relatively cohesive elite. They successfully pursued a wide range of activities once aptly described as the elements of "twentieth-century urban promotion." It was the Chamber of Commerce, not local governments, that originated a concerted program to expand manufacturing facilities in the Bay Area. The development of the Islais Creek district as a combined industrial park and port facility, perhaps the most comprehensive project of its type in the Bay Area during the period, began as a chamber idea as early as 1906. It was the Chamber of Commerce, even before the merger in 1911, that initiated what later became a common front in the Bay Area on behalf of expanded military-related urban development. City Hall did not begin the programs of advertising and promotion designed to attract tourists and convention goers to San Francisco; these measures came in the first instance from the Chamber of Commerce, and by the 1930s, the chamber was carrying out these publicity activities under contract with the city and county government. Of the large-scale infrastructure projects of the period (the Hetch Hetchy water and power project; highways, streetcar lines, and tunnels; the expansion and modernization of port facilities), all were the product of close and cooperative work between the chamber and its affiliates and the city and county government.[13]

In the case of the harbor, bridge, airport, and Hetch Hetchy projects, the chamber's role in initiating policy and its detailed participation in the day-to-day decision making was so extensive that it literally shared policy implementation and monitoring responsibility with local governments. The chamber also played a leading role in the implementation of New Deal development projects, a subject that, along with the building of the Golden Gate and San Francisco–Oakland bridges, will be considered in the next chapter. The chamber was likewise instrumental in beginning to shift city-building projects out of the private control of its own and affiliated organizations into new public agencies such as the local housing authority and the regional service agency. Aggressively using personal lobbying, as well as newspaper, magazine, radio, film, and telephone advertising, the chamber also accumulated an impressive record of success on local and state ballot measures related to urban economic development and even cultural projects such as the Panama Pacific International Exposition and the War Memorial Opera House.[14]

Business power was a political reality in San Francisco from the 1890s to the 1930s, but business did not operate as a unified political bloc or wield political power without challenges to its claim to best represent the public interest. This claim was rejected as early as the 1890s by a discourse according to which the public interest in a democracy required governance to be shared by all male—and, after the passage of women's suffrage in 1911, all male and female—members of the white population. Typically elected for two-year terms and frequently answerable to the voters, public officials were thus predisposed to take into account the expressed interests of all elements of the white polity. It was only after Phelan and his fellow reformers took into account the criticism of representatives of this viewpoint—such as the Catholic priest Father Peter C. Yorke's charge that city government "does not exist for the well-to-do alone"— and reformulated their proposed charter to address it that their new framework of government was approved by voters in 1898.[15]

Father Yorke's rhetoric included a ringing critique of the alleged upper-class bias written into the failed reform charter rejected by voters in 1896, but he was equally, if not more, incensed with a clause in the document that required all teachers in the city's public schools to be graduates of California public schools. No Catholic applicants who had graduated from parochial schools needed to apply—this in a city in which some 30 percent of the female teaching staff was Irish, and most of the Irish were Catholics. For Yorke and like-minded Irish-born residents of San Francisco and their adult children, as well as for Germans and Italians, ethnicity and the Catholic religion were mutually reinforcing cultural markers that deserved a place of respect in community affairs. And while it was true that applicants who were Protestant graduates of, say, public schools in Cambridge, Massachusetts, would also be ineligible to apply for teaching jobs in the city of Saint Francis under the provisions of the first version of the reform charter, that fact did not lessen the offensiveness of the alleged anti-Catholicism that played a role in its rejection in 1896.[16]

Catholic San Franciscans insisted on having a voice in the city's public affairs and were able to exercise influence by virtue of both their numbers in the population and the fact that they had arrived and staked a claim in the city when "the world rushed in" during the Gold Rush. No "Protestant Establishment" lorded over Catholic residents of the city, as was the case in New York City and Boston, and Irish San Franciscans (and, for that matter, Italian San Franciscans) were "white on arrival" in California and never faced ethno-racial prejudice and discrimination of the kind that marked daily life in many other U.S. cities and towns.[17] At the turn of the twentieth century, the city's total population reached 342,782; of that number, 101,000 were German, and 95,000 were Irish. Many of the Germans were Catholics, as were most of the Irish; at the time of the great earthquake and fire of 1906, only 22,000 of the city's 143,000 churchgoers were Protestants, and 116,000 were Catholics.[18]

Given the numbers of Catholics in the population, it is little wonder that their traditions of morality and ethics found a way into the city's discussions of how to define and practice the public interest. Catholic participation in public leadership roles in elected and appointed positions, and their unpaid (often behind-the-scenes) advice and counsel to public officials made San Francisco distinctive during these years. The same was true of Jewish residents, who in San Francisco were predominantly from Germany rather than from Poland, Russia, or Lithuania, and were generally well-to-do. Few were blue-collar workers. Jewish San Franciscans, who made up 6–8 percent of the population from 1870 to 1930, proudly referred to San Francisco as "Our City."[19] Of the seven candidates elected mayor between 1895 and 1944, only two were Protestants. One of them, James Rolph Jr., who served from 1912 to the end of 1930, projected such an acceptable image that many Catholics thought he belonged to their faith until he turned up leading a Masonic parade. Adolph Sutro, the mayor in 1895 and 1896 and a self-described freethinker, was of Jewish parentage and received a religious funeral. Besides occupying the chief executive office, Catholics and Jews routinely held office as members of the Board of Supervisors, heads of city commissions, and members of state and national legislatures. When San Francisco celebrated local and state anniversaries, and when crowds turned out to celebrate the Fourth of July at the Civic Center or in Golden Gate Park, Catholic, Protestant, and Jewish divines read the official prayers. In 1934, when residents by the thousands filed past Mayor Rolph's coffin in the City Hall rotunda, the services were read by Catholic Archbishop Edward Hanna, as well as by Rabbi Irving Reichert and Episcopal Dean J. Wilmer Gresham.[20]

By the time of the campaign for the new charter, twenty years had passed since the great railroad strike of 1877, the nation's first coast-to-coast collective demand that white workers be treated with dignity and respect and that their voices be taken into account in defining the public interest. San Franciscans contributed to the subsequent discourse about the rights of labor, and their prescriptions for the future drew on religious as well as secular moral principles. Trade unionists, public officials, religious leaders, the press, and a critical mass of business owners also insisted on faith-based moral grounds that wage earners had a right to participate in defining the public interest before the city's Union Labor Party existed and long past its brief regime from 1902 to 1907 and then from 1909 to 1911. The positive reception San Franciscans offered to the papal encyclical *Rerum Novarum* (On Capital and Labor) of 1891 foreshadowed the robust labor movement that would soon be built by the city's predominantly Catholic wage earners. The official Catholic newspaper dramatically displayed Pope Leo XIII's picture on its front page and devoted most of the June 17 issue to an English translation of the pontiff's letter. Although he condoned private property and insisted on harmony between capital and labor, Leo also condemned laissez-faire business practices and insisted on government guarantees of working-class interests. San Francisco's Pacific Coast Laborers Union quickly sent the first formal American acknowledgment to Rome thanking the pope. The encyclical, wrote William M. Willey and George D. Gillespie, was "in a measure a joyful surprise to us." The union leaders were pleased "that the cries of distressed labor would be heard in Rome" and grateful for the prompt and kind attention to our needs accorded by our most revered and beloved friend, his Grace, most Reverend P. W. Riordan, Archbishop of San Francisco . . .

We find it difficult to fully express our pleasure and gratitude for the Encyclical. It comes to us like rays of the sun, dispelling the gloom of our Despair. It brings us an assurance that fills our breast with hope. It nerves us on to the battle against injustice with renewed energies.[21]

Two months later, owners of firms that employed 40,000 workers established the Board of Manufacturers and Employers, the city's first organization aimed at coordinating labor relations. They presented their statement of purpose in language that paralleled the official principles of *Rerum Novarum*:

> Its policy is not dictated by a spirit of aggression, but it shall be the earnest endeavor of its members to prevent friction, and to peacefully settle all disputes that may arise between employers and employees. We . . . have no wish to interfere with the indisputable right of labor to organize, but believe in the organization and the federation of employers of labor, to the end that neither party shall tempt the other to overstep the bounds of right, reason, and justice.[22]

By asserting the equal rights of business and labor in its 1891 declaration, the new business association assented to the rhetoric of *Rerum Novarum,* but it then moved aggressively to eliminate labor as a community force by refusing to bargain with all but one of the city's unions. The transparent hypocrisy of this strategy, coming as it did so soon after the popular new Catholic pronouncement on labor relations, became especially obvious during the summer of 1901. For almost a decade, the city's heavily Catholic wage workers had been signing membership cards in labor unions, and in the summer of 1901, restaurant workers, metalworkers, teamsters, and the City Front Federation, a coalition of fourteen other waterfront unions with 13,000 members, went on strike. The organization representing waterfront employers refused to bargain with the striking workers and hired non-union men to take the place of the teamsters to haul the attendees at a convention and their baggage.[23] Mayor Phelan gave his police commissioner, who was also president of the Chamber of Commerce, free rein to appoint special police officers to guard the strikebreaking teamsters, who needed protection from catcalls and dangerous objects. By this act, Phelan invited charges that he had repudiated the principle that the city's working class deserved to be treated with dignity and respect, a principle that he had honored since he won election to the first of his three terms of office in 1897. The son of Irish Catholic immigrants, as well as a millionaire banker, Phelan had been educated by Jesuits and enjoyed a grand tour to Great Britain and continental Europe before entering politics. His stump speeches hit all the right notes, announcing his sympathy with those who hoped and prayed (and sent money) for Irish independence and promising to represent the interests of labor as well as business.[24]

Like most Irish from coast to coast, Phelan was a Democrat, but when his Populist Party predecessor, Mayor Adolph Sutro, left office, he made it a point in his farewell address to include an encomium to Phelan, who would "stand by the people's interest, and during his administration the poor man will have an equal chance with the rich."[25] From 1897 to mid-1901, Phelan's conduct in office was exemplary according to such criteria. But during the strike, by seeming to take the side of an employers' organization that refused to bargain with its workforce, he made himself vulnerable to charges that he had violated his public trust to govern impartially. In fact, the employers had spurned Phelan's attempts to mediate; given the physical attacks on the strikebreaking teamsters, he decided that he could not in good conscience leave them unprotected—hence, his approval of the special officer bodyguards riding the wagons.

The differences between the 1891 and 1901 positions staked out by organized employers reflected their growing sense of unease as workers flocked to join unions in that decade. In 1891, employers quietly conducted what one historian has described as "a campaign of extirpation" against city unions, but their public statements announced their support of the Catholic principle that unions were positive and morally desirable community institutions. In 1901, the employers coupled their refusal to bargain with the strikers with a public condemnation of the very existence of labor unions. By their intransigence, they triggered a community consensus that repudiated unilateral business dictation of labor relations policy. Previous accounts of the 1901 strike have emphasized the lack of support by the city's newspapers, except for William Randolph Hearst's *Examiner* (Hearst was a Democrat), for the union side. It would be more accurate to say that while the press universally condemned strike *violence,* only the daily *Chronicle* (an anti-Phelan, Republic Party paper at a time when newspapers were fiercely partisan) and the ultra-laissez-faire weeklies *Argonaut* and *Town Talk* firmly supported the employers' refusal to meet with union leaders, submit to compromises, and end the strike. In fact, most of the public discussion during the strike criticized both the waterfront employers association for its unwillingness to tolerate collective bargaining and the strike leaders for their failure to condemn physical violence against strikebreaking workers. Both capital and labor, according to this discourse, should have respected each other's legitimate rights, tolerated each other's different needs, and bargained together peacefully as equal partners with a mutual interest in the long-term prosperity of the city.[26]

The Chamber of Commerce supported the position of the employers, but the Merchants Association was reluctant to declare a similar blanket approval of the employers' uncompromising stance. While it rejected a proposal to appoint a committee to seek arbitration without even taking a formal vote, the Merchants Association also tabled a motion condemning the strike leaders for making unreasonable demands. In his speech to the Merchants' Association at a meeting in September, President Frederick W. Dohrmann pointedly reminded the group that in San Francisco, businessmen did not generally reject the right of labor unions to exist and represent their members.[27]

The Retail Dealers Association rejected the waterfront employers' position altogether. The message of this group, which represented grocers, butchers, and livery stable owners, who were directly dependent on wage-earning customers, emphasized the issue of fairness. According to this point of view, the particular businessmen holding out against compromise were the sons of rich men, had never worked for a living, and had no right to claim to represent San Francisco business. Refusal to compromise, these small-business owners argued, might benefit the short-term interests of the city's largest industries, but the wage cuts demanded of the striking workers ultimately would cripple retail trade, lower the value of real estate, increase taxation, and stimulate higher rates of crime and poverty.[28]

The retailers put their description of the situation in language similar to that of an anonymous contributor to *Organized Labor,* the newspaper of the building trades unions. "If the corporations were allowed to 'hog' all the profits that are created by labor, the wage earner will have no money to spend with the merchants." But "if the working element is prosperous, the merchant thrives from his trade. When the laborer's wages are cut it takes that much cash from the till of the businessmen." *The Monitor,* the official newspaper of the Roman Catholic Archdiocese of San Francisco, asserted, "There is something manifestly wrong with an economic condition which spells enormous profits on invested capital yet omits from the list of beneficiaries the vast bulk of the wage earners." Five days later, on August 8, the paper's editor, Father Peter C. Yorke—who was also the spiritual adviser to Michael Casey, president of the teamsters' union—spoke at a strike rally at Metropolitan Hall. To the accompaniment of "prolonged and loud applause and cheering," Yorke urged his audience to remember that employers lacked the moral right to run their businesses any way they pleased without ongoing cooperation with their employees. When a member of the Employers Association named Andrew Corrigan demanded that Archbishop Patrick Riordan silence Father Yorke, Riordan refused, reminding Corrigan that his priest was "merely explaining the Encyclical of the Pope."[29]

With the archbishop's approval, Yorke seized control of the moral leadership of the striking teamsters and waterfront workers, who, it happened, were predominantly Irish as well as Catholic. He appealed to their masculine pride as Irish patriots when he urged them to keep fighting until they could obtain "peace with honor." Paraphrasing *Rerum Novarum,* Yorke condemned "the manifest disposition betrayed by the favored money class to disregard the sentiment of 'the common people'":

> The instinct of justice and sympathy, which formerly bound all classes and conditions of men in this country closely in the bonds of a common brotherhood, under the broad, democratic principles of our political and social organization, is steadily losing its force as a factor for the perpetuation of conditions that have nobly distinguished the internal life of this republic from that of other nations. These labor conflicts are but surface indications of a diseased condition of the body politic. They are a warning against the causes that breed them. The removal of these causes is a matter for the intelligent American voter.[30]

For two months after Father Yorke's speech at Metropolitan Hall, the employers association continued to refuse to bargain with the strikers. Violence between union supporters and strikebreakers, aggravated by the presence of the special officers hired by the Police Commission, left five dead and 336 wounded. When President William McKinley was assassinated in Buffalo, New York, on September 6, several Protestant ministers and the Protestant presidents of Stanford University and the University of California—Benjamin Ide Wheeler and David Starr Jordan, respectively—complained that the murder of the president was symptomatic of a national decline in respect for authority, with particular local application. Their remarks contained a decided anti–Irish Catholic subtext. Wheeler urged citizens to join "the vigilance-men, against disorder, lawlessness, and every form and guise of anarchy." Jordan appealed to "real Americans" who found themselves caught between "grasping trusts and lawless unions" to learn the "Lessons of the Tragedy: "under democracy all violence is treason," including the actions of anybody who "throws a stone at a scab teamster." The anti-Phelan *Chronicle* put the alleged link between the assassin in Buffalo and the striking workers in San Francisco in blunt terms: attempts to interfere with nonunion workmen were "unjust, cruel and un-American."[31]

Archbishop Riordan, delivering a eulogy for President McKinley before the largest congregation ever assembled in St. Mary's Cathedral, forthrightly condemned anarchism and reminded the public that "the Catholic Church has been in all ages the great teacher of submission to authority." His newspaper, *The Monitor,* was more explicit when it chastised the university presidents Wheeler and Jordan by name for having implied that foreign-born Americans had a propensity for anarchism. The paper lectured the academics: "Anarchy and sin are peculiar to no land or people" and went on to condemn "the hysteric cant over the iniquities of 'foreigners' and [the] calls for the suppression of criticism of the United States government."[32]

By mid-September, the employers association and its supporters found themselves in a weakened position. Their financial strength made them the party most likely to last out the strike, but their base of support in the city had become increasingly limited. The mayor had tried to mediate, only to be rebuffed by the employers; the Board of Supervisors now blamed the length of the strike on the employers' refusal to bargain. The Catholic Church had pronounced their position morally bankrupt, going as far as to suggest that if a vigilante crusade against anarchy were to be organized, as some businessmen suggested, it should be directed not at the strikers in San Francisco but at the racists in "the lynching belt" of the Deep South.[33]

Father Yorke expanded his criticism of the employers' strategy into a rough-hewn philosophy of government based on *Rerum Novarum*. He condemned the "noxious growth" of an elitist notion of policymaking based on the assumption that "rich men . . . have made this city . . . and that no man in this city should raise up a voice for anything . . . because they are our lords and masters." He urged San Franciscans to embrace a principle of the public interest rooted in the legitimate rights of working-class residents: "The true interests of a city are not to be found in the clubs . . . amongst its merchants [or] clustered about its banks. . . . [The city's interests should include especially] those who have to labor for their daily bread."[34]

On October 2, Father Yorke and Governor Henry Gage met secretly in the rectory of St. Peter's Church to consider Mayor Phelan's request that the governor declare martial law in San Francisco. Yorke convinced the governor that martial law would only worsen the situation without ending the strike. Then Gage, pointedly ignoring the employers association, presented an ultimatum to the Draymen's Association (owners of freight companies): settle with the teamsters and the City Front Federation of unions or submit to martial law. The leaders of the three groups agreed to end the strike, thereby snubbing the employers association, which was thereby discredited in the eyes of the public. Although neither party to the strike won its demands, the struck employers could resume business, and the striking workers could return to work, albeit alongside the non-union workers who had been hired to take their places. Opponents of labor unions who had refused to accept the Catholic Church's philosophy that endorsed unions as legitimate institutions still condemned them as illegitimate monopolies rather than moral guardians of workers' rights. They would continue to battle union power in the workplace, in the press, and at the ballot box.[35]

The city's labor movement, realizing its continuing vulnerability both at the job site and in City Hall, created the San Francisco Union Labor Party. In the election in December, voters put Eugene Schmitz, president of the musicians' union, in the Mayor's Office. In a pointed snub to anti-union business owners, Schmitz declined to speak at the annual dinner of the Merchants Association, thereby breaking with the practice of former Mayor Phelan. But Schmitz sent the association a statement to be read at the gathering. He began by assuring them that his election at the head of an explicitly pro-union political party "does not mean an industrial or social revolution . . . a destruction of vested interests or the injury of property rights." Then he lectured them, saying "The constantly reiterated imputation of the irresponsibility of the honest working class is without foundation." Finally, Schmitz announced the principle that he intended to practice during his tenure: "All elements of our community are entitled to fair and equal consideration [and] peace and prosperity will reign without interruption in this great city of ours."[36]

Voters returned Schmitz to office twice and even expanded the hold of the Union Labor Party government by giving its candidates a majority on the Board of Supervisors. But the Labor Party officials proceeded to abuse their positions by engaging in what would be called today a "pay to play" policy of issuing business franchises; they were identified, convicted, and removed from office by prosecutors appointed by a self-selected cabal of wealthy capitalists led by James Duval Phelan. But the graft trials' exposure of corruption among the Union Labor Party officials also brought to light the corporate executives whose bribes had proved irresistible to the disgraced supervisors. Public opinion remained strongly behind the continuing efforts of the labor movement to demand an effective role in the city government and in the city's labor relations. And given the pressing need to rebuild the city, the skilled trades and many other unions were able to drive a hard bargain with employers that included a requirement that union members fill the available jobs.[37]

Archbishop Riordan expanded the Catholic Church's public commitment to San Francisco's labor movement by designating Labor Day an occasion for special religious ceremonies honoring working men and women. Father J. R. Newell of St. Dominic's Church pointed out in a typical Labor Day sermon that "the wealthy employer must not treat his workmen as mere chattels to make money by" because "human labor is superior to capital and deserves the higher consideration." But several anti-union firms, the Market Street Railway, and the Pacific Telephone and Telegraph Company refused to quietly submit to labor power; their provocative wage cuts and lockouts set off strikes that sapped the morale and the resources of the unions involved. After nearly a year of often violent struggle, the unions had ceased to exist, thirty-one people had died, and thousands had been injured. The Union Labor Party made a brief comeback in the 1909 election, a feat made possible partly by the upwelling of pro-labor sentiment in the electorate after the bitter strikes of 1907–1908. Patrick H. McCarthy, president of the Building Trades Council, was elected to the Mayor's Office in 1909. He served one term and was then defeated by James Rolph Jr. in November 1911. A shipping company owner and banker, Rolph promised to be "the mayor of all the people" by providing executive leadership in a municipal government that would look out for the interests of labor and the working class without jeopardizing the interests of businessmen. Rolph continued to support government and business cooperation in the six-year-old efforts under way to restore San Francisco after the devastation of the fire and earthquake of 1906 and presided over an extensive program of expanded city services, including the world's fair in 1915 and the Hetch Hetchy water and power project, during his twenty-year tenure.[38]

San Francisco's business organizations had effectively joined forces in 1911 to elect Rolph, a former director of the Chamber of Commerce, to the Mayor's Office, but Rolph had no intention of being a puppet of capitalist power. In 1916, when the newly revitalized chamber declared war on organized labor, arguing that the unions had developed too much power over hiring, wage rates, and conditions on the job, Rolph refused to support their "open shop" campaign. The longshoremen and restaurant workers were on strike, and Frederick Koster, now president of the Chamber of Commerce, declared the strikes an extremist power play, not a legitimate grievance. Koster announced his organization's determination to free San Francisco of its reputation as "a class-ruled city" even if it took a twentieth-century version of the Vigilance Committee of Gold Rush days to do so. The chamber proceeded to organize such a group, dubbing it the Law and Order Committee, and it successfully broke the strikes. Then the city was rocked by an explosion at the foot of Market Street during the largest parade in San Francisco's history; ten people were killed outright and forty were injured. Two socialists, Thomas Mooney and Warren Billings, were arrested, charged with the bombing, and eventually convicted (wrongfully, as we now know) and sent to San Quentin.[39]

In the aftermath of the bombing, Mayor Rolph rebuffed the Chamber of Commerce's offer to help apprehend the perpetrators, and he declined to accept the organization's aid in prosecuting Mooney and Billings after their arrests. He suffered charges that made the rounds in some downtown offices and at Nob Hill clubs that he had become "the walking delegate of the longshoremen's union." The anti-union paper *Town Talk* editorialized that that the strikes and the bombing could have been expected, given a city government that had made San Francisco "the Utopia of organized labor." Rolph replied that "all classes of the community are equally intent that law and order shall be maintained. All shall be treated alike, and only through the representatives of the people." The mayor repudiated what he called a "strong effort . . . to destroy organized labor," and he lectured his fellow business owners that San Francisco needed "more men of vision and insight—men who can think in terms of human right as well as in terms of property."[40]

Rolph's refusal to legitimize the Chamber of Commerce's claim to exercise coequal authority with the municipal government during the days after the Market Street bombing matched the stand taken by Fremont Older, editor of the *Bulletin*. Older was a personal friend of Phelan's, who along with Rudolph Spreckels, had masterminded the graft prosecution with Phelan ten years earlier. Older regarded the Law and Order Committee as an undesirable return to frontier vigilantism and used the pages of his newspaper to oppose Koster and his group throughout the crisis. Rabbi Jacob Nieto of Temple Sherith Israel, Father Peter Yorke (now editor of his own weekly newspaper, *The Leader*), and Archbishop Edward Hanna all joined Older in defending Rolph and criticizing Koster. Yorke used sarcasm and ridicule when describing the chamber's activities to his predominantly Irish Catholic working-class readers. Business, he declared "has no more right to say how San Francisco shall be run than the Chambermaids Union or the Printing Committee of the Academy of Science." Archbishop Hanna (served 1915–1935), like his predecessor, Patrick Riordan, grounded his demand for workers' access to fairness and equality in "facts deep in those eternal truths which rule man's relations with man." Quoting from Pope Leo XIII that since "it is ordained by nature that different classes of men should live in harmony and in agreement," then "labor organizations [will] ever be at the forefront in advancing those things which will make truly great the mighty metropolis that reigns by the western sea."[41]

In 1916, as in 1901, San Franciscans who rejected the claim of the city's business organizations to the free and undisputed use of the title "defender of law and order" had friends in high places. Mayor Rolph refused to countenance the vigilante tactics and leadership claims of the Chamber of Commerce's Law and Order Committee. Archbishop Hanna bestowed the Catholic Church's moral authority on the labor unions to which men and women paid their membership dues. But in the decade to come, San Francisco moved beyond the rebuilding phase that followed the disaster of 1906; the city no longer had a shortage of workers; and city employers could hire labor in a buyers' market. The Industrial Association of the Chamber of Commerce pushed forward with its program of ridding the city of a labor movement powerful enough to bargain on equal terms with employers. As the power of the employers in labor relations waxed and labor's power waned, Archbishop Hanna agreed to serve on the Industrial Association's Impartial Wage Board "to prevent labor from getting a rough deal." Organized labor's power in labor relations experienced a decline during the 1920s, but working-class residents maintained their access to municipal government, and the discourse upholding the rights and dignity of white workers—under construction during the previous twenty years—persisted during the "lean years" of the 1920s and would undergo revitalization in the 1930s.[42]

The series of contests that began in the 1890s had demonstrated labor's ability to challenge the right of businesses to dictate the terms of labor relations, and a Catholic moral economy and labor relations discourse was well established by the 1920s. White residents, regardless of gender, income, ethnicity, or religion, had successfully claimed access to public-policy making institutions. Catholics and Jews lived free from the social discrimination that was the norm in other U.S. cities at the time; they enjoyed economic power and social status and held city, state, and federal political offices. And by the 1920s, white women who felt confined by the domestic roles considered normal by most Catholics (and many Protestant and Jews) were also making claims on the public sphere, even though, for the most part, they were predominantly working in the fields of health, education, and welfare. Their ranks included the Catholic Sisters of Mercy, who ministered to the sick, the unemployed, and the homeless, and the Protestant Katherine Felton, who operated the city's Children's Agency. A partial exception to the tendency of public women to work in the "doing good" professions was Florence Kahn, a Jewish Republican U.S. congresswoman from 1925 to 1937. But then, she had commenced her term when she took the seat of her deceased husband, Julius. And women had successfully achieved suffrage in 1911, despite the fact that the (male) voters of San Francisco, in contrast to the state as a whole, voted "no" on the measure. Women also played a leading role in the successful campaign to close down the city's red-light district and to regulate women's participation in commercial dancehalls.[43]

By the 1920s, it was no longer possible to exclude women and women's self-defined interests from consideration in San Francisco's public sphere. Non-white residents, however, were a different story; they remained outside the charmed circle made up of those able to claim the right to participate in defining the public interest. Chinese and Japanese residents together made up 4.6 percent of the city's total population in 1900 (15,735) and 3.6 percent in 1930 (22,553). Asian immigrants could not become citizens through naturalization; could not marry a white person; could not live outside the segregated Chinatown, Japan town, or Manila town; and could not obtain jobs in many occupations. And while it would be inaccurate to claim that Asian San Franciscans had no defenders among the city's white residents, or that they did not succeed in pushing back against some of the discriminatory social customs and public laws designed to keep them on the margins, it would also be incorrect to exaggerate their agency to the point of claiming that they could exercise political power effectively on their own behalf.[44] The Japanese population quadrupled between 1900 and 1930, from 1,781 to 6,250. Many Chinese residents, however, returned to China; their numbers declined by about half between 1890 and 1900 and continued the downward slide until 1920. In the State of California, the Chinese share of the population dropped by about a third during that decade.

Black San Franciscans doubled as a share of San Francisco's population, from 1,654 in 1900 to 3,803 in 1930. They faced racial discrimination in jobs, housing, education, and access to health care, as in other American cities, but the consensus among African American historians is that "prejudice was mild compared to anti-Chinese sentiments or Negrophobia in the south."[45] Mild or not, racist discrimination kept black residents out of most positions in both private and public institutions; black men might find low-paying jobs in factories or on construction sites as laborers, but nearly half were domestic workers (that was also the case for 80 percent of female workers). Neither men nor women could break through the color line to teach in schools, operate streetcars, or serve customers in downtown retail stores, not to mention serve on the Board of Supervisors or on city commissions. In 1921, white residents of the Sunset District organized a neighborhood association that included on its agenda activities "to help rid the district of undesirables, many families of whom had moved into Sunset within the past year. Colored families are now located on 10th, 12th, 18th, and 33rd Avenues." In 1925, the president of the Central Council of Civic Clubs, an umbrella organization that covered the various neighborhood associations, endorsed an informal proposal for "obtaining a section for colored people" in the city, but although his organization "was working along that line." nothing came of this plan for a purpose-built black ghetto in the city of Saint Francis. The Sunset association itself seems never to have attracted more than one hundred members (who discussed among themselves the need to stop advertising their membership in the thousands based on *potential* strength), and it folded well before its tenth anniversary.[46] The city's African American press and black civil rights organizations exposed housing discrimination when they identified it, but it "was not a conspicuous feature of San Francisco race relations before 1940."[47]

This chapter began with James Duval Phelan asking the Merchants Association in 1897 to help him identify citizen volunteers to assist him and his Democratic Party's program for an institutionalized system of cooperation between local government, private enterprise, and individual entrepreneurship. This cooperative relationship was intended to create more efficient and more honest government, more manufacturing, more imports and exports, more business and residential construction, and more cultural infrastructure in the city of San Francisco. Phelan's progressivism made room for the members of labor unions, provided that they followed the lead of their more far-sighted businessmen neighbors, and Jews were welcome to participate on equal terms. Women, however, would be expected to know their subordinate place and act accordingly.

The chapter ends with James Duval Phelan running for reelection to the U.S. Senate in 1920 under the banner "Keep California White." Like the members of San Francisco labor unions who organized the Asiatic Exclusion League in 1905 and the city residents whose objections to sending their children to school with Japanese students caused an international scandal in 1907, Phelan believed that "this is a white man's country" and "we cannot make a homogeneous population out of people who do not blend with the Caucasian race." In his view, the same principle applied to black Americans; they were "a non-assimilable body, a foreign substance." Phelan lost his bid for a second term in the Senate, but he remained active in the immigration restriction movement, and in 1924 he agreed to serve as treasurer of the new California Joint Immigration Committee. In answer to a question about what he would do "if [he] were given Heaven and California," he replied that he would rent out Heaven and live in California. What this "Native Son of the Golden West" did not say was that his better-than-Heaven Golden State would be off-limits to all non-whites.[48]

Phelan died in 1930, so he never lived to see the landslide victories of his Democratic Party at the national, state, and local levels of government beginning in 1932. And he would undoubtedly have been pleased, after years of Republican dominance, to be able to witness the inauguration of the New Deal. One imagines him even more pleased to discover that much of the economic development and government reform program that he had described as "progressive" would now reappear as central themes of a New Deal and World War II–era "liberal" persuasion. He would have been less pleased to see that post-1930s liberalism contained the seeds of an ultimately successful campaign to disassemble the extensive cultural and institutional racism that still marked San Francisco through the 1930s and beyond.

2

"THE NEED FOR COOPERATION"

The Origins of the Liberal Growth Regime

On September 1, 1941, a small crowd of curious bystanders and committed union members gathered under sunny skies in the small park at the foot of Market Street for the unveiling and dedication of the memorial to Andrew Furuseth. The Norwegian-born Furuseth, president of the International Seamen's Union, had achieved legendary status long before his death in January 1938. Now the larger-than-life bronze bust, which faithfully captured his hawk-like profile and craggy features, stood watch atop a marble pedestal across from the city's Ferry Building. The white-capped sailors who gathered around the memorial with their sleeves rolled up ready for work may have appreciated the symbolism implicit in Furuseth's placement facing up Market Street toward City Hall, as if on the lookout for dangerous waters ahead. Joining Harry Lundeberg, president of the Seafarers International Union, at the microphone was Angelo J. Rossi, who had become the mayor of San Francisco in January 1931. Rossi was the son of Gold Rush–era Italian immigrants, and Lundeberg had left Norway when he went to sea at fourteen. They both took pride in their families and boasted that they were proud to be American citizens. Rossi's most recent campaign, in 1939, was a hard-fought affair during which he was accused of being a fascist sympathizer by the newly established Communist Party newspaper the *People's World*. Lundeberg's seafarers' union, affiliated with the American Federation of Labor (AFL), was battling attempts by a communist-influenced Congress of Industrial Organizations (CIO) rival, which was determined to bring all West Coast sailors under its auspices.[1]

Lundeberg's and Rossi's anticommunist sentiments existed side by side with their dedication to a premise that their Communist Party rivals regarded as anathema, given the party's commitment to spreading the Stalinist gospel of socialist transformation. Rossi and Lundeberg believed that the future progress of the San Francisco Bay Area could best be achieved by reforming American capitalism along the lines of Franklin D. Roosevelt's New Deal. The New Deal was a Democratic Party program, but some of Roosevelt's innovations were compatible with, and some were expanded versions of, the policies of his Republican Party predecessor, Herbert Hoover, including Hoover's Reconstruction Finance Corporation. These programs were meant to help end the worst economic depression in the nation's history by putting the federal government in the business of stimulating the economy of cities and regions, thereby restoring confidence among investors and putting the unemployed back to work. The onlookers at the dedication of the Furuseth memorial needed only to raise their eyes to see one of the tangible results of such innovation: the five-year-old San Francisco–Oakland Bay Bridge. That the bridge, and the adjacent Trans-Bay Terminal, completed in 1939, existed at all was the result of a deliberate bipartisan effort by business leaders of the local Republican and Democratic parties to create a pro-growth coalition with the support of anti-communist unionists and the backing of city voters. They resolved to work their way out of the crisis of the Great Depression by downplaying their partisan and class differences, emphasizing the benefits to the region and its residents that could come with economic growth, and stressing the patriotic American character of their efforts. They created a liberal growth regime in San Francisco that was a politically centrist and moderately liberal enterprise. It developed incrementally in a contested and conflicted manner during the 1930s and wartime years, and it was influenced by local as well as national dynamics and by wartime sentiment and war-related events.[2]

At the time of the Wall Street crash in 1929, San Francisco was still showing the signs of its relative loss of economic power to Los Angeles and nearby Bay Area counties. Alameda and Contra Costa counties were outdistancing San Francisco in manufacturing output, and the value of trade to other San Francisco Bay ports ranked higher than that loaded and unloaded on the city's finger piers. But San Francisco still far outstripped the rest of the Bay Area as a wholesaler, and it still unquestionably deserved its title "Wall Street of the West." Fifth in the United States in the dollar value of its bank clearings, behind New York, Philadelphia, Chicago and Boston, the city had seventeen state banks with 171 branches, compared with sixteen state banks and fifty-six branches in Los Angeles. The headquarters of the Twelfth Federal Reserve District was in San Francisco, as was the Pacific Coast Stock Exchange.[3]

The city's business elite responded aggressively to the impact of the Great Depression. James Duval Phelan died in 1930, but Frederick J. Koster and several other members of Koster's generation were still active in the Chamber of

Commerce and the Industrial Association. They met the challenges of deflation, unemployment, declining tax revenues, and loss of confidence by drawing on the same combination of civic nationalism and noblesse oblige that Phelan had modeled after the earthquake and fire of 1906. Mayor Rolph turned to these men when hard times hit the city; they served on his Citizens Committee to Stimulate Employment, made donations to the San Francisco Community Chest, and volunteered to serve on the Financial Advisory Committee of the San Francisco–Oakland Bay Bridge.[4]

When some 1,000 demonstrators marched under the banner of the Communist Party to City Hall to protest against unemployment on March 7, 1930, Mayor Rolph upstaged their leaders and turned the protest parade into a rally for future progress. When the unemployed from all over Northern California came to San Francisco, the executives of major commercial banks and the Chamber of Commerce reached out to the city's labor unions for help and established private relief organizations; when the private money ran out, they lobbied the Board of Supervisors to propose city-financed relief funds. When the board agreed and sought voters' approval for the necessary expenditures, the business and labor advocates successfully campaigned citywide for voters' approval. Thanks to this coalition-based leadership, San Francisco coped with rising unemployment in 1930, 1931, and 1932 more effectively than Los Angeles, Seattle, and Portland. San Francisco came closer than any other West Coast city to "fulfilling, at least for a time, Herbert Hoover's faith in the ability of a local community to survive and take care of its own."[5]

By the time the nationwide crisis came to the Bay Area, Mayor Rolph and his successor, Mayor Rossi, had already developed extensive policymaking relationships with San Francisco's business elite. In addition to their work as officers in the Chamber of Commerce and Downtown Association, they involved themselves in the revitalization of the California Development Board, a statewide organization whose goals included boosting the Panama Pacific Exposition of 1915. The board placed "agents in every country in Europe to advertise our State and the exposition and to encourage the right kind of people to immigrate to our shores." During the 1920s, the activities in California achieved national prominence when Secretary of Commerce Herbert Hoover (a graduate of Stanford, with many continuing ties to the state's business community) backed a federal government initiative to create an "American System," intended to combine the old free-enterprise philosophy with the new management and engineering by means of the work of private associations cooperating with state and local government.[6]

Hoover's "Associationalism" was intended to be a private voluntary alternative to economic development policies and programs directed by the federal government. He mobilized his Commerce Department to coordinate the activities of the nation's trade associations, research agencies, and professional bodies to work closely with, and provide leadership to, state and local governments. In the Golden State, the renamed California Development Association pulled together the state's various business organizations on behalf of such a vision of cooperation between business and government, with the former as the senior partner. Koster provided leadership for the group all through the 1920s and 1930s. By 1923, the association had a budget of $120,000 (more than $1.4 million today) and operated a research department and a service department. In 1927, Koster took pains to reassure the more than 2,000 member firms of the association that they should "continue through voluntary organization, to work out problems essential to our progress. Let us refrain . . . from placing upon government any new responsibilities. Let us continue to carefully watch proposed legislation and hold new legislation down to the lowest minimum. Keep the government out of business whenever it is possible to do so."[7]

Wigginton Creed, president of Pacific Gas and Electric, one of San Francisco's leading corporations, warned, "We cannot afford to be apathetic and leave to the manufacturers of political hokum the determination of what ought to be done in the interests of the state." R. Earl Fisher, the utility corporation's vice-president, invoked Hoover's ideas explicitly in describing "The Responsibility of Organized Business." According to Fisher, "Sound development can no longer proceed along the lines of an unguided unlimited promotion of industries and population." Fisher quoted Hoover's belief that "the solution of the problems of the American people lies wholly in our ability to build up a cooperative spirit in the communities themselves." Koster expressed great pleasure at Hoover's public commendation of his California organization as the most effective of its kind in the United States.[8]

Throughout the Rolph years (January 1912–January 1931) and during Rossi's administration (1931–December 1943), San Francisco's Chamber of Commerce and Bureau of Governmental Research played a direct role in every important discussion of municipal policy. Rarely did they lose on an issue they considered important, and on perhaps the most important issue of the period, the shaping and passage of the 1932 Charter, they achieved nearly all of their objectives (despite opposition from the Labor Council and the Catholic Church, both of which objected to the increase in appointed officials and corresponding decrease in elected officials). Organized business's record on general obligation bond issues is also instructive. Between 1928 and 1948, city voters acted on sixty-four bond issues, and the chamber made recommendations on all but one. Of these, the voters turned down all thirteen on which the chamber recommended a "no" vote. On the fifty bond issues supported by the chamber, voters passed thirty-one (62%). The chamber boasted that its recommendations matched the results forty-four of sixty-three cases (70%).[9]

When the election of 1932 put the Democrat Franklin D. Roosevelt in the White House and a Democratic Party majority in Congress, Koster was still active in San Francisco affairs. He was also president of the California State Chamber of Commerce and a member of the national chamber's executive board. When Roosevelt began signing the economic reform legislation passed during the first hundred days of the New Deal, Koster urged his fellow businessmen to take charge of the reform process to maintain control of future policymaking. Koster was a devout Catholic as well as a seasoned business leader. He described the crisis and the responsibility of business in language derived from the critique of laissez-faire capitalism embedded in Roman Catholic moral teaching, first in Pope Leo XIII's encyclical *Rerum Novarum* (On Capital and Labor) of 1891 and then reiterated and expanded in Pope Pius XI's *Quadragesimo Anno* (On the Reconstruction of the Social Order) in 1931. "If the individual is to intelligently care for his own interests, he cannot escape being, in some measure at least, his brother's keeper. . . . [H]is advantage in the long run cannot possibly be at the expense of others' disadvantage. This is no longer academic. The proof of this is all about us." Noting "distress and actual starvation in the midst of plenty," Koster complained that it was "unbelievable that such stupidity, such utter lack of intelligent leadership could have prevailed as to have rendered such a thing possible; all the result of adherence to the doctrine of laissez faire, and evidence of the lack of intelligent organized business leadership." He stressed that "how the new deal is to be handled, what the new deal is to be, what success is to be achieved toward obtaining its objectives, will very positively depend on the degree of intelligent cooperation that is developed through organizations of business."[10]

Koster, like his co-religionist Catholic Mayor Angelo J. Rossi, disagreed with many San Francisco businessmen who regarded Roosevelt in the argot of the time as "a traitor to his class" and refused to acknowledge the new terrain of politics and policy that the new Democratic national administration was creating. Rossi gradually shed his Old Guard Republican convictions, accommodated himself to the reality of the New Deal, and sought ways for San Francisco to benefit from its policies. Koster addressed the concerns of the skeptics when he urged them to use the new federal legislation to facilitate regional economic development. Admitting that "it is regrettable that circumstances have forced the necessity of this [National Recovery Administration] partnership between industry and government," Koster argued that "it is now definitely before us, and the important consideration is what steps to take to gain the best results from that partnership."[11]

In the decade that followed, Koster and R. Earl Fisher, a colleague in the California State Chamber of Commerce, pushed ahead with their strategy of "partnership between industry and government," and in the winter of 1944 and spring of 1945, their work bore fruit in the form of the San Francisco Bay Area Council. The council was organized at the end of World War II, but it was an outgrowth of more than a decade of preparatory activity. During the 1920s, the California State Chamber of Commerce, in an explicit attempt to follow Hoover's Associationalism model, had created six Bay Area regional councils made up of representatives from county Chambers of Commerce. They met during May and June 1933, before the National Industrial Recovery Act (NIRA) was signed, to coordinate the writing of proposals by local governments in connection with the public works and highway construction funds anticipated in Title II of the legislation, which created the Public Works Administration. The regional councils then worked continuously during the mid- and late 1930s in a cooperative partnership with city and county governments on urban development issues.[12]

Alexander Heron, a vice president of Crown-Zellerbach Corporation from San Francisco, was part of Fisher's and Koster's network of New Era boosters, and Heron had served as director of finance in the administration of the progressive Republican Governor C. C. Young. Heron was an industrial relations pioneer renowned for his record of "not one hour lost" due to labor disputes between 1900 and 1938; he returned to government service under the Republican Governor Earl Warren in 1943. He used his new position as Warren's director of the state's Reconstruction and Reemployment Commission to establish the greater degree of coordination in business–government cooperation that Koster, Miller, and other advocates of the "cooperative standpoint" supported. In late 1944 and early 1945, Heron presided over the process by which the new Bay Area Council replaced the state chamber's regional councils as the vehicle for "unity of action in solving postwar problems of the Bay Area." Heron also initiated, with the assistance of trade associations and the state chamber, the legislation that created the state's Community Redevelopment Act.[13]

Considered in its historical context, the Bay Area Council can be seen as more than merely a reaction to wartime conditions and part of a nationwide anxiety over possible postwar recession. The council also represented a successful conclusion to the long campaign to create a particular kind of corporatist approach to the process of local urban economic development, something that was sanctioned both by Hoover's Associationalism and by Pius XI's call for "Reconstruction of the Social Order." The regional councils were deliberately modeled by Koster on Hoover's blueprint, then he and his colleagues refashioned them to take advantage of opportunities presented by federal subsidies under the New Deal and did so with the pope's moral teachings in mind. The councils were intended to be cooperative local endeavors bringing businessmen and local, regional, and state government officials together in pursuit of economic growth. Frank Marsh, the first executive vice president and general manager of the new Bay Area Council, came to his duties fresh from his stint as manager of the San Francisco chamber's office in Washington, D.C.[14]

It is not surprising, in this light, that businessmen played a leading role in the Bay Area Council. Nor is the absence from its membership of city planners, who thus far had not figured prominently in civic affairs. But a more striking characteristic of the organization was the participation of labor union leaders, which testified to changes under way in the relationships among businessmen, government officials, and labor leaders as they participated in an emerging liberal growth regime from the late 1930s through the years of World War II.[15] In 1934, dedication to laissez-faire principles and practices persisted among Old Guard Republican business leaders who followed the lead of William H. Crocker, Roger D. Lapham, and others who were antagonistic to the New Deal and resistant to labor's demands for a greater share in decision making in labor relations. During the waterfront strike of that year, moderate employers lost control of strike strategy to the faction that, in the words of Thomas G. Plant, president of the Waterfront Employers Union, had "urged war from the beginning." When these employers tried to break the strike and open the port by force, they set off a melee during which police officers shot and killed two men on July 5. Most writing on the waterfront strike of 1934 interprets the three weeks following "Bloody Thursday" as a triumph of labor solidarity expressed in a general strike that forced capital to give the striking workers their most important demands. These events will be analyzed in detail in the next chapter, but here it is important to note that the reigning interpretation fails to take into account another development—one that is especially important to the origins of the liberal growth regime. Abhorrence of the radicalism attributed to the strike leaders, shock following the murders, and the fear of worse to come gave moderate business leaders the opportunity to take back control of the bargaining process from the hardliners and to come to an agreement with the strike leaders to end the strike.[16]

The character of the strike settlement, as much as the strike itself, set in motion significant changes in economic development politics and policymaking in the subsequent decade and beyond. These changes would reinforce the importance of communitywide cooperation in defining and implementing measures to advance it. Settlement of the strike did not put an end to contention between business and labor, and the waterfront employers would not finally relinquish their hope for a return to pre–New Deal conditions until the late 1940s. However, many local businessmen, including some influential shippers, decided to deal with the unions given the new reality of labor unions' legal legitimacy. Several factors contributed to the change. San Francisco businessmen, like their counterparts elsewhere, were put on the defensive by passage of the National Labor Relations Act of 1935 and by the Supreme Court's upholding of its constitutionality in 1937. Local labor initiatives added to the pressure. In April 1935, leaders of unions active in the 1934 strike founded the Maritime Federation of the Pacific Coast. In January 1937, a reform "New Deal Slate" won election to the San Francisco AFL's Labor Council.[17]

The Maritime Federation's one-hundred-day strike in 1936–1937 forced the Pacific Coast shipowners to transform what had been a tenuous and informal alliance into a temporary, then a permanent, parallel and formal organization in early 1937. By June 1937, both local and statewide business leaders had become increasingly fearful of the potential damage of continued labor strikes to the growth potential of the local and regional economy. Searching for a strategy to limit the economic damage of future strikes, lessen the appeal of radicals, and restore nationwide confidence in San Francisco's business leadership, the California State Chamber of Commerce adopted "A Program for Labor Peace." This program went beyond Koster's call in 1933 for pragmatic accommodation to the New Deal. It established a ten-point "formula for labor peace and social progress that, if followed by employers not only in California but elsewhere in the United States, will almost surely bring to an end the period of strife and strikes though which we are passing." In the same month, the presidents of the Bank of California, the American Trust Company, the Anglo California National Bank, and the Bank of America met privately with the president of the city Chamber of Commerce. They demanded that the chamber take the lead in establishing a new organization to replace the Industrial Association, whose previous intransigent support of the waterfront employers had generated public criticism and whose more recent support of diehard hotel owners had kept a strike against them going for three months.[18]

Then, in November 1937, city voters rejected a ballot measure initiated by the Chamber of Commerce that had proposed to reinstate a two-decade-old anti-picketing ordinance that the Board of Supervisors had overturned in March. By March 1938, the Industrial Association, a fixture in the city's public life for nearly twenty years, had been replaced by the Committee of Forty-Three. The new group announced its intention to both defend the prerogatives of capital and acknowledge the rights of labor. Basing its strategy on the belief that business must organize to compete effectively with the newly revitalized labor movement, the Committee of Forty-Three made a public appeal for cooperation between labor and capital as a necessary means for the restoration of public confidence in business and for the resumption of city and regional economic growth.[19]

In June 1938, the county council of the CIO convened a town meeting with an audience of some 12,000 San Franciscans in the Civic Center Auditorium. Harry Bridges of the CIO-affiliated longshoremen's union, who had served as the head of the strike committee in the 1934 strike, appeared on the platform along with Roger D. Lapham of the Waterfront Employers Association. Bridges denied he was a member of the Communist Party but with studied insouciance declared that he found many of the party's notions admirable and had adopted some of them before the party did. Bridges had switched from opposing the New Deal when the Communist Party adopted its Democratic Front line, and in mid-1938 he was an ardent Roosevelt man. Lapham had been among the most intransigent of the shippers during the strike, but now he affirmed his belief in future harmonious labor relations and cooperative civic enterprise.[20]

In the post–Wagner Act drive to build membership and increase union strength, San Francisco's AFL-affiliated Labor Council delegates regarded the CIO unions as rivals. They were also skeptical about declarations of good faith by the Chamber of Commerce; AFL representatives did not attend the town meeting. Their official newspaper, the *Labor Clarion,* responded to the event with a mixture of sarcasm and ridicule. Privately, however, John F. Shelley, president of the AFL Labor Council, signed an agreement with the Committee of Forty-Three to establish the Joint Labor Committee, which brought the AFL unions into the same new system of collective bargaining and economic growth policy as the CIO. In 1939, the Committee of Forty-Three changed its name to the San Francisco Employers Council. The director of the renamed organization, dramatizing the degree to which business cooperation with labor was premised on the fear of continued labor conflict and business stagnation, as well as hope for future growth—and even conformity with Catholic doctrine and the current Communist Party line—announced: "Visitors to the Golden Gate Exposition will find San Francisco at labor peace not at war."[21]

By the time the Nazis invaded Poland on September 1, 1939, some of San Francisco's most intransigent anti-labor business leaders—notably, William H. Crocker—were dead, and a critical mass of the local business elite had adopted the strategy suggested by Ira B. Cross, a labor economist at the University of California (UC), Berkeley, in 1934. Cross had urged business to take the lead in reforming labor relations and economic development policy to "prevent the growth of revolutionary beliefs and movements." By the time the United States entered the war, Lapham of the waterfront employers, Bridges and other CIO leaders, and Shelley of the AFL had established new institutional relationships premised on the need for cooperation in the pursuit of future economic growth.[22] One week after the Japanese bombing of Pearl Harbor, Bridges addressed the 300 members of the executive board of the California State Industrial Union Council, stating that this was "a people's war, and it is labor's war. This is no time for post mortems," using the language of the Communist Party's Democratic Front as resuscitated by Joseph Stalin after Adolf Hitler violated the Nazi–Soviet nonaggression treaty. Bridges also stressed "the need for cooperation with employers and proper governmental agencies in carrying out our plans." In early June 1942, delegates from 500 unions filled Wheeler Auditorium at UC Berkeley for the weekend-long California Conference on Labor and the War. Jonathan Daniels of the Office of Civilian Defense enunciated one of the two most widely discussed themes of the conference when he criticized San Francisco's Junior League and Chamber of Commerce because they had "represented themselves to be the whole town" and urged the union members present "to get your community to be a democratic community." Frank P. Fenton, director of organizing for the AFL, stressed the other key conference theme: "The American workman is conservative. . . . [L]abor believes in our present system of free enterprise. We want to preserve it. We can preserve it if organized industry and organized labor join hands together."[23]

Throughout the war years, the Employers Council and the AFL and CIO councils conducted negotiations in a centralized, coordinated process that was typically marked by conservatism, civility, and mutual toleration. However, the long-established mutual antagonism between labor and business did not disappear. In June 1940, the AFL Labor Council expressed a general sentiment when it warned each member of the Employers Council against using "this general [national emergency] hysteria as a means for avoiding responsibility to the social problems of his workers." And several rancorous labor disputes occurred during the war, despite the wartime ban on strikes endorsed by both the AFL and the CIO. In 1941 and 1942, retail clerks struck department stores for six months, and hotel workers stayed out until ordered back to work by the War Labor Board after eight months. In the spring of 1944, a seniority dispute broke out between two AFL streetcar operators' unions after the consolidation of the private and public streetcar companies. Also in the spring of 1944, AFL machinists—known for their tradition of militancy and radicalism—demanded a wage increase and refused to accept overtime work. When the local machinists did strike after the war, in the fall of 1945, the International Association of Machinists, working cooperatively with the organization representing machine shop owners in the Bay Area, placed the local union in receivership and ended the strike.[24] In the case of relations between waterfront workers and employers, the war years fostered an armistice, but genuine labor peace was not achieved until after settlement of strikes in 1946 and 1948. Nonetheless, in the maritime industry, as in the city's labor relations generally, the New Deal and wartime conditions combined to create opportunities for institutional interaction that, in turn, began the process of moderating old resentments and enhancing opportunities for cooperative action central to the liberal growth regime.[25]

New political and policy processes for the construction of urban infrastructure, like those in regional economic development and labor relations, also came into being during the 1930s in the context of business activism, economic depression, the national shift from a Republican to a Democratic majority, and the revitalization of the labor movement. Leland W. Cutler, a three-term president of the Chamber of Commerce, played the leading role in securing financing for the San Francisco–Oakland Bay Bridge during the first years of the 1930s. Cutler had been a close personal friend of Herbert Hoover's since their days at Stanford University and a strong supporter of Hoover's Associationalism. Cutler was also a zealous believer in what he called "the magic of friendship" that could link together "citizens outside the government" like him with public officials in charge of urban development projects.[26]

Cutler made the transition from the Hoover administration to the Roosevelt administration relatively easily. Before he had become governor of New York, Roosevelt had been Cutler's counterpart in New York City: vice president and director of a regional office of the Fidelity and Deposit Company of Maryland. In his position as vice president of the Financial Advisory Committee of the trans-bay bridge project, Cutler relied first on Hoover's and then on Roosevelt's help in convincing the Reconstruction Finance Corporation to purchase revenue bonds for the construction of the bridge. A similar process, begun in the Bohemian Grove encampment, an exclusive men's getaway near the Russian River north of the city, involved Cutler's friend, the Democrat George Creel. He gave Cutler a personal introduction to Harry Hopkins, which eventually resulted in a $3.8 million Works Progress Administration grant that allowed the city to reclaim the shoals off Yerba Buena Island and begin construction of Treasure Island, site of the Golden Gate Exposition, of which Cutler served as president.[27]

When Cutler wrote his memoirs twenty years after the beginning of the New Deal, he sharply distinguished between friends such as Roosevelt and George Creel, who shared his philosophy about the proper relationship between government and business, and New Dealers such as Harry Hopkins: "Hopkins was an idealist, almost a fanatic; I think his philosophy of government was all wrong . . . terrible and dangerous." Philosophy, however, was one thing; business was another. Cutler was as willing to use Hopkins's help to boost San Francisco and Bay Area economic development as he had been to depend on Hopkins's boss and fellow Democrat Roosevelt.[28] In 1939, Cutler and the Chamber of Commerce launched a campaign to improve San Francisco's role as the leading regional metropolis for business services (a "Hub of Western Industry"), bolster its tourist industry, and improve its transportation connections to the rest of the nation and the world at the time of the exposition. The chamber continued to sponsor such business-oriented growth initiatives during the war and in 1943, with the support of sympathetic members of the Board of Supervisors, began calling for an official postwar planning committee. In 1945, Mayor Roger D. Lapham established such a committee and appointed as chairman Adrien J. Falk, president of the Chamber of Commerce and one of his colleagues who had participated in the town meeting of the CIO in 1938. In 1945, the mayor's committee, like the Bay Area Council, contained representatives of both labor and business, and its program—beginning with its number-one priority, airport expansion—followed the lines laid out in the earlier Chamber of Commerce priorities.[29]

The importance of the developing growth regime agenda, beginning in the 1930s and continuing during the war years, can be seen in its impact on the revenue and expenditure patterns of the municipal government from 1933 through the 1940s. During the years 1933–1939, the share of the municipal budget derived from state and federal funds, as well as the proportion and size of departmental expenditures for general governance and for public safety (i.e. fire and police), education, and hospitals, increased appreciably. That kind of expansion was stopped by wartime austerity measures. Even then, two of the four bond issues submitted to voters during the war were for major improvements to the city's sewer system and the construction of a juvenile court building. These measures had the solid support of the business and labor network established in 1938; Mayor Lapham also undertook extensive publicity campaigns on behalf of the bonds. He used a similar coalition-based publicity campaign to win voters' approval in a special election in 1944 for the city's purchase of the Market Street Railway and the merger of the private firm with the Municipal Railway. Between November 1945 and November 1948, the same strategy was used to secure the passage of nine out of twelve infrastructure-construction bonds.[30]

Lapham came to the Mayor's Office in January 1944 after playing a key role in setting in motion the détente between business and the AFL and CIO unions in 1938 and 1939, and after serving as an industry representative on Roosevelt's National War Labor Board. He did not partake of the faith-based commitment to Catholic "Social Reconstruction" principles of his predecessor, Angelo Rossi, but his experiences in the decade after the 1934 strike had made him a believer in the importance of defining the public interest around the importance of economic growth and development.[31] Such a strategy, de-emphasizing economic class and political party loyalty and emphasizing instead the short- and long-term benefits of cooperation in the service of growth, also shaped electoral politics. Roosevelt's win in 1932 and Upton Sinclair's defeat in 1934 prefigured the central themes of San Francisco municipal politics from the mid-1930s to the 1960s: the gradual and largely nonpartisan victory of supporters of centrist growth liberalism over critics from both the left and the right.

The growth liberals were Republicans, Democrats, and independents. Several key participants were central figures in the revitalization of the Democratic Party during the years of its recovery in the mid-1930s who went on to play important roles in San Francisco politics during World War II. Maurice E. Harrison, Edward Heller, Elinor Heller, William Malone, and Julia Gorman Porter were among the most important of this group. Maurice Harrison, former dean of the Hastings College of the Law and president of the Bar Association of San Francisco, served as chairman of the Democratic State Central Committee from 1932 to 1934. Like thousands of San Franciscans of more modest means in 1934, Harrison voted for the Republican candidate for governor, Frank Merriam, rather than for Upton Sinclair.[32] The persistence of a robust anti-radical strain at the center of liberal coalition work can been seen in the fact that Harrison's law firm, Brobeck, Phleger, and Harrison, had represented employers during strikes they attributed to radical agitation rather than legitimate employee grievances: the Industrial Association in the city carpenters' strike of 1926, the Bay Area Waterfront Employers Association, and the Hawaiian Planters Association in the 1934 strikes, and the DiGiorgo Corporation in the Central Valley farmworkers' strikes of the late 1930s.[33]

During the war years, Harrison, a Catholic, served as chairman of the Bay Area chapter of the National Committee against Persecution of the Jews. His friend and fellow Catholic Frederick Koster chaired the San Francisco Conference of Christians and Jews. Harrison's belief in a corporate commonwealth along the lines laid out by Koster in 1933 was grounded in similar Roman Catholic principles. In the late 1930s, Harrison helped organize the St. Thomas More Society of San Francisco. The society attracted the city's leading Catholic attorneys who believed that a study of More's life could provide "the true answer to the problems which confront the world today," because Saint Thomas "was the great witness against totalitarianism of his day." In an address to the society two months before the attack on Pearl Harbor, Harrison emphasized the importance of seeing in More's life a model of the kind of reform activity that was compatible with "the integrity of the Christian view of life." He stated: "In the true sense of the word he *was* a reformer. He had no fear of change as such; he advocated and welcomed whatever changes were called for by the requirements of justice. His life is proof that such sympathy is consistent with fidelity to fundamental truth when prevailing trends of thought go beyond rational bounds and when fundamental error masquerades for a while as legitimate reform."[34]

Advocacy of a growth-oriented centrist reform strategy, part of the national Democratic Party program during the 1930s and 1940s, also appealed to Edward and Elinor Heller. Harrison's association with the Hellers began in 1928, when they traveled together to the Democratic Party convention in Houston. In contrast to the Republican Party affiliations of most of San Francisco's Jewish business elite, the Hellers were Democrats, in major part because of the party loyalty of Edward Heller's family in Atlanta. Among his cousins in New York were Herbert Lehman and Henry Morgenthau, one the governor of New York state during the 1930s and the other Roosevelt's Treasury Department secretary. Edward Heller's mother was a delegate to the Democratic convention in 1932, and his wife later became a member of the party's National Committee. Like Harrison, Edward Heller voted for Frank Merriam for governor of California in 1934, and like Harrison, Heller and a handful of the California delegation to the Democratic Party convention in 1940 voted for Harry Truman rather than Henry Wallace as the vice presidential nominee because they regarded Wallace as too radical. (In 1939, when Harrison was put forward as a possible associate justice of the Supreme Court by his friends William McAdoo and George Creel, Roosevelt placed him on the short list, but criticism by John L. Lewis of the CIO that Harrison was "anti-labor" led the president to remove him from consideration.) Edward Heller's support for the centrist Republican Merriam in the governor's race of 1934 earned him a place on the California State Emergency Relief Commission. His support in 1938 for the liberal Democrat Culbert Olson was rewarded by an appointment to the Golden Gate International Exposition Commission.[35]

Another of Olson's appointments to the commission was the San Franciscan William M. Malone, chairman of the Democratic County Central Committee from 1937 to 1952 and chairman of the state's Central Committee in 1940–1942 and 1944–1946. Malone and Heller met for the first time during their term on the exposition commission; in their social backgrounds, they could hardly have been more different. Malone hailed from St. James Parish in the heart of the Irish Catholic Mission District, whereas Heller was part of the Pacific Heights Jewish elite. But they agreed on the need for Democratic Party leaders to build and deploy a centrist growth coalition that would limit the appeal of the leftist and rightist critics of New Deal measures. They shattered decorum in the 1940 convention when, standing on their chairs and shouting to be heard, they and ten other delegates refused to make unanimous the nomination of Henry Wallace for vice president.[36]

Their agenda included the expansion of women's participation in the party's work. The Democratic State Committee, prodded by women like Elinor Heller, created a "fifty-fifty" rule, which required equal representation of men and women in the committee's membership. Julia Gorman Porter, president of the San Francisco League of Women Voters in 1939–1940, joined the State Central Committee in 1941 and served as chair of the Northern California Democratic Party Women's Division throughout the war years. In 1944, Porter served as vice chairperson of the Franck Havenner for Congress Committee. Porter was a native San Franciscan whose grandfather had arrived even before the Gold Rush; Havenner was a transplanted Easterner who had lived in Arizona before coming to the Bay Area. Like Porter, who had come to her political party work by way of a network of Progressive-era reformers that included Lincoln Steffens, Havenner had impeccable progressive credentials. He had been secretary to Senator Hiram Johnson and the California manager of the La Follette campaign in 1924. He also had a decade of service on the city's Board of Supervisors marked by steady criticism of the Pacific Gas and Electric corporation and by staunch advocacy for turning over distribution of gas and electricity from the private company to the city government. Elected to Congress in 1936 on the Progressive and Democratic tickets, Havenner registered as a Democrat in 1939 after deciding that Roosevelt's program best "represented [his] Progressive philosophy."[37]

In 1939, with William Malone as his campaign manager, official backing from the Democratic county committee, and the promise of support from the moderately liberal San Francisco News, Havenner entered the mayoral race. However, the friendly editor at the News died before the campaign, and the paper's promised endorsement never materialized.[38] Havenner's chances probably were hurt even more by the unsolicited endorsement he received from Harry Bridges, leader of the longshoremen's union. Bridges's endorsement of Havenner and his attacks on the incumbent, Rossi, came in the weeks following the signing of the Nazi–Soviet pact and the Communist Party's repudiation of the Democratic Front line. Between September 1939 and July 1941, when Hitler attacked the Soviet Union, Bridges and other CIO organizers and officials whose discourse derived from or coincided with the Communist Party line were outspoken critics of cooperative relations with business organizations and government officials, the latter presented as merely the minions of American capitalism.[39]

Havenner was no puppet of radical unionism, but he failed to aggressively repudiate Bridges's endorsement and found himself the target of red-baiting that portrayed him as a tool of international communism. Rossi's supporters scattered billboards throughout the city that showed City Hall after a Havenner victory with red paint covering its French Renaissance dome. When a Havenner campaign march up Market Street was led by a brass band wearing longshoremen's caps and dockworkers' shirts, pro-Rossi publicity took it as proof that Havenner would be the mayor of radical labor rather than—in the phrase originated by James Rolph Jr. and appropriated by his successor—"the mayor of all of the people." Voters returned Rossi to office with a plurality of more than 20,000 (48% to 41% in a six-person race).[40] One year later, when Havenner fought to keep his congressional seat in a campaign against Thomas Rolph, brother of the late mayor and governor, voters repudiated him again. While Roosevelt was the city voters' choice for president by 60 percent to Wendell Willkie's 40 percent, Havenner was the choice for congressman of only 44 percent of the voters in his district.[41]

Catholic anticommunist appeals to moral order and patriotic nationalism, evident in the Rossi and Rolph campaigns that defeated Havenner in 1939 and

1940, continued to be central to liberal political rhetoric during World War II and in the postwar era. So did the idea of civic virtue, an older concept central to a discourse dating back to early American political culture that had played a role in debates about the public interest in San Francisco politics beginning in the decade after the Gold Rush.[42] The idea that longevity in office made officials "professional politicians" and automatically rendered them less able to serve the public interest dated from the early days of the republic, and it was used again quite deliberately in 1935, the first election after the dramatic increases in Democratic Party registration stimulated by Upton Sinclair's campaign. In that election, a slate of young aspirants to the Board of Supervisors who called themselves members of "the New Order of Cincinnatus"—a "New Guard" that would topple the incumbents—won one seat on the board. They repeated their modest success again in 1939, when the slate included Edmund G. "Pat" Brown, who had been one of the organizers of the group, as a candidate for district attorney. (Brown was proud of his nickname, earned for his success as a schoolboy orator along the lines of Patrick Henry.) In 1941, four members of the five "New Guard" slate won seats on the board, and two years later Brown defeated Matthew Brady to become district attorney.[43]

The New Guard, a bipartisan group that included several labor union activists, advertised itself as interested solely in honesty and efficiency in government, explicitly declaring its James Duval Phelan and Progressive-era roots. William Malone and the Democratic Party regulars not only tolerated the insurgents; they encouraged them. Years later, Malone likened Pat Brown to "a flower that's budding, I never interfered with him."[44] In 1943, Malone drew on the rhetoric of the young New Guard challengers when he put the Democratic Party behind Lapham's candidacy for mayor. This was done on the grounds that Lapham would be a "citizen mayor" who would not be influenced by professional politicians and who would limit himself to one term, thereby demonstrating a disinterested public service-oriented desire to benefit all of the people rather than any special interest.[45]

Malone's support for Lapham's candidacy had origins in the factionalism within the California State Democratic Central Committee, as well as in his commitment to the faith-based centrist growth liberalism he shared with his Catholic colleagues Maurice Harrison and Frederick Koster. In 1942, Governor Culbert Olson supported Malone's rival in the party election to choose a new vice chairman of the committee; the rival was George Reilly, who won by a vote of 218 to 182. A year later, when Reilly decided to run against Angelo Rossi in the mayoral election, Malone refused to support him and joined Harrison and Edward Heller in backing Lapham. Harrison's law partner, Herman Phleger, attorney for the Waterfront Employers Association, broached the idea with Lapham and his wife during a visit by the couple to his room at the Hotel Carlton in Washington, D.C., where Lapham was living while he served as a member of the War Labor Board.[46]

Determined to limit the influence of the CIO Political Action Committee, which had launched a well-publicized social-democratic program that had, in turn, moved the AFL to create a parallel organization, Phleger and Harrison were also cognizant of the potential appeal of a candidate who would carry Roosevelt's endorsement, who would draw conservative and centrist trade unionist voters, and who would promise to be a citizen-mayor. The backing for Lapham was bipartisan: Harrison and Heller, along with Malone and Julia Gorman Porter, all moderately liberal Democratic Party insiders, joined with the leading Republican conservatives Jerd Sullivan of the Crocker Bank; James Lockheed of the American Trust Bank; William S. Maillard Sr., president of the Chamber of Commerce during the 1934 strike; and Elmer Robinson, a Republican Party insider who had been active in Merriam's gubernatorial campaign.[47]

San Francisco's labor movement, not yet willing to endorse a candidate who had called for bloodshed to end the waterfront strike in 1934, officially opposed Lapham and endorsed Reilly in 1943. Labor took this position despite Lapham's move to the center in his work with the San Francisco Employers Council between 1938 and 1941 and his work from 1941 to 1943 as Roosevelt's appointee to the National Defense Mediation Board, the Labor Management Conference, and the War Labor Board.[48] The voters gave Lapham a strong plurality, putting him 33,000 votes ahead of Reilly and 43,000 ahead of the incumbent Rossi (i.e., 42% to 26% to 22%, with the balance, under 10%, going to City Supervisor Chester McPhee).[49] In a postmortem on the election, CIO strategists admitted that "the CIO [had] made a large number of bad mistakes in the campaign, which must be learned from immediately." Noting that "our literature was too 'labor' in character . . . not beamed in such a way as to appeal to the middle class, showing them a program which the whole community could agree upon," the strategists' report went on to describe "a real isolation between the labor movement and the rest of the community." Finally, the report argued, "We attacked Lapham too much on the old labor issues, which he was able to parry by pointing to a change of heart and the War Labor Board."[50]

Lapham's victory, as the confidential CIO report recommended, moved both the AFL and the CIO organizations toward the center in an attempt to compete more effectively for greater influence in city governance. During 1944, in response to the national CIO-PAC campaign and the defeat in 1943 in San Francisco, the labor federations agreed to co-sponsor a voter registration drive with the Junior Chamber of Commerce. The successful registration drive coincided with Mayor Lapham's careful co-optation of numerous Democratic Party, AFL, and CIO leaders. Many of the CIO and CIO-PAC activists had come to the Bay Area during the war, and in 1944 they were leaders in the local Communist Party (renamed the Communist Political Association on the orders of the national Communist Party leader, Earl Browder). Oleta O'Connor Yates, a UC Berkeley graduate who was a local Communist Party activist and the party's candidate for the Board of Supervisors, served on Mayor Lapham's personal Civic Unity Council, which was chaired by Maurice Harrison. Daniel Del Carlo of the AFL joined the Public Utilities Commission, now chaired by Marshall Dill, a former president of the Chamber of Commerce. George Miller of the CIO served on the Postwar Planning Committee. Julia Gorman Porter became a planning commissioner.[51]

Shortly after the war, from early to mid-1946, Lapham faced a recall campaign initiated by Henry F. Budde, editor and publisher of the *San Francisco Progress*, a twice-weekly newspaper distributed free in city neighborhoods. Budde's organization, the Recall Lapham Committee of 1100, Inc., accused Lapham of reneging on his promise to serve as a citizen-mayor and attacked his record in 1944 and 1945 with a crude appeal to "Lunch-bucket Joe" and "Secretary Sue." "We who are fighting for the little fellow's rights earnestly seek your endorsement and active support in recalling a mayor who has NO LOVE for LABOR."[52] Budde's motives remain a subject of speculation, but he was evidently convinced that Lapham's successful purchase of the Market Street railway was an irresponsible drain on city resources, and he appears to have developed personal animosity toward Lapham. There is no evidence to support the *San Francisco Chronicle*'s accusation that Budde was merely a front for CIO-PAC "puppet-show masters . . . out to fool the people of San Francisco about Roger Lapham." In fact, while Paul Schnur, secretary of the CIO Council, had threatened a recall campaign against what he called "the reactionary clique which dominates City Hall" in February, by April the PAC leaders had decided on pragmatic grounds to oppose the recall, even as they "look[ed] forward to the time when Lapham and his friends [could] be eliminated from public life." The recall campaign thus lacked the support of both labor federations, most of the city's neighborhood associations, the mainstream press, and both major political parties. Throughout the city, Lapham received greater voter support than he had in his 1943 election. Even in voting precincts where large numbers of blue-collar union members had voted against him in 1943 and then voted to recall him in 1946, his margin of victory had increased by nearly 20 percentage points.[53]

Lapham's defeat of the recall campaign was a victory for the liberal growth coalition that had become a force to be reckoned with in San Francisco even before the Cold War began. Two years later, the scope of the liberal center expanded when shipowners and waterfront employers finally accepted the permanence of labor unions in their industry; a combination of debilitating strikes and the reelection of Harry Truman in November 1948 convinced them to endorse a "New Look" on the waterfront. On the labor side, some of the Communist Party activists in the CIO left the labor movement at the time of the red scare and the purge of left-led unions, as in the case of Paul Schnur, executive secretary of the CIO Council from 1942 to 1949. Others—most dramatically, Harry Bridges after the negotiation of the "New Look" in 1948—became both defenders of "bread and butter" unionism and growth liberals on urban economic development issues.[54]

When Harry Lundeberg presided over the ground-breaking ceremonies for the new headquarters of the Sailors' Union of the Pacific on September 29, 1947, he asked Nick Hjortdal to dig up the first shovelful of earth and Father Edward B. Lenane to bless the site. Hjortdal was an eighty-eight-year-old charter member of the union; Father Lenane was the Catholic chaplain of the Port of San Francisco. When the imposing three-story Art Deco building opened in June 1950 at the top of Rincon Hill, a few hundred yards from the San Francisco–Oakland Bay Bridge's western terminus, it became the most recent addition to the city's postwar downtown skyline.[55] The ground breaking took place eighteen months after Winston Churchill had warned that the Soviet Union was threatening the freedom of the world by building "an Iron Curtain," and seven days after the building opened, the Cold War turned hot when North Korean troops crossed the Forty-eighth Parallel and attacked South Korea. The Cold War context would indeed contribute to the shaping of San Francisco's urban liberalism during the 1950s, but even before the Cold War, a particular strain of anticommunism—one rooted in the transnational Catholic Action movement— had powerfully influenced the discussion about how to define the common good in San Francisco. From World War I to the Cold War, a significant dynamic in the city's public life was the clash between Catholics and various anti-Catholic interest groups, including the Communist Party, over what role religious values should play in defining the public interest in the second largest city of the American West.

3

"NO QUARTER CAN BE GIVEN"

Catholics, Communists, and the Construction of the Public Interest

On November 24, 1936, a St. Mary's College student from North Beach named Joseph L. Alioto delivered a prize-winning speech in San Francisco. Alioto would go on to graduate in 1937 and then to earn a law degree at the Catholic University of America in Washington, D.C. In an address entitled "The Catholic Internationale" to the St. Ignatius Council of the Young Men's Institute, Alioto, who would later be elected mayor of San Francisco, warned his audience: "Communism has attained the position of a universal power [and] stands today as a cancer in the world's social organism." Given its international scope and its appeal as a "counterfeit religion," only a true religion "that is likewise international," he argued, would be able "to cut away this cancerous growth . . . There is only one power in the world which answers that description: the Roman Catholic Church. The battle lines . . . are clearly marked: It is to be the Catholic Internationale arrayed against the Communist Internationale; Rome against Moscow; Christ against Anti-Christ."[1] Alioto's speech propelled him into the front ranks of Archbishop John J. Mitty's Catholic Action "crusade." Participants called themselves "soldiers" enlisted in the cause of "Christ the King," and they took their cue from the archbishop's urging that "no quarter can be given" in the battle against communism. The struggle between Catholic Action activists and the Communist Party profoundly influenced the debate over how to define the public interest in San Francisco from the early 1930s through the 1950s.

During this period, the Catholic Archdiocese of San Francisco contained more than 400,000 Catholics living in thirteen Bay Area counties from Santa Clara in the south to Mendocino in the north, organized into 174 parishes served by 600 priests. Catholic leaders claimed that the city's sixty parishes embraced fully half of San Francisco's population, but a Census Bureau count made in 1936 put Catholics at 28 percent of the population and 68 percent of all church members. While the size and proportion of San Francisco's Catholic population cannot be described with complete assurance, there is no doubt about the city itself, which increased in size from 634,394 to 775,357 during the period. Only Los Angeles among Western U.S. cities ranked higher in population than San Francisco; number 11 in the nation in 1930 and 1950, it had twice the population of Seattle in 1930 and was 25 percent larger than Houston (number 14) in 1950.[2]

Religion was intertwined with ethnicity in the history of San Francisco during the 1930s and 1940s, but the city's ethnic and religious makeup then was dramatically different from what it is today. During the Depression and World War II years, Irish, German, and Italian immigrants, their children, and their grandchildren made up nearly two-thirds of a population that was 94 percent of white European background. Not all of those Irish, German, and Italian San Franciscans were Catholics, but Catholics were predominant in the blue-collar workforce, and they filled executive, middle-level, and lower-echelon positions in business, government, and the professions. Not all Catholics practiced their religion, but a sizeable number—a "critical mass"—of the city's Catholics took their faith seriously by attending Sunday Mass, by providing financial support to their parish churches and the archdiocese, and by participating in outdoor neighborhood and citywide religious ceremonies. Devout Catholics brought their faith-based convictions to bear in the public realm, as well.[3]

Catholic activism in San Francisco's public life did not begin in the 1930s; rather, it evolved by means of episcopal leadership and lay initiative in response to the encyclical letters of popes Leo XIII, Pius X, and Pius XI. And the popes' doctrinal pronouncements were themselves intended as religious resources to be deployed in a transnational struggle against socialism, communism, and other expressions of the "modernism" that appeared to threaten Catholic Christianity. Archbishops Patrick W. Riordan (served 1884–1914), Edward J. Hanna (served 1915–1935), and John J. Mitty (served 1935–1961) recruited and trained new priests; enlisted laymen and laywomen in the work of the church; built new schools; and used sermons, homilies, and the archdiocesan weekly newspaper, *The Monitor,* to communicate the meaning and the significance of the papal encyclicals and to implement Catholic doctrine in both private life and public policy.

Pope Leo XIII (1810–1903) issued his encyclical *Rerum Novarum* (On Capital and Labor) in 1891. He condemned socialism and communism and defended the right to private property. At the same time, he condemned laissez-faire business practices and defended the right of workers to organize labor unions; called on government to protect working-class interests; and urged businessmen, workers, and government to ensure harmony between capital and labor.[4]

Papal pronouncements also set the parameters for early-twentieth-century Catholic activism in San Francisco beyond labor relations, beginning with a call for "Catholic Action" by Pope Pius X (1835–1914) in his encyclical *Il Fermo Proposito* (On Catholic Action in Italy) of 1905, which urged the Catholic laity worldwide to become actively engaged in what might be called applied Christianity. The message was straightforward: "Bands of Catholics [will] aim to unite all their forces in combating anti-Christian civilization by every just and lawful means." Pius XI (1857–1939) reiterated the call to revitalize Catholic religious practice and to convince Catholics to participate more actively *as Catholics* in public life when he issued two letters at a time when the victory of the Fascists over the Italian Communist Party, and the organization of a Catholic political party, challenged the papacy to provide guidance to its communicants both inside and beyond Italy. In 1922, Pius XI issued *Ubi Arcano Dei Consilio* (On the Peace of Christ in the Kingdom of Christ) and reiterated Pius X's definition of Catholic Action. In 1925, in *Quas Primas* (On the Feast of Christ the King), the pope announced a new Catholic feast day, to be held on the third Sunday of October, as "an excellent remedy for the plague that now infests society . . . the plague of anti-clericalism, its errors and impious activities." Filled with martial rhetoric, the encyclical chastised Catholics generally, not only those in Italy. Pius XI was displeased because Catholics showed "a certain slowness and timidity," and he noted that they were "reluctant to engage in conflict or oppose but a weak resistance." Catholics were told that "it behooves them ever to fight courageously under the banner of Christ their King, then, fired with apostolic zeal, they would strive to win over to their Lord those hearts that are bitter and estranged from him, and would valiantly defend his rights."[5]

This spirited martial prescription for living as a Catholic marked the tenure of John J. Mitty (1884–1961), the former bishop of Salt Lake City, who had come to San Francisco as coadjutor archbishop in 1932. When Archbishop Hanna left office three years later, Mitty assumed leadership and served until his death in 1961. Mitty was a former battlefield chaplain who had participated in the Meuse-Argonne offensive in France during World War I. His leadership style combined efficient administration of archdiocesan business affairs with zealous evangelism in connection with the message of the papal encyclicals. He chose as the official motto of his episcopal office the phrase, "*Mihi vivere Christus est* (To me, to live is Christ)."[6]

Mitty's arrival in San Francisco coincided with a nationwide discussion among Catholic clergy and laity about how to best implement the teachings contained in two papal encyclicals published in 1931. *Non Abbiamo Bisogno*

(On Catholic Action in Italy) contained a robust criticism of the Fascist government's attempts to limit the scope and effectiveness of lay Catholic organizations, especially those of children and young adults. Pius XI reasserted the legitimacy of the church's attempts to shape moral education and to ensure Christian morality in public affairs. *Quadragesimo Anno* (On Reconstruction of the Social Order) reasserted the principles of Leo XIII's encyclical on labor and capital of 1891 that had urged Catholics worldwide to insist on a moral economy. Pius XI condemned what he considered utopian left-wing ideologies and social movements and materialist business practices backed by laissez-faire governments that ignored the general good of the community. He urged Catholics to take the lead in organizing new community institutions designed to foster cooperation among workers, business owners, and government officials, and he excoriated the notions that class conflict was natural, that irreconcilable differences separated working people and the business class, and that an overthrow of all existing things would accomplish paradise on earth for the workers of the world.[7]

Scarcely a year after the Vatican promulgated the two encyclicals of 1931, Archbishop Mitty launched a Catholic Action campaign in San Francisco that continued through the 1930s and into the World War II years and beyond. Meeting with members of the local branch of the National Council of Catholic Women on May 7, Mitty called for "greater effort and activity on your part" to monitor and shape the work of "our State Legislature and our National Congress" to ensure the defeat of "bills [that] totally ignore fundamental Christian and American principles." Mitty then moved beyond political action and called for a broad campaign on several fronts. "Catholic Action," the archbishop reminded his audience, "has been preached to us in season and out of season," and it was time to move beyond rhetoric to practice. The "purpose and object" of lay organizations, Mitty stressed, "is not political. Neither as a Church nor [as] an organization are we interested in any political aim or any political party." However, "We cannot live as if we were not part of the country," and we must "work unceasingly for both Church and country, for both Cross and Flag."[8]

Mitty could not know, as he spoke in May 1932, that a series of events would soon occur in San Francisco that would challenge the church and its lay activists to define more carefully the boundaries between the political and the nonpolitical in Catholic Action work. These events, a local expression of the national contest between labor and management in the context of Depression-related labor relations reforms of the New Deal, were the tumultuous waterfront strike of May–July 1934 and the four-day general strike of July 16–19, 1934. The Pacific Coast maritime strike and the San Francisco general strike challenged church leaders and laymen and laywomen to confront an ambiguity created by the pope's agreement with the Fascist government of Italy of September 1931. Pius XI had agreed to shrink Catholic Action by removing it from electoral politics and restricting its remaining activities to diocesan boundaries. But he issued no corresponding reduction in the theory of Catholic Action; the scope and limits of Catholic Action theory had, in fact, expanded with the Vatican's call for "reconstruction" of the social order contained in the encyclical *Quadragesimo Anno* of May 15, 1931. What did this ambiguity portend for Catholics in the United States? Did the papal agreement regarding Catholic Action in Italy cause bishops, priests, and laymen and laywomen in the United States to reduce the efforts of Catholic Action interest groups in education, labor and capital, anticommunism, and other areas, such as birth control and public morals?

American bishops responded by actually intensifying their attempts to create more effective diocesan Catholic Action work nationwide along the lines of the encyclicals of Pius XI. The coordinating agency for this work was the National Catholic Welfare Conference, an interest group that represented American bishops with headquarters in Washington, D.C., and its chairman during this period was Archbishop Edward Hanna of San Francisco. It was in this context that Coadjutor Archbishop Mitty called for a revitalization of Christian practice by means of a robust new Catholic Action initiative. Mitty's call demonstrated that he and Archbishop Hanna intended to increase, not reduce, faith-based public activism in the city. This decision set the stage for an aggressive assertion of Catholic principles that would occur two years later when San Franciscans confronted the tumultuous events of the maritime strike of May–July 1934. But even before those events transpired, Catholic Action work moved steadily forward.[9]

In September 1932, four months after Mitty issued his call for a Catholic Action initiative to the women of the local branch of the National Council of Catholic Women, laymen in New York City organized the Catholic League for Social Justice and sent out calls to their counterparts in cities across the nation to follow suit. Six months later, Catholics in fifty-four dioceses in the United States, including the largest, had established branches. The Italian American attorney Sylvester Andriano, a former member of the Board of Supervisors, and his law partner William R. Lowery took up the call and organized a San Francisco branch called the Academy of San Francisco, which operated out of the partners' office at 550 Montgomery Street, in the heart of the city's financial district. By April 1933, archbishops Hanna and Mitty had approved the academy's work, and it had enrolled three dozen members, including several judges, numerous attorneys and physicians, and Gordon O'Neill, the editor of the archdiocesan newspaper *The Monitor*. This response in San Francisco to the call for intensified Catholic Action work attracted the attention of the pope's representative in the United States, Apostolic Delegate Archbishop Amleto Giovanni Cicognani, who praised Archbishop Hanna's efforts "to prepare laymen for Catholic Action." It "is becoming urgently necessary," Cicognani wrote, "to prepare laymen who under the guidance of the Bishops and priests will speak for the Church."[10]

On March 3, 1934, the union representing dockworkers on the Pacific coast set in motion a series of events that gave Catholic Action activists an opportunity to demonstrate that they were a force to be reckoned with in public life. Emboldened by the Roosevelt administration's support for union organizing and collective bargaining, the longshoremen's associations demanded worker-controlled unions, union-controlled hiring halls, higher wages and a bonus for overtime work, and a thirty-hour week. Two months later, on May 9, their demands were still unmet, and some 10,000 dockworkers left their jobs after voting to strike in port cities up and down the coast. The following day, May 10, thousands of San Francisco strikers demonstrated their strength when they marched in a picket line along the San Francisco waterfront.[11]

By the end of the first month of the strike, despite personal attempts at mediation by Mayor Rossi and Assistant Secretary of Labor Edward J. McGrady, the conflict had intensified. Seamen and other maritime workers joined the strike, and sympathetic teamsters refused to move "scab" (non-union) cargoes. The Waterfront Employers Association flatly refused to consider the key demand for a union-controlled hiring hall and enlisted the support of the city's Chamber of Commerce and its union-busting Industrial Association. The employers' organizations condemned the strike as a communist-inspired revolt, not a genuine labor dispute, and they urged the mayor to crush it with military force. Archbishops Hanna and Mitty acknowledged the role of communists but insisted that the strikers had legitimate grievances that should be addressed by the employers and condemned their intransigence. Sylvester Andriano, serving on Mayor Rossi's informal citizens' committee, urged the mayor not to use force against the strikers, and Andriano's San Francisco Academy endorsed the demand for a union hiring hall. The academy joined archbishops Hanna and Mitty in criticizing the employers for their refusal to consider moderating their position on the strike demands.

Communist activists did play a role in setting the strategy and tactics of the strike. The Communist Party district organization decided to build up its membership in San Francisco at a meeting in spring 1932, and several experienced agents, including Sam Darcy and Harrison George, then moved to the city to recruit new members, especially waterfront and maritime workers, into the communist movement. To attract the attention of radical and potentially radical maritime workers, party agents decided to publish a mimeographed newspaper, the *Waterfront Worker* (coincidentally, this was one week after

Archbishop Mitty called for the Catholic Action program). For two years, the Communist Party built up the circulation of the newspaper and recruited new members. Several in the *Waterfront Worker*'s inner circle became members of the executive committee of the dockworker's union, Local 38-79 of the International Longshoremen's Association, and one of those men, Harry Bridges, was elected chairman of the strike committee in March 1934.[12]

Bridges, an Australian-born longshoreman, came under attack both because of his alleged communist affiliations and because he had lived in San Francisco for more than a decade but had never become a U.S. citizen. Bridges was a secret member of the Communist Party who went by the name "Rossi" in clandestine communications with the Communist Third International organization (Comintern), but he never admitted to being a member of the party, never explained why he chose the party name "Rossi," and never slavishly followed "the party line." The independent Catholic newspaper *The Leader*—continuing the policy of its founder, Father Peter Yorke, of supporting the rights of labor as vigorously as it did full and complete Irish independence from England— condemned the charges of communist influence as "vicious misrepresentation [by] callous capitalists and the servile press and radio stations." *The Monitor,* while critical of "materialists on both sides," especially castigated the "rugged individualists among the shipping executives who hate resistance to their lust for power and for profits." *The Monitor* warned that settlement of the strike would come only when business agreed to "break away from the code of hate and contempt that has characterized too many American captains of industry and finance."[13]

On June 9, at the end of the first month of the strike by longshoremen and sailors, *The Monitor* presented the Catholic Church's point of view in a front-page editorial titled "The Maritime Strikes." "The rights of the ship-owners over their ships do not give them the right to impoverish the whole community; nor do the rights of the striking workers include the right to pursue their aims regardless of the consequences to the third party in the dispute, namely the people who are not directly involved, but whom depend upon cargoes for their livelihoods and sustenance." Sounding a theme that would prove continuous through the events of 1934, *The Monitor* urged "all Catholics, who are employers, or who are in any way directly connected [with management] to read and know the contents of the encyclicals . . . that treat of the problems of capital and labor . . . and to acquaint their associates and acquaintances with the contents of these encyclicals and to give them copies of them." Should Catholic San Franciscans fail in this duty, according to the editorialist, "then those Catholics will be held to answer."

In addition to prescribing the moral responsibility of all San Franciscans to involve themselves personally in helping to settle labor conflicts according to Catholic principles, the editorial alerted Catholics to the particular danger posed by extremism:

> Shipowners have a perfect right to refuse to deliver the management of their business to a soviet. Longshoremen have a perfect right to organize in a union and to bargain collectively for wages and hours that will enable them to support their families in frugal comfort, to educate their children, and to lay something by for sickness and old age. But these rights are obscured because of the laissez faire extremists on the one hand and the communist fanatics on the other. The public has had enough of both. . . . We regret that hate motivates both of these groups. The Communists hate injustice more than they love justice. The ruthless "individualists" among employers do not consider justice at all, but hate all who check their lust for power and money.

San Franciscans, the newspaper continued, needed to organize a Catholic counterforce:

> If Christian workers would stem the tide of Communism, they must bring to the workers' cause as devoted an energy and as strict a discipline as members of the Communist Party manifest. Communism is a religion—a materialistic religion [and] appeals to many workers because the apostles of Communism work with a zeal worthy of a better cause. They can be challenged and checked only by men, who for the love of God study the Catholic teaching as thoroughly as Communists study the Communist theory; who devote as much energy to the propagation of the principles contained in the encyclicals on labor as the Communists do in spreading the doctrine of Marx; who labor as industriously to apply Catholic principles as the Communists work to apply the principles of Lenin.[14]

Given the influence of Catholic social teaching on labor activism in the city, San Francisco's Catholics had long regarded principled anticommunism and militant trade unionism as fitting together as comfortably as the two halves of a walnut. Mayor Rossi, determined to discredit communism, also took steps to educate the public about the differences between legitimate union activity compatible with Catholic teaching and illegal radical violence. Presiding over a meeting at City Hall, in the midst of the business paralysis induced by the strike, Rossi proclaimed the week of June 21–28 "American Legion Week." Flying squadrons of "three minute men" would take their patriotic message, with musical accompaniment, into all the downtown and neighborhood theaters.

This effort "to stamp Communism out of American life . . . represents crystal-lized efforts of civic, religious, labor and group leaders . . . brought to active educational functioning through the exigencies of the situation, locally and nationally." At the end of the week's events, a committee representing the waterfront employers met with the mayor and his advisory committee and demanded that the city break the strike by forcibly opening the port. Andriano, the Catholic Action leader, disagreed and argued, against the objections of the majority of the group, not to approve of such a plan; nor, he said, should the city to be a party to it.[15]

Andriano was the mayor's friend as well as his personal attorney, but he also commanded a degree of influence because of his previous service on the city's Board of Supervisors and his extensive nongovernmental civic activities. He was singled out as a model of impartial judgment on May 27, when the board unanimously supported a resolution by Supervisor Andrew Gallagher that Rossi appoint a commission to investigate the role of the police during the strike to that point; the commission, the board stated, should include "one or two public spirited citizens whose sense of social justice and of fair play has appealed to me as much, for example, as that of my two former and undefeated colleagues on this board, Supervisors Andriano and Harrelson." Rossi never appointed such a commission, but he decided to follow Andriano's advice and announced that the city's fight was against communists, not labor unions, and that it would not put its authority at the disposal of the Chamber of Commerce and the Industrial Association.[16]

Archbishop Hanna, whom President Roosevelt had appointed as the chair-man of a National Longshoreman's Board with authority to oversee a settle-ment of the strike, joined the mayor in asking the Industrial Association to postpone its attempts to force open the port. When time ran out on the post-ponement, on July 3, the Industrial Association, with the most anti-union employers now calling the shots, began moving freight from the docks to ware-houses, and that action precipitated battles all that day and on July 5 (all parties observed the July 4 holiday). Strikers tried to stop the trucks by intimidating the non-union drivers, threatening to turn over their vehicles, and raining bricks and cobblestones on them. When the city police used tear gas and clubs to dis-courage such behavior, the predictable result was outrage that the police had violated the mayor's promise to maintain neutrality. And when police resorted to shotguns, riot guns, and pistol fire, killing two men who were bystanders at an intersection filled with unruly demonstrators, Mayor Rossi was blamed along with his police department. The governor of California ordered the National Guard to occupy the waterfront and warehouse districts, and the employers reopened the port with non-union workers.

The killings on July 5 ("Bloody Thursday") generated a huge wave of sympathy for the strikers, who held a dramatic funeral procession on July 9 (by agreement with a chastened Police Department) that marched solemnly up the entire length of Market Street to the accompaniment of Beethoven's funeral march. Then on July 13, Archbishop Hanna addressed San Franciscans in a speech broadcast over the radio stations KGO, KPO, and KFRC. He approached the issues of the strike by reemphasizing the principles of Pope Pius XI's "Reconstruction of the Social Order" encyclical of 1931: "A bargain cannot be just unless the human character of the worker is fully recognized," and "rights must be religiously respected wherever they are found and it is the duty of the public authority to protect each one in the possession of his own rights." Returning to the themes enunciated in *The Monitor*'s editorial of June 9, Hanna explicitly endorsed both labor unions and collective bargaining and condemned exploitation by employers that ignored "the human character of the worker." Then, in a blunt rejection of the Communist Party's slogan "Class against Class," he criticized unionists who premised their activities on the necessity of "conflict between class and class." Both sides in the waterfront strike, Hanna insisted, should move quickly to accept the results of arbitration, keeping in mind the "underlying principles which have ever been the teaching of Christianity during 2,000 years." The teamsters, then one after another of each of San Francisco's AFL unions, put themselves on the side of the striking longshoremen and maritime workers by carrying out a general strike that lasted from July 16 to July 19. For seventy-seven hours, the city experienced what the Joint Maritime Strike Committee, in a statement of July 20, described as a "mass strike of organized labor and the united sympathy of the public at large."[17]

Two business groups—an Ad Hoc Citizens Committee, with headquarters at the Palace Hotel, and the Junior Chamber of Commerce—requested a declaration of martial law during the general strike. National Guard troops were already posted on the waterfront, but putting the entire city on a wartime basis would have satisfied those employers described by the president of the Waterfront Employers Association as having "urged war from the beginning."[18] Roger D. Lapham, president of the American Hawaii Steamship Company, expressed the point of view of this faction in a telephone conversation on July 18 with Secretary of Labor Frances Perkins: "We can cure this thing best by bloodshed. We have got to have bloodshed to stop it. It is the best thing to do." The governor, however, refused to declare martial law unless Mayor Rossi made the request. Rossi consulted his Citizens Committee of 25, and, according to Sylvester Andriano, who attended the meeting, "I was the only member of that committee on the side of labor and vigorously opposed the almost unanimous

attempt of the committee to terrorize and brow-beat Mayor Rossi into petition-
ing the Governor to call in the militia."[19]

On July 20, Francis J. Neylan, a Catholic attorney close to Archbishop
Hanna who represented the Hearst interests on the West Coast, hosted a meeting of the employers at his home in Woodside and reminded them of the future
damage to the city's business reputation should they continue their uncompromising stance. The Academy of San Francisco reiterated its argument that
Rerum Novarum and *Quadragesimo Anno* mandated approval of the strike
committee's major outstanding demand: a union hiring hall controlled by the
International Longshoremen's Association. Archbishop Hanna's arbitration
board continued its deliberations as the teamsters returned to their jobs on July
21, and nine days later Hanna announced an end to the strike after negotiating
a jointly operated hiring hall.[20]

Mayor Rossi's refusal to give in to the pressure to declare martial law earned
praise from the labor press and the Catholic papers. *The Leader* described Rossi
as "the mayor of all the people of San Francisco," not "an ineffectual tool of
vested wealth and a foe to honest labor." *The Monitor* argued that businessmen
in San Francisco needed to develop a new approach to labor's demands for
reform: "Just businessmen . . . must present some other group of principles
than those upon which the two brutalizing programs of laissez-faire and Communism are to be founded." The time had come for "The Parting of the Ways,"
and the choice was clear: "Society must be reconstructed on the lines set out in
the Communist program and initiated in Russia, or on definitely Christian
principles."[21]

Mayor Rossi received praise from the Catholic Church leadership and from
the Catholic Action activists, but he received more criticism than credit from
the quarters of conservative business and radical labor. By agreeing to arbitration, J. Ward Maillard Jr., president of the Chamber of Commerce, demonstrated a pragmatic accommodation to the upwelling of sympathy for the strikers that followed the killings of Bloody Thursday. But Maillard continued to
describe the general strike as "treason" and demanded that, in the future, "constituted authority be upheld and that the rights of every man and woman in San
Francisco from this day on shall be protected." He also minimized the responsibility of business for the conditions that had led to the strike demands, admitting only that "it is our duty to see that those isolated instances in which labor
has been exploited . . . be corrected." The Communist Party, whose national
leadership secretly visited San Francisco during the strike, regarded the city as
"the party's greatest organizing success in 1934," but the party's ability to build
on that success was jeopardized by Mayor Rossi and the clerical and lay Catholic activists on whose support he depended. And the hostility of the radical left
toward Rossi and Catholic activists would only grow as Archbishop Mitty and

Sylvester Andriano expanded the Catholic Action program in the months after the settlement of the strike of 1934.[22]

The determination of San Francisco's Catholic Action activists to define the city's public interest according to Catholic moral principles put them on a collision course with the members and supporters of San Francisco's Communist Party. Catholic Action work evolved in response to Vatican policy, archdiocesan direction, and lay activism; Communist Party work developed in response to Comintern policy, district leadership, and local initiative. The party developed a growing presence in the Golden State at the very time that Catholic Action was moving from theory to practice, and the local Catholic campaign against communism, which reflected a long-established Vatican policy, underwent revitalization during the waterfront and general strikes of 1934. While Communist Party activists helped to shape the dockworkers' strategy and tactics, Archbishop Hanna, Mayor Rossi, Andriano, and other Catholic activists, especially the attorney John Francis Neylan, planned the city's strategy and participated in the strike settlement. In the aftermath, Harry Bridges, who denied the charges that he was a member of the Communist Party, and Communist Party activists who openly admitted their party affiliation became particular targets of the Catholic Action mobilization.[23]

The Communist Party made things more difficult for its Catholic critics in the five years after the waterfront strike by closing down its separate Red unions and moving toward selective cooperation with, rather than repudiation of, the new CIO unions, some AFL unions, and the Democratic Party. The new "Popular Front" strategy saw Communist Party publicists praising "progressive Catholics" while condemning those lay Catholics and clergy who were "reactionary" or "fascist." Catholic Action activists, such as Father Raymond T. Feely, a professor at the University of San Francisco, were now required to take pains to educate members of their faith who might be tempted to believe the assertions of Communist Party members they worked alongside or cooperated with in political campaigns "that there is probably some part of the Soviet system that is 'worth a try.'" Catholics in contact with Communist Party members "might be misled by the denials of any concerted religious persecution [in the Soviet Union] and the assertion that 'religion is a private matter' and no concern of the Soviet government." That being the case, "It really should be counted as a duty . . . as a part of Catholic Action" to understand "that the very essence of Communism is violent atheism, and consequently no part of the Soviet philosophy can be tenable for an American citizen."[24]

San Franciscans who read the summary of Father Feely's series of pamphlets titled *The Case against Communism* on the front page of the May 4, 1935, issue of *The Monitor* found a three-column cartoon alongside the article on communism that announced, "This is the May Day Celebration We Want"—

a straightforward call for using the day to honor the Catholic moral economy approach to labor relations and an equally unambiguous rejection of the communist and socialist May Day celebration of working-class solidarity against capitalist oppression. It was almost exactly fourteen months since the beginning of the West Coast maritime strike, and while a truce existed between the longshoremen's unions and the employers that would last until the autumn of 1936, a cold war of considerable scope was taking place between Catholic Action activists and their Communist Party enemies.

The origins of the Catholic and communist cold war went back to 1934, when Mayor Rossi wrote to Governor Frank Merriam requesting additional National Guard troops in anticipation of the general strike, informing the governor, "I am advised by the chief of police that it is feared they will be unable longer to compel obedience to the law" and that he was "convinced that the situation . . . is largely due to the efforts and activities of Communists who have no regard for our American form of government and are desirous of breaking down and destroying law observance. Due to the activity of this particular class of persons, unlawful and riotous assembly exists in the city and county of San Francisco with intent to offer violence to persons and property therein." Three days later, on the second day of the general strike, vigilantes carried out a series of "red raids" on the office of the *Western Worker,* the headquarters of the Communist Party, and other alleged nests of radical activity; carloads of leather-jacketed men drove up to the buildings, broke the windows, trashed the offices, and then moved on to the next site to repeat the exercise. City police followed the vigilantes and arrested the presumed "public enemies" who happened to be present and filled the city jail with several hundred men and women arrested for vagrancy. The vigilantism and accompanying police action on July 17 provided Communist Party critics with additional evidence of the alleged "Fascist" character of the Rossi administration and the Police Department, especially since the mayor did not repudiate the attacks on the Communist Party. Instead, he announced: "I pledge to you that as Chief Executive in San Francisco I will, to the full extent of my authority, run out of San Francisco every Communist agitator, and this is going to be a continuing policy in San Francisco."[25]

Rossi exaggerated the role of Communist Party members in the waterfront and general strike, but he was not alone in his estimate of their influence, which was shared by Archbishop Mitty and his Catholic Action activists. They included Police Chief William J. Quinn, vice president of a newly formed state-wide anticommunist police officers' association, who believed that communists were "the greatest propagandists that ever cursed the earth. They put out propaganda [during the strike] that influenced the conservative men—and the majority of them in that strike were conservative labor men, desirous of bettering their positions, insofar as their hours of work and earning capacity were concerned. But unfortunately for them, when they got out on strike they found in some instances at least that their organizations were controlled by Communistic leaders and they were powerless to do anything but follow."[26]

Chief Quinn and Mayor Rossi may have been innocent of charges that they ordered the violent raids on July 17, but other San Franciscans shared their sentiments about the dangers posed by the Communist Party to the city's well-being, and they used a variety of tactics to monitor communist activity and influence. Hugh Gallagher, operations manager for the Matson Navigation Company and chairman of the Pacific American Shipowners Association, hired private investigators to spy on Communist Party members, as did the American Legion; they both shared their investigators' reports with the Chancery Office and enlisted the archbishop's support in following up on the results of their investigations. Archbishop Mitty's opposition to the Communist Party derived from both faith-based and nationalist-inspired foundations. A World War I chaplain-veteran, Mitty secured membership in the American Legion soon after its founding in 1919. In 1935, he was chaplain of the California chapter, and in 1936, he participated in planning a "United Front" for "combating Radical and Communistic Activities" made up of the legion and representatives of the Knights of Columbus, the Ancient Order of Hibernians, and the Young Men's Institute (in which Andriano had served as "Grand President").[27]

Archbishop Mitty kept himself informed about the investigation of several Communist Party members, including Oleta O'Connor, a twenty-five-year-old native San Franciscan who had been raised Catholic but was now described in a surveillance report as "one of the most radical firebrands among local Communists." By 1935, O'Connor had been a member of the Communist Party for two years, following a year in the Socialist Party, and she was serving as the part-time organizational secretary for the San Francisco party. Her early life mirrored that of many children born into Irish Catholic families of modest means. Her father was a twenty-six-year-old shoe salesman, and her mother was a twenty-year-old housewife when she was born, and they were living in the South of Market working-class district in a basement apartment on a street no bigger than most city alleyways. As their fortunes improved, they moved to Eureka Valley (today's Castro neighborhood), where Oleta enrolled in Douglas School (now the Harvey Milk Civil Rights Academy) and then transferred to Convent of the Sacred Heart grammar school run by the nuns of the Religious of the Sacred Heart. After finishing Girl's High School, O'Connor attended the University of California, Berkeley, where she was president of the Women's Debating Club. She graduated in 1931, earned a master's degree in Slavic languages in the following year, then joined the Socialist Party, which she left after a year in favor of the Communist Party. Twenty years later, she described how "those things that I believed the Socialist Party should be doing and was not doing were being done by the Communist Party; that the Communist Party, so far as I could see then, was really earnestly and sincerely fighting to help improve conditions within the framework of the existing social system; and that in addition to this and growing out of these struggles, they were educating the people to understand the need ultimately of moving toward a socialist society."[28]

In her busy first two years in the Communist Party, O'Connor worked with the American League against War and Fascism, a Communist Party front organization, then on the staff of the *Western Worker*. She subsequently was put in charge of neighborhood organizing in the Marina and the Fillmore neighborhoods before being assigned as citywide organizational secretary. At the time of the general strike, she helped put out the *Western Worker,* and after the vigilantes wrecked its office at 37 Grove Street, near City Hall, she "carried typewriters and paper up and down Telegraph Hill to the private residence where work was being done to prepare the material so that the paper could be put out, despite the destruction of the headquarters and despite the fact that the printing shop had been told not to publish it any more." At the same time, O'Connor was teaching a class on "Americanism" at a Catholic orphanage in the city's Bayview district under the auspices of the Emergency Education Project, a public relief program run by the State of California' Emergency Relief Administration (SERA).[29]

According to an American Legion investigator, O'Connor "had no legitimate need for relief but was placed on the rolls in one of the many Red plots and obtained a position," after which, instead of communicating "the patriotic ideas she was supposed to teach" students, she proceeded "to feed them Communist doctrines, glorifying Russia and her leaders." The director of the Emergency Education Project fired O'Connor after following her and discovering that "she had been visiting Communist headquarters at the *Western Worker* offices in the Civic Center." O'Connor landed other jobs, first as a typist in one of the departments of the SERA office itself, and then as a writer in the federal Works Progress Administration (WPA) writers' project, and the surveillance continued. By November 1936—more than a year after her first firing—an agent reported, "Although this woman is on the WPA payroll and receives the regular weekly stipend from the government, she spends her entire day, with the exception of checking in in the morning and at night at WPA headquarters, at 121 Haight Street [Communist Party headquarters]," where "she is a teacher at the Communist worker's school on the subject of atheism and Catholicism (as applied to Communist policies)." There is no indication in the report that the agent knew that O'Connor was now serving in the position of county educational director of the Communist Party.[30]

While O'Connor was critiquing Catholicism at the Communist Party school, Archbishop Mitty was teaching his own lesson about Americanism in the Washington's Birthday edition of *The Monitor* in 1936. On the front page, over a picture of Washington, readers found a banner filled with tiny American flags and the headline, "Communism, a Monstrous Evil," plus an article describing Pope Leo XIII's denunciation in 1878 of "that sect of men who, under various and almost barbarous names, are called socialists, communists, or nihilists, and who, spread over all the world, and bound together by the closest ties in a wicked confederacy, no longer seek the shelter of secret meetings, but, openly and boldly marching forth in the light of day, strive to bring to a head what they have long been planning—the overthrow of all civil society whatsoever." In the same issue, the archbishop reprinted "Condemning the Totalitarian State," his speech to the golden jubilee dinner of the St. Vincent De Paul Society in January, in which he cited with approval the U.S. Supreme Court's decision in 1922 that invalidated an Oregon law requiring attendance at public schools, thereby preserving parents' rights to send their children to Catholic schools. Mitty asserted that the "inalienable rights" of Americans "are given to us not by the State but they are given to each individual soul by God Himself, and no group of people and **no State has any right to take these inalienable rights away from any individual**." Mitty decried the fact that "in other nations these principles ['the State the supreme arbiter in matters of education and in matters of human relations'] are being put into practice."[31]

Mitty did not specify which countries deserved the appellation "totalitarian," but Pope Pius XI singled out several regimes for criticism in a speech three months later in Rome that was reprinted on the front page of *The Monitor*. Germany, he said, was "known to be particularly dear to Us," but he criticized the Nazi government because it had decided "in violation of all justice and through an effort artificially to identify religion with politics, [that] the Catholic press is not wanted." But the pope especially condemned the Soviet regime, "where a real hatred of God is destroying all that belongs to religion and particularly all that belongs to the Catholic Religion." The pope informed the audience that "he spoke not only as the head of the Church . . . but also as a 'son of our times,' and with solicitude especially for 'human, earthly institutions' which are also menaced by communism." Making reference to the Comintern's official adoption of the Popular Front strategy in the summer of 1935, Pope Pius XI argued that communist "propaganda is the more dangerous when, as in recent days, it assumes an attitude less violent in appearance, less impious in its aim to penetrate into places which would be less accessible were that violence continued. And, alas, it obtains in places incredible success, or, at least, is met with the silence of tolerance, an inestimable advantage for the cause of evil and one of the unhappiest consequences for the cause of good."[32]

In San Francisco, the new Communist Party strategy arrived at the same time as a new district organizer, William Schneiderman. After attending the

Seventh World Congress of the Comintern in Moscow in July and August, Schneiderman returned to the United States, and in October he moved to California. He explained to readers of the *Western Worker* that the new approach meant the Communist Party should make coalitions with "the poor and middle farmers and the city middle class, the professionals, intellectuals, etc.," and the result would be "a broad People's Front. . . . We must change our sectarian methods of work which are an obstacle to winning the masses." By the beginning of 1936, the new approach was making a difference: the Communist Party newspaper advertised non–Communist Party events by organizations such as the American Civil Liberties Union, and its own "United Front" activities included labor leaders and politicians who qualified as progressives but were not party members. By the election campaign period in the summer and early fall, the Communist Party was fielding candidates for political office who claimed that their program promised a more attractive alternative for beating back conservative Republican and right-wing candidates than the policies offered by liberal Democrats.[33]

The perceived threat of the new policy of the Popular Front, combined with the party's determination to compete for political office, galvanized the Catholic Action activists into renewed militancy in the summer and fall of 1936. Hugh Gallagher kept the Chancery Office up to date with his various investigations, sometimes meeting with the archbishop in the company of "my informant." It was likely Gallagher who supplied Archbishop Mitty with the five-page "Special Memorandum in re: Harry Bridges," which contained a chronological report describing "beyond the question of any doubt the direct contact between Harry Bridges and the Communist Party, as well as the affiliation of Harry Bridges with members of that party who are primarily identified with subversive tactics as relate to labor organizations along the Pacific Coast." Several others—who, in contrast to Bridges, made no bones about their Communist Party membership—received special scrutiny from the Chancery Office, including O'Connor, Schneiderman, the district organizer of the party, and Archie Brown, a Young Communist League organizer who would soon travel to Spain and fight on the Republican side in the International Brigades. The archbishop established regular communication with the American League against Communism, which had recently opened its office in the city; its executive director boasted that the increasing number of memberships required him to double the office space after the first nine months. And the Chancery Office filed one report from an informant who reported on a meeting in which the speaker announced that "the Communist Party must make 1936 their objective to gain control in California. He stated that the whole United States is watching the west coast and that if the party is successful in controlling California, the rest of the States will be forced to follow. When these remarks were made every one almost went crazy from happiness."[34]

The informant's account of the meeting may or may not have been accurate, but there is no denying that as the election campaigns of 1936 moved into high gear in the late summer and early fall, labor relations on the Bay Area waterfront once again attracted national attention, this time in connection with the expiration of the agreements of 1934 between the waterfront employers and the maritime workers' unions. Archbishop Mitty called on the two sides "to submit disputed points to an impartial board of arbitration. When conciliation and mediation have failed, this appears to be the only justice and equity, rather than on the basis of the economic power of the employers or the numerical strength and organization of the employees." Mitty quoted Pope Leo XIII's encyclical on capital and labor in support of "the work of arbitration . . . a function that is proper to government." Mitty insisted that "San Francisco wants not a temporary truce but a permanent peace."[35]

Mitty's assumption that a San Francisco community interest existed above and apart from the interests of particular factions, and that the interest of the community as a whole required employers and unions to submit to government arbitration, was shared by neither party to the dispute. The maritime unions were now represented by the Maritime Federation of the Pacific, a coalition of seven unions organized in 1935; its slogan was "An Injury to One Is an Injury to All." Some AFL leaders regarded the federation as "a communist conspiracy" out of keeping with the limited "hours, wages, and working conditions" goals of their craft-centered tradition. The waterfront employers were now party to a campaign to deport the Australian-born Bridges that had support from a variety of anticommunist organizations on the grounds that he was a Communist Party member and not a citizen of the United States. The financial editor of the *San Francisco Chronicle* stormed out of one meeting of employers in outrage after getting the distinct impression that the employers were seriously considering assassinating Bridges. Edward F. McGrady, the Department of Labor's troubleshooter who visited the Bay Area in early September, reported to President Franklin Roosevelt on September 20 that "after two years of bickering and violations of the contracts on the part of both sides, hatred has developed, and there is a determination on the part of each side to smash the other."[36]

The Pacific Coast waterfront strike began on October 29, 1936, and lasted ninety-eight days—fifteen days longer than the strike in 1934, with neither the employers nor the workers achieving an unqualified victory. In the weeks leading up to the strike, during the months that the ports were closed and the pickets marched, and after the resumption of shipping on February 4, 1937,

Communist Party activists and Catholic Action militants raised the temperature of the local cold war that had been going on between them since 1934. In August, some 9,000 people turned out for the appearance in San Francisco of Earl Browder, the Communist Party candidate for president. In October, nearly 50,000 people attended the annual observance of the Feast of Christ the King at Kezar Stadium. Pope Pius XI had established this liturgical event eleven years earlier, dedicating the last Sunday of October to services intended to remind all people, not just Catholics, that Christ was their rightful ruler in things of the spirit.[37]

San Francisco Catholics had celebrated the Feast of Christ the King since 1925, first at the San Francisco Seals baseball stadium and then at Kezar Stadium, adjacent to Golden Gate Park. But Archbishop Mitty broke with tradition in 1936 when he announced, in a message carried in San Francisco's daily newspapers, that the observance on October 25 would be dedicated not only to the cause of world peace but also to the campaign against the Communist Party. A week before the event at Kezar Stadium, Mitty used the pages of the *San Francisco News* to denounce the new Communist Party slogan that equated communism with patriotic Americanism. Mitty insisted that backers of the Communist Party were "false prophets" who would "reduce man to the state of slavery by denying the noblest quality of his nature. He becomes a mere puppet, his individuality being entirely submerged in the totalitarian state. Russia, Mexico and Spain speak eloquently of the evils of such a philosophy of government." Communism was not Americanism at all but, rather, un-Americanism: "No citizen worthy of the name can subscribe to those false and destructive principles of government which have been imported from Russia." Communism jeopardized the church as well as the state: "The teachings of Stalin are in direct opposition to the doctrine of Christ, our King, and it is our sacred duty to endeavor by all the power at our command to stem the tide of this pernicious system, which if allowed to spread, will destroy Christianity. No quarter can be given." In the *San Francisco Sunday Chronicle* on the day of the observance, the keynote speaker of the day, Father Richard Hammond, invited Protestants to join with Catholics in protesting both "the great sums being spent on armaments throughout the world" and "appeals to class warfare." Father James McHugh, spiritual adviser to the Holy Name Societies in the archdiocese, criticized the Communist Party for "the spread of harmful propaganda" and assured readers that "no Holy Name man can countenance for a moment a philosophy that at once blasphemes Christ and aims to destroy our Government."[38]

Archbishop Mitty's call for an anticommunist crusade brought an immediate response from the Communist Party, which, since the adoption of the Popular Front strategy, had been advertising itself as the essence of patriotism; the party had scrapped its old "Class against Class" slogan in favor of the new

"Communism Is the Americanism of the Twentieth Century." The Communist Party printed the broadside "An Appeal to Catholic People, a Reply to Archbishop Mitty."[39] It was widely distributed by party members and presented a three-part argument designed to counter what they had "read about Communism in the Hearst papers." First, it stated,

> Your enemy is not the Communist Party, which puts forward a program growing directly from your daily needs. Your enemy is the Liberty League—the Mellon–Morgan–Du Pont clique working through the Republican Party—which would smash our living standards and destroy every vestige of liberty and democracy, freedom of press, and religious worship. . . . We Communists are men and women seeking to eliminate the crying injustices perpetuated against the people by a handful of industrialists and bankers. Jobs, social security for all, freedom of speech, press and worship, the preservation of democratic liberties—these are the things we stand for.

Second, it argued that readers needed to appreciate the Communist Party's viewpoint on "Hitler Germany and Spain Today." In Germany,

> Fascism has been victorious. Catholics as well as Jews have been thrown into concentration camps, imprisoned, tortured and murdered. Today German Catholics are joining with Communists in an underground movement to smash Hitler's reign of terror. In Spain the common people—mainly of Catholic faith—are fighting desperately to defend their democratically-elected government. While the wealthy Church hierarchy in Spain are supporting the fascists—who have been financed and armed by Hitler and Mussolini—hundreds of propertyless priests are fighting shoulder to shoulder with the people against reaction.

The final point urged readers to acknowledge and reject Archbishop Mitty's allegedly erroneous and dangerous views. In his call for the Christ the King rally, the broadside said, Mitty had presented the Communist Party as an alien force whose message was contrary to church teachings and inimical to the public interest. But the truth was that

> because the Communist Party is recognized as the steadfast champion of the people, . . . the Communist Party is the main target of fascist attacks in the United States. . . . When Archbishop Mitty calls for a drive against Communism, he is lining himself up with the reactionary enemies of the people: the Wall Street group, the Republican Party

which sponsors Black Legionism and its program of extermination of Catholics, Communists and Jews! There is a way to defeat American fascism. That way is the independent political action of trade unionists, Communists, Socialists, workers, and middle-class people of all religions, united in a People's Front.

One of the People's Front candidates in the state election of 1936 followed up on the Communist Party's printed attack on Archbishop Mitty by delivering a speech critiquing him on KGO radio the day before the rally at Kezar Stadium. Vernon Dennis Healy, a construction worker and member of the pile drivers' union, had first run for office on the Communist Party ticket in the 1934 election for State Senate District 12; Healy received 4.6 percent of the vote, attracting 1,134 votes compared with the 23,312 won by the incumbent, a Democrat named Herbert W. Slater. Now Healy was the Communist Party candidate for Congressional District 1, and he would lose again (and later in 1938 when he ran for a seat in the Assembly), this time garnering a mere 1.1 percent of the votes and losing to Clarence F. Lea, a Democrat and former district attorney of Sonoma County.[40]

Healy adopted a "guilt by association" rhetorical strategy in a radio address he made on October 24, arguing that Mitty had aligned himself with the "Radio Priest" Father Charles Coughlin, a notorious anti-Semite who broadcast from Royal Oak, Michigan, with "William Randolph Hearst—the enemy of all lovers of peace and freedom, the enemy of every person who stands for the democratic rights for which our forefathers fought and died 160 years ago," and with "the Wall Street reactionaries." According to Healy, Mitty had added his voice to "those who shout Communism the loudest [and] who are trying to bring about in this country a fascist dictatorship . . . and are preparing, together with the Hitlers and Mussolinis, to plunge the world into another imperialist war." Whereas Mitty criticized the Soviet Union, the Republican government in Spain, and the regime of Lázaro Cárdenas in Mexico on the grounds that "our Church can accept no system of government that enslaves men," Healy defended them as "democratically elected governments" that were "anti-fascist, dedicated to the preservation of the democratic rights of the people." Healy concluded his broadcast with a call to "Fellow Catholic people" to understand that "there is nothing in our program that is un-American, un-Christian, or contradictory with the needs of the Catholic people. We are sure that you will agree with us now that Communism is really the Americanism of the Twentieth Century."[41]

In fact, very few Californians agreed with Healy, judging by the small number who registered to vote as communists or who voted for Communist Party candidates in November (not all of whom were party members), and while

Roosevelt won reelection by a landslide of historic proportions, Earl Browder garnered only 10, 877 votes in the Golden State, a mere 0.4 percent of the total. Five months later, Archbishop Mitty, unfazed by the Communist Party's charges that he was helping to prepare the way for a Fascist America, considered making his relationship with the American League against Communism official. The organization had received "criticisms and suggestions that we add the word 'Fascism' to our title," but instead of explicitly indicating in its name that it opposed fascism, as well as communism, the group renamed itself the National Americanism Foundation. But after contacting colleagues in New York City and getting "the dope on them," Mitty decided that the foundation was "just another organization against Communism, of which there are so many."[42]

4

"A GREAT TRAGEDY"

Catholics, Communists, and the Specter of Fascism

San Franciscans kept informed about and were deeply concerned with, disturbed by, and divided over the political crises that roiled European affairs, from Benito Mussolini's March on Rome in October 1922 to Adolf Hitler's Blitzkrieg against Poland in September 1939. City residents turned out in the thousands for competing Catholic and communist events, especially after March 19, 1937, when Pope Pius XI published his encyclical *Divini Redemptoris* (On Atheistic Communism). A scathing indictment of "bolshevistic and atheistic Communism, which aims at upsetting the social order and at undermining the very foundations of Christian civilization," the pope's message also contained a reassertion of the importance of grassroots Catholic Action workers throughout the world—"Our beloved sons among the laity who are doing battle in the ranks of Catholic Action." According to the pope, the "task [was] now more urgent and indispensable than ever," and "militant leaders of Catholic Action . . . must organize propaganda on a large scale to disseminate knowledge of the fundamental principles on which, according to the Pontifical documents, a Christian Social Order must build."[1]

On April 27, San Francisco County Sheriff Daniel C. Murphy joined the attorney Joseph Scott of Los Angeles and Joseph J. Rosborough, former postmaster of Oakland, at the podium during a Catholic Action rally against communism at San Francisco's Civic Auditorium. Sponsored by the Knights of Columbus and the Catholic Daughters of America, the "mass meeting" drew thousands to the Civic Auditorium, where they heard Scott (a popular figure in Knights of Columbus circles who in the mid-1920s had appeared with Sylvester Andriano on programs critical of the government of Plutarco Elías Calles in

Mexico) declaim about the incompatibility of communism and Christianity. Sheriff Murphy reminded the audience that Catholic Action required agitation for social justice as well as vigilant anticommunism: "Every man that works is entitled to security for himself and his family." Rosborough deplored the anticlericalism and atheism of the Republican government in Spain and its Soviet and Soviet-sponsored volunteer allies in the civil war, but he also stressed that "if the ruling class in Spain hadn't been so selfish and ruthless with the human multitude, violence and death wouldn't now be stalking through that tragic land." John D. Barry, a local newspaper columnist known for his skeptical, free-thinking views, initially feared that the mass meeting would "play communism up as far more important than it really was [and] make it better known." But he concluded, "The meeting will do good. It's making communism serve as a challenge to our own short-sightedness and inhumanity."[2]

Barry served as the moderator of another "mass meeting" the following evening at the Dreamland Auditorium, this one sponsored not by Catholic organizations but by the American Friends of the Soviet Union. The warm-up address came from Beatrice Kincaid, who used her time to ridicule the Catholic event the previous evening, which she described as "dull and sluggish." The audience, she said, had "had such a bewildered look on their faces. The speakers knew nothing at all about Communism." Kincaid was a veteran of a Soviet program that recruited volunteers who moved to Russia and devoted a year or two to help build socialism in one country under Stalin. She insisted that "there is no such thing as persecution in Russia. And they told [us] last night that there is." Archbishop Mitty's informant, a professional stenographer named Carmel Gannon, could not resist a touch of retaliatory ridicule: "And the cut of the people at Dreamland: Many of the men before the meeting opened sat with their hats on and thought nothing of it. And the women chewed gum. The man just ahead of me had hair that looked as if he cut it himself, and never combed it." The main speaker at the American Friends of the Soviet Union rally was Victor A. Yakhontoff, a political exile who had served as a major-general in the czarist army and as assistant secretary of war in the social democratic government of Alexander Kerensky before the Bolshevik victory in the Russian Revolution. Yakhontoff urged the audience to befriend the Russian people in the hope that rivalry between Japan and the Soviet Union would turn Stalin toward the United States, which would lead to a defensive alliance and eventual liberalization of the Soviet regime.[3]

For Archbishop Mitty and his Catholic Action leaders, just then preparing the ground for two new organizations in San Francisco—Catholic Men of San Francisco and the St. Thomas More Society—the notion that an eventual convergence of values could develop as a consequence of future mutual diplomatic interests was anathema, given Pope Pius XI's encyclical of March 1937. Earl

Browder, general-secretary of the national Communist Party, discovered this after he received no takers among militant Catholic Action activists for his offer, made during a speech to the tenth national convention of the national Communist Party, to extend "the hand of brotherly cooperation to Catholics." And San Francisco's new daily Communist Party newspaper, *People's World,* merely played up the exception to the rule when it quoted approvingly the speech of the liberal Catholic Father James M. Gilles, who criticized "red baiting" and urged greater attention to matters of social justice, including the "fight for Tom Mooney's freedom." (Mooney and Warren Billings were in prison serving long sentences for trumped-up charges that they had been responsible for carrying out the bombing at the Preparedness Day Parade that killed ten people and injured three dozen more in San Francisco on July 16, 1916.) Archbishop Mitty informed the shipping company executive Hugh Gallagher, "I cannot see that there is any possibility of comradeship between the Communists and the Catholics. Their Teachings are both atheistic and immoral." And Martin H. Carmody, supreme knight of the Knights of Columbus, whose organization stressed its commitment to "a Crusade for Social Justice as well as a Crusade against Atheistic Communism," told Archbishop Mitty that he was pleased that San Francisco had hosted one of the 6,000 meetings across the country dedicated to "a correct presentation of this menace to Christianity and Christian civilization."[4]

Carmody boasted to the archbishop that his organization had also made progress in thwarting the activities of the Communist Party front called Friends of Spanish Democracy, the purpose of which, he argued, was "primarily to spread Communistic propaganda." The "real purpose of this subversive movement," according to Carmody, was to support the anticlerical, socialist Republican regime in Spain, which in his view was an enemy, not a friend, to democracy in that country. Carmody was proud that his group had been responsible for having the permits for more than fifty meetings canceled by local authorities. The Knights of Columbus, and Archbishop Mitty, also supported the national Catholic campaign to get the U.S. government to honor the arms embargo by Britain and France against the Spanish Republic. The embargo drove the Republican side closer to Stalin's Soviet Union, which alone provided weaponry to the Republicans, while Hitler and Mussolini supplied arms to the rebel forces under General Francisco Franco. A relative handful of American Catholics worried about what they regarded as the moral dilemma of choosing either the anticlerical Republicans or the fascist-backed rebels. But most American Catholics followed the lead of their bishops and chose the latter, seeing the conflict not as a moral dilemma at all but, instead, as a simple choice between godless communists and courageous defenders of the church. The National Catholic Welfare Conference established the Keep the Spanish Embargo Committee in Washington, D.C.; Mitty's confidante Agnes G. Regan was active in the committee and kept him abreast of its work. When the committee decided to establish a national network of Catholic Action laymen to create grassroots support for its lobbying, Mitty appointed Sylvester Andriano as the "contact man" in San Francisco.[5]

Andriano and Archbishop Mitty followed the lead of the vast majority of Catholic Action activists in the United States, clerical and lay alike, who perceived the Second Republic's attitude to the church to be as hostile as Mexico's in the previous decade and rejected the Second Republic's claims to be the legitimate government of Spain. They were acutely mindful of the fact that "the character and extent of the breakdown of public order under the left Republican government in 1936 had no historical precedent of such proportions in western Europe, being equaled (and in fact exceeded) only by the situation in 1917 in Russia, where there was no effective government at all." In a six-page, single-spaced memorandum on communism prepared for Archbishop Mitty in September 1937, Father Hugh A. Donohoe remarked: "Ten years ago it would have appeared incredible that the religion and civilization of Spain rested on insecure foundations. Now Spain is passing through the dark night of a civil war in which the supporters of Sovietism and Communism are striving to drag it down to the irreligious, unmoral, and barbarous condition of Russia."[6]

American Catholics were appalled by the social chaos under the republic, which included the takeover of churches and church property, the closing of Catholic schools, and the expulsion of priests, and they were outraged by the republic's treatment of the Spanish Church. Critics of the republic reasoned that in a genuine democracy, James Madison's and Thomas Jefferson's concept of freedom of religious worship would have a hallowed place and its practice would be ensured, but the Spanish Republic failed to provide such guarantees to Catholicism. Worse, the critics argued, the republic had made public pronouncements about the Catholic Church no longer existing in Spain, which went well beyond disestablishment, and it allowed—if not encouraged—murders of thousands of priests and nuns and the desecration and destruction of churches. In fact, between July and December 1936, in "the greatest anticlerical bloodletting Europe has ever seen," the Republicans killed almost 7,000 clergy, which was about 10 percent of all deaths attributable to republican action during the Spanish Civil War and some 12 percent of Spain's Catholic personnel. Most Catholics took the position that the defenders of the republic had been deluded by phony democrats and that the claim by the government in Madrid and its defenders to be the true democrats was simply a mendacious and fraudulent assertion of no value whatsoever.[7]

A relative handful of dissenting American Catholics defended the legitimacy of the republic while criticizing its anticlericalism and its failure to check the leftist violence against the church and its clergy while at the same time denouncing the fascist support for, and the violent excesses of, Franco's rebellion against the republic. But they were few and far between during the nearly three years of bloody and often vicious fighting between July 1936 and April 1939. Archbishop Mitty denounced the dissenters as naïve and dangerous, as did his Catholic Action associates Bishop John F. Noll of Fort Wayne, Indiana, and Monsignor Michael J. Ready, executive secretary of the National Catholic Welfare Conference in Washington, D.C. Noll accused the dissenters of "collaborating beautifully, even if unwittingly," with the forces of Satan, and Ready announced that they had bought into the "Red game" of confusing the issue. Donohoe, writing for Mitty, criticized "those who profess to see in the present conflict a struggle between a legitimate and democratic government on the one hand and a party of self-seeking Fascists on the other."[8]

By the time the Vatican recognized Franco in August 1937, Catholic Action stalwarts in San Francisco had already established their own anti–Spanish Republic front in the form of a Spanish Relief Committee headed by Monsignor Charles A. Ramm. A convert to Catholicism whose Lutheran parents had immigrated to San Francisco, Ramm had graduated Phi Beta Kappa from the University of California, Berkeley. He served as secretary to Archbishop Patrick William Riordan (archbishop from 1884 to 1914). He was also assistant pastor of St. Mary's Cathedral under Mitty and served on the state Board of Charities and, for more than thirty years, on the Board of Regents of the University of California. Ramm was thirty years older than Sylvester Andriano in 1937, as was Richard M. Tobin, the San Francisco banker who served as treasurer of the Spanish Relief Committee and a member of the national Keep the Spanish Embargo Committee. Tobin came from the city's Irish Catholic "Old Money" crowd with close ties to the national Republican Party (he had served as minister to the Netherlands in the administrations of Calvin Coolidge and Herbert Hoover), whereas Andriano and Ramm were Democrats, and Andriano had roots in Little Italy rather than Nob Hill. But their ethnic and partisan differences did not interfere with solidarity on the question of the illegitimacy of the Spanish Republic and the lack of credibility of the Communist Party's defense of that government.[9]

Three months after the Spanish civil war began, the Communist Party's presidential candidate, Earl Browder, criticized the arms blockade of Spain in a radio broadcast on the NBC Red Network; he urged Americans to lobby for the repeal of the embargo and insisted that the Spanish republican government was democratic and the Franco rebels were fascists. Four days later, William F. Montavon, director of the National Catholic Welfare Committee's Legal Department and a member of the Knights of St. Gregory, a prestigious lay Catholic honorary society, answered Browder on the same radio network with a point-by-point rebuttal. Montavon recited "a record of mob violence, march-ings [*sic*] of Marxist militia, arson, robbery, [and] assassination" that, he insisted, proved that the republic was "a government in political bankruptcy." Where Browder had "denounced the upper Hierarchy as big land owners, cruel exploiters of the peasants, fighting with the rebels," Montavon asserted that "there is no scrap of evidence to warrant even a suspicion that any member of the Hierarchy in Spain is a big land owner, an exploiter of peasants or is fight-ing with rebels."[10]

The San Francisco Spanish Relief Committee set out to answer the Com-munist Party's argument that Americans had a duty to defend the Spanish Republic, a democracy, and a duty to oppose the Franco rebels, who were fas-cists. The committee announced its purpose as "to present to those who will read them the facts and the causes of the present struggle in Spain," and it pub-lished several pamphlets by local scholars. Aurelio M. Espinosa, the fifty-seven-year-old chairman of the Department of Romance Languages and Literature at Stanford University contributed *The Second Spanish Republic and the Causes of the Counter-Revolution,* a dispassionate recounting of events from the procla-mation of the republic by Alcalá Zamora on April 14, 1931, to the murder of the conservative leader Calvo Sotelo on July 13, 1936, and the aftermath of the army uprising four days later by generals Miguel Cabanellas and Francisco Franco—"not a revolution," he concluded, "but a counter-revolution." The sec-ond publication of the Spanish Relief Committee came from one of the com-mittee members, Umberto Olivieri, whose work, in contrast to Espinosa's, was an exposé intended to demonstrate that it was Joseph Stalin's rather than Thomas Jefferson's "brand" of democracy that was practiced by the regime in Madrid. Olivieri was a fifty-three-year-old veteran of World War I who had earned a law degree from the University of Rome and then served as a captain in the Italian Army during World War I. He left Italy for San Francisco in 1921, after the defeat of the Catholic Popular Party in the jockeying for political power that resulted in Mussolini's success the following year. Olivieri's first position was in the Bank of Italy's Legal Department, where he worked with James A. Bacigalupi, Sylvester Andriano's first partner, and where he met Andriano, whose offices were upstairs from the bank's lobby. Olivieri, possibly in collaboration with Andriano, organized the seventh centenary of St. Francis of Assisi, the patron of San Francisco, and Olivieri left the Bank of Italy for Santa Clara University and a position as professor of romance languages.[11]

Sylvester Andriano wrote the preface to Olivieri's pamphlet "Democracy! Which Brand, Stalin's or Jefferson's?" Andriano began with a statement that matched those of the Communist Party, asserting as the party did that "the historic soil of that country [Spain] has become once more the battleground for the clashing ideals of the world. Upon the outcome of the cruel struggle now raging in the land of Cervantes, Calderon, Murillo, Balmes and Isabella, the future of civilization depends. Whether or not we realize it; whether or not we will it, the truth is, we are all involved in that struggle. The issues at stake are too fundamental, too vital, too universal for anyone to remain neutral." But while the Communist Party chose the Republican side, Andriano opted for the Nationalists: "Order or Chaos; Christianity or Communism; Civilization or Barbarism; God or No-God—that is the one and only issue involved in this titanic struggle. On one side or the other of that single issue each must align himself." In his pamphlet, Olivieri presented a list of the "faults of the Spanish government," compared General Francisco Franco to General George Washington, and characterized the "tenets of the Third International of Moscow" as "the false pretenses of a hypocritical democracy . . . for whom democracy is the Trojan Horse for the establishment of communism." Olivieri concluded by warning readers who shared his and his committee's views to be prepared to defend themselves against anti-Catholic and even personal attacks, because "if we speak in favor of the Nationalists—or rebels—we run the risk of being accused of being fascists because every opponent to communism, right or wrong, is in the current conception a contemptible fascist."[12]

In fact, anti-Catholic attacks by the Communist Party were already under way in 1937, and they would intensify as San Franciscans felt more and more obliged to take sides as the conflicts in Europe spread beyond Spain to involve Germany, Austria, and Czechoslovakia. The local attackers zeroed in on a variety of alleged Catholic shortcomings, including "the great scandal of silence"— the failure of Catholics to condemn the bloody purges and reprisals carried out against the Republicans in Spain by the Catholic Francisco Franco. One critic dispatched letters to Archbishop Mitty and Father Raymond Feely of the University of San Francisco arguing, "The Pope blessed Franco, who is using Mohammedan Moors in his war against Spanish Catholics[,] and also blessed Mussolini (the Supreme Fascist), in his rape of Ethiopia." F. R. Fuller argued that there was more to fear from "the Catholic Octopus (the Hierarchy) with its tentacles spread all over the earth" than from the "Red Octopus"; that "'Roman Catholicism' is a foreign 'Ism' run by a foreigner,—the Pope"; and that if one asked, "Why all this Knights of Columbus Crusade against communism?" the answer was to distract the public from Catholic malfeasance. "Can it be possible that the flare-up (temporary or otherwise) caused by the present 'Graft Investigation' has threatened to expose those Catholics who are in the majority as the rulers of our fair city (both civil and industrial)?"[13]

Fuller ended his litany of the "train of abominable machinations and terrorism as practiced by the 'Catholic Hierarchy' all down the centuries" with an exhortation to "Read the 'People's World'!!" Three weeks after it published its first issue, the official Communist Party newspaper *People's World* editorialized that "Pete [McDonough] was not the Fountainhead." The press had popularized the phrase "Fountainhead of Corruption" to describe the bail bondsman McDonough, who was the chief target of the Atherton graft investigation in 1937. *People's World* now argued that the phrase fit "the corrupt Rossi administration," of which Sylvester Andriano was a member, better than it did McDonough. Nine months later, *People's World* wrote that "unkind critics of Rossi call Mr. Andriano the Mayor of San Francisco" in an exposé that pilloried Andriano as "the 'front man' behind which the Italian government teaches California born school children to 'Believe, Obey, Fight' for Mussolini and be disloyal to democracy and America."[14]

The targeting of the Catholic Action leader Sylvester Andriano and Mayor Rossi in January–October 1938 took place amid both the continuing attempts by the Communist Party to get its candidates elected to local offices and the deepening political crises in Europe. Germany annexed Austria on March 11, and on September 29, Hitler and British Prime Minister Neville Chamberlain signed the Munich Agreement, followed by German occupation of the Czech Sudentenland on October 5. Then came the night of November 9, Kristallnacht (the Night of Broken Glass), when Nazis attacked Jews and their homes, businesses, and synagogues throughout Germany. Oleta O'Connor, who had married a San Francisco plumber in 1937 and changed her name to Yates, now served as the Communist Party's state election campaign manager. After the elections in 1936, she and her colleagues faced more formidable competition from Catholic Action, because Archbishop Mitty and his lay activists were drawing strength from Vatican actions that called into question the party's argument that Catholicism equaled fascism. That Communist Party argument had already become tenuous for those San Franciscans who were well informed enough to know that the Lateran Accords with Italy were a pragmatic accommodation to the fact of Mussolini's regime, not a principled endorsement of the theory of fascism. But the equation of Catholicism with fascism faced an even more daunting challenge after Pope Pius XI issued his robust repudiation of Nazism on March 14, 1937, in *Mit Brennender Sorge* (On the Church and the German Reich).[15]

The encyclical, which was sent by special Vatican envoys rather than by public post to frustrate Nazi censorship and was written in German rather than Latin for maximum effect in Germany, was read to congregations by the bishops instead of their delegates and created maximum consternation among Nazi officialdom. The pope condemned the "aggressive paganism" of the Third Reich because it "exalts race, or the people, or the State . . . above their standard value and divinizes them to an idolatrous level, [and] distorts and perverts an order of the world planned and created by God. . . . None but superficial minds could stumble into concepts of a national God, of a national religion; or attempt to lock within the frontiers of a single people, within the narrow limits of a single race, God, the Creator of the universe, King and Legislator of all nations before whose immensity they are 'as a drop of a bucket.'" Nazi secret police confiscated all of the copies they could find, and Hitler's government did what it could to minimize the impact of the encyclical in Germany. Overseas, it was widely distributed and favorably received, especially in the United States, where the German ambassador complained that 25 million Catholics "stand united and determined behind their Church."[16]

Nowhere was that assessment more accurate than in San Francisco, where for decades the Jewish population had lived relatively free of the anti-Semitism that plagued their co-religionists in most American cities. In 1930, Archbishop Edward Hanna put Catholics officially on the side of American Jewish well-being by making an archdiocesan donation of $500 to the campaign for a Jewish Community Center. In 1931, Hanna received an American Hebrew Medal, given each year to those who "achieved most in the promotion of better understanding between Christians and Jews in our country." And in 1936, to advance "justice, amity, and understanding among American Catholics, Jews, and Protestants," Archbishop Mitty supported a "Good Will Tour" around the country by the Jesuit Father Michael J. Ahern, the Presbyterian minister Dr. Everett Clinchy, and Rabbi Morris Lazaron. This effort aimed at "combating and diminishing religious and racial bigotry" and reached more than 50,000 people in twenty-seven cities in ten different states.[17]

On New Year's Day of 1938, the archdiocesan newspaper paired an article condemning anti-Semitism as "contrary to Catholic Doctrine" with an editorial that condemned Nazi and fascist attacks on Jews as contrary to San Francisco Catholic traditions, as well as a violation of Catholic Church teachings. The editorial was titled "The West Coast" and announced, "We are really a different people. We do not need to follow as the East leads. *We* should lead because we are still free to express our principles, to admit the truth and to follow where it leads." In November, Archbishop Mitty participated in a twenty-seven-minute radio address on CBS condemning Kristallnacht. The broadcast went out on the evening of November 16 and was sponsored by Catholic University in Washington, D.C. Mitty was one of five Catholic clergymen and laymen, including former Governor Alfred E. Smith of New York, who denounced the Nazi attacks. Father Maurice S. Sheehy, chairman of Catholic University's Religious Education Department opened the broadcast by saying that the world was "witnessing a great tragedy in Europe" and that Catholics were determined "to raise their voices, not in mad hysteria, but in firm indignation against the atrocities visited upon the Jews in Germany." Mitty was the first to speak after the introduction: "As Catholics we have a deep and immediate sympathy with the Jewish men and women who are being lashed by the cruelty of a fierce persecution, especially in Germany. They for racial reasons and we for our religion are writhing there under the same intolerant power."[18]

Mitty's call for solidarity between Catholics and Jews fit nicely with San Francisco traditions, but it was a bold tactic, since many Catholics still opposed expressions of amity with Jews as an unacceptable admission that their religion was equal to Catholicism in God's eyes. "Thank God," Mitty continued, "that at last a careless world has waked up, and knowing what is going on across the waters, denounces persecution of race or religion everywhere with one vast united voice that rings around the earth. It is the voice of a better humanity, whose latent sense of justice, freedom and fellowship has at last been aroused by a fundamental appeal." Mitty ended his appeal for Catholic solidarity with the Jewish people with a familiar denunciation of "all class feeling" because it "has in it the dangerous element that sets one man against another. It may be hostile feeling against race or religion or economic conditions. Let us honestly search our own hearts and if we find this evil thing [class feeling] there, do our best in all our dealings with our fellow-men, in all the relations of life, to root it out of our being."[19]

People's World did not provide coverage of Archbishop Mitty's radio broadcast on November 16 denouncing Kristallnacht. Nor did it carry the story of Pope Pius XI's formal protest to the Italian state condemning the Nazi-inspired anti-Semitic racial laws adopted by Mussolini's government on November 10. But throughout the winter, summer, and early fall of 1938 the Communist Party hammered away at the alleged corruption of Rossi's city administration, explicitly asserting a nefarious community of interest that joined city officials, Catholic Action, fascism, and Nazism. In January, *People's World* exposed to its readers what it considered to be the true character of Mayor Rossi's administration: Rossi and his minions, not McDonough, deserved the title "Fountainhead of Corruption." In February, the paper rejected the argument in the *Catholic Herald* newspaper of London that "a worldwide trend [was under way] on the part of the Vatican and the Catholic hierarchy away from the Rome–Berlin–Tokyo axis and toward the democratic powers." The real story, according to *People's World,* was that San Francisco's Catholic newspaper was "parroting the reactionary cry of 'Communists.'" And the Catholic Action League of Decency-inspired raid on a city pornography publisher by Police Chief Quinn was denounced as interference with freedom of speech rather than "a police matter." In March, Andriano's friend Amadeo P. Giannini, founder of the Bank of Italy and chairman of the Bank of America, was excoriated in the headline, "Giannini in Plot to Aid Mussolini: Coast Banker Wants Billions for Fascism." The news story claimed that by participating in a British-led consortium to invest in an Italian government project, the banker was a fascist sympathizer. An editorial three days later claimed that Giannini "moved heaven and earth to aid Mussolini" and that "the exposure of Giannini shows how expansive and intricate is the network of conspiracy among these plotters for world Fascism."[20]

In May, Rossi's "reactionary government" was accused of colluding with the private Pacific Gas and Electric corporation, because Rossi refused to support public ownership of utilities. "It is not too early to think of a real civic house-cleaning next year, when Mayor Rossi, the real 'fountainhead of corruption' will come to you seeking reelection," *People's World* stated. An editorial on May 28 suggested a campaign slogan for the mayoral race in 1939: "Shine in 39: Oust Rossi." In July, Catholic leaders in the Italian community who had failed to condemn the Mussolini regime's adoption of the Nuremberg racial laws found themselves condemned as "ItalianAryans." And two days after the signing of the Munich Agreement, *People's World* announced that Mayor Rossi's planned appearance at the annual United German Societies meeting, which would also be attended by German Consul-General Baron Manfred von Killinger, would take place "under the swastika" and would signify that the mayor was joining "Nazis in Celebrating Czech Deal." Rossi did attend, a demonstration organized by the Communist Party took place, and city police officers removed and arrested numerous anti-Nazi pickets, including Oleta O'Connor Yates, from the streets surrounding California Hall. According to the Communist Party, "Mayor Rossi [was] a Fascist," and his participation in the event was an "outrageous insult . . . to the Democratic and Freedom Loving people of San Francisco." It was three weeks later that *People's World* published a three-part story with titles reading, "Mussolini Money Subsidizes Fascist Schools in California," "[Children] Told Their Mission in Life Is Armed Conquest for Fascism," and "Rossi Police Commissioner [Andriano] 'Front' for Fascist Schools."[21]

Twelve days later, Communist Party candidates for state offices met defeat at the hands of California voters. Oleta O'Connor Yates, running for a seat in the State Assembly, received only 845 votes (2.3%), compared with 20,379 votes for the winner, the Democrat George D. Collins Jr. But while the Communist Party candidates were rejected all over the state, voters embraced the Democratic Party cause, ending a long period of Republican Party control by electing Culbert Olson as governor, Ellis Patterson as lieutenant-governor, and Sheridan Downey as a senator. All three were liberal Democrats, as were a large proportion of the Democrats who captured the majority in the State Assembly. The Communist Party, which had thrown most of its assets into the campaigns of liberal Democrats rather than those of its own standard bearers, interpreted the election results as a vindication of the People's Front strategy. An election worker who exulted at a post-election party, "We won!" was told to calm down by William Schneiderman, the district organizer, because "we did not win, comrade. The Democratic Party won." But even Schneiderman could not deny that "a certain euphoria was prevalent in Party ranks." The editor of the *People's World* later recalled, "I was swept up by the same exuberance as the young woman, and was jolted, therefore, by the sudden confrontation with what I knew, of course, was the reality."[22]

The reality that intruded on the comrade's enthusiasm included the daunting spectacle that had occurred ten days before the election, when Archbishop Mitty's Catholic anticommunist crusade had once again attracted more than 50,000 celebrants to the annual Feast of Christ the King rally at Kezar Stadium. The Chancery Office advertised a special feature of the 1938 rally, one that distinguished it from earlier such celebrations: it served as the capstone event in the first weekend conference of Andriano's new organization, the Catholic Men of San Francisco. The archbishop presented his audience with the strongest yet exhortation to join "the Crusade to which Pope Pius XI summons you—to a Crusade of Catholic Action . . . in order that we might do something to save Christian civilization and Christian principles." Mitty bemoaned the "loss of faith on the part of so many people" and said:

> We have seen since the World War the rise of the Totalitarian state. . . .
> We see what has happened in Russia, what was attempted in Mexico. We see what has happened in Germany, what is happening in Spain. . . . Throughout the world there is this vast avalanche coming upon humanity which threatens to wipe out Christian civilization, which threatens to destroy nineteen centuries of Christianity. . . .
>
> We have developed a certain double conscience: Do not bring your religion outside of the four walls of the Church. They say they do not want political churchmen without defining what 'political' means. If religion has nothing to do with the things of human life it is not worth much. Christ wants us to bring our religious principles into our recreation, into our social activities, into industrial and economic matters, into legislative problems, into international relations. We have the fundamental principles that will solve all of these problems.[23]

Two weeks after Mitty's address at Kezar Stadium, *The Argonaut,* a local public affairs journal, published Father Hugh A. Donohoe's article "Communism: Anti-Religious and Anti-American." Donohoe, now teaching at the archdiocesan seminary, took aim squarely at the Communist Party's People's Front slogan "Communism Is Twentieth Century Americanism." He argued that "the high democracy of the founding fathers" was based on the principle that the "state receives its authority from God, not directly but through the medium of the people." Thus, "American democracy means more than the fickle rule of the many; it is something more than simple arithmetic; it means the rule of the majority in harmony with eternal law." Donohoe quoted Browder's own *What Is Communism?* to the effect that "we Communists do not distinguish between good and bad religions, because we think they are all bad for the masses." Donohoe argued that the Communist Party denied "the basic truths that are the essence of the Christian heritage" when it rejected belief in "a Creator, a personal God" and "the belief that marriage is a life-long union between man and woman." The Communist Party's call for "complete liberation of women from all inequality" demonstrated that "Christian teaching on woman's place in society is likewise subjected to persistent attack." Referring to the fact that "in Russia today there are political purges because some Communists fail to conform to the new code of 'democratic' principles," as more evidence of party perfidy, Donohoe concluded that opposing communism should go hand in hand with "the renewed acceptance of the Christian heritage in private and in public life" and that Americans who joined the crusade against communism were thereby "serving God and country."[24]

Two months later, Pope Pius XI died in Rome. As Catholics throughout the world mourned his passing, San Franciscans rededicated themselves to his Catholic Action principles as they geared up for another city election season. They did so as events in Europe moved the world inexorably toward war. In March, Hitler dismembered Czechoslovakia and occupied Bohemia and Moravia. France and England then reconsidered the Munich Agreement, and Chamberlain declared that if Poland was attacked, Britain and France would respond. In April, the people of Spain saw their civil war come to an end, but in the United Kingdom, men faced a new conscription law. Then Italy invaded Albania. Germany and Italy agreed to aid each other in case of a war involving either country—the so-called Pact of Steel—in May. On August 23, the improbable occurred: Germany and the Soviet Union agreed to a nonaggression pact, and one week later, Hitler and Stalin began dividing up Poland, setting off a declaration of war against Germany by Britain and France.

To Catholic Action activists in San Francisco, the Molotov–Rippentrop Pact represented yet another instance of Stalin's perfidy and communism's essential moral bankruptcy. To San Francisco Communist Party activists, the Nazi–Soviet agreement posed a challenge: how could they remain faithful to the sharp turn in Moscow's strategy and at the same time continue their search for political power in local government? Andriano worked to get his friend and client Mayor Angelo Rossi reelected, while the Communist Party backed a candidate whose credentials met their revised standards of anticapitalist commitment. Franck Havenner, the Communist Party's choice for mayor, was defeated, as indicated in the previous chapter, and voters rejected the three Communist

Party activists candidates for city office: Oleta O'Connor Yates for city assessor and Elaine Black and Archie Brown for the Board of Supervisors.[25]

In its spring 1939 issue, the *Moraga Quarterly* published the article "The Catholic College Graduate and Labor." The author was John F. (Jack) Henning, a recent graduate of St. Mary's College who would go on to become the head of the California State Federation of Labor, as well as Undersecretary of Labor in the administrations of John F. Kennedy and Lyndon B. Johnson. Henning announced, "The army of the Church is today engaged in a stern struggle," and he warned Catholics to reject both "American Way" individualism and the "painted panaceas [of] the land of Communism or the land of Fascism." Henning was addressing male graduates of St. Mary's College, but both men and women followed his lead, and their activities created a distinctive Catholic liberalism in San Francisco as they worked to define the public interest in relation to both homegrown American traditions of secular individualism and imported European ideologies of fascism and communism.[26]

5

"WITH MALICE TOWARD NONE"

Catholic Liberalism in San Francisco

W hen young Joseph L. Alioto urged Catholics to borrow grand strategy from communists and organize a "Catholic Internationale" in 1936, he immediately joined the front ranks of San Francisco's Catholic Action cadre of dedicated men and women determined to bring public life into alignment with the values of their religious faith. His public work and that of a like-minded network of men and women contributed to a distinctive Catholic liberalism in San Francisco, a project that generated deep concern among critics of such a faith-based program. Catholics argued that nothing in the First Amendment prohibited a citizen's drawing on his or her faith when participating in local, state, or national politics; in fact, they pointed out (correctly) that freedom of conscience (and to act accordingly) was itself explicitly protected by the nation's "First Freedom." Catholic liberals insisted that they were good Catholics and good Americans. But many Communist Party members and secular liberals in San Francisco worriedly asked, echoing the liberal Protestant magazine the *Christian Century*, "Can Catholicism Win America?" The question was "of special concern because, unlike members of nearly all other churches, these millions of American citizens are subject to the spiritual direction of an Italian pontiff who represents a culture historically alien to American institutions." Because of the aggressive program of Catholic liberalism that Alioto and his colleagues promoted in San Francisco, tensions arising from disagreements between those who argued that it represented the highest stage of Americanism and those who regarded it as an insidious anti-American import were at the heart of discussions about how to define the public interest for a generation after the New Deal.[1]

In 1943, Alioto was back in San Francisco after a period of law school and war-related work in Washington, D.C., and the United States was allied with the Soviet Union in a struggle to defeat the Axis powers. Father Hugh A. Donohoe (1905–1987) reminded readers of *The Monitor,* the official weekly newspaper of the archdiocese, that according to Catholic doctrine, "We must hate evil principles but not the persons who uphold those principles. Communists teach many principles that we hate but not only do we not hate Communists, we admire many of their qualities. We admire above all their unswerving devotion to a course in which they probably believe: making this war an anti-Fascist war."[2] Donohoe's admiration of the "unswerving devotion" practiced by communists appeared in the "As the Editor Sees It" column, which he contributed to each weekly issue of *The Monitor* from November 1942, when he became editor, to November 1947, when he stepped down to assume new duties as the city's auxiliary bishop and pastor of St. Mary of the Assumption, the cathedral church of the archdiocese located adjacent to the chancery office on Franklin Street. Donohoe served as pastor of St. Mary's, and as auxiliary bishop under Archbishop John J. Mitty, until he left San Francisco in 1962 to become the first bishop of Stockton, California.[3]

Donohoe began his service as editor of *The Monitor* in 1942 with a rhetorical strategy that invoked both Abraham Lincoln and Catholic Christian principles. "Your editor," he wrote, "begins this work with malice toward none." Readers were urged to consider Lincoln's famous phrase from the second inaugural address as "more than a catchy phrase. It sums up the Christian concept of living—at peace with God, with self and with neighbor." Donohoe asked readers to avoid demonizing the nation's enemy populations:

> It is hatred of principles not of persons that the Christian code allows.
> . . . Hatred of principles sharpens the wits. It makes men think; it
> makes them alert in the defense of the principles in which they believe.
> . . . What principles are the proper objects of hatred? There are many:
> that man exists for the State; that any one State has a special 'mission'
> that calls for the subjugation of all other States; that the State is a law
> unto itself; that the moral law is for persons, not for governments; that
> men are essentially different by reason of blood or color or nationality.
> These are but a few of the principles for which the Christian holds no
> brief.[4]

Donohoe served as Archbishop Mitty's unofficial and informal coordinator of the work of the Catholic Action cadre in San Francisco, a role that was facilitated by his appointment as editor of the official weekly newspaper and as pastor of St. Mary's Cathedral. He began his work immediately after being ordained in June 1930; when the school year began that fall, the twenty-five-year-old Donohoe commenced teaching at the archdiocesan preparatory seminary for aspiring priests, St. Joseph's College. Two years later, he began doctoral studies at the Catholic University, then received his doctorate in 1935. His dissertation was written under the direction of the nationally eminent scholar of Catholic social justice theory, Monsignor John A. Ryan (1869–1945). Donohoe then began a seven-year tenure as a professor of social ethics at St. Patrick's, the archdiocesan seminary in Menlo Park, some thirty miles south of San Francisco. During that time, he organized the local branch of the Association of Catholic Trade Unionists and served as its chaplain from its founding in 1938 through the 1940s. From 1935, when he returned from Washington, to 1962, when he left to become bishop of Stockton, Donohoe served as Archbishop Mitty's chief spokesman on Catholic Action in general and on issues of labor relations, social justice, and political socialization in particular.[5]

Like several of the most active members of the Catholic Action cadre, Donohoe was a product of the heavily Irish Catholic Mission District. He was born in 1905, the third child of Patrick and Frances Brogan Donohoe. Patrick hailed from Longford, Ireland, and Frances, born in California, was the daughter of Irish immigrants. As co-owner of Donohoe and Carroll Monuments in Colma, a small town just beyond city boundaries that housed Holy Cross Cemetery, Patrick provided headstones and mausoleums for Catholic burials. He died in 1923 when Hugh was eighteen.[6]

Hugh Donohoe's sister Patrice recalled that "there was lots of joy in our family but that didn't last after my father died." What did last was the Catholic religiosity and devotion to the church that Patrick had fostered. "We said the Rosary together every solitary night. My father had great devotion and I attribute our vocations to that." Two of Hugh's four brothers became priests in the Jesuit order, and three of his five sisters became Catholic nuns. Patrice, a life-long member of the Sisters of Notre Dame de Namur, recalled Hugh as "devoted to the Pope and his teachings" and "always positive" rather than negative when it came to spreading the Catholic Action message.[7]

From the time he assumed his duties as a professor at St. Patrick's, Donohoe prepared outlines for Archbishop Mitty's labor-related sermons; wrote drafts for the archbishop's correspondence on social ethics; organized conferences on social policy matters; and founded, managed, and taught in a diocesan labor school. The archbishop also called on him to serve as a mediator in a case of labor-management conflict in Notre Dame Hospital, an archdiocesan institution. One of his first duties was the organization of a Social Action School for Priests in the San Francisco Bay Area. After the national meeting of U.S. bishops in November 1936, a call went out to set up summer schools of social action for the clergy that would operate under the direction of local bishops. Mitty responded by asking Donohoe to create a month-long school in San Francisco, which was the fourth in the nation after Toledo, Milwaukee, and Los Angeles. Designed to give local priests an opportunity for "the serious study of the Social Encyclicals and of their practical application to the American condition," the Social Action School enrolled twenty-eight priests for the four-week course in June 1937. In residence at St. Patrick's Seminary, the priests divided their work into five courses: Principles of Social and Distributive Justice, Catholic Social Philosophy, The Labor Problem, History of the American Labor Movement, and The Agricultural Problem. Donohoe taught the Labor Problem course.[8]

In his course on the Labor Problem in 1937, Donohoe drew on his studies with Monsignor Ryan (who was popularly known as "the Right Reverend New Dealer") and the research for his doctoral dissertation. A study of collective bargaining under the 1933 National Industrial Recovery Act (NIRA), the work assessed the record of the New Deal law's operation in the light of scholarship on Catholic labor relations. Section 7(a) of the NIRA was of particular interest to Catholic social justice advocates because its language put the force of government policy in service of a central principle of Pope Leo XIII's *Rerum Novarum*: "Employees shall have the right to organize and bargain collectively through representatives of their own choosing, and shall be free from the interference, restraint or coercion of employers of labor, or their agents, in the designation of such representatives or in self-organization or in other activities for the purpose of collective bargaining or other mutual aid or protection." Donohoe concluded that while the law's collective-bargaining provision did "make concrete that right which all employees possess and should exercise," in practice "enforcement of Section 7(a) has been a complete failure." The dissertation included an analysis of pending legislation introduced by Senator Robert Wagner of New York that was intended to replace the NIRA (which the Supreme Court declared unconstitutional in the spring of 1935) with a more effective National Labor Relations Act.[9]

President Franklin D. Roosevelt signed the Wagner Act, which established the National Labor Relations Board, into law on July 5, 1935, and signed the Fair Labor Standards Act (FLSA) three years later. These New Deal measures established federally sanctioned and enforceable collective-bargaining rights for unions, contained federal rules for a minimum wage and a maximum hour workweek, and banned products of child labor from interstate commerce. Donohoe's vigorous defense of the Wagner Act and the FLSA in years to come derived from his conviction that they conformed to "the Catholic approach to the labor question," which he located in "the doctrine of natural rights." "The specific rights include the right of private ownership, the right of reasonable access to the goods of the earth, and the right of a living wage. The processes are two in number: group action that aims at promoting individual welfare and the assistance of the state to effect the same purpose."[10]

Donohoe's assessment of the extent to which federal labor relations policy succeeded in meeting the requirements of *Rerum Novarum* and *Quadragesimo Anno* in his dissertation was a prologue to his monitoring of labor relations practice in his communications with Bay Area Catholics while he taught at St. Patrick's Seminary in the late 1930s and edited *The Monitor* from late 1942 to 1948. He condemned laissez-faire business practice, preached to workers about their moral obligation to join unions, condemned both unionists and employers when they appeared to him to lose sight of the general good as they struggled for the interests of their groups, and insisted on carefully calibrated state participation in the economy while condemning "ruthless State intervention."[11]

While still at St. Patrick's, Donohoe defended labor's gains made since the Wagner Act from attacks by employers who still hoped to turn the clock back to pre–New Deal conditions. In the wake of the congressional elections in 1938, conservative business organizations began a coordinated assault on labor and the liberal legislation of the New Deal. The National Association of Manufacturers (NAM) was especially notable in this regard, because it fostered a campaign to establish open shop conditions by means of state "Right to Work" legislation. One of the NAM's tactics was to win Catholic clergy over to the side of the open shop by means of a Clergy-Industry Education Program designed to persuade Catholic priests that American conditions were so superior to those of Europe that *Rerum Novarum* and *Quadragesimo Anno* should not guide Catholic social policy in the United States. When Archbishop Mitty received an invitation to send Bay Area priests to one such program in November 1941, Donohoe agreed to attend with ten other priests to speak out about the need for local employers to adopt a "broad social conscience" on labor relations matters. One year later, writing from the editor's desk of the official newspaper, Donohoe countered the NAM's complaint that business enjoyed no federal support of the kind the Wagner Act provided to labor by pointing out that business organizations did not need legal protection because the right of association by employers was "not under attack."[12]

Father Donohoe played a key role in Archbishop Mitty's efforts to support moderate alternatives to radical unionism, the third type of activity undertaken by the church that aimed to influence labor relations and shape the character of public life in San Francisco during the period. The Catholic Church undoubtedly enjoyed a high degree of credibility among the working class largely because a great many priests and bishops were themselves from working-class backgrounds and were thus quite sympathetic to the demands of organized labor. At the same time, where issues of labor were concerned, the church also enjoyed considerable credibility among business leaders. Archbishop Mitty supported the struggle by anticommunist unions for greater influence in the city's public life while he simultaneously waged a campaign against communism. The condemnation of communist influence in waterfront labor unions in San Francisco, particularly the charge that Harry Bridges of the International Longshore and Warehouse Union (ILWU) was a member of the Communist Party, was a staple of business and Catholic unionist rhetoric during the period. Recent research in the records of the American Communist Party stored in the Comintern Archives demonstrates the truth of the charges against Bridges and many of his waterfront union comrades. The archbishop's forthright leadership in the campaign against the Reds thus appears to have been based on realistic grounds and was not an instance of the reckless and irresponsible extremist red-baiting endemic in those years.[13]

The church in San Francisco used the same forums through which it promoted mainstream unionism to combat left-wing unionism: *The Monitor*, Labor Day sermons, public lectures, special events and programs, and union functions. It was not uncommon for the church to engage in public defense of management against those who were viewed as radical unionists. During the intra-union strife between communists and anticommunists that accompanied the onset of the Cold War, Archbishop Mitty lent his full support to anticommunists. In at least one instance, he issued explicit instructions to individual priests to use their influence over workers to ensure the defeat of a "communistic organization" in a union election supervised by the National Labor Relations Board.[14]

In addition to promoting the negative by working to combat communist influence in the union movement, the archbishop also accented the positive by supporting Catholic lay activists who established a San Francisco branch of the Association of Catholic Trade Unionists (ACTU). The ACTU was founded in New York in March 1937 by several former members of the Catholic Worker Movement who had grown dissatisfied with what they saw as the utopian character of that organization. The new group proposed to promote unionization and increase the practice of Catholic principles within the labor movement. The organization conducted labor schools, sponsored public lectures, published pamphlets and newspapers, supported strikes, provided legal assistance for the rank-and-file, and solicited church support for union activities. By 1940, Catholic unionists had established eight regional chapters in cities across the nation. While modeled after the New York organization, each chapter emerged under various local conditions and remained essentially autonomous.[15]

San Francisco unionists organized a chapter in 1938, during a strike by retail clerks, in response to an incident in which three nuns crossed a picket line. Angered and frustrated by the nuns' insensitivity to the strike effort, not to mention their apparent ignorance of Catholic teachings, several Catholic unionists formed an ad hoc committee to inform the public of the church's position on labor issues. This committee quickly evolved into a local chapter of the ACTU, the formation of which was announced in a press release dated September 18, 1938. The new organization, its membership restricted to Catholics, ratified a constitution that declared its purpose: "To foster and spread . . . sound trade unionism built on Christian principles." This would be accomplished by supporting union organizing and strike efforts, as well as by sponsoring educational programs designed to increase the influence of Catholics within unions by teaching them how to be more effective organizers and negotiators.[16]

The archbishop's initial response to the formation of the new organization was cautious, a reaction that was no doubt realistic given that suspicion of unions was as common among Catholics in San Francisco as it was in other American cities at the time. One such conservative, a J. J. McDonough, wrote to Archbishop Mitty after receiving a "Dear Catholic Friend" letter calling for support of the retail clerks' strike. McDonough asked whether the archdiocese had approved of the letter: "I was under the impression, that anything with Catholic attached to it could not be sent out, unless endorsed by the Archbishop. I thought it best to return this letter so you could see what is being sent out. I consider myself a good Catholic, but also a loyal citizen to the employer who has given me my livelihood for the past 30 years. I do not believe in biting the hand that is feeding me."[17]

Two months later, Archbishop Mitty moved from a stance of caution to that of "wholehearted approval," and he gave his blessing to Donohoe's request to serve as its chaplain, the only ACTU office that was not an elective position. Initially, the archbishop instructed Donohoe to steer the ACTU away from "political activities and from possible difficulties between various labor organizations." However, as Mitty became convinced of the ACTU's commitment to the spread of unionism based on Christian principles, he quickly recognized the organization's potential to counter the influence of communism within the local labor movement and gave it his unreserved full support. The ACTU received public praise as an excellent example of the type of Catholic worker societies called for by Pius XI in *Quadragesimo Anno*. Business leaders received assurance that the new organization had the endorsement of the archdiocese. Catholic workers received encouragement to join the ranks of the group.[18]

John F. Maguire served as president of the ACTU during its active years from 1939 to the mid-1950s. Like Donohoe and John Shelley, Maguire was a graduate of St. Paul's grammar school in the heavily Catholic Mission District. By 1944, ACTU membership within the archdiocese had swelled to the point at which, with the guidance and encouragement of Father Bernard Cronin, a graduate of the Social Action School for Priests, a second chapter was established in Oakland. After twenty-five years of operation, some 750 applications had been distributed and 599 union members joined and paid dues, though monthly meetings and communion breakfasts typically attracted fewer than two dozen activists. By the time Laura Smith, a member of the retail clerks' union who had been a founding member of the ACTU, closed the checking account in 1963, the group had been largely inactive for five years.[19]

During the first fifteen years, by contrast, ACTU members in San Francisco made themselves a force to be reckoned with, particularly in the longshoremen's unions. The most dramatic evidence of the ACTU's efforts to ensure democracy in union affairs occurred in the ILWU, whose international president was Harry Bridges. The Australian-born Bridges, director of the waterfront strike committee in 1934, survived four deportation attempts and developed an international reputation during the period as a paladin of leftist unionism. Bridges, who we now know was not merely an American Communist Party member but was on the Central Committee, typically scoffed at charges that he operated a communist dictatorship and boasted of his union's democratic procedures. He had a point. In the largest of the locals in the ILWU, Local 10, James Stanley Kearney, who had joined the ACTU in early 1940, defeated the Communist Party member Archie Brown in the election for vice-president of the local in 1943. During the subsequent twenty-seven years, Kearney served nine two-year terms as the president of Local 10. This record is even more impressive in light of the fact that incumbents were required to stand down after each term to keep a president from succeeding himself. When Kearney died suddenly in 1970, he was still serving as president, and the entire waterfront shut down in his memory. Given Kearney's electoral success and that of George Bradley, another Local 10 officer and ACTU activist, it is not surprising that the left-wing director of the Research Department of the ILWU sent an informant to ACTU meetings who took notes on the proceedings.[20]

By the mid-1940s, Bishop Donohoe's name had become synonymous with Catholic Action, particularly with the labor relations agenda of Archbishop Mitty's program, and Donohoe's moral idealism endeared him to San Francisco's Catholic union members and their leaders. By 1947, the NAM and other business lobbyists had succeeded in weakening union power to the point that Donohoe referred to them in his editorial column as "the greatest and the wealthiest propaganda machine in the country." He pointed out that in one year they had spent nearly $3 million financing more than 1,500 talks to women's clubs, civic groups, and student assemblies. They had advertised nationally in more than 500 daily newspapers and 2,000 weeklies and generated daily publicity releases sent to all of the wire services. Pamphlets and even movies rounded out a well-coordinated campaign to win converts to the open shop. Labor, by contrast, lacked such funding and thus could not compete effectively, and claims by business regarding the tyranny of labor unions were nonsense.[21]

The open shop campaign sought to prohibit compulsory unionism. By 1947, fourteen states (mostly in the South and West) had passed the so-called Right to Work laws. Catholic labor intellectuals were divided on the question of whether the open shop or the closed shop best fit papal labor doctrine. Donohoe followed the example of his mentor, Monsignor Ryan (who died in 1945), and strongly opposed the open shop, staying firmly in the left-wing of the Catholic social justice spectrum of opinion. In opposition to Father Edward A. Keller, an economics professor at Notre Dame University from 1933 to 1969, who defended the open shop in *The Case for Right-to-Work Laws: A Defense of Voluntary Unionism,* and Archbishop Henry J. O'Brien (1896–1976) of Hartford, Connecticut, who claimed that the closed shop violated constitutional rights, Donohoe argued that it was "neither immoral nor unethical to require union membership for the greater common good of the group." And when Walter Reuther and the United Auto Workers demanded that General Motors Corporation open its books during contract negotiations so the public could accurately assess its ability to pay its workers, Donohoe strongly agreed: "Surely if the ability to pay is the proper formula in setting wages, then exact knowledge of that ability is the first requisite."[22]

In addition to opposing the corporate campaign against labor, which included an unsuccessful campaign to pass an open shop law in California in 1945 and the successful Taft-Hartley Act of 1947, passed over President Harry Truman's veto, Donohoe worked closely with both American Federation of Labor (AFL) and Congress of Industrial Organizations (CIO) unions as they faced the challenges of converting from wartime to postwar economic conditions. In addition, he was active as a chaplain for the local ACTU, with some 600 members, and he was a popular speaker at both local union meetings and national federation conferences. He continuously reminded his audiences of their responsibilities as citizens of their community as well as their rights as unionists. As might be expected of a clergyman, he urged them to realize that the union cause would succeed best if premised on "forgetfulness of self" of the leaders and "dedication of those they represent."[23]

When Donohoe moved from *The Monitor*'s editorial office to the chancery after being consecrated auxiliary bishop in October 1947, some 700 unionists attended a dinner in his honor in one of the city's premier hotel banquet rooms, the Gold Room of the St. Francis. The dinner was sponsored by the ACTU jointly with AFL, CIO, and independent union organizations in the Bay Area. John F. ("Jack") Shelley, president of both the California State Federation of Labor and of the AFL's San Francisco Labor Council, and a former California state senator, praised Donohoe for having been "a champion who understands us perfectly; a man who has realized our rights; one who has fought for us." Shelley continued, "He has made San Francisco realize that we are not primarily interested in wages but rather we insist that our labor and the conditions of our labor be an expression of our human personalities. . . . [He] has instilled in the minds of the public that we are not mere 'things' but human beings with personal interests clamoring to be recognized."[24]

Like Donohoe, Shelley (1905–1974) was a product of the city's Mission District, and they had known each other since boyhood, having been classmates at St. Paul's grammar school. Shelley was also born in 1905, one of nine children of Denis Shelley and Mary Casey; his father was an immigrant from County Cork who worked on the docks as a longshoreman, and his mother was a native San Franciscan. Donohoe left St. Paul's for the preparatory seminary, but Shelley enrolled in Mission High School, where he was president of the debating club and the student body, captain of the rowing team, head cheerleader, and commander of the ROTC. In 1922, Shelley shipped out as a merchant seaman, and by 1929, when he returned home because of a death in the family, he had worked his way up to first mate and was fluent in Spanish and Tagalog, a Philippine language.[25]

When the twenty-four-year-old Shelley started work that year, he immediately enrolled as a member of the International Brotherhood of Teamsters and drove bread trucks in the city. Restless and ambitious, he delivered bread during the day and studied law at night, and the University of San Francisco—a Jesuit institution—awarded him a law degree in 1932. Three years later, he was elected vice-president of his local union, then president the following year. In January 1937, he won election as president of the San Francisco County AFL Labor Council, the youngest man ever to hold that position, and in 1938, city voters sent him to Sacramento as their sole state senator, a position he held until 1946. Shelley also served as president of the Labor Council through the 1940s, as well as president of the California State Federation of Labor, and would later serve eight terms in the U.S. Congress (1949–1964) and one term as mayor of San Francisco (1964–1968). Shelley was one of the organizers, with Donohoe, of the local branch of the ACTU, and he drew explicitly on the principles of the Catholic encyclicals in his labor union advocacy and as an elected official at the local, state, and federal levels.[26]

Shelley's appeal to voters, from his run for the state senate in 1938 to his campaign for mayor in 1963, drew explicitly on Catholic labor teaching in several ways. He demanded justice for working people and at the same time advocated treating business as a partner, not an enemy of labor. Like Pope Leo XIII in *Rerum Novarum,* Shelley insisted that the community's well-being should take precedence over the interest of any specific interest group. Shelley's first election campaign flyer included a quotation from his campaign manager, City Supervisor James B. McSheehy, that illustrated his approach: "Speaking as a business man, Supervisor McSheehy said: 'Shelley's loyalty to the workers in the

American Federation of Labor has never been open to question. At the same time, he has always been conscious of the general public welfare in labor-capital dispute. He knows San Francisco problems and is pledged to work for their solution.'"[27]

During his tenure as state senator, Shelley sponsored two pieces of legislation that put into practice the Ryan–Donohoe interpretation of the labor encyclicals that called on state intervention for the furtherance of workers' dignity: a labor standards bill for apprentices in the building trades and a disability insurance program. And in San Francisco shortly before being elected to the senate, in his capacity as president of the county AFL labor council, Shelley helped put in place the business and labor cooperative arrangement that mimicked at a local level the industrial council concept of Pius XI's *Quadragesimo Anno*. In 1937, faced with a labor victory in the waterfront strike of 1934 and voters' rejection of a twenty-year-old anti-picketing ordinance, leaders of the city's Chamber of Commerce met with Jack Shelley and together they negotiated the informal arrangement whereby employers would accept the legitimacy of picketing, provided no violence took place. The chamber then disbanded its twenty-year-old anti-union Industrial Association, a subsidiary that had orchestrated the city's successful open shop campaign. A new cooperation-oriented subsidiary was created in its place called, first, the Committee of Forty-Three, and then, in 1939, the San Francisco Employers Council.[28]

By 1940, the CIO unions had joined Shelley's AFL unions in this informal cooperative system for handling labor relations in the future. Disagreements persisted on the particulars, and numerous hard-fought strikes and negotiating sessions took place in the decade to come. However, future conflicts would be settled within the institutional framework informed by Catholic labor theory that Shelley (with Donohoe's advice and counsel) had spearheaded in 1937 and 1938. During the 1940s and 1950s, the Catholic activism practiced by Archbishop Mitty, Bishop Hugh Donohoe, and laymen such as Jack Shelley and Joseph Alioto brought them into competition with various anti-Catholic individuals and groups, including communists and free-market advocates, who advocated undoing New Deal labor legislation. An episode during the presidential election year of 1948 is illustrative. Early that year, frustrated by its inability to limit Catholic political power in local elections and in the labor movement, the San Francisco Communist Party's county committee commissioned the research report "Catholicism in San Francisco." "We Communists," according to the report, "have been negligent in taking this factor into consideration, and while there has been a token recognition of the importance of Catholicism in our community, we have not given it the attention it merits." Party activists discussed the eight-page, single-spaced report at neighborhood branch meetings and then at a day-long conference in September. As they prepared for the elections in 1948, the city's communists were instructed to keep in mind that "Catholicism has a broad mass appeal which has been carefully fostered over the centuries," that "Catholic Action is a world wide movement," and that "the Church through Catholic Action is out to reclaim its lost worlds." The party member who drafted the report probably minimized the zeal of Catholic Action activists while exaggerating the appeal of the church's program.[29]

The Communist Party was troubled not only by the ACTU. It also faced competition with the University of San Francisco (USF) Labor Management School, which, like the ACTU, promoted alternatives to radical unionism. The idea to establish the labor management school emerged in a series of discussions in 1946 between Donohoe and Father Andrew C. Boss of USF. Boss was a graduate of Gonzaga College with a graduate degree in labor economics and industrial relations from Georgetown University. Like Donohoe, Alioto, Henning, McGuire, and Shelley, Boss was a native of San Francisco, one of the six sons of a Mission District barber. Also like Donohoe, Boss saw Catholic labor schools as a way to enhance the status and power of the mainstream labor movement, as well as to compete more effectively against the Communist Party in San Francisco. Donohoe and Boss regarded the new school as one element of a two-part strategy. The ACTU, which was nearly a decade old at the time, would continue to combat communism within the local labor movement, and the Jesuits at USF would operate an educational program that could effectively compete with the California Labor School, which was supported by the Communist Party. Father Boss recalled in an interview in 1972:

It was a bad time for labor, with the depression still a sharp memory and the Postwar turmoil creating fertile ground for the commies. They had a communist labor school in San Francisco, and it was touch and go as to the influence they were beginning to have on the labor movement. We needed something to shift the spotlight onto the sound teachings of the Church about the dignity of the workingman and his rights.[30]

The USF Labor-Management School opened its doors in the spring of 1948 and was greeted with the enthusiastic support of both Archbishop Mitty and new Auxiliary Bishop Hugh A. Donohoe. Father Boss became the director in 1950 and served in that position until his retirement in 1975. In 1978, the institution ceased to operate independently, and its courses were absorbed into the USF Business School's curriculum. As was the case with the ACTU, the school received considerable publicity in *The Monitor,* and Catholic unionists were encouraged to attend. Unlike the ACTU educational programs, one did not have to be Catholic or a union member to attend. The USF school was open to union members and to management personnel who were directly involved in negotiations with unions. This more inclusive admission policy, coupled with greater resources that allowed for a wider variety of courses, allowed the USF program to recruit a broader constituency than the ACTU-sponsored programs.[31]

The USF School offered two ten-week sessions each year to mixed classes of union members and officials, management personnel, and lawyers involved in labor-management negotiations. Jesuits from the USF faculty, union officials, and management executives taught the non-credit evening courses. Topics included practical offerings such as parliamentary procedure, public speaking, and how to take a case to the NLRB, as well as broad offerings such as "Election Year—1948," "Philosophy of Communism" and "Soviet Expansion."[32]

During Archbishop Mitty's tenure, attendance at the fall and spring sessions averaged 120. The largest enrollment came in the spring of 1949 (230), during the adjustment period after the passage of the Taft-Hartley Act. The second largest enrollment occurred in the spring of 1958 (199) during the McClellan hearings into labor union corruption that led to the passage of the Landrum-Griffin Act, which imposed new regulations on unions in the following year. From 1948 through 1950, the first three years of its existence, the school attracted more than 500 students to its programs, and by the beginning of the session in the fall of 1958, 1,500 union and management people in the Bay Area had graduated from the school. By 1969, graduates numbered more than 5,000 and included representatives of approximately 500 different labor unions and 200 businesses.[33]

Besides running the two sessions each year, with four to six evening classes each session, the USF Labor-Management School published a monthly magazine, *USF Labor-Management School Panel,* and sponsored conferences and symposia devoted to particular issues. Before the AFL and CIO merged, the presidents of each organization's county labor councils actively participated in courses and conferences, as did business agents, presidents, vice-presidents, and research directors of individual local AFL and CIO unions. Jack Henning regularly taught courses and spoke at conferences. During the 1950s, the Labor-Management School cooperated with the San Francisco Urban League and the Council for Civic Unity on behalf of liberal racial reform measures, and Mayor George Christopher appointed Henning to the city's new Commission on Equal Employment Opportunity in 1957.[34]

By the end of the 1940s, organized labor had established itself as a legitimate participant alongside business and government in the liberal growth coalition that shaped San Francisco's urban development into the 1970s, but the city's business organizations continued to challenge organized labor's power and influence. Archbishop Mitty continued to put the influence of the church on the side of moderate union labor. This position often placed him at odds with the more conservative business leaders of the city. In 1947, Mitty joined the Republican Party leaders Governor Earl Warren and Mayor Roger Lapham at the opening ceremonies of the AFL's convention in the city. Lapham, who had come a long way from his call in 1934 for violent repression of the waterfront strike, had accepted the legal right of unions to represent their members and to participate in collective bargaining with employers. However, Lapham continued to endorse measures such as the Taft-Hartley Act of 1947 and the unsuccessful "Right to Work" state ballot initiative in 1958. Both aimed to limit the powers available to labor unions. The archbishop, by contrast, put the church on record as being strongly opposed to Taft-Hartley, and *The Monitor* provided considerable space to national and local union leaders who condemned the measure during congressional debates and deplored its passage when it was passed over President Truman's veto.[35]

In the case of State Proposition 18, the "Right to Work" initiative of 1958, which California voters rejected by a substantial margin, Mitty's initial strategy was cautious. In July, he consulted with his counterparts Joseph T. McGucken in Sacramento and Cardinal J. Francis McIntyre in Los Angeles, then announced that the church's official position would be to stay neutral. Lapham was anything but neutral. The former mayor served as Northern California's chairman for the Proposition 18 campaign, and in October he debated the measure on public television with Harry Bridges of the ILWU and, before an audience at San Francisco State College, with Jack Henning, who was then serving as the research director for the California Federation of Labor. Then the attorney Gregory A. Harrison made a move that changed the dynamics of the campaign entirely.

Harrison was the brother of Maurice E. Harrison, one of the founding members of the city's St. Thomas More Society and a staunch supporter of Archbishop Mitty's Catholic Action initiative of the late 1930s. Both brothers were partners in Brobeck, Phleger, and Harrison, the law firm that had represented the shipowners from the early 1930s to the late 1940s. In 1948, however, the shipowners' organization had taken its business to a rival firm, one that was critical of the older tradition of employer intransigence and supportive of the "New Look" in labor relations that had been developing since the settlement of the strike of 1934. Now, just days before the November election, Harrison bought a large ad in all of the major newspapers headlined, "Popes, Prelates and Priests Urge Voluntary Unionism." Pictures of Popes Pius XI, Pius XII, and Leo XIII and of Cardinal Francis Spellman were placed alongside carefully selected quotations that implied that the Catholic Church urged a "yes" vote on "Right to Work." Mitty responded by issuing another, almost full-page newspaper ad that appeared the day before the election. His statement rejected the claim "that so-called 'voluntary unionism' is the official teaching of the Catholic Church. This is a gross misrepresentation of the facts." Printed alongside Mitty's recommendation that voters "vote as they see fit on any issue in accordance with their conscience" appeared criticisms of Proposition 18 by Monsignor Matthew Connelly, the chaplain of the San Francisco Port, and Father Andrew Boss, dean of the USF Labor-Management School. When the election was over and the votes had been counted, the president of the state's labor federation sent a warm "thank-you" letter to archdiocesan headquarters.[36]

San Francisco's Catholic liberalism extended beyond growth politics and labor relations in the 1940s and 1950s due to the efforts of a cadre of young priests who were handpicked by Archbishop Mitty. In 1947, one of the leading members of this cadre, Father Joseph D. Munier (1909–1993), criticized the revival of laissez-faire philosophy and business attacks on labor unions in a speech at the Catholic Conference on Industrial Problems in Portland, Oregon. "Hopeful signs towards the realization of Pope Pius XI's reconstructed social order," Munier concluded, "are all too few." Munier, like Donohoe and Shelley, was a Mission District native, born in 1909 to the French immigrants Marie and August Munier. Joseph attended St. James grammar and high schools before enrolling at the University of California, Berkeley, where he graduated Phi Beta Kappa in 1931. Munier decided to become a priest during a visit with his mother to the shrine at Lourdes after graduating from Berkeley, and he was ordained in Rome after studying at the North American College, a seminary for Americans in the Eternal City, in 1937.[37]

Archbishop Mitty identified Munier as an ideal candidate to replace Donohoe at St. Patrick's Seminary, and he arranged for the newly ordained priest to earn a doctoral degree at Catholic University. Munier's dissertation, "Some American Approximations to Pius XI's 'Industries and Professions,'" was a study of whether any of the pope's recommendations for a cooperative commonwealth had been instituted to any practical degree within American economic life. His dissertation supervisor was Monsignor Francis J. Haas (1889–1953), dean of the School of Social Science at the university, the American prelate who had earned national recognition for his service in positions at a variety of New Deal agencies and who would soon head the Fair Employment Practices Committee. Munier assumed the position of professor of economics, sociology, and social ethics at St. Patrick's Seminary in 1944, with an explicit charge from Mitty to train future priests and "to promote knowledge and interest in Catholic Action."[38]

Munier taught at the seminary for seventeen years and promoted the Catholic Action message in sermons, homilies, speeches, and research reports. He also worked as a consultant to the Christian Family Movement, a lay organization dedicated to Catholic family life, until he retired from his professorship in mid-1961. His forecast for the success of the papal initiatives may have struck his listeners in Portland in 1947 as pessimistic, but he left them with a call for action, as well as with an "either–or"—that is, "Either democratic, mutual cooperation based on Christian principles of justice and charity will prevail or the class struggle leading to dictatorship and based on anarchy and hatred will crush us."[39]

In 1950, Father Munier, now at the center of the San Francisco Catholic Action cadre, took the message overseas as a U.S. State Department consultant to the Religious Affairs Office of the U.S. High Commissioner for Germany (USHCG). The context was the establishment in 1949 of the North Atlantic Treaty Organization (NATO), which marked another turning point in the evolving competition between the United States and the Soviet Union. Munier coordinated his work with Bishop Aloysius J. Muench (1889–1962), the bishop of Fargo, North Dakota, who was serving in Frankfurt as the regent of the Vatican's Apostolic Nunciature in Germany.[40] Munier's assignment required him "to investigate the impact of Christian social teaching upon the solution of the social problems" that postwar Germany faced. In the summer of 1950, he spent three months in Bavaria and Württemberg-Baden consulting, lecturing, and participating in seminars to instill faith in "a spiritual conception of life" to counter the communist alternative of "a godless form of democracy, a diluted, secularistic and materialistic brand of expedient and pragmatic democracy." According to Munier, "The Germans are still looking for the real substance of democracy, the religious, philosophical foundation."[41]

Munier interviewed three dozen bishops, priests, and chaplains of various social action and workers' organizations, and he met with academic specialists in Christian social teaching; he also made visits to Kolping houses for young workers, Hildegarde's Homes for Working Girls, and other, similar institutions. Munier arrived for his initial briefing at USHCG headquarters in Bad Nauheim, near Frankfurt, with "high hopes of finding a post-Hitler church on fire for the [social action and Catholic workers'] cause." What he discovered was very different and seems to concur with the description of the diocese of Münster as researched by Wilhelm Damberg: "Admittedly, in 1945, between theory and practice lay a gaping abyss." Munier reported finding "a few social-minded Bishops, few very exceptional priests who are devoting themselves full-time to the workers, and finally the lay leaders of a variety of worker organizations," but his experience left him "disappointed in not finding a more courageous, a more militant and a more positive presentation of Christian social principles by church institutions in Bavaria and Württemberg-Baden."[42]

Munier's report to the Catholic Affairs Branch of the USHCG contained four pages of detailed suggestions and three recommendations for immediate action. First, he called for reducing the social distance between teachers and students in the Catholic workers' schools by removing university professors and appointing instructors recruited from the working class. Second, he urged the bishop of Rottenburg to appoint a young full-time priest to aid an older priest who was managing the Stuttgart Central Worker Office. Third, he recommended that every diocese establish social action schools for priests modeled on those in San Francisco that Father Hugh Donohoe had established fifteen years earlier.[43]

Father Munier's State Department consultancy coincided with another transnational endeavor of the archdiocese in the years immediately following the end of the Second World War: the resettlement of displaced persons. In 1948, Mitty chose Father Bernard C. Cronin (1910–1987) to head the Catholic Resettlement Committee of the archdiocese. Cronin and Munier were good friends, having both been in residence at the Catholic University of America from September 1939 to the summer of 1942 in Washington, D.C., "struggling together to obtain our doctorates" in the School of Social Science under Dean Haas. Cronin's doctoral dissertation was a richly documented analytical narrative of the role of Father Peter C. Yorke in the labor movement of San Francisco during the tumultuous decade of 1900 to 1910, which included a waterfront strike, the organization of the city's Union Labor Party, the graft trials that took place after the earthquake and fire of 1906, and the election of the first labor party mayor in American history.[44]

Born in 1910, Bernard Cronin was one of seven children born to the Irish immigrants Daniel and Sarah Davey Cronin. The Cronin family lived in the East Bay city of Oakland, a city that experienced rapid growth as many businesses and families relocated there from San Francisco in the years after the devastating 1906 earthquake and fire. Both parents worked for wages: Daniel as a plasterer and Sarah as a domestic. Sarah eventually became the housekeeper in the home of Benjamin Ide Wheeler, president of the University of California, in Berkeley. Like Hugh Donohoe and Joseph Munier, Bernard Cronin graduated from a Catholic elementary school—Sacred Heart Parish School in Oakland—and then attended the preparatory seminary at St. Joseph's.

In 1930, the year that Donohoe became a priest, Cronin began his training at St. Patrick's Seminary. In June and July 1937, one year after Cronin's ordination at St. Mary's Cathedral, the new priest attended Father Donohoe's Social Action School at St. Patrick's while serving as assistant pastor at St. John's Church in San Francisco.[45]

After he finished his doctoral work at Catholic University in 1942, Cronin spent five years doing special assignments for Archbishop Mitty, including serving as chaplain of a new East Bay chapter of the Association of Catholic Trade Unionists, director of health and hospitals, dean of the Religion Department at College of Holy Names, assistant director of Catholic Social Services, and assistant director of the Society for Propagation of the Faith.

Cronin brought something of an evangelical fervor to his duties in these positions, as illustrated in his talk to the East Bay ACTU in April 1945. He urged his listeners to turn out for the address "The Moral Basis of Peace," by Monsignor Fulton J. Sheen (1895–1979), at the Oakland Civic Auditorium during Sheen's visit to the Bay Area in connection with the ceremonies initiating the United Nations. "It is not enough to say that Christian principles must be respected in any and all plans for peace. . . . [T]he press and other public servants could hardly afford to ignore our news and views should we demonstrate by mass attendance at the Auditorium on the night of April 19 that we Catholics constitute more than a fourth of the population of this town." In May 1947, Cronin became the church's representative on the San Francisco Committee for Education on Alcoholism, a position that provided him with experience relating to city officials, as well as to Jewish and Protestant delegates. This work came at a time when Mitty was receiving an increasing number of requests for participation by Catholics with Protestant and Jewish representatives in postwar social policy community projects; the archbishop picked Father Cronin to head one such project, the Archdiocesan Catholic Resettlement Committee.[46]

Concern about homeless victims of the European war first became a priority with the Truman administration in June 1945, and in the late summer and fall of that year the president appointed Earl G. Harrison, former commissioner of immigration, to report on the problem and initiated a dialogue with the U.S. Army leadership about policy alternatives. In his address at the first meeting of the General Assembly of the newly formed United Nations organization on October 23, 1946, Truman announced: "I intend to urge the Congress of the United States to authorize this country to do its full part, both in financial support of the International Refugee Organization and in joining with other nations to receive those refugees who do not wish to return to their former homes for reasons of political or religious belief." In 1948, Truman signed the first Displaced Persons Act, but the legislation contained discriminatory restrictions that were widely condemned. In his acceptance speech at the Democratic Party convention in Philadelphia in July 1948, Truman promised that if reelected, he would "ask for adequate and decent laws for displaced persons in place of this anti-Semitic, anti-Catholic law which this 80th Congress passed." Truman won the election, and on June 16, 1950, he signed an amended Displaced Persons Act.[47]

Given the large number of Catholics among the displaced persons in Europe (estimates varied between 55 percent and 73 percent from 1945 to 1947), it is not surprising that the heads of the National Catholic Welfare Conference and Catholic War Relief Services recommended to Archbishop Mitty that "we should lend wholehearted support and cooperation" to the national campaign to facilitate the entry of displaced persons. Lay activists in San Francisco, headed by Maurice E. Harrison (1888–1951), the attorney who in 1939 had organized the St. Thomas More Society, formed an interfaith Bay Counties Committee for Displaced Persons two months after Truman's United Nations speech. Mitty endorsed the effort and co-sponsored a public statement in February 1947 along with Rabbi Morris Goldstein, president of the Northern California Council of Rabbis, and Abbott Book, secretary of the Northern California Council of Churches. The statement was published in Bay Area newspapers as an advertisement urging the public to lobby for "the liberalization of immigration laws [so that] this nation would be doing its bit to wipe out a bitterness in Europe that threatens to generate new conflicts."[48]

Mitty delegated preliminary work for the resettlement program to Father James Murray, assistant director of the archdiocesan Little Children's Aid organization, and Murray recruited fifty Catholic men and women to lay the groundwork. By the time Cronin assumed his duties in September 1948, each of the thirteen counties of the archdiocese had a working resettlement committee, as did each of the parishes and all of the Catholic "nationality" organizations: French, Italian, Polish, Slovak, Croat, Slovene, and Lithuanian. In addition, each of the dozen or so Catholic religious organizations—such as the Knights of Columbus, the Guadalupe Society, and the Catholic Daughters—had established its own working groups, and so had Catholic members in the two major labor organizations, the AFL and the CIO. Father Cronin headed the Resettlement Committee for ten years, becoming known in the Bay Area as "the priest of displaced persons." He operated his agency cooperatively with Jewish and Protestant counterparts; press photographs show him in numerous appearances, sometimes walking arm in arm, with local rabbis and Protestant ministers. They facilitated the settlement and sometimes—as in the well-publicized case of the Shmerlins, a Jewish family who needed assistance in traveling from Shanghai to Israel—the transfer of some 6,000 displaced persons from camps in Europe and Asia to new homes in the United States and beyond.[49]

6

A "DIFFERENT ERA"

San Francisco Women and the
Pursuit of the Public Interest

When Julia Gorman Porter reflected on her experience in party politics and urban planning in 1975, she described the 1960s as a turning point for women in public life. Porter was not repeating the
familiar refrain about feminists challenging traditional gender roles and exerting more influence in politics. She was instead referring to what she regarded as
the negative consequences for female political activists in San Francisco of
changes in American political culture after the assassination of President John
F. Kennedy: cynicism about politics; distrust of public officials; criticism of
noblesse oblige. Porter was also ambivalent about the rise of single-issue citizen
action groups that seemed to place a higher priority on their particular causes
than they did on advancing the interests of the city as a whole. She confessed to
feeling nostalgic for San Francisco in that "different era" from the 1930s to the
early 1960s.

Porter's identification of herself as a "dedicated Democrat" put her squarely
in the mainstream of pro-growth liberalism, but hers was not the only alternative available to women in San Francisco who chose to involve themselves in
the debates about how to define the public interest in the years from the Progressive era through the 1960s. Women associated with the city's Catholic
Action movement participated with their archbishop in a campaign to purge
the city of what Walter Lippmann called "the acids of modernity" in his book *A
Preface to Morals* (1929). Their faith-based commitment to what they called
their moral and educational apostolate had consequences for both public discourse and public policy. Then there were the communist women active in public life. They may have marched to the beat of a different drummer, but they

also labored to bring public policy in San Francisco into conformity with a faith—a faith in the power of communist theory to open the hearts and minds of city residents and move them to work to create a Soviet-inspired socialist San Francisco. Between the Catholic Action women and their communist opposite numbers, liberal women such as Julia Gorman Porter—who proved more influential and whose efforts produced more lasting results—occupied the mainstream of San Francisco liberalism.

When the Vatican's Cardinal Giuseppe Pizzardo gave formal approval to San Francisco's new Catholic Action program in the summer of 1938, the local response among archdiocesan activists was enthusiastic: "*Dieu le vault*—God wills it, cried the crusaders of old with Pope Urban II and Peter the Hermit when it was a matter of rescuing the Holy Sepulchre and the Holy Places from the hands of the infidels. *Dieu le vault*—we can repeat today in unison with our pastors and priests in answer to the clarion call of our Holy Father and of our own Archbishop when it is a matter of rescuing individual souls, the home, the school, public morals and Christian civilization itself from the blight of the new paganism and the frightful chaos of Communism."[1]

One of Cardinal Pizzardo's calls to action involved "the apostolate of education involving the maintenance of Catholic schools," something that Catholic women had actively pursued for years. Students at St. Rose's girls' high school in San Francisco and St. Mary's boys' high school in Berkeley were the first to organize, creating a Knights of Catholic Action club at their campus, followed by a Bay Area-wide group called the Student Catholic Action Council. The council and an associated Federation of Catholic High School Religious Organizations of the Archdiocese of San Francisco published the *Student Catholic Action* newsletter and *Student's Handbook of Catholic Action*. The students based their work on Pope Pius XI's urging that "centers of Catholic Action should be formed in universities and in secondary schools," and their newsletter quoted the Vatican's apostolic delegate to the United States, Archbishop Amleto Cicognani, about the importance among Catholic youth of "unity of action, harmony of purpose, and union of minds." Because Catholic high school students were segregated, with boys and girls attending separate institutions, the federation hoped to use its publications "to help united Catholic girls and boys in our Catholic high schools to do the great things they can do TOGETHER [*sic*] for Christ and his Church."[2]

Catholic Action work with youth played an important role in the agendas of San Francisco's Catholic women's organizations. Catholic women in San Francisco had organized a Young Ladies' Institute (YLI) in 1887, and in 1920 they established the city's Archdiocesan Council of the NCCW. By 1936, the YLI claimed a membership "11,000 strong" in the thirteen counties of the archdiocese, and they celebrated their Golden Jubilee the following year with a parade down Market Street, the city's major downtown thoroughfare; a program at the War Memorial Opera House; and a solemn pontifical mass at the cathedral. Archbishop John J. Mitty had first announced his Catholic Action campaign at a speech in 1932 before the women of the NCCW. Now, addressing the YLI's members at their fiftieth-anniversary banquet, he reminded them that:

> Conditions have changed considerably during these fifty years. Progress in material affairs has been well-nigh startling. How about the things of the spirit? The public in general, and perhaps, too, some of our own Catholic people, are not putting the same emphasis on spiritual values as our forebearers [sic] did fifty years ago. Throughout the nation there has been a lessening of the grasp on spiritual truth, on religious belief, on moral principles. There is not that same strong recognition of God as our Creator, as our Ruler, as our Judge. The Ten Commandments are regarded as being worn out—a mediaeval idea; moral principles have been thrust in the background. This condition has a tendency to affect many of our own Catholic people who have seen their most sacred traditions supplanted by a new code of morality which is not the code of Christ.

Mitty closed by exhorting the women to "stand out as the right arm of the Church in your parishes . . . participating in the apostolate of Christ himself."[3]

Both the NCCW and the YLI participated in the Catholic Action crusade during the mid- to late 1930s, the women of the NCCW the more active, possibly because of the close working relationship between Archbishop Mitty and Agnes G. Regan. As a board member of the NCCW from the time of its organizational meeting in Washington, D.C., in 1920, and then as executive secretary shortly thereafter, Regan developed effective communications with all of the bishops in the United States. But she was especially close to the San Francisco scene because she grew up in one of the city's wealthiest and most prestigious Irish Catholic families. Her father was a banker who also had served for a decade as the personal secretary to the city's first archbishop, Joseph S. Alemany; two of her three sisters became Catholic nuns (there were nine children in the family); she graduated from a Catholic grammar school and St. Rose high school; and she graduated from the San Francisco State Normal School (today's San Francisco State University). Regan taught in the San Francisco public schools for several decades, eventually serving as a member and president of the city's Board of Education. Archbishop Edward Hanna sent her as a delegate to the first meeting of the NCCW, and she kept close watch on San Francisco affairs from her office in the nation's capital all through her twenty-year tenure as executive secretary.[4]

Archbishop Mitty made no secret of his determination to increase the local influence of the women's groups, writing to one local activist, "You are aware of the fact of how interested I am in the development of the National Council of Catholic Women in this Archdiocese." Mitty appointed Father Eugene J. Shea, a priest assigned to the Catholic Charities office, to work with local Catholic women to implement the youth-oriented programs coordinated by the NCCW's headquarters in Washington, D.C. Father Shea and Margaret McGuire, president of the Archdiocesan Council, organized a series of leadership conferences in the spring of 1937 designed to train "young women who would be interested and helpful in developing activities for girls of high school and college age." By the late summer of 1939, Father Shea had learned that "parish organizations for high school girls are the most difficult to organize and yet most necessary since most of the public high school youngsters have only an elementary knowledge of their religion"—all the more reason, then, for participating in the NCCW's strategy of using radio broadcasts to reach women who might be persuaded to join their local Catholic Action activities. Archbishop Mitty endorsed and publicized Regan's "A Call to Youth" radio programs, which were broadcast on NBC over seventeen weeks during the winter and spring each year from 1937 to 1940—"a leaders' training school for diocesan, deanery and parish youth chairmen, youth leaders and youth officers throughout the country."[5]

In October 1936, McGuire answered Mitty's call "to develop a program for girls." She explained that her organization now had eleven councils and 150 affiliated organizations that operated in the archdiocese as "an official part of the Program of the Catholic Church in the United States." She stated, "Every organization, parish and inter-parish, is a distinct unit yet a very definite part of the great Catholic Federation. In this affiliation no individual organization loses its identity or autonomy. It continues to function for the purpose for which it was founded but through the Federation it promotes a united Catholic Action on a wider scale." McGuire asked the archbishop to approve a plan to hold the national conference of the NCCW in San Francisco in 1939, the meeting to coincide with the Golden Gate International Exposition scheduled to be held on Treasure Island that year. Mitty endorsed the proposal, and the following May he congratulated the NCCW women "for the work you are accomplishing. I feel that with Catholic Action, with earnest effort, with self-sacrificing zeal, we can begin to accomplish some of the things the Holy Father is asking of the laity to do. We can help to bring the spirit of Christ into the environment in which we live and where we function."[6]

McGuire continued to work closely with the chancery office, and on March 9, 1938, she reported that the city's Tourist and Convention Bureau had donated $2,000 to help defray the expense of holding the NCCW's national convention in San Francisco and that she had booked accommodations and meeting rooms in the stately Fairmont Hotel high atop Nob Hill. Preparations for the convention continued through the year, and by the following January Maude Fay Symington, president of the Marin County unit of the organization, reported on the progress of what promised to be "in every way an exceptional convention; not only the first time the N.C.C.W. is meeting in the West, but holding a convention during the great Golden Gate Exposition year. California, so very Catholic, must lead the World Council of Catholic women in its public avowal of united, triumphant, and militant Catholicism; a challenge to the subversive influences and anti-God activities saturating the entire world today." In May, Archbishop Mitty urged the NCCW women to recall that "we are surrounded by an atmosphere of secularism and worldliness" and his determination to present "the Catholic point of view, in showing forth the Catholic principles and Catholic philosophy of life." He continued, "I really want you to realize the amount of dependence that I put upon lay cooperation. The clergy cannot do everything, and the bishop can accomplish only as his clergy and laymen and lay women are willing to do with him . . . the problems of the future, the great things that confront us must be solved by the action of our laity, under the direction of the hierarchy."[7]

The importance of establishing Catholic standards of morality was a recurring theme during the five-day conference in September 1939, at sessions held in the Fairmont Hotel and at a special Catholic Women's Day in the San Francisco Building at the Golden Gate Exposition grounds on Treasure Island. Hitler's storm troopers had invaded Poland on the first day of the month, triggering declarations of war against Germany by England and its allies, and on September 9, the opening day of the conference, the Battle of the Bzura began; it ended ten days later with a German victory that foreshadowed the Polish defeat at the end of the month. Sylvester Andriano addressed the compelling importance of Christian morality in the face of such events during his speech on the last day of the NCCW conference, echoing Cardinal Pizzardo's insistence that Catholic Action included "the moral apostolate concerned with the defense of Christian morality wherever threatened." And so did Pope Pius XII when he spoke to the delegates who attended the annual congress of the International Union of Catholic Women's Leagues in Rome in April. The newly installed pontiff, who took up his duties on March 2, announced his intention to continue his predecessor's "all-embracing program" for "the training and preparation of the Catholic woman in her various fields of apostolate, for the Christian restoration of modern society." He reminded the delegates of "the golden rules outlined by the Pontiff of happy memory who was the great promoter of Catholic Action and who is still its invisible inspiration." And he exhorted Catholics to unify and work against "the absolute denial of invisible realities, of the noble moral values, and of every supernatural ideal."[8]

When Cardinal Pizzardo announced in mid-1938 that "Catholic Action is essentially an apostolate," he included in "the moral apostolate" work aimed at ensuring that the values communicated "in the press, over the radio, in the theater, motion pictures" were compatible with Christian teachings. In San Francisco, the Archdiocesan Council of Catholic Women took action in defense of "decent literature" by launching a "Clean Reading Campaign" focused on magazines for sale in public places. The city's efforts on this front were not unique, linked as they were to both international and national Catholic faith-based activism on behalf of the moral apostolate. In January 1938, Bishop John F. Noll, of the Fort Wayne, Indiana, diocese, published an article describing his city's League for Clean Reading. Noll was the publisher of the nationally distributed newspaper *Our Sunday Visitor, the National Catholic Action Weekly*. He was also a National Catholic Welfare Conference (NCWC) official, and his article appeared in the NCWC's magazine *Catholic Action*. In February, Father William G. Butler, assigned by Archbishop Mitty as the official adviser to the city's Catholic women, suggested to McGuire and her colleagues that the Archdiocesan Council "work out a diocesan scheme" modeled on the Fort Wayne campaign. The council's purpose was clear: it would "assist the law enforcement agencies of this jurisdiction to suppress literature and pictures" and "eliminate from magazine sales racks and tables publications which 1. Glorify crime and criminals; 2. Contain matter which is predominantly sexy; 3. Feature illicit love; 4. Print indecent or sexy pictures; and 5. Carry disreputable advertising."[9]

Archbishop Mitty asked Andriano and Professor James Hagerty of St. Mary's College to work on this front in concert with the Archdiocesan Council of Catholic Women, and they established the Committee on Indecent Literature. Members of the committee and volunteers then contacted the city's major news and magazine distributors, only to discover that "the profit motive is much stronger than any moral urge in all too many retail outlets to guarantee any success from such an approach." Another joint working group made a survey of "legislation on pornographic literature, of postal regulations, law enforcement, the honor system, direct censorship, and the boycott." Three months later, the committees reported that the laws were adequate and the postal regulations were sufficient, "but law enforcement is impractical because of the laxity of some jurists and juries in returning convictions." And "the element of goodwill [on the part of vendors] is obviously lacking, thus reducing our means of attack to some sort of public boycott." The committee called for a politically savvy approach: "If a boycott were to be started as an exclusively Catholic undertaking, there would be the danger of an unfavorable public reaction; therefore it is *absolutely essential* that all representative groups be interested in any public action, and further that all are made to feel themselves as an *initial* and *important part* of the forces that are to be employed."[10]

It was the Catholic women who dominated the leadership and carried out the day-to-day work of this program. They urged Archbishop Mitty to enlist the support of "the Protestant and Jewish church councils," as well as the assistance of city newspapers, officials, and "all other groups who should be interested in decency." Mitty followed up in June with official instructions to the priests of every parish in the entire archdiocese to read his official letter condemning "magazines and other periodical literature which are detrimental to the morals of our people, and particularly to the morals of our growing boys and girls." On Sunday, June 12, the archbishop's letter was read at every mass in all thirteen counties of the archdiocese, and it was repeated the next Sunday, June 19, after which, at every mass, the congregations repeated the clean reading pledge after the priests:

> I pledge myself to refrain from purchasing, reading or spreading such literature and to endeavor to restrain those under my jurisdiction or influence from so doing; I pledge myself to refuse patronage in any form to those places of business which persist in displaying, offering for sale or selling such literature, or providing it for the entertainment of patrons who are waiting to be served; I pledge myself to refuse patronage in any form to those firms which use such literature as an advertising medium; I pledge myself to patronize those places of business which cooperate in the campaign.[11]

Thousands of San Franciscans took the clean reading pledge during the summer; some of them presumably also boycotted the purveyors of "pernicious literature" filled with "pagan manifestations" of "flagrant evil." But the female Catholic Action activists in the Clean Reading Campaign were hampered in their efforts because, as Florentine Schage, one of the lay activists, complained to the assistant chancellor, they found "it very difficult to ask retailers to remove literature we consider objectionable when they have no list to use as a check." Archbishop Mitty had such a list, and he invited Schage and several colleagues to pick up copies at the Chancery Office. In November, Bishop Noll and his like-minded colleagues established the National Organization for Decent Literature (NODL), which drew up what it called "our black-list" for use in dioceses across the nation. Noll's organization issued *Catechism Dealing with Lewd Literature,* which announced its purpose on the title page: "A Comprehensive Treatise for Use by Men and Women Engaged in the Drive against Indecent Literature and for Radio Broadcasts." The *Catechism* took pains to remind its readers that "there would be a danger if we designated 'indecent' the magazines on our black list. We have adopted a Code in keeping with that adopted by the Legion of Decency in relation to Motion Pictures, and we charge the magazines with violation of that Code." Bishop Noll urged readers to "understand [that] we do not attach the 'immoral' charge to all these magazines. They are on our banned list because they offend against one or more of a five point Code adopted by the N.O.D.L." In addition to *French Night Life, Illustrated Japanese Sex Relations, and Savage Arts of Love Illustrated,* magazines included on the black list were *The Facts of Life* and *Your Body.*[12]

The Catholic women targeted "indecent pictures" as well as print media and radio broadcasts, and in November 1938, neighborhood theaters in San Francisco were screening the short film *The Birth of a Baby.* First Lady Eleanor Roosevelt recommended the movie for its public health benefits, but the San Francisco activists "made a spirited protest" against the showing and complained directly to the nation's official movie censors in Hollywood. This was four years after the founding of the Catholic Legion of Decency and eight years after the adoption of the Motion Picture Production Code by the film industry's trade association, which remained in effect for nearly forty years. The production code is associated with the president of the Motion Picture Producers and Distributors of America, Will H. Hays, and with the head of the Production Code Administration that did the actual work of vetting films, Joseph I. Breen. But the code itself was written by a Jesuit priest, Daniel A. Lord, S.J., with input from the Catholic Action advocate Martin J. Quigley and the Archbishop George Cardinal Mundelein of Chicago. Breen was himself an active Catholic, and James Hagerty and Sylvester Andriano confided to him that they hoped for a sympathetic response from his office to their complaint rather than, as in the Clean Reading Campaign, a situation in which it was necessary to make "endless protest to parties who may be helpless to improve the situation or uninterested or irresponsible."[13]

Archbishop Mitty provided his own assessment of the campaign against indecent media to Archbishop Cicognani the Vatican's apostolic delegate. Writing in March 1939, Mitty reported that he was "happy to say that the results were quite satisfactory in the residential districts. A great deal of difficulty was encountered, however, in the business sections." Mitty's report was prompted by Cicognani's official notice that "the Supreme S[acred] Congregation of the Holy Office, in keeping with the competence conferred upon it by the Code of Canon Law (can. 247, #4), feels the need of reminding the Most Reverend Ordinaries of their obligation to censure pernicious writings (cf. can. 1395, #1) and to denounce them to the Holy See (cf. can. 1397)." The Vatican official's concern was prompted by "the continuous and constantly increasing diffusion of all kinds of publications which spread erroneous doctrines, deprave the mind and pervert morals, imposes an obligation upon the Shepherds of Souls to be ever more watchful and prompt in keeping the Faithful from such poisoned sources and so 'to defend sound and orthodox doctrine and to defend good morals' (can. 343, #1)."[14]

Mitty and his Catholic Action women continued the decent literature campaign "with greater zeal and thoroughness" by developing closer working relationships with the city's police department and by joining forces with their counterparts in Los Angeles. This strategy benefited from the fact that, Andriano, the head of the Catholic Men of San Francisco organization, was now a member of the Police Commission, having been appointed by Mayor Angelo Rossi in July 1937. Andriano, whose reputation for probity had been acknowledged by the president of the Board of Supervisors during the strike crisis of July 1934, and former Chamber of Commerce President J. Ward Maillard Jr. replaced two members of the commission who had been discredited in a grand jury investigation into police corruption in the city. The report of the investigation by the former FBI agent Edwin Atherton laid bare a variety of malfeasance (including abortion mills, gambling, and prostitution) that netted some sixty-seven crooked police officers and two dozen city officials an estimated $1 million per year. One hapless patrolman who was discovered on the take shot his wife and children, then took his own life, rather than face up to his disgrace. The post-grand jury Police Commission set out to demonstrate its trustworthiness, with two Catholic Action stalwarts on board: Andriano and Police Chief William J. Quinn. Quinn was not included in the Atherton Report, and he had been a member of Andriano's organizing committee that worked with the archbishop to establish the new Catholic Men of San Francisco organization.[15]

The cooperative relationship between Catholic Action moral apostolate activists and the city's police department had been under way for several years when Archdiocesan Chancellor Thomas A. Connolly received a tip from Joseph J. Truxaw, chairman of the Los Angeles Campaign for Decent Literature. Truxaw's source, a municipal judge in Los Angeles, passed on information about a printing firm in San Francisco that was allegedly "the 'HOME' on the Pacific Coast of pornographic cartoons and pictures. Distributions from that place are made by trucks to all parts of California, Nevada, Oregon and Washington." Connolly informed Quinn that "it certainly would be an excellent move for public morals" to close down the firm and replied to Truxaw that he could "rest assured that the police will not involve the Catholic Church in this matter in any way whatsoever." Three months later, Chief Charles W. Dullea (who succeeded Quinn when he retired after thirty-five years of service) informed the chancery office that the department's "surveillance and investigation" yielded arrests that he expected would close down "the source of the printing of indecent literatures, pictures and booklets, distributed throughout this city and the bay counties." Dullea assured Assistant Chancellor Edwin J. Kennedy that the San Francisco Police Department was "pledging [its] fullest support in the suppression of lascivious literature and other immoral booklets."[16]

The moral apostolate won another victory when the administration of the Golden Gate International Exposition canceled an exhibit in the Hall of Science sponsored by the Birth Control Federation of America. Margaret Sanger happened to be speaking to the League of Women Voters of San Francisco the same week that the exposition announced the cancellation of the exhibit. Sanger expressed her disappointment to a reporter for *People's World,* the local Communist Party newspaper: "Wherever I go I meet the same opposition—and I must say that it is most insidious and effective." But Anna E. McCaughey of Los Angeles, national chairman of the NCCW, used cancellation of the birth control display as an occasion to remind Archbishop Mitty that the members of her organization "look upon San Francisco as a focal point where East meets West in developing national service for God, Church, and Country."[17]

The clash between competing Catholic and communist definitions of the public interest evident in the birth control issue played out in women's participation in a variety of public events in San Francisco. Two years before the women of the Archdiocesan Council marched up Market Street to commemorate their golden anniversary, the women of the Young Communist League celebrated May Day with a different Market Street parade. The parade on May Day 1935, like the series of outdoor rallies that had recently been put on by the Communist Party on behalf of the repeal of the California Criminal Syndicalism Act, an anti-radical measure that dated to 1919, demonstrated both the party's growing strength of numbers and women's leadership in party work. Police Chief Quinn, committed to purging the city's public spaces of Communist Party influence, routinely arrested the organizers and broke up the meetings. So on St. Patrick's Day, Elaine Black, who was scheduled to speak on freedom of speech for communists, arrived at Dolores Park dressed in green and prepared for trouble. Born on the Lower East Side of New York City to Jewish immigrants from Russia, Black grew up in Los Angeles and joined the Communist Party's International Labor Defense (ILD) organization in 1930 at twenty-three.[18] By 1935, she had moved to San Francisco and had made herself so indispensable to the legal defense work of the party that the hardened sailors and longshoremen she bailed out of jail had taken to calling her their "Red Angel." Her arrest on St. Patrick's Day and subsequent trial (she was acquitted on appeal) followed similar experiences during the strike of 1934 and foreshadowed the harrowing experience of finding herself the target of vigilantes when, in Salinas during the farm workers' strike in 1936, a lynch noose was dangled from the door of the garage where she had parked her Model A Ford.[19]

By 1936, Black had married a party comrade named Karl Yoneda, a native of Glendale, California, whose parents were immigrants from Japan. The couple married in Seattle because antimiscegenation laws barred them from marrying in California. They lost their Communist Party membership when the party purged all Japanese American members and their spouses from its rolls after the Japanese attack on Pearl Harbor. Then the U.S. Army ordered Karl Yoneda and the couple's three-year-old son to be interned at the Manzanar War Relocation Center, one of the ten internment camps built to house Japanese Americans excluded from the West Coast by Presidential Executive Order 9066 on February 19, 1942. Outraged by the prospect of her husband and son living without her in the harsh desert location in the Owens Valley, 400 miles from San Francisco, Elaine refused to be separated from them, and eventually the Army allowed her to join them in the camp. Because they were outspoken American patriots, as were all Communist Party members during the war, the Yonedas were terrorized by the "Black Dragon"—pro-emperor Japanese-born internees—until they left the camp. Karl volunteered for military service and served as a frontline interpreter for military intelligence in Burma, and Elaine worked as an office manager for the United Electrical Workers union until he returned. After the war, the couple resumed their active membership in the Communist Party after moving fifty miles north of San Francisco to a six-acre chicken ranch in Penngrove, where Elaine was president of the Communist Party-affiliated Civil Rights Congress in Sonoma County. She raised money for a branch of the party's California Labor School and supported the campaigns for the state Fair Employment Practice Committee. After their son graduated from high school, Elaine and Karl moved back to San Francisco, and Elaine remained an active party member involved in a variety of labor, anti–Vietnam War, and women's rights activities into the 1980s.[20]

During the 1930s, when Elaine Black worked with the ILD, she met Oleta O'Connor Yates when they both worked in the campaigns to organize farmworkers in the San Joaquin Valley. They also supported the campaign to free Thomas Mooney and Warren Billings from San Quentin State Prison, where the men were serving their sentences for the Preparedness Day Parade bombing in 1916. In the San Francisco election in 1939, Elaine Black ran for a seat on the city's Board of Supervisors and Yates ran for the office of city assessor with the backing of the Communist Party. During the war, while Black was still in Manzanar, Yates ran again for supervisor, this time emphasizing the need to "Gear San Francisco to the Attack [on the Axis powers]" and promising that, if elected, she would "Strike a Blow at Hitler and Jim Crow."[21]

Richard Lynden and John Pittman campaigned with Yates in 1943, using radio broadcasts on the stations KYA and KGO to publicize her patriotic qualifications. Lynden was the left-wing president of Local 6 of the longshoremen's union, and Pittman was a black graduate of Morehouse College with a master's degree in economics from UC Berkeley. Pittman edited the Communist Party newspaper *People's World*. According to Lynden, Yates was "the only candidate for the Board of Supervisors with a strong program against racial discrimination and segregation," and Pittman appealed to voters' pride in San Francisco's presumed cosmopolitanism. "Mrs. Yates," according to Pittman, "thinks the city needs a committee on race relations to work for unity among all peoples of this great cosmopolitan center. I stand for that. I'm sure the city's Irish-Americans, Negroes, Chinese, Mexicans, Filipinos, Italian-Americans, Greek, Armenian and other national minority groups stand for that. But I'm also sure that Hirohito, Tojo, and Hitler don't want that." Lynden also appealed to female voters with the argument that a vote for Yates was a vote against the city's tradition of political patriarchy. Lynden praised Yates as a "native daughter trained in political service and with experience that ably fits her for the position. At a time when women are playing an increasingly active and important role in the life of our nation it is hardly likely that anyone can be prejudiced against a woman in the city administration."[22]

Yates ran for supervisor for a second time in 1947, this time in a Cold War context. Her wartime appeals to patriotism were replaced with a program that stressed both the party's continuing support for racial equality and the importance of "sweeping big business out of city hall [and] elect[ing] a woman to the Board of Supervisors." Yates promoted equality for women within the Communist Party, as well as in City Hall, at a time that women accounted for approximately 43 percent of the membership but found it difficult, as she had, to rise into leadership positions beyond the local level. The Communist Party was committed in theory to providing opportunities for leadership to women, and the party "maintained a vision of women as active agents within the working class." But in practice, women usually worked at the grassroots, from staffing school lunch and similar programs to running for local office. Communists, both men and women, typically regarded feminism in and of itself as a bourgeois affectation—selfish, individualistic, and too far removed from important issues of political economy and class power. Many women acknowledged discrimination by men against women as an institutionalized reality in the Communist Party, but those who proposed a separate feminist agenda were censured or forced to resign from the party.[23]

In her campaign for the Board of Supervisors in 1947, Yates was able to take advantage of the national Communist Party's increased emphasis on the importance of women's equality and stressed "the great importance of the fight for women's rights." She pointed out that no woman had served on the board since Margaret Mary Morgan's one term in 1921–1925. In one of her radio broadcasts, Yates discussed the issue with "Mrs. Orton" and "Quinn": "Why that's outrageous! What's the idea? Do they think that women are only good enough to cook the meals and clean the house and take care of the kids? As a woman I feel personally insulated." Mrs. Orton chimed in, "Women are just as able as men—in the Board of Supervisors or anywhere else. I am fighting mad about the high cost of living, and about there being no women on the Board of Supervisors and I am going to change it."[24] Ten days later, in another radio broadcast, Yates argued, "We cannot have a truly representative government in San Francisco without a woman on the Board of Supervisors. For far too long, women have been relegated to a sort of second class citizenship in our society." She was also careful to note—and referred to Congresswoman Helen Gahagan Douglas of southern California to illustrate her point—that a female supervisor should both represent the women of the city and "be a representative of the trade union men, the small businessmen and the little people in general."[25]

Yates lost her bid for the Board of Supervisors in 1947. Then, five years later, she tried a third and last time, but only after overcoming the FBI's attempts to keep her off the ballot on the grounds that she had been arrested for violating the Smith Act of 1940 and was incarcerated in the Los Angeles County Jail awaiting trial. Yates was in jail because as early as her campaign in 1943, she had attracted the scrutiny of State Senator Jack Tenney, chairman of the California Assembly's Joint Fact-Finding Committee on Un-American Activities. For Tenney, Yates's ability to run for office at all "was an example of the present dangerous trend" toward the importation of Soviet-inspired socialism into the United States after the war. Superpatriots such as Tenney regarded Yates's Communist Party line attack on big business and her promise to stand up for "the little people" as un-American and pro-Soviet, and Yates and other communists in California found themselves increasingly on the defensive after the war ended and the Cold War began. On July 26, 1951, Yates was awakened by federal agents at the door of her home, arrested, and taken into custody for conspiring to overthrow the U.S. government.[26]

When city residents opened their *San Francisco Chronicle* on the morning of July 27, 1951, they encountered a banner headline that announced "FBI SEIZES TOP WEST COAST REDS." Yates and her comrades were accused of being part of a "conspiracy" to overthrow the U.S. government because "they wrote, published and circulated books, magazines and newspapers, including the *Daily People's World* here and *The Daily Worker* in New York. It was [also] alleged that the Communist leaders conducted secret schools, recruited members in basic industries and plants, and held conspiratorial meetings." Yates was flown to Los Angeles, and she spent more than four months in the county jail until bail was reduced from $50,000 to $25,000. She was the first to testify when the trial began in February 1952. Dorothy Healey, known as the "Red Queen of Los Angeles," who chaired the Southern California Communist Party, later recalled being impressed with Yates's testimony because "she gave a remarkable presentation on the witness stand of the real nature of our theory and practical activities."[27]

As it happened, Yates was the only defendant to testify; hence, the case became known as *Yates et al. v. United States*. When the prosecutor tired of her disquisition on Marxist theory, Yates has said, "He asked me to name people who were present at Communist Party meetings—people who are not even defendants in the case. I refused." The judge cited her for contempt each time she refused to divulge names. The trial ended on August 6, 1952, when the jury, after six days, found the defendants guilty. Judge William C. Mathes sentenced each defendant to five years in jail, adding an extra year to Yates's sentence to cover the eleven charges of contempt of court; after a series of appeals, the U.S. Supreme Court ruled on June 16, 1957, that the indictments of five of the four-teen defendants had been illegal and ordered new trials for the remaining nine, but the Justice Department declined to retry the nine in question.[28]

Although the court's decision did not declare the Smith Act unconstitu-tional, it did rule that Communist Party members who merely proselytized on behalf of a Soviet-inspired socialist alternative could not be prosecuted for con-spiracy. Party members who had previously been convicted had their convic-tions overturned, and Yates and her comrades, who had claimed all along that they were both communists and good Americans, considered themselves vindi-cated by the Supreme Court. As it happened, however, American communists' faith in their cause had already been sorely tested, and many had already decided to leave the party. Nikita Khrushchev's speech revealing the magnitude of Sta-lin's murderous practices was made public at a party meeting in New York City in April 1956; then, in November, Soviet T-34 tanks rolled into Budapest, and Khrushchev himself ordered the crushing of the Hungarian people's revolution against Soviet control. From Yates's point of view, the American Communist Party, given the degree to which it functioned as the official agent of the Soviet Party, needed to find a way to distance itself from these blows to Soviet credibil-ity, and she decided that the American party had failed in this important task. On March 26, 1958, Yates and twenty-six other party leaders officially tendered their resignations, announcing that the party was incapable of overcoming its "isolation from the American people" and could no longer command their con-fidence. Yates and her fellow signers were among the three-quarters of the American Communist Party members who dropped out in the two years after the unsettling events of 1956. According to Yates's husband, he and Oleta "came to reject the absolutism of communism . . . the kind that has pat answers for everything—party line answers. After we made our decisions, we felt truly liberated [and] felt no attraction for Khrushchev's brand of communism."[29]

Margaret McGuire did not waver from her belief that Catholic faith-based values should provide the standard against which public policy in San Francisco should be measured. Oleta O'Connor Yates rejected her girlhood Catholicism, embraced the Communist Party's cause, and then lost faith in the party during the Cold War. Julia Gorman Porter, the third woman from San Francisco whose life and work are profiled in this chapter, was a lifelong Democrat, played a leading role in the Democratic Party's California branch, and then served for twenty-four years on the San Francisco Planning Commission. Porter was a pragmatist through and through, and like many other women active in Democratic Party politics and policy work from the 1930s through the 1960s, she was skilled at trimming and compromising when necessary. Her work exemplified the cooperative bargaining necessary among government, business, and labor officials that she believed would best produce the high rates of economic growth necessary for progress that benefited the entire society.[30]

Porter's involvement in politics had roots in the social welfare activism of the Progressive era and the urban design initiatives of the City Beautiful movement. Born in 1897 to a pioneer-era Irish Catholic business-class family, Gorman enjoyed a comfortable childhood, including private schooling at the Convent of the Sacred Heart.

Like Oleta O'Connor Yates, Porter was raised a Roman Catholic, and like Yates, she grew estranged from Catholicism. By the World War I years, she had become part of the city's genteel bohemian cultural scene. The character of her marriage to Charles B. Porter, a dentist and instructor at the University of California Dental School, in 1924 made it "natural" for her to become active in urban policy work. Her husband was thirty-three years older that she; the couple was childless, and both of Porter's brothers-in-law had become involved in urban planning and social policy work. Robert Porter, an attorney married to the daughter of the philosopher William James of Harvard University, served on the board of the Telegraph Hill Neighborhood Association, the city's first settlement house. Bruce Porter, an architect and graphic artist, had been one of the founders of the Association for the Improvement and Adornment of San Francisco, the private organization that commissioned Daniel Burnham to draw up the "city beautiful" plan of 1905. Encouraged by Laura Suggett, the sister of Lincoln Steffens, and inspired by Franklin D. Roosevelt's campaign, Julia Gorman Porter became a director of the city's Democratic Women's Forum in 1932, and in 1939, she became president of the local chapter of the League of Women Voters.[31] She continued to play a leadership role in the California Democratic Party during the 1940s, 1950s, and 1960s.

Soon after taking up the presidency of the League of Women Voters, Porter joined members of the Junior Chamber of Commerce in conducting an economic and social survey of Chinatown. The survey brought her into a working relationship with a network of seasoned social activists from the Progressive era and younger newcomers who involved themselves in policy work for the first time during the Depression. They shared a belief that social and urban policy legislation of the New Deal provided an opportunity to reverse economic decline and halt the deterioration of the built environment, as well as to improve the condition of the poor and limit the human suffering caused by the Depression.[32]

A leading figure in the reform network was Alice Griffith, the well-to-do San Francisco native who had organized the Telegraph Hill Neighborhood Association in 1902. In 1911, Griffith and her colleague Elizabeth Ashe organized a nongovernmental social policy agency called the San Francisco Housing Association. Griffith, Ash, and San Francisco's state senator led the campaign to pass the state's first tenement law and building code enforcement program. By the Depression decade, Griffith had become a leading member of California's community of social policy reformers.[33]

When the San Francisco Board of Supervisors established a local Housing Authority following federal and state legislation in 1937, Griffith was appointed one of the five commissioners. One year later, Griffith, the Junior Chamber of Commerce, and volunteers from a study group led by the social reformer Alexander Meiklejohn began the Chinatown survey. (Meiklejohn and his wife were part of Julia Gorman Porter's social circle.) Then, in 1940, Porter and Griffith, with the financial assistance of Morse Erskine, Morgan Gunst, and several other business executives, revived the San Francisco Housing Association to create an information clearinghouse and contact point for publicity, public speaking, and lobbying. It was these "Civic Minded Women," to use Porter's own language, who transformed a Progressive-era nongovernmental planning and social policy agency into an institution capable of linking city planning work in San Francisco with New Deal-era federal urban policy legislation.[34]

The association's orientation to urban policy included a new and forthright emphasis on the necessity of considering slum clearance, housing improvement, transportation planning, and downtown revitalization within the context of the need for comprehensive urban planning and to plan cities in relation to their natural environment. With Gunst as president and Porter serving as vice-president, the organization incorporated in 1943 and changed its name to the San Francisco Planning and Housing Association. The new emphasis came at the suggestion of a group of local architects who had recently graduated from the School of Architecture at the University of California, plus a recently arrived lecturer at Berkeley.[35]

The architects included Francis Violich and T. J. (Jack) Kent Jr. They worked under the name Telesis to signify their conviction that the human and the natural environment could be brought into harmony by means of intelligent planning. The Telesis group had the support of an older generation of Bay Area architects, including William Wurster, and was influenced by the ideas of

Lewis Mumford. Kent had formally sought out Mumford to be his mentor after his graduation in 1938. Mumford had also influenced the new lecturer at Berkeley, Catherine Bauer, the author of *Modern Housing* (1934), an activist on behalf of the passage of the Housing Act of 1937, and the first director of the new federal Housing Authority. Bauer arrived in Berkeley in January 1940 as the Rosenberg Lecturer in Public Social Service, and in August she married Wurster. The Rosenberg Foundation, which supported Catherine Bauer Wurster's faculty position, also provided a $4,000 seed money grant for the new Planning and Housing Association.[36]

In the view of Julia Gorman Porter and her associates, the voluntary work of the association would stimulate, and monitor, a reconceptualized and more effective partnership arrangement between the private and the public institutions involved in urban development. In previous decades in San Francisco, business associations, especially the Chamber of Commerce, had taken the lead position in urban policy planning.[37] In the future, Porter and her colleagues reasoned, intellectuals, professionals, and citizen volunteers, both inside and outside government, would take over that position. This elite planning coalition, informed by grassroots preferences as expressed by the electorate, would bring a broad-minded, aesthetically aware, environmentally conscious, communitywide perspective to what had been a parochial process rooted in the bargaining between economic and neighborhood interest groups and city government officials. They grounded their work in a desire to protect and enhance the quality of life of all of the people of the city and to preserve the unique natural and physical amenities of the city and the region. They believed that future economic growth constituted a high priority, but growth needed to be guided by environmentally conscious professional planners in cooperation with public-spirited volunteers serving at the request of elected officials.[38] Their point of view was ambitious in view of the historically fractious and politically polarized political culture of San Francisco.

For Porter and her circle, active involvement in Democratic Party electoral politics went hand in hand with urban policy activism. In 1941, Porter became the chairwoman of the Northern California Women's Division of the state Democratic Party; her vice-chair until they both resigned in 1943 was Catherine Bauer Wurster. The regional office of the National Resources Planning Board provided Jack Kent with his first job after he earned his degree in architecture and before he began studying planning at the Massachusetts Institute of Technology (MIT). When Kent moved to Cambridge, Massachusetts, in 1943 to complete his graduate degree before being drafted, he joined two of his associates from Berkeley who had also moved to Cambridge. Wurster, who was forty-five, and his new wife had also come to MIT because Wurster wanted to train himself in city planning in anticipation of the demand for planners, given the urban revitalization he imagined would be necessary after the war. The Wursters returned to Berkeley during the war, as did Kent after completing his service when the war ended.[39]

Ironically, it was a Republican city administration that provided Porter and Kent with an opportunity to put their planning and policy ideas into practice, and it was a factional fight within the Democratic Party that brought Porter into a Republican administration. In 1943, George Reilly, the leader of the rival Democratic faction, ran for mayor. Rather than endorse Reilly, Porter and Catherine Bauer Wurster resigned from their party offices, and Porter campaigned for Roger D. Lapham, a Republican. President Roosevelt also endorsed Lapham, who had transformed himself from an Old Guard Republican into a moderate Republican and had served on Roosevelt's War Labor Board. Porter referred in campaign speeches to the "outpouring of women" who were helping to get out the vote for Lapham. She argued that women especially admired Lapham because they knew he would ensure there would be "no more muddling of such problems as transportation and housing." A Lapham administration, she stressed, would invite the "best brains in our community and business to apply sound business methods" in addressing the city's needs in the "extraordinary times" after the war.[40]

After Lapham won the election, he appointed Porter to his new Planning Commission, and the commission, riding a "great wave of idealism" that coincided with planning for the drafting of the United Nations Charter, moved quickly to implement a program of revitalization guided by comprehensive planning. Porter believed that planning for growth was a vital necessity: "a city either goes ahead or retrogrades, and you do not stand still."[41] She excelled at the delicate task of moving the growth agenda forward while insisting that development projects be compatible with the city's natural beauty, the health of its citizens, and the well-being of the people of the entire region. Porter worked closely with the city's planning director (the first in its history), L. Deming Tilton, who had been appointed in 1942. Tilton had been trained as a landscape architect, had worked as a planner for Harland Bartholomew's firm, and, during the 1920s, had earned high praise for his work with Los Angeles, San Diego, Santa Barbara, and Orange counties. In 1934, he became the planning director for the California State Planning Commission and helped draft the state planning act of 1935.[42] Tilton's philosophy was close to that of Porter and of Kent and his Telesis group, and he hired Kent as one of his assistants when the young planner left the Army. However, Tilton's personal style clashed with the mayor's; he lacked experience in the give and take of bargaining among agencies in the municipal government;[43] and his efforts to implement a master plan met a solid wall of resistance by Old Guard bureaucrats in City Hall.[44]

In contrast to Tilton, Porter, a San Franciscan by birth and a consummate politician, was skilled in the fine art of building allegiances, repairing broken alliances, maintaining coalitions, and brokering compromises. During the Lapham years (1944–1948), and again between 1956 and 1976 (during the terms of George Christopher, Jack Shelley, and Joseph Alioto), Porter served on the Planning Commission, with one term as the commission's president.[45] During the second half of the Lapham administration, and again in the mid-1960s, Porter's friend Jack Kent worked with the Planning Commission, first as planning director and then as the mayor's special deputy for planning. During the Christopher and Shelley years, Porter worked closely with Deputy City Planner James Redmond McCarthy, another advocate of growth liberalism. Kent and McCarthy, like Porter, claimed native birth, and both were well connected, like Porter, through family, friendship, and political party ties to influential decision makers who could make or break a particular initiative by the Planning Commission. During her tenure, Porter supported the scaled-down and landscaped freeways along San Francisco's northern waterfront and through part of Golden Gate Park, which were never built, as well as the Transamerica Pyramid, which has become a world-famous feature of the city's skyline.[46]

When Porter dictated her oral history in 1975, she tallied up her defeats and victories. Both the biggest defeat and the greatest victory, in her mind, occurred on the waterfront. Her defeat (by a one-vote margin) in the campaign to stop the construction of the Fontana Towers apartment building near Fisherman's Wharf still rankled after more than a decade. At the same time, she took pride in using the Fontana defeat to rally citywide support for a permanent forty-foot height limit for buildings on the waterfront. She was pleased that her friend, the businessman and philanthropist William Roth, had purchased the old Ghirardelli chocolate factory. Roth's move kept the previous owners from turning the site into more high-rise apartments and allowed architects associated with the Telesis group to convert the factory into an environmentally friendly retail center serving local and regional residents and tourists from beyond the Bay Area.[47]

By the mid-1960s, because of opposition to crosstown freeways and an outcry against what critics dubbed the "Manhattanization" of the city, the Planning Commission found itself confronted by a new breed of neighborhood politics and a new and robust environmentalist movement. Many of the new environmentalists challenged the equation of development and progress altogether. Bruce Brugmann, founder of the free weekly *San Francisco Bay Guardian* newspaper, publicized this reform agenda. His neo-progressive muckraking weakened the political influence of the *Examiner* and the *Chronicle*. The environmentalists challenged the qualifications of incumbents whose careers had been premised on "growth liberalism," and they mobilized to replace them with more ecologically minded candidates. Phillip Burton led the new breed of environmentalists, and they successfully worked to displace many of the older generation of Democratic Party officials in local and state government positions. Burton went to Congress, where he became a leading national environmentalist leader. His brother, John Burton, worked with Jean Kortum, one of a new breed of women younger than Porter who were active in land use reform. Kortum later organized the successful campaign against building the Golden Gate Freeway along the city's northern waterfront. John Burton went to the State Assembly and later served as the speaker pro-tem of the State Senate. Willie L. Brown Jr., a protégé of Phillip Burton's, went to the State Assembly, where he served as speaker for many years and then moved to the Mayor's Office.[48]

For what are perhaps understandable political reasons, the men and women who led the new urban environmentalist movement ignored the degree to which the reforms pioneered by growth liberals such as Julia Porter had prepared the way for their own activism. By the time Porter died in 1990, San Francisco had earned a national reputation for its "Downtown Plan" of the mid-1980s that established thoroughgoing height and bulk limitations on office buildings. In the publicity surrounding that accomplishment and similar innovations in planning with the environment in mind, no credit was given to Porter's work. Eight years after Porter's death, Sue Bierman recalled her not as a forerunner but, rather, as "a lady of the old school." Bierman had organized the successful campaign against the Golden Gate Park Panhandle Freeway, a campaign that operated out of Willie Brown's campaign office in 1964, and she later served on the Board of Permit Appeals, the Planning Commission, and the Board of Supervisors.[49] When queried about Julia Porter's influence, Bierman could not recall any positive accomplishments associated with Porter's planning work and remembered her only as a proponent of an outmoded approach to planning who had been disturbed by the uncompromising character of the anti-freeway movement and upset by the confrontational tactics of the activists. It is ironic that Julia Porter's work has been forgotten, because her brand of growth liberalism—albeit seasoned with a strong dose of "progressive" populism—has proved remarkably resilient since the 1970s.

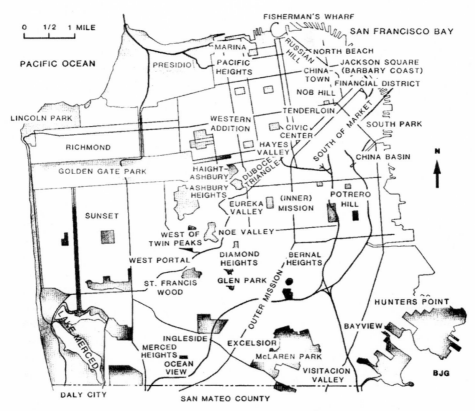

Map of districts and neighborhoods in San Francisco. *(Courtesy of University of California Press.)*

Father Peter C. Yorke, who provided spiritual leadership to the unions during the strike of 1901 and advocated for social justice until his death in 1925. *(Courtesy of Chancery Archives of the Archdiocese of San Francisco.)*

San Francisco's white male public sphere included members of Local 85 of the International Brotherhood of Teamsters, shown here at a union picnic. The devout Catholic Michael Casey, president for more than thirty years, during the waterfront strikes of both 1901 and 1934, is in the center pouring from the bottle. *(Courtesy of Labor Archives and Research Center, San Francisco State University.)*

May Day Parade of the San Francisco Communist Party in 1935. Archie Brown, who served in the Abraham Lincoln Brigade during the Spanish Civil War and was an active party member into the 1960s, leads the Young Communist League contingent. *(Courtesy of San Francisco History Center, San Francisco Public Library.)*

Annual Christ the King Rally in 1935, which attracted more than 50,000 Catholics to Seals Stadium. Archbishop Hanna officiated at the event, which was attended by city officials as well as the leaders and supporters of the Catholic Action crusade. *(Courtesy of San Francisco History Center, San Francisco Public Library.)*

From right to left: David Jenkins, founding director of the Communist Party's California Labor School, which offered city residents opportunities to hear from both local and national figures; the singer and actor Paul Robeson; the playwright and screenwriter John Howard Lawson; and the ILWU longshoremen's union activist Revels Cayton. *(Courtesy of Labor Archives and Research Center, San Francisco State University.)*

Officers of the Young Ladies Institute of the Archdiocese of San Francisco at their annual communion mass in 1939. The YLI worked to implement the Catholic Action moral apostolate program. *(Courtesy of Chancery Archives of the Archdiocese of San Francisco.)*

The Catholic activist Terry Francois and demonstrators protesting housing discrimination by the Standard Building Company, June 5, 1961. *(Courtesy of San Francisco History Center, San Francisco Public Library.)*

Audley Cole in 1942, wearing his San Francisco Municipal Railway hat after overcoming the Municipal Carmen's Local 518 union's opposition to his becoming a motorman on city streetcars. *(Courtesy of Labor Archives and Research Center, San Francisco State University.)*

San Francisco's nonpartisan liberal pro-growth regime, which operated from the late 1930s to the early 1960s, enjoyed widespread support from city residents. The Democrat Joseph L. Alioto (*left*) and the Republican Walter A. Haas Sr. (*right*) served as co-chairmen of the Reelect Mayor George Christopher campaign in 1959. Christopher was a Republican. *(Courtesy of San Francisco History Center, San Francisco Public Library.)*

Mayor Joseph L. Alioto with a group of African American supporters during his campaign in 1971. The ILWU union leader LeRoy King is standing at the far right. *(Courtesy of San Francisco History Center, San Francisco Public Library.)*

7

"HUMANITY IS ONE GREAT FAMILY"

Jews, Catholics, and the
Achievements of Racial Reform

On August 12, 1957, Mayor George Christopher presided over the swearing-in ceremony for the seven members of San Francisco's new Commission on Equal Employment Opportunity (CEEO). Approved by the Board of Supervisors after more than a decade of lobbying by civil rights activists, the CEEO became the first such agency in a major city in California. Three years later, the commission ceased operations when the state pre-empted its duties after the California Fair Employment Practice Act of 1959 went into effect.[1] In the twenty-year period prior to the passage of the state's fair employment act, as the world reeled from a global conflagration followed by a Cold War, the practice and preservation of civil rights and civil liberties became an increasingly pressing issue in both world affairs and domestic politics. In San Francisco, site of the dramatic signing of the United Nations Charter at the War Memorial Opera House on June 26, 1945, the campaign for civil rights took center stage in municipal politics and policymaking. The participation of white Jewish and Catholic reformers in a multiethnic/racial coalition for civil rights contributed new dimensions to the debate about how to define the public interest in San Francisco during World War II and the early Cold War years.[2]

During the late 1930s and the 1940s, Jews and Catholics in San Francisco shared the nationwide outrage at the murderous consequences of Adolf Hitler's European and North African wartime regime and the postwar repression practiced by Joseph Stalin in Poland, Hungary, and other Soviet satellite countries. Jewish and Catholic calls for combating racism and anti-Semitism took on a new urgency beginning in 1938 after the Nazi Anschluss (connection) with Austria on March 12 and Kristallnacht on November 9–10.[3] Even before the

Japanese attacked Pearl Harbor, San Francisco Jews, operating on the assumption that no one can be safe unless everyone is free, played the leading roles in assembling a racial justice coalition that also included Catholic liberals, as well as those who were neither Jewish nor Catholic.[4] Like their counterparts in Los Angeles, the white racial reformers coalesced with non-white civil rights organizations in the early 1940s and created an interracial council that revitalized the civil rights movement in the Bay Area. A new Bay Area Council against Discrimination began its work in early 1942, making San Francisco one of the first cities in the nation to establish a citywide interracial and multiethnic civil rights organization during the war years.[5] According to Hilda Taba, who conducted interracial human relations workshops throughout the nation during the late 1940s and 1950s, some 400 civic unity councils sprang up during the war years, but nearly all of them had expired without tangible accomplishments by the end of the 1940s. However, the civic unity movement proved successful in San Francisco.[6] The San Francisco Council for Civic Unity (CCU), which succeeded the Bay Area Council against Discrimination in 1944, made legislative gains in the 1940s and 1950s, and it created the institutional and ideological foundation for the later civil rights work of the 1960s.[7]

The city's tradition of religious toleration played a role in shaping the character of Jewish and Catholic participation in the civil rights movement in the 1940s and 1950s.[8] To Americans today, influenced by events since the 1960s, San Francisco may appear to be a "natural experiment in the consequences of tolerating deviance."[9] In fact, until after World War II, San Francisco—for all its vaunted reputation as a raucous wide-open port city—did not welcome racial diversity, gays, lesbians, or political radicals any more than did the rest of urban America. However, the city's reputation for religious toleration was well deserved.[10] In 1931, Archbishop Edward Hanna of San Francisco received the annual *American Hebrew* Award for the Promotion of Better Understanding between Christians and Jews in America. In 1950, Earl Raab visited San Francisco and interviewed residents for one in a series of articles on "The American Scene" for *Commentary,* the monthly magazine of the American Jewish Committee. "San Francisco, for cities of its size," Raab concluded, "is the nation's 'white spot' of anti-Jewish prejudice," with a "startling poverty of anti-Semitic tradition."[11] Raab described how Jewish residents had created a remarkably assimilated, and unusually secular, community while they forged a century-long record of business, professional, and cultural achievement. Historians have subsequently described how Jewish and Catholic participation in business and political leadership set the urban West apart from the rest of the nation generally, and San Francisco may well have perfected the model.[12]

The Jewish and Catholic response to the racial justice campaigns occurred in the context of dramatic changes in San Francisco's population and a consequent twenty-year battle over the extent to which government policy should be used to break down existing barriers to racial equality in the private and public spheres. From the beginning of the twentieth century until World War II, nonwhite residents constituted a very small number in and proportion of San Francisco's population. Irish, German, and Italian immigrants, their children, and their grandchildren made up nearly two-thirds of a population of which some 94 percent had a white European background. But in the 1930s, only about 3 percent were Chinese, Japanese, and Filipino; 1.2 percent were born in Mexico or were of Mexican descent; and .6 percent were African American.[13]

New demographic realities in the decade after Pearl Harbor brought unexpected challenges to San Francisco's white population and its customary social relations practices. San Francisco's population increased from 634,536 in 1940 to 775,357 in 1950 and then declined to 740,316 in 1960. Newcomers and their children made the city more diverse; the black population increased from 4,846 to 43,502 to 74,383; the Chinese population grew from 17,782 to 24,813 to 36,445; and the Japanese population increased from 5,280 to 5,579 to 9,464. By 1960, the city also housed 51,602 Hispanic residents and 12,327 Filipinos. The white population increased and then declined in size, from 602,701 to 693,888 to 604,403 and—foreshadowing later trends—declined as a proportion of the total from 94 percent to 89.5 percent to 81.6 percent.

At the end of World War II, the city's Chinese residents, Japanese families returning from internment camps, Filipinos, Hispanics, and tens of thousands of black newcomers found themselves confronted with both a severe housing shortage and San Francisco's historical pattern of robust racial prejudice and institutionalized racial discrimination. Entire neighborhoods were still off-limits to all but white residents; gaining access to jobs, health care, education, and cultural opportunities continued to be difficult and sometimes impossible unless one qualified as white. Many, if not most, white residents expected Chinese, Japanese, Filipino, African American, and Hispanic residents to continue living within their segregated enclaves and acquiescing in their subordinate status. Mayor Roger D. Lapham asked Thomas Fleming, the editor of the *Sun Reporter,* an African American newspaper at the end of the war, "How long you think these colored people are going to be here"? Fleming replied, "They're here to stay, and the city fathers may as well make up their minds to find housing and jobs for these people. Because they ain't going back down to the Jim Crow South."[14]

Resumption of the status quo *ante bellum* was not to be, because liberal reformers in San Francisco had launched a wartime assault on theories of racial superiority and on the social, economic, political, and cultural expression of such notions in the conduct of public affairs and private business in the city. Prominent Catholic clergy and lay men and women, with the support of their archbishop, participated in the mobilization against the discrimination faced by the city's ethnic minorities at a time when the nation proclaimed to the world its abhorrence of doctrines of racial superiority and its revitalized definition of human rights—as applying to all regardless of race, religion, color, and creed. San Francisco Catholics did not speak in one voice then any more than they do today, but in early 1942, Catholic racial liberals joined with Protestant and Jewish civil rights activists, and made common cause with ethnic/racial minority rights organizations, when they helped establish the Bay Area Council against Discrimination.[15] This was nine months before American Catholic bishops expressed "paternal solicitude for American Negroes" working in the war industries in their "Victory and Peace" statement of November 1942.[16] One year later, the bishops issued another pastoral letter acknowledging the "millions of fellow citizens of the Negro race" who deserved "not only political equality, but also fair economic and educational opportunity, a just share in public welfare projects, good housing without exploitation, and a full chance for social advancement." The bishops also declared that it was the "duty of a citizen to try to relieve racial tension."[17]

The civil rights coalition in San Francisco during this period originated in and received its greatest support from the liberal center. When judged by such criteria as the sources of financial support for the civil rights coalition, outspoken advocacy by official representatives of religious institutions, and willingness to accept leadership positions in legislative work, the conclusion is unmistakable. Jews played the leading roles, and Catholics occupied secondary roles in the 1940s and 1950s. The coalition depended on the fundraising talents of members of established families, such as the Levi Strauss executives Daniel E. Koshland Sr. and Walter A. Haas Sr. Two Jewish philanthropies provided grants for operating expenses in the first years: the Columbia Foundation and the Rosenberg Foundation. Postwar Jewish migrants to the city also excelled in drumming up financial support, particularly Benjamin H. Swig, owner of the Fairmont Hotel, and Rabbi Alvin I. Fine of Temple Emanu-El, who arrived in 1946 and 1948, respectively.[18]

The liberals believed that well-meaning men and women could put aside their different class, religious, and ethnic loyalties in the interest of civic pride and national progress. Their goal was not to "change the system" but, rather, to make incremental reforms in the system. They sought to protect Americans in the exercise of their constitutional rights and to improve the everyday lives and future opportunities of thousands of disadvantaged and underprivileged Americans. The liberals saw themselves as building on the work of the previous reform generation of the Progressive era and New Deal, and several of the founders of the civil rights coalition began their public careers as Progressive-era activists.[19]

The Progressive era's heritage appears clearly in the origins the Survey Committee, a Jewish defense association of the 1930s that produced offshoots that supported African American, Asian, and Mexican American civil rights during and after World War II. In 1937, Judge M. C. Sloss, Jesse Steinhart, Walter A. Haas Sr., and Daniel E. Koshland Sr. established a San Francisco branch of the American Jewish Committee's Survey Committee. Sloss, the son of one of the city's most influential Jewish business leaders of the late nineteenth century, served on the California Supreme Court from 1906 to 1919. Sloss, Steinhart, Haas, and Koshland brought in their contemporary, Eugene Block, to direct the daily affairs of the Survey Committee. Block was a journalist who had started his career as a protégé of Fremont Older, editor of the muckraking afternoon paper the *San Francisco Bulletin*. The Survey Committee, together with the Anti-Defamation League of B'nai B'rith and a newly established branch of the American Jewish Congress, launched a counterattack on the local Nazi Bund and other anti-Semitic organizations. Then Japanese relocation threatened the liberties of Issei and Nisei residents, debates intensified over citizenship status for Chinese residents, and wartime migration brought nearly a 1,000 percent increase in the African American population of San Francisco. Activists in the Survey Committee, the International Institute, and other local groups addressed the protection of civil rights generally. The Bay Area Council against Discrimination began its work in 1942 and was active until 1944. Lapham established a Mayor's Civic Unity Committee in 1944, which operated parallel to the CCU for several months and then disbanded. The CCU then began more than twenty years of work with local and state African American, Asian American, and Mexican American organizations on behalf of racial equality in education, employment, and housing.[20]

Daniel E. Koshland Sr., Eugene Block's associate in the Survey Committee, characterized Harold J. Boyd as "the real founder of the Council for Civic Unity."[21] Boyd, the city's controller in 1940, was born in 1890, but whereas Block grew up in the French American Jewish community, Boyd came of age in the Irish American Catholic Mission District. A labor union activist as well as a city official, and a "champion of the underdog" since the Progressive era, Boyd stirred the community when he made an outspoken public speech at the Golden Gate Exposition at Treasure Island in 1939, condemning Nazi attacks on Jews and Catholics. Boyd assumed leadership in the local Citizens Committee for Democratic Freedom in North Africa, the Bay Area Committee of the National Committee against Persecution of the Jews, and the local branch of the National Conference of Christians and Jews (NCCJ).[22]

The president of the NCCJ during the war years, the Catholic manufacturer Frederick J. Koster, also began his career in the Progressive era, serving as president of the local Chamber of Commerce. He had played a leading role in establishing the Law and Order Committee of 1916, following the Prepared-ness Day Parade bombing that killed ten and wounded forty people on July 22, 1916. A businessmen's association dedicated to eradicating violence, eliminat-ing class enmity, and banning all collective bargaining agreements produced by "duress or coercion," the Law and Order Committee operated according to the principles of Pope Leo XIII's labor encyclical. Koster's California Barrel Com-pany developed a reputation for fair management practices, including the establishment of the eight-hour workday, and the coopers' union honored him with a certificate of appreciation at the height of local hysteria about the Pre-paredness Day Parade bombing. During the 1930s, Koster championed New Deal reforms and vigorously condemned fascism and Nazism.[23]

Party loyalties did not keep supporters of the civil rights movement of the 1940s and 1950s from coalescing on behalf of local and state legislation. As Benjamin Swig recalled in an interview in 1978, "In those days there wasn't so much stress [among liberals] on whether you're a Democrat *or* a Republican. So I went to anybody I knew [when I was raising money]."[24] The founders of the Jewish Survey Committee possessed impeccable Republican Party credentials, as did Koster, whereas Harold Boyd prided himself on being a New Deal Dem-ocrat. Nonetheless, Walter A. Haas Sr., who, like Koster, presided over the local Chamber of Commerce, regarded Boyd as "a special friend."[25]

Robert and Lucy McWilliams, both left-of-center Democrats, brought a Catholic point of view to the civil rights coalition during the 1940s. Superior Court Judge Robert L. McWilliams, who, like Koster, was active in the local chapter of the NCCJ, took his law degree from UC Berkeley. He began his career at the high point of the Progressive era as an assistant district attorney before opening his own practice and teaching at Hastings College of the Law and the San Francisco Law School. Among the many students influenced by his commitment to Catholic principles of social justice, future Governor Ed-mund G. (Pat) Brown is the best known. Both Robert and Lucy McWilliams frequently publicized their support for interfaith cooperation and for civil rights legislation.[26] Lucy McWilliams, an honorary member of the Zionist organization Hadassah, also served as the vice-chairman of the Democratic State Central Committee. In 1935, she led a campaign to establish healthy migrant worker camps at the Pescadero and Half Moon Bay farms in San Mateo County. In 1942, she chaired the Bay Area Council against Discrimina-tion, and in 1944, she served as one of the founders of the CCU.[27]

During the second half of the 1930s and the first years of the 1940s, a new and younger contingent of white liberal activists joined the older veterans of the Progressive era in the civil rights coalition. Some, as mentioned earlier, were neither Jewish nor Catholic, but they all brought to the coalition a politi-cal consciousness forged in the heat of New Deal debates over the failure of

American capitalism and the use of government policy to secure the American dream for all. Many had embraced the socialist cause before the war.[28] When they moved to what Arthur M. Schlesinger Jr. in 1949 called "the vital center," their work expressed a continued commitment to economic equality as well as racial justice.[29]

Three leading activists in the coalition typified this process. David Selvin moved from work at the Pacific Coast Labor Bureau to the Jewish Survey Committee and then became the executive secretary of the Bay Area Council against Discrimination. Selvin, a Jew, grew up in Utah and was sensitive about his minority status and sympathetic with those forced to live on the margins of society. Edward Howden worked for the San Francisco Planning and Housing Association and the California Housing Association. After three years in military service, he became the director of the CCU. Earl Raab, who worked with Eugene Block in the Jewish Community Relations Council, also represented this new, younger cadre of civil rights activists. Like the Bay Area Council against Discrimination, the Community Relations Council evolved out of the Jewish Survey Committee. Raab's writings, sometimes with the political sociologist Seymour Martin Lipset, reached a national audience. He also chaired the Bay Area Human Relations Clearing House.[30]

Neither Selvin nor Raab, who was also of Jewish background, had grown up in an actively religious household. Each, however, drew on the tradition that represented the Jews as a people with a historical destiny to alleviate suffering and right wrongs. They used their academic training in research and writing—Selvin at Berkeley and Raab at City College in New York—to further the cause of economic justice and racial and religious freedom. Howden grew up in Oakland, attended University High School near the Oakland–Berkeley border, and graduated from the University of California. Howden found himself drawn to the liberal activism of Harry Kingman and Ruth Kingman. Harry Kingman served as general-secretary of Stiles Hall on the UC Berkeley campus, the only location where members of the Young Communist League could meet. Born in China to Protestant missionaries, Kingman counseled hundreds of future activists about the importance of protecting civil liberties and civil rights. Harry and Ruth Kingman worked as partners, and their inspiration directly influenced Howden, as well as Yori Wada, a Japanese American student who would go on to become the director of San Francisco's Japantown YMCA and to have a long career as a civil rights activist and a stalwart liberal Democrat. In September 1958, Edward Howden left the CCU to head the city's new CEEO and a year later was appointed by Governor Brown to head California's new Fair Employment Practices Commission (FEPC). At the same time, Harry and Ruth Kingman established their Citizens Lobby in Washington, D.C., with Koshland serving as treasurer. Harry and Ruth Kingman and Edward Howden worked closely with Clarence Mitchell, director of the Washington, D.C., division of the NAACP in the lobbying campaign to pass what became the Civil Rights Acts of 1964, 1965, and 1968.[31]

San Francisco's large and active communist community developed an ambivalent relationship with the liberal civil rights movement. Communists worked with liberals on civil rights during the period of the "Popular Front" line of World War II and before the Cold War. This common front approach was evident in the Bay Area Council against Discrimination in 1942–1944, in Mayor Lapham's Civic Unity Committee in 1944, and in the first two years of the CCU in 1944–1945. Devout Catholic anticommunists such as the attorney Maurice Harrison and the Reverend Thomas F. Burke served on these committees. So did Communist Party officers and activists such as Oleta O'Connor Yates and Aubrey Grossman. They investigated rumors of an impending race riot in Hunters Point (it never happened), and they listened to complaints filed by black tenants against the city's Housing Authority (the discriminatory policy was eventually outlawed).[32]

Tension developed in late 1945 and 1946, and the common front collapsed. The party line changed and forbade cooperation with liberal reformers, and the Communist Party's credibility suffered as knowledge of Soviet repression of civil liberties increased. Liberals distanced themselves from communists by declaring that their determination to eradicate racial injustice did not call into question their loyalty to America. For these reasons and because of the social and ideological changes in the city's African American community after the war ended, the coalition experienced a variety of tensions and challenges during the years of its most widespread appeal. Many on the left—and on the right, as well—remained outside the liberal coalition, opposed to its reformist principles, critical of its legislative strategies, and determined to eliminate its influence.[33]

In 1938, Elliot M. Burstein, rabbi at Temple Beth Israel from 1927 to 1969, and Saul E. White, rabbi at Beth Sholom from 1935 to 1983, founded the Northern California Branch of the American Jewish Congress. Then they organized a boycott of German goods in protest against Nazi repression. Burstein and White stood out as outspoken advocates of the establishment of a Jewish state in a Jewish community that generally eschewed Zionism.[34] The principles of freedom and self-determination central to their work earned White and Burstein a wide following among civil rights activists. Both men appeared frequently before non-Jewish audiences and spoke to local radio audiences. Rabbi White developed a close personal and professional relationship with Howard Thurman, African American minister of the Church for the Fellowship of All Peoples, a pioneering Protestant interracial church in the heart of the Fillmore District.[35]

Burstein's sermons and lectures from the late 1930s and the years of World War II exemplify the ideological connection linking the defense of Jewish freedom, the struggle of the Allies against the Axis powers, and the campaign for civil rights. On March 27, 1937, a year after Hitler demilitarized the Rhineland and seven months after the Anschluss with Austria, Burstein presented the lecture "Slavery in Modern Times" to the audience of the KFRC radio station. He exhorted the audience to "eternally give battle to every robber of human freedom" and argued that the story of Moses leading his people out of Egypt was everyone's heritage, not just that of the Jews. "The story of the Exodus is a warning to be eternally vigilant against all lash-masters. . . . [Th]is why we regard with dismay the mushroom growths of fascistic movements in the world today." Speaking at Odd Fellows Hall on "What Is Americanism?" ten days after Hitler opened the Balkan campaign and the day before Yugoslavia surrendered to the Nazis, Burstein anticipated the civic unity council efforts that marked the war years. "There is still plenty of prejudice against the negro, the Jew, the Catholic. As long as this exists, our democracy will be sick and needs a good dose of tolerance. But even tolerance is not enough. Tolerance is arrogance. Our Americanism should include definite efforts made to unite all Americans on their common tasks and to urge groups not to capitalize on their differences."[36]

On June 30, scarcely a week after Adolf Hitler danced for joy before photographers after forcing a humiliating armistice on France, Rabbi Burstein addressed an audience at the First Methodist Church. "The Christian–Jewish answer to the World's Crisis," he insisted, is to stand up to the "force, trickery, ruthlessness . . . of communism, nazism, or fascism." However, he said, "We must not, if we value our democracy and liberties they allow us, employ their tactics. . . . We must bend over backwards and give sympathy and love in greater measure than ever. . . . World conditions are such that shortly they will demand tremendous sacrifices from all of us. But the greatest sacrifice of all is a subjugation of passion to reason. We must not lose our wits. We must fight not with hate and vengeance, but with a calm sense of a serious duty to perform."[37]

By the summer of 1944, one month after the Allied invasion at Normandy, Burstein spoke on "Religion and Democracy" over radio station KSFO. He suggested that "the religious idea . . . that humanity is one great family—a family of equals in its own eyes and the eyes of God . . . will not be established unless the democratic idea is first established." In a democracy, "man must at least respect his neighbor, his person, his opinions, his wants and his rights. If this cannot be achieved positively by persuasion, it can at least be achieved negatively by legislation."[38] Burstein summed up his talk about the link between religion and democracy with a call for "not love of neighbor, but an understanding of, a sympathy with, a healthy respect for, our neighbor."[39] The social theorist Horace Kallen had for years popularized this model of social relations as "pluralism" or "democratic pluralism." As Burstein explained, "Discrimination or attacks against any group anywhere, no matter what its beliefs, origin, or skin pigmentation, is an attack against humanity as a whole."[40]

Burstein's endorsement of pluralism found an echo in the sermons and lectures of the Paulist priest Thomas F. Burke, pastor of Old St. Mary's Church and brother of Monsignor John J. Burke, the general-secretary of the National Catholic Welfare Conference and a prominent national spokesman on Catholic social justice. Archbishop John J. Mitty, whose term of office extended from 1935 to 1961, frequently delegated Burke to represent the archdiocese at interfaith gatherings. Burke's Thanksgiving Day sermon at the Civic Auditorium in 1937, under the auspices of the NCCJ, urged San Franciscans to "gather for common interests and for common action [against] bigotry and intolerance and bitterness and war."[41]

By the time Father Burke died in 1947, his prewar message about the need for pluralism as the basis for cooperation to protect "the very soul of America" had even greater appeal for liberal Catholics and Jews. Raab recalled that when he involved himself in the civil rights coalition in 1951, he did so because he "had a great interest . . . in strengthening democracy in this country, coming out of the experiences of the 1930s for the Jews. . . . My underlying philosophy and this related to my main interest in Jewry, was that the important objective of [this work] was to strengthen democratic pluralism . . . and civil rights demonstrated this principle at the time more than anything."[42]

In the spirit of Rabbi Burstein's conviction that "our big positive guns are persuasion and education"—and, if that failed, then "negatively by legislation"— the civil rights liberals used the CCU to educate and inform the public and lobby for new civil rights laws. The CCU adopted an inclusive strategy, bringing together representatives of established groups and new organizations. From Chinatown came Henry Shue Tom, executive secretary of the Chinatown YMCA, and Lim P. Lee, a lawyer and Democratic Party activist who became San Francisco's postmaster in 1967. The Chinese American Citizens Alliance sent Kenneth Fung, an attorney who had been born in San Francisco; Fung served three terms as president of the alliance and lobbied for immigration law reform on its behalf in Washington, D.C. The CCU also worked with Robert B. Flippin of the National Association for the Advancement of Colored People (NAACP) and Seaton W. Manning of San Francisco's new branch office of the National Urban League, which was established in 1946.[43]

During and after the war, new migrants to the city added their voices and energy to the emerging coalition. By the time the American Catholic Bishops issued their pastoral letter "Discrimination and Christian Conscience" in November 1958, reminding Catholics that "discrimination based on the accident of race or color cannot be reconciled with God's creation of man," liberal Catholics in San Francisco had more than a decade of experience as civil rights advocates.[44] Terry A. Francois, an African American Catholic who had graduated from Xavier University in New Orleans in 1940, moved to San Francisco after his discharge from the U.S. Marine Corps in 1946. Francois immediately immersed himself in civil rights activity. In 1950, with a degree from Hastings College of the Law in hand, he joined the boards of directors of both the local NAACP and the national Catholic Interracial Council. He and his law partners Loren Miller and Nathaniel Colley carried the NAACP's suit against the San Francisco Housing Authority that culminated in the banning of its so-called neighborhood pattern policy of segregation. Francois served as president of the local NAACP branch and with Edward Howden and Irving Rosenblatt conducted the negotiations with the San Francisco Employers Council in 1957 that resulted in their endorsement of the city CEEO ordinance. In 1964, Francois became the first African American to serve on the Board of Supervisors when Mayor John F. (Jack) Shelley appointed him to that position.[45]

Mayor George Christopher appointed Francois to the new CEEO in 1957, where he served with Peter E. Haas, the son of one of the founders of the Jewish Survey Committee. The son and the father, incidentally, disagreed about liberal civil rights legislation. "I remember big arguments with my father," Haas recalled in 1992. "[He] said you can't legislate these things. You can't legislate morality."[46] Richard L. Sloss, the son of another of the four men who organized the Jewish Survey Committee, served on the board of the National Urban League after World War II and brought his liberal point of view to his work on behalf of its projects. In his lay sermons at various synagogues during the 1940s and 1950s, Sloss returned again and again to the importance of eradicating prejudice and fostering pluralism, as in this talk from 1948: "Differences in thinking are not only inevitable, they are healthy signs of freedom of the mind; but they need not, and should not, become the basis for groundless suspicions and unreasoning distrust. Let no man believe unkind generalizations about groups other than his own."[47]

Sloss belonged to the Temple Emanu-El congregation. Alvin Fine, a staunch liberal from Cincinnati who arrived in San Francisco in 1948, served as senior rabbi at Emanu-El until 1964. A native of Portland, Oregon, Rabbi Fine quickly moved to the center of the civil rights coalition, playing an active public role in a variety of initiatives, including the campaigns to establish a city and state FEPC.[48]

Fine also took active leadership in the NCCJ. Throughout the 1950s, quietly and with considerable tact, he nudged Archbishop Mitty to place the Catholic Church actively in the forefront on interfaith cooperation and civil rights reforms.[49] One example particularly reveals Fine's strategy: when the criticism over Harry Truman's appointment of an ambassador to the Vatican made headlines across the country in late 1951 and early 1952, the local NCCJ met behind closed doors for a confidential discussion of how to limit the damage to interfaith relations in San Francisco. When several of the Protestant representatives "vehemently" declared their opposition to Truman's action, Rabbi Fine "told [them] that he didn't think it was any of their business whether the Vatican was a State or not a State." The archbishop's representative to the meeting, Father James N. Brown, the superintendent of Catholic schools, confided to Mitty that while Fine's arguments expressed "the Jewish attitude toward religion in the public schools . . . he is one of the Zionists who does not believe in a Church–State set up there."[50]

The controversy over the Vatican ambassador, like the concurrent battle over whether tax monies should be allowed to support Catholic schools, underscored the longstanding mutual suspicions between the Catholic Church and Jewish and Protestant organizations that persisted during the period. Archbishop Mitty, who had served as bishop in Salt Lake City in 1926–1932, brought to San Francisco considerable experience in negotiating interfaith tensions. He facilitated the practice of "mixed marriages" between Catholics and non-Catholics, and he led the successful campaign to reform the church's national policy to allow such marriages to take place in parish churches. During and after World War II, Mitty received a crescendo of requests from Protestant and Jewish organizations and Catholic laymen for greater interfaith cooperation and support for domestic civil rights. The archbishop allowed the formation of an Interracial Communion League at St. Benedict the Moor Church in 1952. Father Bruno Drescher, the pastor of the church, which stood in the heart of the African American community in the Western Addition, was a civil rights stalwart who served on the CCU's board. However, attempts to obtain Mitty's approval for a citywide Catholic Interracial Council did not succeed until 1960.[51]

Given his experience in Salt Lake City, where he had coexisted with the Mormon majority and expanded efforts to make converts to Catholicism, Mitty responded to calls for interfaith cooperation with ambivalence. He was determined to refuse a forum to unfriendly liberal and left-leaning Protestant and Jewish ministers and rabbis who might vilify the church because of its support for General Francisco Franco in Spain. "Catholics," as he put it in a confidential letter, should not be placed "in a compromising position." In addition, "There is the possibility that the ordinary rank and file of the people may begin to feel, as a result of these meetings, that one faith is as good as another."[52] The archbishop resolved his ambivalence in a way that typified his administrative practice generally. He made almost no public statements about either the interfaith movement or the civil rights movement. At the same time, he delegated to trusted priests and laymen the authority to act on behalf of the archdiocese. Mitty began this policy in 1941 and did not change course during the nearly twenty years that followed. He explained to a colleague on the faculty of Holy

Redeemer College that he had been influenced by the opinions of "a very splendid Catholic judge" and "a very splendid Catholic lawyer." No doubt he referred
to Judge Robert L. McWilliams and Maurice E. Harrison, both of whom were
on close personal terms with the archbishop. "Their opinion," Mitty confided,
"makes me a bit slow in condemning these meetings." Besides, he said, "The big
difficulty I foresee in not giving some participation in these meetings is the possibility of a charge of un-Americanism."[53]

The question of how to define and practice Americanism took center stage
in American political culture during these years. The Jewish community, heterogeneous in outlook, debated the question of whether support for a Jewish
homeland in Israel could be compatible with loyalty to America. The Catholic
community, heavily Irish American, questioned whether racial prejudice and
discrimination could coexist with its profession of Christianity.[54]

Amid these tensions and ambiguities, the most public Catholic *institutional*
support for the civil rights movement in San Francisco came not from archdiocesan priests but from priests associated with particular religious orders. The
activism of Father Burke, whose Paulist order might be expected to take the
vanguard on these matters, given its program of interfaith cooperation, has
already been noted. In addition, the Jesuit University of San Francisco (USF)
developed institutional relationships with the NAACP and the Urban League
during the first decade after the war, and these relationships increasingly
brought Catholic lay and clerical civil rights activists together with a variety of
African American leaders. The connection came about largely through the initiative of Father Andrew C. Boss, director of USF's Labor-Management School.
Boss grew up in a working-class family in the city's Mission District. By the late
1940s, Boss (like Raab, who first clashed with the communist left during his
student days at City College of New York) was a principled anti-Stalinist as well
as a firm advocate of civil rights. The Labor-Management School opened its
doors in the spring of 1948, after Boss and Father Hugh A. Donohoe decided
that the city needed a Catholic alternative to the California Labor School, whose
administration and curriculum were dominated by the Communist Party.
Donohoe wore several hats. In the late 1930s, he began twenty-five years of
service as chaplain to the Association of Catholic Trade Unionists. During the
war years, he edited the official newspaper *The Monitor*. And in 1948, Archbishop Mitty appointed Donohoe auxiliary bishop and delegated him to represent the archdiocese on the board of the CCU.[55]

During the decade between the founding of Labor-Management School and
the passage of the city and state FEPC laws, Father Boss opened the pages of the
school's periodical, *Labor Management Panel,* to articles by local African American leaders. He also organized conferences to expose discrimination in
employment and generate support for fair employment legislation.[56] The USF

events provided a forum for opponents of liberal civil rights legislation, as well as an opportunity for its supporters to spread their gospel. In an Institute on Minority Group Employment held in April 1951, for instance, Adrien Falk, president of the California Chamber of Commerce, criticized the legislative approach and called for voluntary job training and skill-development initiatives by employers. Falk, a confidante to mayors Roger Lapham and George Christopher, would persist in this argument all the way to the passage of the city fair employment ordinance in 1957.[57]

One of the Labor-Management School's civil rights programs, a panel discussion broadcast on the radio station KNBC in January 1954, featured D. Donald Glover, industrial relations secretary of the city's Urban League. Judge Sylvester McAtee, another discussant, raised the issue of the Communist Party's influence in the civil rights movement. John F. Henning, a graduate of St. Mary's College who was serving as the research director of the California State Federation of Labor, also appeared on the program. In August 1957, Henning would join Haas and Terry Francois on the city's FEPC, and in 1959, Governor Brown would appoint Henning to the position of director of the California Department of Industrial Relations. Now Henning bristled at McAtee's claim that fair employment legislation "provides the ideal opportunity for propaganda by [communists] who wish to create racial animosities, and employer–employee conflict." Henning responded "on this matter of associating the drive for racial justice in this country with any Communist purpose. The Communist apparatus must be opposed if democracy is to survive but to exploit the issue and associate the campaign for racial justice with the Communist movement is actually the last refuge of those who are morally sterile and philosophically bankrupt."[58]

The state FEPC bill passed five years later, on April 16, 1959. The campaign to pass the legislation began with the Bay Area Council against Discrimination and the CCU in the early to mid-1940s. Then the CCU and its counterparts in Southern California, along with the California State Labor Federation and the Jewish Labor Committee, all worked with the NAACP's "Fight for Freedom" program of 1953 and revived the campaign. Augustus Hawkins and Byron Rumford, African American members of the California State Assembly, saw the bill through the legislature. C. L. Dellums of the Brotherhood of Sleeping Car Porters, the uncle of future Congressman Ron Dellums, served as chair of the labor, minority, and religious coalition. The white liberals William Becker and Max Mont from the Jewish Labor Committee managed the day-to-day operations.[59] By the time the state FEPC began its work in 1959, the liberal coalition had desegregated San Francisco's public housing projects, won an antidiscrimination clause in urban redevelopment housing policy, and successfully campaigned to establish the city's CEEO.[60]

The white Jews and Catholics who participated in the civil rights movement of the 1940s and 1950s prepared the ground for an expansion of interfaith cooperation, as well as for further legislative victories for racial liberalism at the state and local levels during the 1960s. But these later accomplishments did not represent a simple continuity with the racial liberalism of the postwar years. On the morning of November 4, 1964, headlines in the *San Francisco Chronicle* proclaimed, "Big Johnson Victory; Solid Murphy Lead; Prop[osition] 14 Passes." The United States expressed its confidence in the incumbent president as Lyndon Johnson crushed Barry Goldwater in a sweeping victory. The Golden State gained a new senator when the movie star George Murphy defeated Pierre Salinger, former press secretary to John F. Kennedy. And California lost its newly established fair housing act as voters endorsed a constitutional amendment to nullify the law by a two-to-one margin. Given the morality-play character of this no-holds-barred contest between the defenders of a state law requiring racial equality in housing and opponents of such a mandate, it is not surprising that Northern California's leading daily newspaper announced the passage of Proposition 14 in front-page headlines. California voters' rejection of legislative protection for racial equality in housing was a statewide expression of an increasingly rancorous national debate over the role of government in ensuring social justice in an increasingly diverse multiethnic society. Focusing in on the ways in which Catholic San Franciscans negotiated these troubled waters demonstrates some of the limits of racial liberalism at the very time of its most impressive victories.

The United States experienced considerable turmoil during the 1960s—if not quite the "civil war" that some historians have asserted—and the Catholic Church itself underwent significant change related to the Second Vatican Council (Vatican II).[61] Several local developments between the fight over the FEPC in 1959 and the campaign for Proposition 14 in 1964 complicated the ways in which San Franciscans experienced what has been characterized as a period of "frenzied agitation, whose intensity was heightened for Catholics by the merging together of the religious crisis and the society-wide political cultural crises."[62] In April 1963, Professor Raymond Sontag of UC Berkeley identified the complexities that were emerging when he noted that at the very moment Catholics might be experiencing a desire to "fit in" as they became more accepted in the American mainstream, they had a duty to be "different" from the mainstream by insisting on the kind of uncompromising racial justice called for by church teachings on race.[63]

Archbishop Mitty approved the establishment of a local branch of the Catholic Interracial Council in 1960. Mitty died in 1961, and his successor, Joseph T. McGucken (served 1962–1977) established an official archdiocesan Social Justice Commission in 1964. Behind the seeming continuity, considerable change took place. Between 1960 and 1964, several charismatic leaders left San Francisco. Bishop Donohoe, whose leadership in the CCU had legitimized Catholic participation in the city's equal rights campaign, left to become the head of the newly formed Diocese of Stockton. John F. Henning, whose leadership in the fair employment fight had inspired Catholic working men and women to participate in civil rights work, left to become the undersecretary of labor in Washington, D.C.

Also, a local grassroots challenge to the church's authority emerged even as the Vatican II proceedings encouraged the displacement of the traditional deferential mode of Catholic Action by a new, change-oriented, critical approach. This occurred when the new archbishop's $9 million cathedral that replaced the burned-down neo-Gothic St. Mary's was picketed by a small but media-savvy cadre of angry Catholic clergy and laymen and laywomen. They claimed that the cathedral was an ostentatious architectural showpiece out of place in the City of Saint Francis; worse, they alleged, it was built at the expense of poor African American families who had been displaced by the redevelopment of the area. The protesters also criticized the archbishop for failing to publicly condemn the segregated skilled building trades unions whose members were building the cathedral; McGucken, they argued, should have seized the opportunity to demand faster progress toward racial integration in the labor movement.[64]

Members of the relatively new local chapter of the Catholic Interracial Council were among the most outspoken critics of Archbishop McGucken. The new organization had been approved by Archbishop Mitty in 1960, and Father Eugene Boyle became its chaplain two years later. At the time, Boyle was a forty-one-year-old diocesan priest who had caught Mitty's eye in the mid-1950s. Mitty assigned him to the archdiocesan Mission Band, the adult-education outreach program that recruited Cesar Chavez into labor and civil rights work. Boyle also founded and moderated a dialogue program on KCBS radio that analyzed "the moral aspects of current issues," including civil rights and civil liberties. When Martin Luther King Jr.'s room at the Gaston Motel in Birmingham was destroyed by a bomb in May 1963, Boyle overcame his reservations about protest marches and joined other religious leaders and laymen and laywomen at a demonstration at San Francisco's City Hall.[65] The following year saw Boyle, and his Catholic Interracial Council colleague John Delury, a graduate of USF, assume leadership of Archbishop McGucken's new archdiocesan Social Justice Commission. At the same time, following in the footsteps of Bishop Donohoe, Boyle co-founded the citywide Catholic, Protestant, and Jewish Conference on Religion, Race, and Social Concerns. The new organization's purpose was to revitalize connections between churches and synagogues with groups such as the NAACP and the National Urban League and to expand on the work that the Bay Area Council against Discrimination and the CCU had begun twenty years earlier.[66]

The year 1964 witnessed a quickening in civil rights activism by a new cadre of clerical and lay activists. It also saw growing strength of the opposition to government-imposed equal rights legislation that had existed for twenty years. In San Francisco that year, Mayor Shelley proposed to the Board of Supervisors a permanent Human Rights Commission. The board established the commission on July 13, and Shelley quickly appointed the fifteen commissioners, including the religious activists Sister Rose Maureen Kelly, Father Boyle, and Rabbi Alvin Fine. Outspoken critics of the new city Human Rights Commission disliked it for the very reason its proponents demanded its establishment: the commission wielded subpoena power and soon developed a national reputation as an aggressive advocate of racial, religious, gender, and sexual-orientation equality in education, employment, and housing.[67]

The increasingly robust property-rights-based libertarian opposition to racial liberal legislation was a national as well as a local phenomenon. Racial liberals by the thousands marched down Market Street on July 11, 1964, to protest the scheduled appearance of Senator Barry Goldwater of Arizona at the Republic Party convention in San Francisco the next day. The demonstrators excoriated Goldwater as the "anti-civil rights candidate" because he had voted against the federal Civil Rights Act. But Goldwater's supporters cheered when he exhorted delegates that "extremism in the defense of liberty is no vice. And let me remind you also that moderation in the pursuit of justice is no virtue." The California Real Estate Association and like-minded property owners throughout the Golden State were similarly inclined when they renamed the state's antidiscrimination housing legislation the "forced housing," not "fair housing," acts. Their remedy for such "government tyranny" was the voter-initiated constitutional amendment designed to block government bans on discrimination in housing that would become Proposition 14.[68]

The events associated with Proposition 14 began in 1959 when California passed its first fair housing laws. The Hawkins Act of that year barred discrimination in public housing; the same year, the legislature passed the Unruh Act, which banned discrimination by realtors when they were acting "independent of the owner's request."[69] Four years later, in April 1963, Assemblyman Rumford introduced Assembly Bill 1240. This proposed ordinance aimed to prohibit owners from inquiring as to the race, color, religion, national origin or ancestry of prospective buyers or tenants, and expanded existing law to include about 70 percent of the state's housing. The "public" aspect of preceding law was to be expanded to include "publicly assisted" housing—that is, housing financed by the GI Bill or federally assisted mortgage money. Transactions involving realtors and brokers were also to be included.[70]

Shortly after Assemblyman Rumford introduced the legislation, *The Monitor* ran an expansive article supporting the proposed legislation. Housing discrimination threatened the "social health of society" because segregation created immoral "hermetically sealed" ghettoes that interfered with a morally acceptable future of integrated cities and suburbs. Several other states had already bested California's record of fair housing legislation, and the claim that prejudice could not be overcome by legislation was disproved by data from New York. "Laws change community patterns and changes in community patterns change attitude."[71] The *Monitor* disparaged the argument that marshaled the Fourteenth Amendment's due process clause in defense of presumed citizens' property rights as a misguided resuscitation of a long-dead, antebellum states' rights ideology.[72] The *Monitor's* support for racial equality in housing was followed two months later by a pastoral letter from the American bishops titled "On Racial Harmony." The bishops declared unambiguously that racial segregation was a violation of Christian teaching and argued that "respect for personal rights is both a moral duty, and a civic one."[73]

By the end of September, the California Assembly and Senate had approved the Rumford Fair Housing Act, and liberal Democratic Governor Pat Brown signed it into law. Immediately, the California Real Estate Association announced plans to gather signatures for a ballot referendum leading to a constitutional amendment to nullify the new law. In November, the National Catholic Conference for Interracial Justice urged Californians to defend the Rumford Act when it resolved that "no Catholic in good conscience can sign petitions or support laws or ordinances that deny minorities a full and equal opportunity to secure decent homes on a non-discriminatory basis."[74]

San Francisco's Archbishop McGucken signed a full-page advertisement in the *New York Times* urging voters to withhold support for the repeal petition. State Controller Alan Cranston, speaking at a testimonial dinner for Byron Rumford, argued that Rumford's new law had not been found lacking; it had not been given an opportunity. Cranston agreed with the argument that we "can't legislate morality, but we can and must uphold legislation that provides conditions conducive to morality."[75]

At the grassroots, conservative voters avidly signed the petitions, and by February 25, 1964, enough signatures—half of them from Los Angeles County— had been confirmed to put the measure on the ballot. Governor Brown, a San Franciscan and a practicing Catholic, tried to derail the future success of the measure by persuading lawmakers to place it on the fall, rather than the spring, ballot. Brown imagined (wrongly, as it turned out) that the larger liberal turnout expected in the November presidential election would condemn the measure to defeat. Like the San Francisco Catholic Interracial Council, Brown realized the potential significance of repealing the Rumford Act. If California approved a constitutional amendment barring further local or state legislation on behalf of housing rights regardless of race, color, religion, ancestry, or national origin, the forces of conservative reaction would win a substantial national victory.[76]

Most of the Catholic bishops of California went on record in opposition to Proposition 14, but Cardinal McIntyre of Los Angeles refused to condemn the measure, declaring that "the Roman Catholic Church doesn't take a stand on political matters." He advised Catholics to vote their conscience, as "the teaching of the Church is clear."[77] According to Monsignor Francis A. Quinn, who edited *The Monitor* during the Proposition 14 campaign, Archbishop McGucken respected "the tradition that clergy did not take the forefront in these matters" at the same time that he believed it was "right for the Church to be involved but with prudence and moderation." McGucken therefore declined invitations to appear in person and declare his position forthrightly and instead designated or allowed those who would speak uncompromisingly against Proposition 14 to represent the church.[78]

When McGucken did act, or speak, he avoided outright attacks on the supporters of Proposition 14 while arguing that the measure deserved repudiation. He insisted that newspaper ads asking voters not to sign the petition to get the measure on the ballot avoided all "accusation" of the real estate industry. At the same time, he insisted on strengthening the language of the ads to make explicit that "the initiative now proposed would not only kill existing California law, but would prohibit legislative, and other agencies of state and local government, including the courts, from dealing with acts of religious or social discrimination in housing." The changes were made, and the full-page ad ran in the *New York Times,* the *San Francisco Examiner,* and the *San Francisco Chronicle* on December 23, 1963.[79]

The archbishop hoped the proposition would be declared unconstitutional by the courts and removed from the ballot, thereby relieving him of the need to make a public condemnation of the measure, but in the meantime he cautiously provided support for the anti–Proposition 14 forces from behind the scenes. When Rabbi Joseph Glaser of the Union of American Hebrew Congregations threatened that "Protestants and Jews will go it alone" if McGucken would not personally participate in interfaith efforts to stop the repeal of the Rumford Act, the archbishop designated Father Boyle the archdiocesan representative. Glaser was no doubt unaware that the archbishop would send a check drawn on archdiocesan funds, for twice the amount requested, to his co-religionist Benjamin Swig, the director of Californians against Proposition 14.[80]

McGucken was invited to give the invocation when Dr. Martin Luther King Jr. appeared at an anti–Proposition 14 rally at the Cow Palace on May 26, 1964. Following past practice, he declined, once again sending Father Boyle in his place. Boyle condemned Proposition 14 as representing "an alien, un-American and unchristian concept of property which must be rejected."[81] In late May, the archbishop himself was quoted as saying that Catholics who supported the proposition made "errors in conscience" (in which a person can perform an objectively immoral act while remaining subjectively free of guilt because his conscience is sincere and free of immoral intent).[82] He was personally opposed to repeal, but he would not go so far as to say that Catholics had a moral duty to vote against it. Edward Keating, publisher of the local left-wing magazine *Ramparts,* publicly criticized the archbishop, calling him "derelict in his duties" for opposing the measure on constitutional, rather than on moral, grounds.[83]

The archbishop's hope that the courts would remove Proposition 14 from the ballot was disappointed. By September, the measure still had not been taken off the ballot, and McGucken established the archdiocesan Social Justice Commission to promote and coordinate racial justice education in connection with the anti–Proposition 14 campaign.[84] Leadership fell to Father Boyle, John Delury, Monsignor Francis Quinn, and Monsignor Bernard Cummins, superintendent of archdiocesan schools, with one pastor as a representative from each county in the diocese. The archbishop asked all pastors to form committees of six to ten members to discuss issues of social justice in their parishes and recommended that each pastor preach twice on racial justice before the election. According to a partial follow-up survey, thirty-two parishes had several sermons on the topic; nine had one; and six had none.[85]

Two weeks before the election, on October 22, 1964, McGucken published the "Letter on Christian Justice and Love" on the front page of *The Monitor.* Sent from Rome, where he was attending a session of Vatican II, the letter did not mention Proposition 14 directly, but it stated plainly that "inequality in opportunity to enjoy housing because of race is an insult to human dignity."[86] The archbishop ordered that the letter be read from every pulpit in the archdiocese. The chancery office did not object when the *San Francisco Chronicle,* the daily with the largest circulation in the city, reported that the "pastoral letter from Rome urges 750,000 Catholics in the Archdiocese to vote 'no' on 14."[87]

Archbishop McGucken had participated in the opposition to repealing the Rumford Act in December 1963, and he personally urged defeat of Proposition 14 two weeks before the election, but he made no attempt to restrain or moderate the editorial content or the reportage on the controversy over fair housing by the official diocesan newspaper. In September 1963, *The Monitor* published a non-discriminatory statement on its real estate page; it continued to appear, and was praised in the "Letters" column, regularly.[88] Lengthy articles appeared on the issue of race. Many did not address the Rumford Act or repeal efforts directly, but they nonetheless promulgated the church's antiracist teaching. In a full-page article, Professor Richard R. B. Powell of Hastings College of the Law, wrote, "Property rights cease when civil rights involving the public interest is at stake."[89] Father Joseph Farraher contributed four articles that appeared in September and October elaborating the thesis that "it is a sin against charity and justice to refuse to sell a house on the basis of race." He insisted that since the Rumford Act was fully in accord with church teaching, "Catholic moral teaching requires a 'no' vote."[90] As the length and quantity of these articles increased, one reader was prompted to complain; he counted eleven articles related to race, civil rights, or the Rumford Act in the August 27, 1964 issue, "each giving a one-sided [anti–Proposition 14] view."[91]

The Monitor endorsed the Rumford Act after its passage and called for a "no" vote on Proposition 14. Commenting on the divisions among San Francisco Catholics, the editor acknowledged "tension between members of the Church" but also insisted that the "law which went into effect on September 20 is a moderate one; give it a chance."[92] An editorial cartoon published on December 27 revised the story of the Magi; instead of gold, frankincense, and myrrh, the Three Kings brought the infant Jesus racial justice, a ban on nuclear testing, and a successful outcome for the second session of the Ecumenical Council.[93] In January, the editor challenged conservative readers who quarreled with Catholic civil rights activism by asking, "What is the Church's function if not to make its voice known on moral issues?"[94]

By late August 1964, with Goldwater campaigning for president and the Proposition 14 campaign in high gear, *The Monitor* editorialized that "no California voter should vote 'yes' on 14," citing the authority of Bishop Floyd L. Begin of Oakland that "Prop[osition] 14 contradicts what is clear and universal Catholic social teaching."[95] In his column on October 10, Monsignor Bernard Cummins, superintendent of archdiocesan schools, addressed "the uneasiness of many in the Church in dealing with social issues," pointing out that "the Church is a newcomer to the area." Cummins traced the development of the church's stand on public issues from Leo XIII's encyclicals to John XXIII's "continued emphasis on the role of the Church in the World." When Catholics found themselves uncertain about "the relationship of the Church to the world, i.e. politics," they should listen for guidance: "The Bishops will speak."[96] Archbishop McGucken spoke out strongly against Proposition 14 in his pastoral letter of October 22, and the accompanying editorial instructed readers that although the measure "has split the state and has also created differences within the Church," the archbishop speaks for the church, which does not use its authority "recklessly."[97]

Several members of the local Catholic Interracial Council criticized the archbishop for his cautious strategy and tactics during the campaign. They faulted the archdiocese for failing to take a more active stand in the community at large and called for an all-out campaign to defend fair housing. These critics wanted the archdiocese to make public common cause with anti–Proposition 14 efforts of the Jewish Community Relations Council and the San Francisco Council of Churches.[98] Mac Hull of San Rafael, an officer with the Catholic Interracial Council, envisioned a door-to-door campaign "reaching every Catholic household in California. . . . The character of the Civil Rights movement could proceed to success if full religious witness can be brought to bear on those who say they believe, but are prejudiced."[99] Council members who distributed anti–Proposition 14 literature after Sunday mass sometimes found themselves criticized for being too aggressive by parishioners who complained to Archbishop McGucken.[100] John Riordan, another Catholic Interracial Council activist, addressed the issue of how to proselytize among his coreligionists when he argued that the group needed to find "positive ways" to spread "Church teaching on race."[101]

Catholics who objected to sermons against Proposition 14 and the distribution of anti–Proposition 14 literature after mass gave tacit approval to the point of view announced by Robert Miller, head of the Northern California Committee for "Yes on 14." Miller insisted that the issue was political, not religious, and discussion of its merits did not belong in the pulpit. In Los Gatos, a town in Santa Clara County sixty miles south of San Francisco, Catholics claiming to represent sixty parishes organized a "Yes on 14" group, but such organized support for the measure did not exist in San Francisco.[102] Shortly after the Rumford Act took effect, the St. Thomas More Society's Catholic attorneys established their own Lawyers' Committee on Interracial Justice. The San Francisco Archdiocesan Council of Catholic Men (a successor to the Catholic Men of San Francisco) called for the defeat of Proposition 14 at their convention at Riordan High School, and the Archdiocesan Council of Catholic Women, in "only the second time this group ha[d] taken a public stand on an issue," also came out against the measure. The chairman of the Theology Department at USF bluntly informed Catholics that if they voted in favor of Proposition 14, they were putting their salvation at risk.[103]

On November 3, 1964, California voters passed Proposition 14 by a two-to-one majority. In San Francisco, the measure passed, but by a much narrower margin: 150,314 "yes" votes to 134,611 "no" votes. Only two counties—Humboldt and Inyo—rejected the proposition, as did the city of Palo Alto. Governor Brown declared that he would not enforce the law until its constitutionality was verified, and California's secretary of state refused to certify the vote. The federal government threatened to hold further federal funds for slum clearance in view of the victory of Proposition 14. John Delury of the Catholic Interracial Council and the Social Justice Commission and Earl Raab of the San Francisco Human Relations Clearing House immediately set to work in support of the ultimately successful legal campaign to overturn the voter mandate in the courts. Eventually, the California State Supreme Court declared Proposition 14 unconstitutional, and the U.S. Supreme Court upheld the ruling.[104]

Assessments of the Catholic participation in the fight against Proposition 14 fight, and the Catholic role in civil rights work more generally, began even before the election in November. In an op-ed article published on January 31, 1964, Father James Gaffey criticized the church hierarchy because it had "preached, but not led" in the racial justice campaign. When *The Monitor* polled local Catholics on October 22 on the church's conduct in racial matters, 55 percent replied it was "weak"; 20 percent that it was "too strong"; and 25 percent that it was "just right." Further, 18 percent of the respondents believed that civil rights and race relations were "improper" subjects for the church. When asked to predict the outcome of the Proposition 14 vote, 51 percent expected a "no" vote, while the remaining 49 percent felt the proposition would pass. The poll showed that 61 percent of the respondents felt that race relations had improved since the beginning of the decade, and fully 89 percent believed that the highly publicized sit-ins at the Sheraton Palace Hotel in the spring of 1964 had "not helped" the cause of racial justice. Judging from this admittedly impressionistic survey and from sentiment expressed in the letters to the editor column of *The Monitor,* the sit-ins seem to have been a pivotal event in influencing positions. Before the sit-ins, letter writers often described themselves as conscience-stricken over racial justice issues; afterward, many described themselves as repelled by "lawlessness."[105]

Retrospective analyses of the Catholic role in civil rights work also noted the gap between the liberal clerical and lay racial justice activists who spoke out in favor of fair employment and fair housing laws and the conservative grass-roots parishioners who opposed them. Father George Kennard, who had preached at numerous Bay Area churches on the bishop's pastoral letter of 1958, believed that the effort to defeat Proposition 14 was lost at the parish level, because priests and pastors alike refused to speak out forthrightly for civil rights for fear of offending conservative members of their parishes. According to Kennard, churches in the Haight-Ashbury and Western Addition neighborhoods of San Francisco, which were more racially mixed than other areas, were the most active, but in the upper-middle-class Richmond District, pastors and their congregations were apathetic and perhaps even hostile to racial reform laws. In such parishes, according to Kennard, a "curtain of silence" descended, and the church's stand against racial injustice was not actively promoted.[106] Father Boyle and John Delury, leaders in both the Catholic Interracial Council and the Social Justice Commission, looked back on their efforts as an instance of doing too little, too late. Boyle praised the energy and commitment of his racial justice activist colleagues, especially the Catholic nuns who spread the gospel of equality in parish schools, but his overall assessment was negative.

The activists "had minimal influence on the Catholic population generally," he said. "[They] failed to make members understand the facts of discrimination," and church teaching on racial justice remained "relegated to library shelves."[107] Reflecting on the fact that a mere 1.4 percent of the local Catholic population were African American and that San Francisco's white Catholics consequently tended to minimize the seriousness of racism in their midst, Delury ruefully concluded that racial justice activism may have reached only a "dedicated fringe."[108]

The historian Clay O'Dell concluded his study of the Catholic Interracial Council effort with a mixed verdict that mirrors the split among the twenty-six veteran activists he surveyed. "Those advocating greater action and more controversial tactics," he wrote, "tend[ed] to see the group as less successful than those who tended towards pointing out the value in 'raising awareness.'" Mary Anne Colwell was one of the former activists in the San Francisco Catholic Interracial Council who participated in O'Dell's survey. Like Father Boyle, Colwell stressed the role of women in the racial justice movement; in her estimation they "did at least half and probably more of the organizational work" in the council. "There were plenty of people who did not support the work of the [Catholic Interracial Council] and a few hostile priests—but in [*sic*] the whole most people recognized our work as necessary. I would say most laity and clergy were passively supportive."[109]

The downbeat assessments by Kennard, Boyle, and Delury have been echoed in recent critical commentary on racial reform from the 1940s to the 1960s. According to this interpretation, a negative rather than a positive assessment must be levied, given the dispiriting chasm between high hopes and modest accomplishments. The experience of San Francisco recounted in this chapter demonstrates that the achievements of the racial reformers, though noteworthy in the context of the time, were indeed limited. This conclusion is reinforced by the story of the politics of urban development in the Western Addition neighborhood of the city, the subject of the next chapter.[110]

8

"NOT FOR . . . REAL ESTATE VALUES ALONE"

Urban Redevelopment and the Limits of Racial Reform

T he nearly 5,000 fans who turned out for the Golden Gloves boxing tournament at the Civic Auditorium in 1948 cheered, shouted, whistled, and applauded when "Singing Sam" Jordan accepted the Diamond Belt after winning the light heavyweight championship fight. Jordan acquired his nickname after he began singing "The Star-Spangled Banner" before his fights; sometimes he even gave the crowd a tune after one of his winning bouts. Like so many black men and women who helped boost the African American population from 4,846 to 43,502 in the decade of the 1940s, Sam Jordan decided to settle down in the city rather than return to his Southern home town—in his case, Diboll, Texas. He retired his U.S. Navy uniform and sported an ILWU Local 6 union button on his work shirt, like the other members of the racially integrated longshoremen's and warehousemen's union. When he hung up his gloves after winning eleven fights, losing five, and fighting two to a draw, he opened Sam Jordan's, a bar on Third Street in the Bayview–Hunters Point District in the southeastern corner of the city, where a growing black population lived in low-cost houses and apartments adjacent to San Francisco's district of slaughterhouses and auto-wrecking yards.[1]

Sam Jordan's place was some four miles from the site of the annual Golden Gloves tournament in the Civic Center, in the 7,000 seat exposition hall that Mayor James Rolph had dedicated in 1915, when it had served as one of the attractions of the Panama Pacific International Exposition. The office of Carleton Goodlett's newspaper, the *Sun-Reporter,* was located only a mile away from the auditorium, in the city's Western Addition neighborhood that, by the late 1940s, was also known as "the Fillmore" because of the eight-block retail strip along a street of that name in the heart of the district. Goodlett was a thirty-four-year-old African American physician and native of Omaha, Nebraska, who had earned a doctorate in psychology from UC Berkeley in 1937. He went on to earn his medical degree in Nashville and moved back to San Francisco in 1945, when he became the owner of the *Sun,* which he merged with Thomas Fleming's year-old *Reporter.* Goodlett practiced medicine and fought to overturn the racial caste system that kept San Francisco hospitals off-limits to non-white physicians. Fleming edited the new paper, the *Sun-Reporter.* The paper became an influential source of news and opinion in the city's burgeoning African American population in the Fillmore District, home to 2,144 of the city's 4,846 black residents in 1940; 14,888 of 43,502 in 1950; and 14,631 of 74,383 in 1960. The Western Addition was also the site of the city's traditional Japanese and Japanese American settlement, which numbered 5,087 in 1940 and 5,383 in 1950. In 1947, nearly two-thirds of the area's residents were white; some 26 percent were African American; and about 5 percent were Japanese. The district also housed growing numbers of Chinese and Filipino residents.[2]

On June 3, 1948, the Board of Supervisors convened a special public meeting to hear from residents of the Western Addition before deciding whether to designate the neighborhood a redevelopment area. The meeting took place at the Civic Auditorium, and Goodlett was among the estimated 3,000 men and women who turned out for this first public hearing on an urban redevelopment project in the State of California. The California Community Redevelopment Act of 1945 stipulated that before a local agency could begin a project, it had to seek the advice of residents of the target area. The audience that June evening was smaller than for Sam Jordan's Golden Gloves victory, but the *San Francisco Chronicle* was on to something when it noted that, when a similar meeting was held two years earlier, only 125 people had showed up. The Western Addition redevelopment hearing in June 1948 was the first round in a long fight over which principles should guide the redevelopment of neighborhoods in San Francisco, which values should take priority in developing planning principles, and who should have a voice in the decision-making process about setting the values and principles of future land use. Complicating these questions was the two-sided reality of whites' access to economic and political power and growing determination among non-white residents to acquire such access.[3]

The hearing was the beginning of the long struggle to define the city's responsibility for insuring racial justice in its redevelopment policy that would unfold as San Francisco's population became more diverse after World War II. But even before the demographic changes, several white female social reformers and their businessmen allies initiated new institutional avenues for the redevelopment of the Western Addition. They were intent on remaking the area through what they considered desirable and long-overdue improvements in the area's heavily pre-1906 earthquake residential and commercial properties; they were confident that the outcome would create long-term benefits for future residents of the district and the city as a whole, as well as opportunities for investment and income for the businesses related to real estate that were involved in the process.

This process began in 1938, but its roots extended back to 1910, when the Commonwealth Club, Catholic Settlement and Humane Society, Council of Jewish Women, Women's Public Health Association, and Telegraph Hill Neighborhood Association created a new, quasi-public agency called the San Francisco Housing Association. Like other Progressive era "citizens outside the government" enterprises in San Francisco, the group enlisted the support of business, organized labor, and academic health and welfare professionals and lobbied for model legislation and stronger enforcement of health and safety laws. And like similar organizations, the San Francisco group enjoyed only moderate success and languished from the World War I years to the early 1930s. Then, in response to their awareness of hardship on the streets of San Francisco and their desire for financing from New Deal agencies, the city's social welfare reformers revived the dormant San Francisco Housing Association. Alice Griffith, a veteran reformer since 1910, supervised three survey projects intended to provide the data necessary for the city to apply for federal aid from the newly established Public Works Administration, Civil Works Administration, and Public Emergency Housing Corporation. San Francisco did not receive a federal housing-related project in the subsequent five years, but another opportunity beckoned when Congress passed the Federal Housing Act of 1937. The State of California immediately followed up by allowing cities to create special agencies that could participate in the competition for federal funds to improve local housing, and San Francisco's Board of Supervisors created the San Francisco Housing Authority on April 18, 1938. Two months later, the Housing Authority received permission from the city and county government to get rid of "unsafe or insanitary dwelling units."[4]

Griffith moved ahead with preparatory work for housing reform by recruiting eighteen members of a social policy study group associated with an adult education center operated by Alexander Meiklejohn, a civil-libertarian activist and advocate of progressive education. His pedagogy emphasized "group process" and "taking part in the action of your community or shaping things, making things happen the way you hoped they would." Along with Elizabeth Ashe, a Progressive era colleague, and Florence Richardson Wyckoff and Dorothy Erskine, two younger activists, they conducted a housing survey of Chinatown. Then, between March 1939 and January 1941, they completed a more comprehensive land use survey intended to provide a data base for the first proposal of a city master plan by the San Francisco Planning Commission in August 1941.

This work was coordinated with the Junior Chamber of Commerce and the newly organized California Housing and Planning Association, headed by Edward Howden, who later directed the San Francisco Council for Civic Unity (CCU). Howden's presence, and the character of the advisory board that was dominated by Bay Area social welfare liberals, led to an explicit emphasis on bringing racial-minority residents into the process of land use planning. The white reformers imagined that a broad ethnic/racial coalition would work together to eliminate shack towns, slum dwellings, and blighted neighborhoods, with all in agreement that such conditions were morally offensive and objectively definable obstacles to humane living conditions.

The discussion that led up to the state's enabling legislation emphasized that "blighted districts, slums, and areas of low-value, useless property exist in almost all cities of California. They block civic progress and handicap business. Buildings are in various stages of decay. They fall down and burn up, endangering life and other property. Housing is bad and family life crowded, insanitary and disagreeable. People leave such areas for suburbs." The Housing and Planning Association agreed that "areas in the city which lose to the suburbs decay and go to seed—these are the *blighted areas* which must be replanned and rebuilt and bring the suburbs back to the city." Also, redevelopment would foster "*long-term investment, employment for the Building Trades, as well as decent housing for the middle income group.*" This perspective also informed Alexander Heron, an executive at the paper manufacturer Crown-Zellerbach, who had played a lead role in creating the pro-growth Bay Area Council and now chaired the working group that drafted the California Community Redevelopment Act. The legislation was premised on the principle that housing and land use reform was compatible with the business priorities of the real estate and home building industries.[5]

The Community Redevelopment Act of 1945 established the procedures that cities used to designate redevelopment sites and transfer powers of eminent domain to new local redevelopment agencies. The subsequent availability of funds from the federal government set the framework for the city's programs. The framework included attention to the rehousing of residents displaced by redevelopment and cooperation between public agencies and the private sector in the process. As outlined by the Community Redevelopment Act, approval of a redevelopment plan was to be contingent on the availability of comparable housing for those displaced. This issue became a highly contentious one, because the actual method of determining "availability" was not clearly defined. Another area of contention derived from disagreement about the division of responsibility. The public sector's involvement extended to planning, site acquisition, and site preparation, such as clearing old buildings and putting in new streets and sewers. Private developers were then expected to purchase most of the redeveloped land and carry out the actual building (in compliance with the approved redevelopment plans).[6]

The call for urban redevelopment occurred against the backdrop of significant changes in San Francisco as large numbers of African Americans moved into the Fillmore District during and after the war. Fleming exaggerated when he characterized the neighborhood as "a ghetto for minority groups" in a *Sun-Reporter* editorial, but he echoed an increasingly popular stereotype that the Fillmore was a "ghetto" and a "colored district." The black population in the district had increased significantly, from 2,144 to 14,888, but at the time of the redevelopment hearing, the district was still almost two-thirds white. The area had indeed visibly changed as more black business establishments sprouted up along the retail strip on Fillmore Street and several thousand Issei and Nisei residents returned from wartime camps. But the restaurants, retail stores, and bars all attracted a diverse, ethnically and racially mixed clientele, especially on Friday evenings, when the sidewalks overflowed with the predominantly white but decidedly diverse blue-collar residents of the district who cashed their paychecks, bought groceries at several discount outlets for canned goods, and took in the latest movie at the New Fillmore Theater.[7]

The changing character of the Fillmore District—specifically, its *physical* character—was in the forefront of Mel Scott's thinking as he prepared the "Western Addition District Redevelopment Study" for San Francisco's recently established City Planning Commission. Scott's primary focus was on the built environment of the neighborhood, which he compared unfavorably with the open spaces and wooded hills of the Bay Area. His report contained very little about the social and cultural character of the Fillmore and nothing about how the varied residents of the Western Addition experienced their daily lives and how they might wish to live in the future. Scott had earned a bachelor's degree in English literature from the University of California, Los Angeles. He became fascinated with landscape design as a graduate student at UC Berkeley, where he served as a lecturer for twenty years, beginning in 1949, while also playing a leading role in the local conservation movement. Scott's report laid down the parameters that guided the recommendations presented at the public hearing in June 1948, as well as subsequent redevelopment activity in the Western Addition. His report contained a definition of the public interest that was both influential and limited in its capacity to advance the racial reform agenda associated with redevelopment that some of the participants in the process—particularly Edward Howden, Carlton Goodlett, and Thomas Fleming—would come to regard as primary. "Most important of all," Scott wrote, "this report seeks to interest private enterprise in investing in the rebuilding of San Francisco's older areas. . . . [N]ever before has private enterprise had such magnificent opportunities to serve the people while assuring itself reasonable return on long-term investments."[8]

When Scott addressed social issues, it was to promote redevelopment as a solution to poverty, crime, juvenile delinquency, and poor health and safety conditions; this was a "social control" agenda that had been a key feature of many Progressive era and New Deal reforms. His more central theme was the importance of identifying and removing evidence of the "confusion" inherent in an intermixing of various types of buildings that was a mark of "irrational" land use. "An unmistakable indication of the character of the district is the large number of second-hand stores and junk shops that it contains," he wrote. "Their dusty confusion symbolizes the area. Amid the cast-off paraphernalia from thousands of households, one finds an occasional 'antique,' some bit of craftsmanship that will give pleasure for a long time, but all the rest speaks of a disenchanted yesterday and is as outmoded as the hand-me-down dwellings in the surrounding blocks. It is time to begin sorting out the good buildings among all the old and battered structures . . . and to place them in a new setting, orderly and protected by desirable standards from every becoming overcrowded, squalid, and dispiriting."[9]

Scott echoed the Chamber of Commerce's vision of San Francisco in 1939, which now also informed the Bay Area Council's regional strategy, centered on the city's becoming "to the Bay Region what the Island of Manhattan is to the New York Region." The key sectors would be "shipping, retail trade, finance, entertainment of tourists and visitors, specialized services, food processing, manufacture of small, high quality goods with high market value." The result would be "increasingly a city of professional and semi-professional workers, managers and officials, clerical workers, craftsmen, and service workers." In an extensive catalogue of recommendations, Scott addressed four additional points. First, while redevelopment should be primarily residential, he urged the city "to study the possibilities of redeveloping blighted areas that would be suitable for industry." Second, he argued for the creation of a "city-wide housing program embracing both public and private housing." Third, he noted the importance of building new public housing units for those who would be displaced by redevelopment, given the lack of replacement housing. In a fourth but related point, he argued that the city's Housing Authority had an obligation to rehouse "colored and foreign-born families," because "only a relatively small proportion of them may be expected to be in a position to occupy quarters in the new development." Implicit in his recommendations was an admission that redevelopment planners declined to accept responsibility for insuring that those displaced would be rehoused in their former neighborhood.[10]

Scott's report did not address the potential negative response that would be articulated by residents of the Western Addition who would find themselves ejected from their neighborhood when the city demolished their housing. Instead, he drew on a Progressive era discourse that stressed how redevelopment in the Western Addition would promote long-term benefits for the city as a whole: "[The] Courts have agreed that the eradication of blight is a public purpose and that all society gains when deteriorated areas are replanned and rebuilt." Scott's emphasis on private sector leadership in redevelopment and the importance of focusing on a concept of the public interest embedded in an elite reform discourse complemented the belief of the Chamber of Commerce and the AFL's county labor council that what was good for their members was good for the public at large. They were convinced that the state's Community Redevelopment Act contained sufficient protection for those low-income and racial/ethnic-minority residents who would be displaced by demolition of their neighborhoods.[11]

In contrast to the AFL council, with its fifty-three building trades unions, which was satisfied with the safeguards written into the state redevelopment law, the county council of the CIO announced it would provide only "reserved support" for Western Addition redevelopment, even before the Planning Commission made the Scott report public. The CIO called for greater public attention to the city's overcrowded housing, the need for rent control, and the pervasive racial discrimination in the city. In 1945, its housing committee warned that "the end of the war does not mean the end of the housing crisis" and urged prompt and vigorous action" to counter "a wild, speculative housing boom." In March 1946, the organization upgraded its ad hoc three-person housing committee into a seven-member standing Committee on Housing and Planning, and Paul Schnur, the secretary-treasurer, refused to support the "Slum Clearance Revolving Fund" that the city's Housing Authority had requested from the Board of Supervisors. Schnur assured the board that his organization agreed with the general idea of redevelopment, but "[any] slum clearance proposal must go hand in hand with a housing program. If the housing needs of residents displaced by redevelopment were not taken into account in the design of the project, then shortages caused by the war would intensify and worsen the conditions in other existing slum areas."[12]

The CIO had first insisted that housing for those displaced by redevelopment be made a top priority when discussions took place in connection with the state legislature's passage of the Community Redevelopment Act in the last months of the war. The Chamber of Commerce and the Bay Area Council envisioned redevelopment as an integral part of a long-term regional economic development strategy; the AFL looked forward to the opportunities for employment involved; the CIO agreed these were positive benefits but also demanded guarantees related to social and racial justice. In January 1945, they announced a three-part set of "necessary safeguards" and "positive guarantees" that needed to be written into the state's redevelopment legislation: "persons displaced as a result of condemnation proceedings are furnished adequate, sanitary, suitable housing at rentals which they can afford to pay"; "projects [must] meet the needs of the citizens of the community in which the projects are constructed and . . . no speculative profits can be gained by realtors and builders"; and "there will be no discrimination because of race, creed, or color in any of the projects constructed as a result of the legislation or in connection with the displacement and rehousing of people arising from the condemnation proceedings."[13]

The San Francisco Communist Party took a parallel stance on Western Addition redevelopment. In its platform for the municipal elections in 1945, the party endorsed an "urban redevelopment program to clear the slums and provide low cost housing for all who [were] in need of it." In addition, the party's platform called for a ban on restrictive racial covenants or any other form of discrimination or segregation in the designated area and adequate replacement housing for those displaced (within their original neighborhoods), and it recommended that residential redevelopment should take precedence over all other land use improvement projects. The Communist Party and CIO stance on redevelopment matched the views of Reverend Frederick Douglass Haynes, pastor of the Third Baptist Church in the Western Addition. Goodlett convinced Haynes to be the first African American to run for a seat on the city's Board of Supervisors in the 1945 election. Haynes had built his church up from a congregation of 150 in the early 1930s to more than 3,000 by 1947, and he was a leading member of the city's African American social elite. The Ministerial Alliance of San Francisco, the Fillmore Democratic Club, the CIO, the AFL's Union Labor Party, and the Communist Party all endorsed his candidacy, and an enthusiastic multiethnic cadre of election workers from the Fillmore and CIO member unions mobilized voters.[14]

Haynes lost his bid for office in 1945, as well as a second attempt in 1947, but he effectively communicated his views on redevelopment to a citywide audience by using both the print media and the radio station KYA. He endorsed redevelopment provided it served the interests of the Fillmore District's population. The primary purpose of redevelopment, he insisted, should be to expand the supply of affordable housing. "I will push through a low rent housing program to alleviate the shameful conditions now existing in our city," he said. "I propose to see low-income dwellings erected with the aid of city and federal funds, to assure these people of homes. My program includes immediate use of the Redevelopment authority to build homes in our blighted areas." The vision of how the future redevelopment of the Western Addition could best serve the public interest that was articulated by Haynes, like those put forward by the CIO and the Communist Party, contrasted with the vision of the Planning Commission and its allies in the social reform, business, and AFL union communities. Haynes, the CIO, and the Communist Party endorsed Fillmore redevelopment, but they insisted that it should be formulated primarily to meet the housing needs of low-income San Franciscans and a high priority should be placed on the promotion of the rights of non-white residents who might be adversely affected.[15]

Forty years after Haynes lost his run for the Board of Supervisors in 1947, two of his supporters at the time—Fleming and Daniel Collins, founder of the San Francisco branch of the National Urban League—looked back on the late 1940s as a time of lost opportunity, when the African American residents of the Western Addition failed to rouse themselves sufficiently to influence the redevelopment of the district along the lines that Haynes had supported. As they recalled it, very little community opposition was evident prior to the actual tearing down of buildings in the 1950s, but the large turnout for the public hearing on June 3, 1948, demonstrated that a change was under way. The two campaigns by Reverend Haynes had stimulated a flurry of political organizing in the Fillmore that was marked by an uptick in the work of the NAACP, the formation of the Fillmore Political Club and the Urban League branch, and the voter registration and voter turnout efforts of the CIO's Political Action Committee (CIO-PAC). Residents of the Fillmore District and owners of property in the Western Addition made up the vast majority of the audience at the Civic Auditorium, and the reporter who covered the event for the *San Francisco Chronicle* noted that the audience "frequently burst into applause for points made by the opponents. Little handclapping was given advocates of the measure." The speakers who challenged the Planning Commission's plans for the Fillmore indicated that the debate over how to define the connection between redevelopment and the public interest was moving in a more contentious direction.[16]

State Senator Gerald O'Gara, who chaired the Interim Committee on Redevelopment of the State Senate, had also been one of the leading figures in the passage of the Community Redevelopment Act. O'Gara explained in blunt language why he regarded the Western Addition as an ideal location for California's first redevelopment district. This is where the "worst blighted condition exists in the City," he said, with "the most [*sic*] number of people crowded together in a square mile, the oldest houses, the most unsanitary conditions, the place where crime and juvenile delinquency and domestic difficulties, and all the other things that grow out of blight and slum exist in the worst degree." O'Gara acknowledged that there were "very grave problems connected with community redevelopment" (including "the minorities") and agreed that such issues "must be fully explored, and, if necessary, fought over." But, he stated, "They are not insurmountable problems." He urged the audience to realize that Western Addition redevelopment not only was "a matter of good business for San Francisco; it [was] a good buy, a good investment." Finally—and O'Gara earned applause for this conclusion—"We feel that this is one way to fight such things as Communism; to preserve this American way of life; and we ask you to adopt the resolution tonight."[17]

In addition to the Chamber of Commerce and Building Trades Council, the American Legion, the Veterans of Foreign Wars, and the League of Women Voters sent representatives to the hearings to urge the supervisors to declare the Western Addition a redevelopment site. The District Attorney's Office, which had recently completed a survey of buildings that violated health and safety codes, strongly endorsed slum clearance as a deterrent to crime. It argued that clearing and redeveloping the Fillmore would reduce crime, which, it asserted, was higher in the Fillmore District than the size of its area and population warranted and was caused by the outdoor toilets, broken plumbing, deteriorating stairways, and overcrowding that its study had identified. Edward Howden of the CCU also spoke in favor of redevelopment, but he called for more safeguards against possible racial discrimination than were already built into state legislation and the city's plans. "Large-scale, well-planned development is necessary and desirable," he said, and the CCU approved of the city's plans "*provided* reasonable and adequate safeguards of minority rights and interests are contemplated." Howden did not go on record demanding that such safeguards be incorporated into the city ordinance designating the redevelopment area. Instead, he called on the supervisors to enact them in the near future: nondiscrimination in the redevelopment district; rehousing for those displaced; low-rent public housing in the redevelopment area; priority in re-entry to the redevelopment area for those who were displaced; support of minority business; and minority representation in the proposed San Francisco Redevelopment Agency. Howden took issue with the notion that benefits would accrue to low-income and non-white residents of the district by virtue of the mere operation of the redevelopment process and insisted on supplementary provisions that would safeguard their interests.[18]

The representatives of the Veterans of Foreign Wars and the American Veterans Committee also recommended the designation proposal, but they joined Howden in urging stronger provisions. Daniel F. Del Carlo, spokesman for the building trades unions, assured the supervisors that "we are for this plan," because he was convinced that safeguards against "displacing of people" and protections for "minority groups [and] low income groups" were already "in the law." None of the thirteen who testified along with Del Carlo in favor of approving the redevelopment designation lived in the area; none were African American or Japanese American, the two largest non-white population groups in the Western Addition. Twelve testified against the Board of Supervisors' proposal to designate the area a redevelopment site before the hearing ended at 11:20 P.M.; half lived and worked in the neighborhood, three were African

American, and one was Japanese American. Ulma Abels, a white resident of the neighborhood who had been educated at USF, represented the Business and Professional Alliance of San Francisco. He owned a small business in the Fillmore and confessed to being skeptical that the "safeguards" under discussion for the protection of displaced residents and owners of businesses and the rights of non-white residents would be enacted by the Board of Supervisors. He lectured the supervisors on ethics, recalling, "I was always taught that in order for the end to be good, the means to the end had to be good. I was wondering, 'would the means be good, considering the circumstances in the Western Addition?'" Abels also questioned the ethics of having "private enterprise stepping in and redeveloping this area" and urged instead a different, mixed process. "I think if the government is going to subsidize private enterprise [by clearing the land and preparing it for rebuilding]," he argued, it "should also subsidize the parties to be displaced."[19]

Goodlett, representing the NAACP, began his testimony by assuring the supervisors, "We agree that the Western Addition is a blighted area that should be rebuilt." But, he continued, the NAACP did not approve of the current proposal because "urban redevelopment, as envisioned in this law [the state's Community Redevelopment Act of 1945] is not adequate. We feel that it is undemocratic [because] it places the burden upon the minority people . . . to see that their rights are protected." To those who argued, "Let's go into this thing and revise it after we take this step [to approve redevelopment]," Goodlett replied, "Experience has taught minority people that if we don't start out right we might not end up right." The NAACP believed that the city "has a moral obligation to recognize the fact that you cannot take 86,000 people out of one neighborhood and put them in another neighborhood. We will stand in the way of the implementation of it until we are convinced that it is a democratic act. We are interested in a first-class citizenship, first class living conditions for all Americans, irrespective of race, color and creed."[20]

Goodlett's forthright demand that the decision to redevelop the Fillmore would have to be based on an affirmative response by the residents of the neighborhood had been supported by the CCU and the CIO after the passage of the state's enabling law, months before the hearing in June 1948. The CCU now approved the designation plan, hoping to successfully revise it after passage. The CIO expanded its critique of the law and would not support the designation, even suggesting that a conspiracy might be at work, because "the real moving forces behind this ordinance are only interested in using this law for the purpose of making huge profits, with the taxpayers' help, [and] unless the Board of Supervisors rejects this ordinance and adopts one which will prevent misuse of this law, the crime of segregation and the disease of blight will further spread over our city."[21]

Another recent migrant to the Fillmore District, Cecil F. Poole, offered another point of view at the hearing. Poole, an African American attorney with offices at 1805 Fillmore Street, stated his "qualified opposition" to designating the Western Addition a redevelopment area. He disagreed with those opponents who accused the state's legislature and the Board of Supervisors of bad faith and conspiratorial intent. He also praised the board's skill in bringing the various constituencies to the table to the point at which "you have your representatives from the Apartment Owners' Association teamed up with the members of the Communist Party" urging the supervisors to vote down the city ordinance that would set the project in motion. Poole was a thirty-three-year-old native of Birmingham, Alabama, who had grown up in Pittsburgh; attended high school in Washington, D.C.; received his bachelor's and law degrees from the University of Michigan and a master of law degree from Harvard University; and then served during the war as a military lawyer for the Tuskegee Airmen who flew in the 332nd Fighter Group of the U.S. Army Air Force. Poole and his wife had lived in the Fillmore District for three years, and they had recently started a family; he told the supervisors that he and many of his colleagues and neighbors would "heartily endorse this proposal [if] urban redevelopment was going to proceed along generally fair lines, insofar as the treatment of all the people affected by urban redevelopment is concerned." But he had concluded that "very little serious effort [was] going to be made to see that implementation proceed[ed] along the lines that [would] really have teeth." He finished his testimony by insisting that the public interest could be effectively served only when both the process and the product of redevelopment included "the people of San Francisco without regard to race, color or creed. . . . They will have an opportunity to apply for housing based upon their need, based upon their previous occupancy of these areas, and based upon the fact, first and foremost, that they are not Japanese or Negroes, or even poor whites, but American citizens in the City of San Francisco."[22]

Poole's skepticism turned out to be justified when, seven weeks later, the Board of Supervisors approved the redevelopment designation ordinance by a vote of ten to one at the regular Friday meeting on July 19. The board's passage of the measure without the amendments demanded prior to designation at the public hearing played into the hand of those Western Addition residents who distrusted the political process and had accused public officials and private sector speculators of a conspiracy "to get Blacks away from the area." This charge of hypocrisy and perfidy on the part of white public officials who headed redevelopment haunted the politics of redevelopment for years to come.[23]

In the immediate aftermath of the board's actions, critics demanded the delay of the project until the city revised the legislation to protect the interests of neighborhood residents. The Ministerial Alliance, composed of African American ministers in the Fillmore District, argued that redevelopment was necessary but urged that the "project be defeated in its entirety with its *present* provision" because, as Reverend William Turner pointed out, "*This* proposal for redevelopment disregards in too great a degree, the rights and welfare of the present inhabitants of this area as over against the alleged benefits which would accrue to the city as a whole." Yukio Wada, president of the San Francisco chapter of the Japanese American Citizens League (JACL), also endorsed redevelopment while urging opposition to this particular plan, his organization having decided at "an open general meeting . . . that a protest must be made now since later may be too late and ineffective." The consensus of the JACL meeting was that "the purpose [of redevelopment] is good in that it can be used to replace the slum dwellings of the Western Addition with new buildings." The group expressed dismay that the Board of Supervisors had failed to modify the city's proposal by building into its language and specifications the explicit criteria for safeguarding the public interest of residents that the residents themselves had suggested over many months since the passage of the Community Redevelopment Act. The JACL expressed itself as "regretful" but determined "to make clear its stand."[24]

The city moved ahead with the redevelopment despite these and other appeals to the supervisors after the public hearing. The San Francisco Redevelopment Agency began operations on August 10, 1948. Howden of the CCU, in a temporary coalition with a variety of other civil rights and neighborhood organizations, lobbied the supervisors to pass a city law banning discrimination in future redevelopment areas. Their proposed municipal law echoed the language of the CIO's housing and redevelopment platform of 1945–1946: "prohibits and provides safeguards against discrimination or segregation by color, creed or ancestry in the sale or use of land to be acquired in San Francisco's blighted areas for redevelopment pursuant to the Community Redevelopment Act of 1945." Howden reiterated one of Cecil Poole's arguments that the best intentions of city government and private developers would not automatically end racism in San Francisco; legislation would be necessary. He was also determined to undermine those free-enterprise ideological critics of the liberal, mixed-public-and-private nature of redevelopment who were cynically using the rhetoric of antiracism to discredit the liberal Community Redevelopment Act altogether. And, in a savvy and prescient observation, he argued that the success of Western Addition redevelopment hinged on passage of the toughest possible law against racial discrimination: "Unless this or a similar ordinance is enacted, it may be predicted safely that the Work of the Redevelopment agency and the approval of the projects during years ahead will be delayed, harassed, and possibly even thwarted by persons and organizations striving to protect the rights of minority groups. This prospect would probably discourage private investment in such projects, and endanger the entire program."[25]

The testimony at the public hearing received extensive coverage in the city's press, and one influential San Franciscan reconsidered his position. State Senator Gerald O'Gara had previously urged that redevelopment should begin without any additional legislation or amendments; if and when instances of racial discrimination occurred, they could be dealt with individually. But the public hearing and Howden's arguments had convinced him to change his mind, and on November 24, he insisted that "the proper time is now. . . . I believe there is no solution but a clear-cut and immediate statement of policy which will insure minority groups of their constitutional rights."[26]

The newly created Redevelopment Agency countered the CCU's measure with a proposal for a non-binding resolution expressing its commitment to racial equity. The agency argued that a binding ordinance might chase away private investors, particularly the builders of new rental housing, thereby causing "builders to continue to seek land which is now available only outside the City's boundaries." The Chamber of Commerce, Junior Chamber of Commerce, and San Francisco Planning and Housing Association backed up the Redevelopment Agency, as did the *San Francisco Chronicle,* which editorialized, "The private builder who could be prevailed upon to invest his money, though hedged about with an ordinance which could send him or his tenant to prison if a jury thought them discriminatory, does not exist. Under such an ordinance, there would be no redevelopment."[27]

Howden and the supporters of the ordinance insisted that the public interest would be served best when the self-defined needs of all of the residents of the Fillmore District, as articulated by the leaders of the interest groups representing them, were protected by law. The African American civil rights organizations, the JACL, and the Chinese American Citizens Alliance—plus Ernest Besig, director of the American Civil Liberties Union, and Lee Dai-ming, editor of *Chinese World*—all lobbied the Board of Supervisors in favor of the ordinance. This "interest group liberalism" process brought civil liberties defense groups into a coalition with ethnic/racial organizations, as well as both San Francisco county labor councils, on behalf of a municipal ordinance. When the Board of Supervisors convened a public meeting on the question, a "jam packed" audience made up mainly of "minority Western Addition residents" expressed its emotions by "boisterously" shouting down those who attempted to speak in favor of the Redevelopment Agency's position. The city attorney, however, ruled that a nondiscriminatory ordinance was unconstitutional, and the Board of Supervisors passed the weaker non-binding measure, Resolution 8660, on May 16, 1949. The resolution called for the inclusion of "covenants against discrimination or segregation" in all Redevelopment Agency leases and contracts. In November, the Board of Supervisors passed a similar resolution banning racial discrimination and segregation in the city's public housing projects.[28]

The Redevelopment Agency devoted six years to preparing a detailed plan for the first phase (A-1) of its Western Addition redevelopment, and the Board of Supervisors approved the plan on May 28, 1956. Eight years after work began on A-1, plans for the second phase (A-2) received the board's approval, on October 15, 1964. The agency began work on it in May 1966. The plan for A-1 covered 108 acres, and it affected 4,190 dwelling units. The plan called for relocating 2,555 households and 350 businesses to make way for new market-rate high-rise and low-rise rentals, cooperatives, and senior citizen units. Nonresidential structures included three medical buildings, two office buildings, a hospital, a convalescent home, a Japanese cultural and trade center, and a cathedral. Residential acreage decreased to 29 acres from 43 acres, and population decreased to 3,724 from 6,112. The second phase, A-2, covered 277 acres and affected more than 14,700 people, with a plan for increasing the population of the area to more than 19,000 residents; 4,100 market-price and privately subsidized housing units were planned, along with 420 public housing units. A-2 also included nonresidential redevelopment: an extension of the Japanese center in A-1 (including four office buildings and commercial space), a seven-square-block Fillmore Center (with some residential units), a four-story office building for the headquarters of the ILWU, and a three-story building for the San Francisco City Employees Credit Union.[29]

In 1963, the Redevelopment Agency concluded that "the great majority of the affected families, individuals, businesses and institutions clearly and unmistakably improved their status. Despite the many problems encountered and notwithstanding the absence of new legal and fiscal devices to facilitate the creation of new housing until the Housing Act of 1961, the Agency's goal of satisfactory housing for all displaced residents, though not completely realized, was approached. Two out of three of the residents moved into standard housing and three out of four bettered their condition." But the agency's tally in 1976 of how the two projects affected what it called "affordable units" of residential housing was frankly downbeat: 3,320 replacement units were constructed in A-2 to replace the 3,216 that were destroyed, but in A-1, 3,208 units were destroyed that were not replaced, and the agency destroyed 4,599 affordable housing units that were not replaced in its three other redevelopment districts.[30]

After the supervisors approved the designation of the Western Addition as a redevelopment area, and as the Redevelopment Agency moved into the planning, demolition, land clearance, and rebuilding stages, interest groups representing African American and Japanese American residents of the district continued to argue for the inclusion of their own definitions of the public interest in the process to shape the district's final land use. Their work was influenced by local, as well national and even international, developments related to the civil rights movement and the Cold War. The red scare played a role in weakening Goodlett's legitimacy as a community spokesman on redevelopment. At the public hearing on June 3, 1948, Goodlett coalesced with the political left; along with the Communist Party and the CIO council, he explicitly favored redevelopment of the Fillmore but not the designation plan that the supervisors would approve on July 19. Then, on August 3, the national press shocked the public with Whitaker Chambers's accusation that Alger Hiss, a high-ranking official in the U.S. State Department, was a member of the Communist Party. On August 25, Hiss and Chambers both testified at the first hearing of the House Committee on Un-American Activities ever to be televised. This dramatic intensification of the red scare gave Goodlett's critics a rationale for resuming their efforts to remove him from the presidency of the San Francisco branch of the NAACP. This followed earlier criticism, dating back to 1946, when the NAACP had cooperated with the John Brown Club of the Communist Party to picket a local movie theater until it hired African Americans. The boycott proved successful, but anticommunists in the regional and national offices of the NAACP complained about the negative publicity that could come from any cooperation with the Communist Party. Other flare-ups occurred over selling the Communist Party newspaper at branch meetings and endorsing Archie Brown, the Communist Party's candidate for governor of California, in the election of 1946. One board member complained about the "sizable portion of the active membership" that he believed was using the organization "for purposes of the Communist Party," and the presence of communists was blamed for the decline in NAACP branch membership from a high of 2,981 to 387 in 1950. When he became the executive director of the NAACP's West Coast regional office in October 1950, Franklin H. Williams moved the San Francisco branch away from what he considered the left-wing extremism of "Goodlett and his gang." The attorneys Cecil Poole and Raymond J. Reynolds and the banker Jefferson Beaver guided the organization in a centrist fashion into the 1950s, and there was little debate when members voted to ban Communist Party members from the branch in 1956.[31]

Opposition to the Communist Party was only one expression of the depth and breadth of both centrist and conservative political viewpoints as the African American community of the city's Western Addition grew in size and influence during the 1950s. In 1958, this point of view was evident when William McKinley Thomas clashed with D. Donald Glover. Thomas, sometimes nicknamed "Mr. Republican," had made himself influential in the city's African American community and in the national Republican Party. He was a delegate to numerous Republican National Conventions, and in 1936 he had given the seconding speech for Alfred Landon's nomination. He was the first African American to occupy a city office in San Francisco when Mayor Roger D.

Lapham appointed him to the board of the San Francisco Housing Authority in 1946. In March 1958, Thomas blocked the nomination of D. Donald Glover, industrial secretary of the San Francisco Urban League, for the position as director of the West Coast office of the President's Committee on Government Contracts. Thomas admitted that Glover was "eminently qualified" for the post, but he refused to support a Democrat and suggested that Glover change his party affiliation and register as a Republican. Thomas's influence with Republican Senator William Knowland led to Glover's being denied the position, to the accompaniment of a flurry of letter writing and name calling among black community leaders. Three years later, the appointment of another Republican, James Stratten, director of the Booker T. Washington Community Center, to the San Francisco Board of Education again highlighted the strength of the center-right point of view among the leaders of black interest groups in the Western Addition. Stratten had supporters, but the *Sun-Reporter* called him "a Negro by birth" who "in ninety percent of his behavior" went out of his way to "appease white folks." Terry Francois, president of the NAACP, attacked Stratten as "a tool and a pawn" of whites who had "demonstrated his lack of qualifications, concerns, or appreciation for the problems of the community."[32]

The national red scare and the local shift of the NAACP toward a more centrist orientation were evident in the editorial posture of the *Sun-Reporter,* which moved from criticism to a wait-and-see point of view regarding Western Addition redevelopment from the early to the late 1950s. In an editorial published in April 1951, Fleming drew on the Communist Party's, CIO's, and NAACP's position of 1948 when he reminded readers that "the City has a plan for housing redevelopment that will presumably eradicate some of the slum areas. Negroes are gravely concerned over these plans. The way that it is presently drawn it appears that its aim is to depopulate the city of Negroes." But Fleming's hints of conspiracy were later replaced with headlines announcing the Redevelopment Agency's promises of "NO BIAS IN REDEVELOPMENT OF WESTERN ADDITION" and a series of articles titled "Urban Redevelopment— What It Means To You" that provided details of the A-1 plan, assurances from city officials, and suggestions for finding temporary shelter. Readers received similar advice on how to accommodate themselves to A-1 in both news articles chronicling the progress of the project and editorials with titles such as "Decent Housing Assured." In October 1952, the CCU reiterated its endorsement of the A-1 project at a public hearing attended by some 300 "quiet and attentive" Fillmore residents, assuring residents that it believed "the rights and opportunities of all families irrespective of color, creed, and ancestry" would be safeguarded.[33]

At the same time, Fleming and like-minded activists—who continued to promote redevelopment, provided it followed a recipe of their own making—

sought to interest community-based institutions in participating in the city's plans. Yet few African American individuals and institutions commanded the capital necessary for such participation. Revels Cayton, a Communist Party member active in the San Francisco ILWU, later characterized this lack of capital as "a spike to the heart" for African American leaders like him who realized that they were witnessing a missed opportunity. Goodlett expressed exactly that regret at the time: "As [A-1] has unfolded itself, the economics of the situation have developed so that if we aren't careful there are going to be few or no members of the Negro group participating in this project. . . . I think it is not an understatement for me to say that the established organizations in our community have been rather disappointed and rather dismayed on our inability among ourselves to raise enough capital to participate in this project."[34]

A similar lack of capital undercut attempts to interest the Redevelopment Agency in a homegrown Japanese American plan to redevelop part of A-1 in the heart of historic "Japantown." This effort began in 1953 when the Nisei attorney Victor S. Abe, who was active in the JACL and the Japanese Chamber of Commerce of Northern California, brought together several merchants who sought the agency's approval for a "Japanese Garden Center" that would attract local residents and tourists. The Redevelopment Agency was lukewarm to the idea, but it provided enough encouragement that the group worked for several years and produced a working plan. By late 1959, however, both Mayor George Christopher and his new redevelopment director, M. Justin Herman, motivated by potential material and symbolic benefits, had decided that this part of A-1 redevelopment should center on a trans-Pacific and Japan-focused, rather than a Western Addition and Japanese American-focused, concept. Abe, his cash-poor Japanese American colleagues, and their more modest, community-oriented project were rejected in favor of the wealthy Hawaii-based banker Masayuki Tokioka, who would go on to create the Japanese Trade Center in A-1. Then, when planning for A-2 began, local Japanese American investors in the ad hoc United Committee for the Japanese Community created the Nihonmachi Community Development Corporation. This second local group would work with the San Francisco Redevelopment Agency during the late 1960s and the 1970s and construct a substantial complex of residential, commercial, and cultural buildings on four blocks east of the A-1 project. The area's redevelopment took place in a relatively contention-free process that contrasts dramatically with the story of most of the A-2 area.[35]

By September 1960, when Masayuki Tokioka flew to Japan and signed leases to bring firms associated with Tokyo Kaikain, Kinki Nippon Railway Company, and Meitetsu Enterprises to the Western Addition, Redevelopment Agency bulldozers had razed entire blocks in the Western Addition. The scale of the destruction and the social dislocation experienced by the displaced residents came at the same time that the civil rights movement in the U.S. South shifted into a more militant phase. One month after students from North Carolina Agricultural and Technical State University began their sit-in in Greensboro in February 1960, white students at San Francisco State College, black and white ILWU unionists, and NAACP members marched in a picket line on Market Street in downtown San Francisco protesting Woolworth's and Kress's segregated stores in the South. In May 1963, 30,000 San Franciscans paraded under a banner that read, "We March in Unity for Freedom in Birmingham and Equality of Opportunity in San Francisco." The author James Baldwin, who had expressed his shock at the devastation in the Western Addition during a tour of the area, addressed the crowd. "We are not trying to achieve anymore 'token integration,'" he said, "and we are not, please God, trying to teach the South how to discriminate northern style. We are attempting to end the racial nightmare, and this means immediately confronting and changing the racial situation in San Francisco."[36]

Six months earlier, a demand for "freedom now" had led Carlton Goodlett and Wilfred Ussery, head of the San Francisco branch of the Congress on Racial Equality (CORE), to form a new organization called the Citizens Protest Committee (CPC) to persuade the state Democratic Party and local Democrats to support a stronger civil rights platform. In January 1963, CPC members picketed the inauguration of Governor Pat Brown, who had been elected to a second term the previous November. The CPC was incensed because Brown had failed to appoint an African American to any of the three openings on the San Francisco Municipal Court; in an open letter to his son, Goodlett explained the larger issues involved: "We are picketing the Governor as a symbol of our real, serious irritation not only over his failure to give us a judgeship, but also over his refusal to appoint capable Negro men and women in other areas of the state government. . . . During the past 15 years we Negroes have been begging and pleading and praying for recognition. At long last, we are convinced that something dramatic must be done to shake up the Democratic Party."[37]

Governor Brown eventually responded to these complaints by appointing Joseph Kennedy to a position on the Municipal Court. Kennedy was a respected African American public defender, but he had critics in the Youth Council of the local NAACP who were unhappy with his appointment. Influenced by an emotional speech by the up-and-coming Willie Brown, a native of Texas who had moved to San Francisco in 1955, they demanded that Kennedy resign from the NAACP and voted to picket his swearing-in ceremony. Officers of the national and regional NAACP demanded that the San Franciscans back down, and the next day, Willie Brown had second thoughts and apologized. No picket line or resignation took place, but the incident demonstrated both the rising temperature of the local civil rights movement and an emerging new cadre of young claimants for leadership in the city's racial reform politics.[38]

Indeed, Ussery believed that "the country [was] on the verge of blowing up over the issue of second class citizenship." In June, he accused Mayor Christopher of being paternalistic and condescending for having issued a call for a biracial commission to study the city's racial problems. "The white community," Ussery responded, "will not be permitted to name our leaders and spokesmen by appointing them to some well-intentioned bi-racial committee which does not have the power to carry out its own decisions." In July, he pulled together an ad hoc committee of African American organizations to "negotiate" with the city's "white power structure." Members of the committee, which included the Student Nonviolent Coordinating Committee (SNCC), stressed that tempers were heating up and that it was up to whites to negotiate in a "realistic and sincere fashion" to redirect African Americans' energy. In addition to the local branches of CORE and the NAACP, the ad hoc committee included the Negro-American Labor Council, the San Francisco State College Negro Students Council, and the Bayview–Hunters Point Citizens Committee. On July 29, the ad hoc committee created the United San Francisco Freedom Movement (USFFM), which immediately demanded "an eyeball to eyeball confrontation with the white power structure of the city." Among the list of demands, including more appointments of African Americans to the police and fire departments, apprenticeship and training programs for black youth, district election of city supervisors, and Afrocentric textbooks in public schools, was one that had particular resonance in the Western Addition: expanding affordable housing and ending racial discrimination in housing.[39]

Well before the formation of the USFFM in July 1963, the NAACP's housing committee had documented both the inability of a majority of black residents to move back to the Western Addition after being forced to move out and the Redevelopment Agency's practice of rehousing the displaced in already congested parts of the city, such as Bayview–Hunters Point. In the spring of 1959, Francois, acting on behalf of the NAACP, filed a discrimination suit against the San Francisco Redevelopment Agency, charging that it was going along with landlords in predominantly white areas of the city, whose refusal to advertise openings for displaced Fillmore residents "only furthers the concentrations of African-Americans living in segregated ghetto conditions." Several months later, Francois called a press conference where he announced that the San Francisco Redevelopment Agency's "bad record" of displacement followed by re-segregation was "so grave that we are asking our national office to send a national housing expert to give us advice" that might lead to further lawsuits or direct action in the form of public demonstrations. Francois's efforts coincided with Ussery's argument that Western Addition redevelopment should be seen as an important front in the civil rights movement more generally. African American and other non-whites in the Western Addition and their white allies, according to this argument, should seize on redevelopment as a two-sided opportunity: an opportunity to stop the San Francisco Redevelopment Agency from implementing its A-2 proposal, and an opportunity to create a powerful community-based political movement that would produce a grassroots alternative to the agency's plan. In September 1963, the USFFM charged that the redevelopment agency's "relocation program is inconsistent with the public policy of the United States, as manifested in its Constitution and laws." The agency's director, M. Justin Herman, replied by asserting that, by calling for a halt to A-2, the CCU, NAACP, and USSF were encouraging "a cruel decision to condemn whites and non-whites to their slums, to deny them a chance to get decent housing, inside and outside the area . . . a needless sacrifice as well in the lack of recognition of the complicated unfolding nature of the redevelopment process itself."[40]

Scarcely two months later, fresh from a victory in pressuring the city's retailers' association into agreeing to end racial discrimination in hiring in December 1963, the USFFM picketed the Sheraton-Palace Hotel, then expanded the campaign with sit-ins in the Van Ness Avenue showrooms of the city's new car dealers. As the newspapers filled up with photos of city police officers arresting several hundred mostly white demonstrators, and CORE prepared for another protest at the Bank of America headquarters, residents of the Western Addition A-2 project area met at the Macedonia Baptist Church and vowed, "We Shall Not Be Moved." In January, members of ILWU Local 6—more than 600 members of the union lived in the A-2 area—organized a meeting to create a Western Addition redevelopment resistance league. Members of the ILWU also lived in the A-1 area, in the recently completed St. Francis Square housing complex west of the Catholic cathedral that had been sponsored by the union and the Pacific Maritime Association. The ILWU declared that it "enunciate[d] the principle of 'An Injury to One Is an Injury to All' in this fight" and urged residents in A-2 to participate "in a mass refusal to budge from present dwellings until each and every family in the area has been provided with a home fit to live in at a price they can afford." On April 16, after a three-day public hearing on A-2 sponsored by the Redevelopment Agency, Mayor Jack Shelley announced to reporters that the San Francisco Redevelopment Agency's record with A-1 had convinced him that "this time the city should first worry about the human factors involved."[41]

The question of how to define "human factors" occupied the CCU, the ILWU, and the USFFM in the weeks leading up to the public hearing. The CCU insisted that "people rather than other aspects of community life should be emphasized more, and that those who bear the brunt of redevelopment should define more of its plans." The ILWU emphasized that "area owners and renters must have the maximum opportunity to participate in planning, decision making, rehabilitation, and rebuilding." In addition to residents' exercising more control over the project, a nonprofit agency would manage the finished redevelopment area for the benefit of the residents, who would live in adequate temporary housing until reconstruction was completed and then return to the Western Addition. These alternative plans constituted blueprints for creating an economically and racially integrated community based on the expressed needs and desires of existing residents. Power would shift from the San Francisco Redevelopment Agency and its for-profit developers into the hands of residents and their own nonprofit, community-based agency. The USFFM, which had established a "Freedom House" where civil rights workers could meet and coordinate their Western Addition work, asked J. Herman Blake, an African American graduate student in sociology at UC Berkeley, to write a critique of the redevelopment agency's A-2 plan. Blake convinced three white fellow students to do the necessary research, which the lead author, Jerry Mandel, wrote up and mimeographed just in time to arrive at City Hall for the presentation. The USFFM's "Critical Assessment" described how the San Francisco Redevelopment Agency's plans called for demolishing most of the buildings in blocks heavily populated by African Americans while restoring and rehabilitating the buildings in blocks populated by whites. Also, most African Americans who were moved out would not be able to afford to move back into the rehabilitated housing. The report concluded that African Americans, small businesses, and storefront churches would be hurt by the plan, but white upper-middle-class residents, large businesses, and churches from the major denominations would be aided by A-2.[42]

The testimony offered by the San Franciscans who spoke at the standing-room-only hearings on the evenings of April 14–16 dramatized how much had changed since the Civic Auditorium meeting in 1948 to discuss whether to designate the Western Addition a redevelopment area. In 1964, while everyone expressed support for redevelopment in principle, speaker after speaker questioned the San Francisco Redevelopment Agency's judgment as to who would be helped by the project, criticized the agency's alleged prejudiced view of area residents, condemned its previous record of unilateral decision making, and expressed skepticism about whether it would build participatory mechanisms into the plan that would ensure participation by residents. As anticipated, the Chamber of Commerce, Junior Chamber of Commerce, and San Francisco Planning and Urban Renewal organization (a successor to the San Francisco Housing and Planning Association) all supported M. Justin Herman's position that more harm would come to area residents and to the city as a whole from delaying the project than from moving it forward. In addition, several churches and social service agencies gave the plan qualified support. The Jones Methodist Church and the Methodist Churches of San Francisco announced approval of the plan, provided that the San Francisco Redevelopment Agency guaranteed the construction of low- and moderate-income private housing and scattered-site public housing (to prevent "ghetto-like" concentrations). Jones Methodist Church, which had begun in a storefront and later expanded into an imposing new house of worship, urged the agency to sell the entire redevelopment area to a nonprofit agency.[43]

Opponents of A-2 who represented civil rights organizations maintained a united front and were supported by two speakers from the ILWU and three speakers from the CCU. One of five speakers representing the NAACP was delegated to present a summary statement for his group, CORE, the USFFM, the ILWU and the CCU: "We do not oppose urban renewal. We welcome a good plan in which the people of the area have been consulted, a plan for the people of the area, a plan not for buildings or real estate values alone, but a plan for those who live in Area 2." The claim that redevelopment was a racist conspiracy, which existed as an undercurrent in 1948, was now forcefully presented by the Fillmore resident Percy Jones, who argued that the plan was "not designed to help the people displaced. It is planned to displace these people permanently and unconditionally, to seize the land they live on and rebuild A-2 with structures which will rent or sell at prices that the majority of the present residents can't afford to pay." Jones promised that "the first bulldozer that comes into my neighborhood is going to have to run over me." Many residents voiced concerns over their potential loss of property and business income, and all stressed what they regarded as an intrusion by outsiders into their neighborhood. Lillian Dixon, owner of a small dry cleaning business in the heart of A-2, described her shock when she discovered that her shop would be demolished and replaced by a parking lot for a proposed shopping center that would include space for businesses like hers but at rents she could not afford. Dixon announced that she would follow Percy Jones's example and lie down in front of the bulldozers.[44]

Jones, Dixon, and other opponents of A-2 redevelopment used the language of the Southern civil rights campaign when they insisted that they could not wait any longer for the city to stop its program of "Negro removal." The ILWU promised to "join in massive resistance unless the plan is changed," and Chester Wright of the San Francisco State College Associated Students threatened "Black Nationalist" direct action if the San Francisco Redevelopment Agency went ahead with its A-2 plans. Ten days after the public hearing, Mayor Shelley released a statement on housing that his office, with Herman's assistance, had been preparing since his inauguration in January. The six-page statement released to the press on April 27 was entirely devoted to Western Addition A-2, which, Shelley, argued had "a very human purpose" but "ha[s] come under increasing criticism for its shortcomings." Shelley promised that the city would revise the plans for A-2 by extending the relocation schedule from three years "to at least five years" and that it would stop "massive bulldozing of wide areas into vacant fields of rubble." The city, the mayor promised, would move faster to provide lower-priced housing, using the ILWU's St. Francis Square project as a model, and would investigate ways to provide direct assistance for moderate-income housing for purchase and rent subsidies "for persons displaced by redevelopment." Additional public housing and a new Office of Housing and Development in the Mayor's Office that would supervise the Redevelopment Agency and the Public Housing Authority were also possible reforms, the mayor indicated. Shelley closed by promising to ask for help from the Governor's Office and the state's legislature "toward solution of a complicated problem that faces our City today" and asked San Francisco residents to "work together for that purpose."[45]

Mayor Shelley's invitation to "work together" proved as unpersuasive to the USFFM, CORE, and the NAACP in San Francisco in April 1964 as did the plea of Birmingham's white ministers in their "Call for Unity" to Martin Luther King Jr. in April of the previous year. King explained "why we can't wait" in his famous letter from the Birmingham jail, which appeared as a chapter in his book of that title in 1964. Wilfred Ussery and William Bradley of CORE and the USFFM, joined by NAACP members, responded to Mayor Shelley's peace offering by demanding that he increase the representation of poor African American residents on his anti-poverty committee. Bradley and Ussery were also frustrated by the limited gains produced by the direct action tactics at the retail stores, the Sheraton-Palace, Auto Row, and the Bank of America, and they became increasingly critical of cooperation with white allies in the movement and "the white establishment" in city government. Bradley's aggressive recruiting of new black members, combined with his assertions that "racism is the prevailing feature of the white mentality," that the white demonstrators were "cowardly" and ineffective, and that "integration is a dirty word," caused a drop in CORE membership among local whites from half at the end of 1963 to 20 percent by mid-1964. The San Francisco Redevelopment Agency held off on any work in A-2 because of uncertainties about future housing laws caused by the passage of Proposition 14 in November, and by the time the law was overturned and the agency was ready to go ahead, the stage was set for a new and more aggressive anti-redevelopment politics that would develop in the context of ideologies of Black Power and Third World Liberation rather than under the sign "An Injury to One Is an Injury to All."[46]

9

To "Alleviate Racial Concentrations"

The Public Interest in Education and Employment

In August 1962, the San Francisco Board of Education voted to cancel the opening of the proposed new Central Junior High School, and in July 1964, the Board of Supervisors established the city's Human Rights Commission (HRC). The cancellation of Central and the creation of the HRC occurred to the accompaniment of contentious debates that dramatized growing divisions among the city's interest groups during the administrations of President John F. Kennedy and President Lyndon B. Johnson. Public controversy over Central marked the politicization of the city's public schooling and began a nine-year battle over how to organize public education in the face of local civil rights challenges to customary practice and state and federal oversight of local educational policy. Organized labor's ambivalence toward the HRC acknowledged the power of new attacks on old traditions of white privilege and workers' control of the labor process and opened a new stage in the debate over the role of government policy in creating and enforcing equality in employment. San Francisco traditions that had developed to guide the work of the public schools and the city's labor relations came under direct challenge, and these events transpired in the context of continuing demographic changes in the city, school desegregation decisions by the U.S. Supreme Court, escalating national civil rights activism, and racial reforms in education and employment in the California legislature and the U.S. Congress.

When President Dwight D. Eisenhower sent National Guard troops to Little Rock, Arkansas, to enforce the integration of Central High School in 1957, Harold Spears, San Francisco's superintendent of schools, announced that the city was an exception to the national norm because "we have all races in our schools." The *San Francisco Call-Bulletin* boasted, "Integration [Is] No Problem Here." Spears was a fifty-five-year-old white native of Indiana who had moved to the city in 1947 and become superintendent the year after the U.S. Supreme Court's decision on school desegregation in *Brown v. Board of Education of Topeka* in 1954. A nationally eminent scholar of school administration theory, Spears committed the city to providing high-quality education for all, regardless of class, ethnicity, or race; colorblindness, for Spears, was a shining principle of educational professionalism. The city followed a policy from 1936 of enrolling students in neighborhood schools—a policy based on the principle that students were better off attending the schools nearest their homes. By organizing school attendance in this manner, the Board of Education aimed to strengthen the bonds among parents, teachers, and administrators, which, it believed, were imperative to a sound educational environment. In addition to this neighborhood pattern of schooling, the city followed a historical institutional tradition rooted in Progressive-era concepts of nonpartisanship and administrative expertise. The mayor appointed the seven members of the Board of Education, and in deference to historic class divisions and ethnic/racial diversity, three seats were reserved for Protestants, two for Catholics, and two for Jews. Two of those seats were also reserved for women, and one each was reserved for business and labor representatives. In 1961, Mayor George Christopher appointed James Stratten as the first African American member of the board. The board operated independently of the city supervisors, determined its own tax rate and budget, and selected the superintendent. Like the city's Public Housing Authority, the Board of Education jealously guarded its autonomy from the Board of Supervisors. Both agencies placed a high priority on their "neighborhood pattern" of operation, which, given San Francisco's dramatic demographic changes after 1942, resulted in the high concentrations of non-white residents of public housing and of non-white students in public schools in some parts of the city. The federal courts declared the housing authority's neighborhood-pattern practice unconstitutional in 1953, but no equivalent challenges to the Board of Education's racial policies had been made since President Theodore Roosevelt pressured the city into scrapping its proposal in 1905 to create separate schools for Chinese and Japanese children. That was about to change.[1]

In December 1961, several white CORE members met privately with Superintendent Spears and asked him to issue a public acknowledgement that de facto segregation was a reality in San Francisco, accompanied by a public statement describing how the Board of Education proposed to remedy the situation. They withdrew their request after consulting with Earl Raab's Bay Area Human Relations Clearing House and decided that CORE's anecdotal information about segregation in a handful of schools was a weak foundation for an attack on the Board of Education. A month later, the white civil rights activists Beverly Axelrod and Frank Quinn asked the Board of Education to provide to the public a detailed census of the racial composition and racial distribution of students in the city's public schools. Quinn had replaced Edward Howden as executive director of the Council for Civic Unity (CCU) and would later become first executive secretary of the city's HRC. Axelrod had been working in civil rights since she joined the National Lawyers Guild in 1948. She moved to California from New York City in the early 1950s, served as the NAACP president in Modesto, and was a counsel for the San Francisco branch of CORE in 1962. Quinn and Axelrod's request for racial data was coordinated with a new national strategy by the NAACP to concentrate on de facto segregation in public schools outside the South. June Shagaloff, the NAACP's special assistant for education, selected San Francisco as a target for an "attack on defacto school segregation," and she recommended several possible tactics in the Bay Area. They included "examinations of school conditions and practices, public meetings, conferences with local school Boards of Education, school 'teach in' demonstrations, school picketing and formal complaints with State Commissioners of Education." The Board of Education responded to the public request for racial data by asking Superintendent Spears to examine the problem in detail and report back to the board as soon as possible.[2]

The NAACP filed formal complaints about San Francisco to the State of California, in addition to requesting information from the city's school board. This tactic enabled the organization to make desegregation and school district boundaries a state, as well as a local, issue; it was used in the hope of forcing an early and relatively easy victory, thus eliminating the need for multiple campaigns at the local level. Shagaloff initiated this divide-and-conquer approach in April 12 with a long memorandum to the State Board of Education. She asked that that state take an "effective leadership" role on de facto segregation by formulating "an affirmative state educational policy requiring all local public school authorities to maintain and operate multi-racial schools in fact and not merely in theory." The NAACP proved successful when, on May 10, the State Board of Education directed State Superintendent Roy Simpson to issue a resolution requiring local districts to adhere to specific rules regarding school attendance boundaries in an effort to avoid de facto segregation. Superintendent Spears immediately condemned Simpson's order, arguing that "the strength of the American public school system has resulted from local interest in and local control of the schools" and that Simpson's action represented "a serious threat of encroachment upon local autonomy."[3]

When Terry Francois of the San Francisco branch of the NAACP increased the pressure on the city's Board of Education to supply the racial data requested, Superintendent Spears pointed out that gathering such information was a time-consuming process. Francois suggested an alternative in the form of an impartial citizens' committee that would draft a report, but Spears disagreed and reasserted the importance of "the long standing policy that schools here shall draw their students from their own neighborhood." The NAACP, CORE, the CCU, and the National Lawyers Guild all joined in condemning such an argument as a transparent defense of racism because, they argued, it was the neighborhood pattern policy that created de facto segregation in the first place. Spears, however, argued—contrary to the legal theory that undergirded the *Brown v. Board of Education* decision—that racial diversity in classrooms and individual schools did not guarantee high-quality education for all children, which could only be achieved by "real equality of teaching throughout the city."[4]

Pressure increased when the NAACP local branch began discussing possible litigation against the Board of Education, and publicity generated by the conflict between Spears and the civil rights organization stimulated interest among the city's large number of neighborhood associations. Among the most active was the West of Twin Peaks Central Council (WTPCC), which represented thirteen homeowners' associations and more than 6,000 households. The council met with Spears and expressed its concern over rumors that the Board of Education was considering a plan to move students among the schools to achieve racial balance. Spears assured the council that no such plan was imminent and explained that he was merely compiling a report on the general topic of race and the schools. The council claimed that the NAACP and CORE were trying "to intimidate honest, decent citizens with public charges of segregation before the Board of Education," and it was determined to put its position opposing the abolition of neighborhood schools on the record.[5]

Superintendent Spears defended San Francisco's system using a definition of the public interest that was increasingly called into question in the early 1960s in the city, as well as in the nation. Spears argued, "We shouldn't pay any attention to race in the schools. Every school in our city gives its students the same high-level teaching and school services. We shouldn't keep figures on racial composition—and we don't." The NAACP, CORE, and the CCU questioned whether high-quality teaching was available where high concentrations of African American students filled neighborhood classrooms in low-income parts of the Western Addition, Merced Heights, Oceanview, Ingleside, and Bayview–Hunters Point neighborhoods. The advocates for African American civil rights also questioned Superintendent Spears's belief that the public interest required equality of opportunity for access to school for all students, including African American children, but not special efforts to create racial balance within schools or special attention after entering school (except for bilingual teachers in schools in Chinese neighborhoods and compensatory programs for students of all backgrounds who needed remedial work). The critics insisted that racial concentrations per se, no matter what the cause, needed to be acknowledged and undone, an outcome that required explicit condemnation of institutional racism, not colorblind denial of racial difference, plus moving pupils out of their neighborhoods if necessary to achieve racial balance. Debate about these contentious issues shaped the controversy over Central Junior High School.[6]

The controversy was the product of the long-anticipated move of Lowell High School to a new campus near Lake Merced. The Board of Education decided to use the old building in an uptown part of the Western Addition to relieve overcrowding in nearby junior high schools, particularly Benjamin Franklin, with its large concentration of African American students. The plans were further developed in April, when the superintendent recommended only a temporary new site, given anticipated population changes due to redevelopment in the Western Addition. Financial considerations also came into play: a complete rehabilitation was estimated to cost $1,406,000, as opposed to the $75,000 estimated to make only urgent repairs for a temporary site. The board accepted the superintendent's recommended alternative and changed the name of the building from Lowell High School to Central Junior High School. These actions mobilized a group of parents of white students at nearby Grattan Elementary School, in the district that included the soon-to-be famous Haight-Ashbury neighborhood. The parents, who included Beverly Axelrod, objected to the proposed new junior high for two, interrelated reasons; first, they disliked the district boundaries established for Central because the result would be to "create a virtually all Negro institution"; and second, since students from Grattan would be expected to move to Central, their white children would be attending a predominantly African American junior high.[7]

Contemporary observers attributed the parents' opposition to Central Junior High to a combination of liberal ideals and racist fears. The parents showed a genuine desire to see their city move away from racial segregation to racial integration; generally, they were moderate- to upper-income white residents who were relatively well educated, humanistic in outlook, and supportive of President John F. Kennedy's "New Frontier" political ideas. At the same time, they were worried about "the threat of engulfment of the ghetto," given that the population in the census tract for Grattan Elementary was 80 percent white, and the population in the proposed Central district drew from two census tracts, one with a population that was more than 50 percent black, and the other with a population that was 25–50 percent black. The white parents of Grattan students allied themselves with the African American civil rights organizations and opposed the proposal for the new junior high school. Their motives were undoubtedly different, but the goals of the Grattan students' parents and those of the NAACP matched sufficiently to allow cooperation on this issue.[8]

As the debate over Central Junior High got caught up in the San Francisco campaign against de facto school segregation, the context changed as the tension that the NAACP created between the State Board of Education and local California school districts intensified. On May 29, State Superintendent Simpson demanded that the state board establish better monitoring of how local school districts drew their boundaries to "result in the highest possible degree of integration in the schools." The state board obliged and promised to implement Simpson's recommendation "with the full thrust of [its] legal authority and moral leadership." Robert W. Formhals, executive secretary of the California School Boards Association, immediately contested the proposed oversight of "attendance practices within local school districts where the governing boards of such districts had traditionally exercised this duty." Public schools, according to his organization's principles, could not be unmindful of social change, but at the same time, "they should not undertake through direct community action to become a major instrument either to divert or impede such change nor to force such change." This position was similar to that of Superintendent Harold Spears in San Francisco.[9]

Three hundred people went to Nourse Auditorium on the evening of June 19 to hear Superintendent Spears's report on "the proper recognition of a pupil's racial background" in the operation of the city's public schools. Spears declared that "the function of the American public school [was limited to] the effective instruction of the pupils therein." The city's neighborhood policy was best suited to the "close school and home relationships between the parents and teacher" that supported the schools' mission. The civil rights organizations and State Board of Education had allowed themselves to be dazzled by utopian visions, he said. "Practices and proposals that may seem promising in print or public forum, so often lose their glitter in the peculiarities of the local situation." Spears then reiterated the colorblind policy of the city, claiming that "pupils have the right to see each other not by color but by what is behind it. And this goes for teachers and parents as well."[10]

Toward the end of his lengthy report, Spears expanded his discussion to address the question of how American society generally, and not just San Francisco, should define the role of public education in the aftermath of *Brown v. Board of Education* and the civil rights legislation of 1960. He acknowledged the need to take seriously the Supreme Court's order to eliminate segregated schools but rejected the argument that "providing the non-white child a proper education is essentially an administrative, legal, or political maneuver." Spears refused to make the city's racial data on school attendance public, and he defended a philosophical perspective that was under attack when he argued that "the school is actually an instrument of social change, but as such an instrument, the children are not to be used as tools. Instead, through their education, and consequently their enlightenment, society is better assured of their adult adjustment as self-paying members of the economy, and as active participants in the civil and cultural affairs of the community." He refused to be party to a policy reform that used the public schools "to correct the inadequacies of out- side community conditions," and he believed this would happen if the city dis- carded its neighborhood-based attendance rules and drew up new boundaries based on race/ethnicity or if it had recourse to busing students to create ethnic/ racially diverse school populations. The superintendent bridled at the prospect of the city schools becoming an instrument of a racial-reform-based social change movement, and he announced that he could offer "no educationally sound program to suggest to the board to eliminate the schools in which the children are predominantly of one race."[11]

Superintendent Spears's robust defense of the status quo in the public schools, coming as it did in the midst of the controversy over Central Junior High, put the dissenting parents of the Grattan students in a quandary: they accepted the superintendent's promise to review the boundaries in the spring of 1963 because it would be difficult to make changes before the beginning of the fall term. Francois, however, announced that waiting was not an option, and during a school board meeting on July 24, he declared, "The NAACP will take action right away to prevent a ghettoized school." He promised picketing, law- suits, and, if necessary, a student boycott, and the Grattan parents then agreed to join the NAACP and "force a showdown" about Central at the next meeting of the board, on August 7. At this point, the *San Francisco Chronicle* joined the NAACP and the parents in their criticism of the school board and the super- intendent. On August 1, the newspaper published an editorial and the first of four political cartoons it would run during the Central controversy. The edito- rial declared the racial pattern of the city schools "an issue of great immediacy" central to the questions about which "the public is concerned." It called on the Board of Education to "put a reasonable proportion of Whites and negroes in every public school, even if this means carrying Negro or White children across neighborhood lines." The cartoon that accompanied the editorial por- trayed two pupils standing before a pair of doorways asking each other, "Which school shall we go to?" Superintendent Spears met with the Grattan parents and with the Haight-Ashbury Neighborhood Council and reiterated his support for the neighborhood schools pattern. The San Francisco chapter of the California Teachers Association announced its support of the superin- tendent, even though it disapproved of de facto segregation, because the asso- ciation believed there were "no sound solutions easily available." Francois expected to file an NAACP lawsuit when Shagaloff, the organization's educa- tion specialist, approved the details when she visited San Francisco during the second week of August.[12]

Mayor Christopher entered the controversy when he urged the Board of Education to follow up on the civil rights groups' requests to draw the boundaries for the new Central Junior High district to reflect as closely as possible the racial composition of the city's entire school population, not the school's immediate area. Christopher acknowledged that the city charter prohibited him from exerting pressure on the board and assured its members that he had no interest in challenging its autonomy, but the board emphasized its independence and refused to budge. At the meeting on August 7, the board member Adolfo de Urioste asked the critics to give Central a "fair chance" to operate during the fall semester and promised that if the fears expressed by the Grattan parents and other critics materialized, the board would consider alternative plans. Another board member, Edward Kemmit, assured critics that he considered the new Central a temporary site and said that the project did not justify the degree of controversy that had already developed. The critics were not mollified, and almost three dozen dissenters refused to leave Nourse Auditorium after the meeting was adjourned. They staged an overnight sit-in and did not leave until the next morning. Two days later, the Grattan Parents Association and a special committee of the Haight-Ashbury Neighborhood Council began planning their own legal action against the Board of Education.[13]

On August 9, the *San Francisco Chronicle* weighed in on the Central controversy a second time with an editorial arguing, "School's Duty Is To Integrate." This time, the paper asserted that if the school board opened the new school without reforming the enrollment rules, the city would "fail to give White and negro youngsters alike the experience which they are entitled of learning in an environment normal to the city." That many white residents were "loath to recognize" the drift toward segregation did not excuse the board from its responsibility to use the public school system to welcome blacks "into the life of the community" by making every school racially integrated: "Most white parents don't mind sending their children to a school where the minority are Negroes. They are going to mind if the proportion is 60 per cent Negro. A school in which a racial minority group predominates practically guarantees that the neighborhood around it will become a minority ghetto." The accompanying cartoon dramatized the increasing political heat on the board by portraying board members at a table refusing to look at roaring flames in the background labeled "growing segregation problem," with one member asking "are we SURE we don't smell smoke?" Members of CORE threw a picket line around the Unified School District's offices on Van Ness Avenue during rush hour, and the San Francisco Labor Council criticized the board and the superintendent for their intransigence and urged the mayor to establish a citizens' committee to recommend solutions to de facto segregation. The NAACP promised a student boycott if Central opened as planned, and four city supervisors urged the school board to settle the "raging Central Junior High controversy" before the fall term began. Members of the Grattan Parents Association announced that they would not send their children to Central on September 5 "unless the student body is predominantly white."[14]

Superintendent Spears called for patience and reminded the public that locating a junior high school in the old Lowell High building was intended as a "purely temporary expedient," saying, "I wish the public realized that Central is not a permanent fixture. It is probable that in a couple of years the City's regular fifteen junior high schools will be able to handle the student load without the help of Central." Then the attorney Aubrey Grossman filed suit in U.S. District Court on behalf of the parents protesting the attendance boundaries of Central. Grossman, a longtime member of the Communist Party who had successfully defended Harry Bridges against deportation charges, had been active in civil rights work since 1944, when he served on Mayor Lapham's personal Civic Unity Committee. Now Grossman sought an injunction preventing the opening of Central. He alleged that Central would effectively be racially segregated, a violation of the black students' Fourteenth Amendment rights according to the *Brown v. Board of Education* decision. The suit charged that Spears and the board were guilty of deliberately drawing school attendance zones to create de facto segregation. Judge Alfonso J. Zirpoli denied the injunction and asked the defendants and plaintiffs to reach a "working accord" and settle their differences outside the courtroom.[15]

Following Judge Zirpoli's request, Samuel Ladar, president of the school board, initiated conversations with the superintendent and representatives of the litigating parents' groups, but none of the parties was ready to change positions. The parents' groups continued to call for a redrawing of the attendance boundaries, and the school district's representatives refused to abandon their existing policy and pointed out that changes could not in any case be accomplished before classes began in September. The Grattan parents did mention that they would be satisfied if Central never opened, but neither Ladar nor Spears was prepared to accept that idea. The *San Francisco Chronicle* published a third political cartoon ridiculing the school board's incompetence. In the cartoon, a stumped "School Board" stands before a blackboard on which the teacher ("S.F.") has written the problem: "Take 102,444 students, divide into 132 schools, maintaining x% negro students and y% white, subtracting de facto housing factors and multiplying by neighborhood patterns and Supreme Court decision."[16]

Adding to the complexity, a group of white parents calling themselves the Citizens Committee for Neighborhood Schools now entered the controversy. They used the direct action tactics of CORE and the NAACP to call for maintaining the neighborhood pattern. Their president, Leon Markel, warned that they would seek an injunction, if necessary, to keep the board from sending white students from other parts of the city to the proposed Central campus to keep it from becoming predominantly black. Markel was active in the liberal California Republican Assembly and had been treasurer of the CCU. He and his fellow Republican Party reform activists had supported the state's Fair Employment Practices Commission legislation, but he drew the line at school busing to create racial balance. Markel's organization announced it would stand for the principle that "those schools are best which are close to home" and challenged the claims of the NAACP and CORE activists to represent the people of San Francisco. "We want a San Francisco solution to a San Francisco problem by San Franciscans, not by imported sit-in specialists, with no threats of boycotts or picketing or recriminations." Markel reminded San Franciscans that it was the Grattan parents and members of the Haight-Ashbury Neighborhood Council who objected to sending their children to a school that would be 60 percent black. If any party was guilty of prejudice, he argued, it was surely those parents. The *San Francisco Chronicle* decried the fact that "San Franciscans, group against group, are now engaged in unseemly controversy over one aspect of a grave community problem that largely spans the city's entire economic and social spectrum. A new school, set up in a new district created by the happenstance that a school building became available through the transfer of Lowell High. . . . Central must now appear to be a less than desirable acquisition to the public school system. As a breeder of hostility and ill will among the citizens, it has, even on paper, proved its potency."[17]

Two weeks remained before the opening of the fall term when the Board of Education met on August 21. Superintendent Spears requested a special order of business and presented a report recommending that the plan to establish Central Junior High School be rescinded. He explained that his decision to abandon the proposal was based solely on his desire to protect the educational welfare of the pupils. The board accepted Spears's argument and promptly voted unanimously to cancel the project; Board of Education President Samuel Ladar said he was deeply troubled by the controversy and expressed his regret that the Central plan had been "made an issue by which certain groups had sought to obtain a hasty decision on the basic problem." In his view, the outcome was "no victory for proponents, or for anyone." The protestors disagreed and interpreted the outcome as "a stunning success." Some of the African American students who would have attended Central were assigned to Aptos Junior High, where the percentage of non-white students increased to 18 percent in 1964, 25 percent in 1965, and 32 percent in 1966. And in 1964, the school board shifted the boundaries of Commodore Sloat Elementary School, which, like Aptos, was located in the predominantly white Lakeside West of Twin Peaks area of the city. At Commodore Sloat, the proportion of non-white pupils increased from 15 percent in 1964 to 22 percent in 1966. Spears hoped by such actions to dampen controversy, which, with its picket lines, pending legislation, and threatened boycotts, was harmful, in his view, to "the stable conditions necessary for a suitable teaching and learning situation." But the NAACP, CORE, the CCU, and their allies regarded the cancellation of the Central project as a victory in their larger campaign to overturn the city's neighborhood pattern of schooling, and it is not surprising, as one contemporary study of school desegregation politics concluded, that the protestors' demands were "more or less met by the school board without reducing any of the pressure for a more general solution."[18]

The Central controversy, coming as it had in the context of the national campaign against de facto segregation, marked a turning point in San Franciscans' struggle over how to define the public interest in education. Civil rights activists had successfully challenged Superintendent Spears's and the school board's tradition of professional expertise and autonomy from political pressure. The consequences of this overturning of the status quo and the politicization of decision making over public schools became apparent when the Board of Education met again on September 18, this time in the auditorium of Galileo High School. Some 1,400 people turned out at the special forum—the *San Francisco Chronicle* sensationally described it as a "hot public debate"—in which individuals and groups responded to Spears's report. Terry Francois called on the board to assent to the principle that "racial composition of the schools [will] become a matter of concern to this board and its administrators" while at the same time preserving "to the maximum extent possible . . . the basic character of the neighborhood schools." White critics of the civil rights groups presented forceful objections that demonstrated a melding of parental concern for their children's welfare and a principled objection to the strategies and tactics of the movement. Albert Vipiana, a white parent and resident of the affluent Marina District, whose wife later became a leading anti–school-busing activist, argued that "forced" and "artificial" integration would harm the city's future race relations: "In short, by introducing or acknowledging race as a criterion for education, you will further prejudice the cause [of civil rights] and destroy its effectiveness." A member of the Alamo School Mothers Club demanded that the school board respect "one of the basic rights of free democracy, the right not to be singled out because of one's race, color, or creed. Just as no child should be denied admittance to any school in our democracy because of race, color, or creed, no child should be forced to attend a particular school because of any of these." Jeanne Bogard, a white parent whose daughter had been slated to attend Central, which was "walking distance" from her home and where she would have studied with "the same classmates she had in the 6th grade," had no qualms about the majority-black student body that would have attended

Central: "I personally was 100 per cent behind Central Junior High." Because of the cancellation of the school, however, the girl ended up being bused to Aptos Junior High on the other side of Twin Peaks. "When I hear the squeal of brakes in bad weather," Bogard said, "I think it could be the school bus." Bogard criticized CORE's tactics, which had included sit-ins at the school board meetings, picketing outside the school board's building, and a telephone campaign that targeted school board members at their homes during the dinner hour, not as grassroots democracy in action but as "a crime."

The board responded to the testimony by African Americans and whites (representatives of the city's other non-white parents, as indicated earlier, had not yet mobilized on this issue by this date) by unanimously endorsing James Stratten's proposal to defer the question of school desegregation by appointing a three-member Ad Hoc Committee to review the entire matter and report to the city the next spring. This is what Axelrod and Quinn had demanded back in January, so setting up the Ad Hoc Committee represented a victory for them. However, the board was determined to maintain control of public discussion in the face of the increasing militancy of the civil rights organizations and insisted that ordering a report did not necessarily mean commitment "to any change in our policy." Wilfred Ussery of CORE demanded to know whether the public would have to wait seven months to find out whether the city would "disapprove of segregated schools," and de Urioste replied, "That's what the resolution means."[19]

The board's Ad Hoc Committee reported in April 1963, and Ussery and many others were surprised by its call for San Francisco to "alleviate racial concentrations" in city schools. The report stated that no change in present policy would be made to transfer students to schools outside their neighborhoods, but the CCU praised the report's explicit statement that the board agreed to "consider race in drawing up school boundaries" and in choosing new school sites, and the NAACP considered the report an acknowledgment of de facto segregation, labeled it "a delightful surprise" and "a step forward," and decided not to pursue its lawsuit. The report, however, insisted on distinguishing between what it called "local racial concentration" and "segregation [which] is an overt act that has not occurred in San Francisco." The report also praised Superintendent Spears's previous compensatory education programs, agreed to expand them and establish new programs to bolster intergroup education, and promised to add a human relations and intergroup relations manager in the central office. The report was officially adopted at the next regularly scheduled school board meeting; here again, however, the board pointedly announced that the proposals in the report would be considered "whenever practical, reasonable, and consistent with the neighborhood school plan."[20]

After winning a symbolic victory in April 1963, with the Board of Education committing itself to "consider race" in drawing school boundaries and choosing new school sites, the civil rights organizations shifted their attention to derailing the Western Addition A-2 project and pressuring downtown hotels, banks, retail stores, and automobile dealers into hiring non-white employees. The members of Ussery's CORE and Francois's NAACP provided the foot soldiers in these two campaigns, but they did not attend, speak out, or sit in at Board of Education meetings in late 1963 and 1964 to the degree that they had in 1962 and the winter of 1963. Beverly Axelrod left the Bay Area temporarily and traveled to the South, where she provided legal advice and representation to students who registered voters in Louisiana and Mississippi in 1963–1964; when she returned, she turned her attention to the legal defense of Black Panther Party members. It was Axelrod who took Eldridge Cleaver's writings from Folsom Prison to *Ramparts* magazine, where they were first published. (They were reissued in 1968 as the bestselling book *Soul on Ice.*) Superintendent Spears did not move aggressively to restructure the racial balance in the city schools, but in the spring of 1964, he did propose a new high school in a location picked to maximize its "being properly integrated." He expected that the civil rights groups would "go along with it" but failed to consult with any of the civil rights leaders before making his announcement. As one contemporary observer noted (and as M. Justin Herman, director of the Redevelopment Agency, learned), "The movement at this point was in no mood to go along with anything." Now, the NAACP, backed by the San Francisco AFL-CIO Labor Council, insisted that new schools should be built *within* areas of African American residential concentration; polls conducted by the school district indicated that African American parents in the Western Addition and Bayview–Hunters Point would rather have better neighborhood schools than have their children bused into other parts of the city. Spears accepted the new demand and sent voters a bond issue that he said "he would never have dreamed of asking for" because it obviously represented an accommodation to, rather than a contribution to undoing, the city's existing pattern of racial concentrations in particular neighborhoods. Inadvertently, the superintendent's agreeing to this demand sowed the seeds of the successful NAACP lawsuit in 1970 that demanded complete desegregation of students and faculty in the city's elementary schools. As one educational policy analyst later concluded, Spears's "accommodation was ultimately a costly one," because "the plaintiffs in *Johnson* [*v. San Francisco School District* in 1971*] would point to the construction of ghetto schools as evidence of the school district's deliberate segregation of black students."[21]

When the *Johnson* suit was filed in 1970, Harold Spears had retired and was living in Indiana, where he remained active as a consultant and writer. He announced his retirement date of 1967 in July 1965, following a new round of demonstrations and picketing by the civil rights front, which had resumed its criticism of the Board of Education for having failed to make good on its promises of April 1963. In August 1965, Spears released to the public the school census data that Beverly Axelrod and Frank Quinn had first requested in January 1962; not surprisingly, the parties involved in the city's politics of education interpreted the results differently. Critics of Spears and the school board emphasized the finding that African American students made up more than 90 percent of the pupils in seven of the ninety-five elementary schools; they de-emphasized the facts that only four of the elementary schools were more than 90 percent white and fully 76 percent of all African American students attended integrated elementary schools. This contrasted with the situation in Baltimore and St. Louis, two other non-Southern cities where similar civil rights fronts had launched campaigns against de facto segregation; there, only 14 percent and 20 percent, respectively, of African American students attended integrated elementary schools. In San Francisco's eight high schools, the proportion of black students ranged from 8 percent to 34 percent, and in the fifteen junior high schools, two had enrollments of African American students of more than 50 percent.[22]

Release of the enrollment data did nothing to end contention over how the city's public interest in education should be redefined in light of the social and political changes of the early and mid-1960s. San Francisco's school board meetings, like the redevelopment hearings described in Chapter 8, would continue to be public spaces where an increasing number of interest groups, more and more focused on racial justice but increasingly divided about how to define it, joined the contest. Francois, now a member of the city's Board of Supervisors, proposed (unsuccessfully) that the city make the school board an elected body, and Willie Brown, now a member of the State Assembly, agreed, pointing out that doing so would increase residents' ability to gain "fundamental participation in the affairs of the school."[23]

Participation was certainly evident in August 1965, when the city's new Human Rights Commission and the Board of Education sponsored two public conferences on how to move forward to address de facto school segregation. California voters had repealed the state's fair housing ordinance the previous November, redevelopment of Western Addition A-2 was on hold, and the courts had not yet overturned the two-to-one voter mandate in favor of Proposition 14. San Franciscans who had supported Proposition 14 and who had voted for Barry Goldwater in the presidential election were now mobilized and energized by the "property rights are civil rights" argument of those high-profile campaigns and joined in the contest over defining the public interest in education. Alice Vipiana, a campaign manager for Goldwater in San Francisco's

19th Congressional District and later a campaigner in Ronald Reagan's successful run for governor, joined Marjorie Lemlow in a new group called Mothers
Support Neighborhood Schools that defended neighborhood schools as exten-
sions of individual and family property rights. Lemlow had been a co-chair of
the Citizens Committee for Neighborhood Schools in 1963–1964. Another new
interest group, Parents and Taxpayers, joined the debate in 1965, and all three
organizations used the language of parents' and taxpayers' rights. Like their
counterparts in Southern California and elsewhere in the nation, Vipiana and
Lemlow decried what they regarded as externally imposed social engineering
implicit in the principles embedded in the *Brown v. Board of Education* decision. They "affirm[ed] it to be the duty of the parents to assure that their children are reared and educated in familiar surroundings and receive a proper and
adequate education. If our children are permitted to leave the family neighborhood, where we cannot control their environment or where certain conditions
are beyond our reach, then good education and the molding of character is
impossible." Critics accused Vipiana and Lemlow of cynically masking racist
values behind hypocritical claims that they were defending liberty of conscience. They retorted that their families' rights could not be overridden by government, ironically foreshadowing the logic of the U.S. Supreme Court's 1965
decision in *Griswold v. Connecticut,* which defended access to abortion as a
constitutionally protected family "right of privacy" matter.[24]

By 1965, questions about when individuals, families, businesses, or unions
and other voluntary associations (such as those representing parents, taxpayers, and racial reformers) deserved privacy—autonomy and independence—to
operate free of government oversight, and when they deserved government
assistance (even to the point of having their interests protected by and enshrined
in law), took center stage in debates in San Francisco about how to define the
public interest regarding racial discrimination in employment, as well as in
education. John F. Shelley, the city's mayor in 1965, first addressed these questions in March 1942, when in his position as president of the AFL's San Francisco Labor Council he responded to critics who charged that "the Labor Movement was practicing race discrimination." The charges derived from the refusal
by one of the council's member unions, Municipal Carmen's Union Local 518,
to train a twenty-four-year-old African American named Audley Cole as a
motorman. Cole had passed the Public Utilities Commission's civil service
exam, which qualified him to operate the city-owned Municipal Railway streetcars, and he was set to begin work after finishing his on-the-job training.
After he was nearly halfway through the lessons, Local 518 voted to impose a
fine of $100 on any member of the union who agreed to continue Cole's train-
ing. The union was allegedly supported by the police and firefighters' associations (which did not deny the charges); they worried that if Cole succeeded in

becoming a city employee, a precedent would be set that could be used to challenge the white-only (Irish-ethnic preference) recruiting in the departments. Negative press coverage led the local to rescind the fine, but Cole's training stopped, and motormen who expressed willingness to resist the racist move by the union found themselves pressured, threatened, and even physically attacked. The manager of the Municipal Railway responded by suspending fourteen motormen and then, after the union reimbursed the men for their lost wages, increased the suspension period and threatened dismissal. Mayor Rossi condemned the union's actions, pointing out, "If the colored person is good enough to be a soldier, he is good enough to work for this city. The man passed his civil service examination and should be able to work. We are not going to turn anyone down because of his race."[25]

In the two weeks that followed Rossi's press conference on the Cole case, his condemnation of Local 518 was echoed by the San Francisco CIO Council, the AFL Labor Council and several AFL local unions, the Bay Area Council against Discrimination, the major daily newspapers and the Communist Party newspaper, and the San Francisco branch of the NAACP. The AFL Labor Council issued strong criticism of the motormen's union, both because its racist actions were "Fascist and Nazi in character" and because it was "giving a false impression of organized labor to the public, and [was] weakening the prestige of all unions and of the San Francisco Labor Council." The AFL Labor Council also asked Mayor Rossi to investigate the *San Francisco Chronicle*'s allegation that the police officers' and firefighters' associations had conspired with Local 518 to bar Cole from the job operating Municipal Railway streetcars. Ten days after the council issued its reprimand to Local 518, Cole was at the controls of a streetcar and working as a full-fledged motorman, but the union that had refused to train him had stuck to its position through the entire controversy. "I guess they mean to wear me out physically and financially," Cole wrote to the wartime federal Fair Employment Practices Committee, "but they won't." He offered the union and the Public Utilities Commission a compromise deal, which they both accepted: he would be trained by the Municipal Railway's education department, not—as was customary—by the union. Ten days later, on March 31, AFL Labor Council President and future Mayor Jack Shelley and Secretary John A. O'Connell issued an extraordinary statement to all of the one hundred plus member unions on the Cole case. Their statement acknowledged the affiliated unions' cherished worker-control principles (the autonomy of the local union, the sanctity of collective-bargaining agreements between the union and the employer, majority rule within the local union, and respect for seniority rights), and they admitted that "it is true that this Council cannot set the policy of the local unions affiliated with it." At the same time, Shelley and O'Connell urged all of the individual unions that belonged to the council to follow "the

policy of the American Federation of Labor, which is 'there shall be no discrimination against persons because of their race, color or creed.' . . . Most
especially is this so in these days when our Country is fighting to preserve our
rights to democratic government and ideals." By the end of the war, several
hundred African American men and women worked as streetcar operators and
in various other Municipal Railway jobs; none had been employed before the
attack on Pearl Harbor.[26]

The practice of the AFL and CIO county councils' taking the high road of
principled commitment to racial equality ("the policy and the thought *mentally
and actively* 'that all men are created equal'") while urging member local unions
to shed racist practices proved a constant in the two decades from the Cole case
to the creation of the HRC in 1964 and beyond. Edward Howden put in nearly
twenty years as executive director of the CCU, on the city's Commission on
Equal Employment Opportunity (CEEO), and on the state's Fair Employment
Practice Commissions during those years. In assessing the relative support for
fair employment reforms from business and labor, Howden reckoned that the
San Francisco Labor Council consistently supported both fair employment laws
and agencies to monitor their implementation at both the local and state levels
as a means to achieve racial equality in employment, often to a greater degree
than many of its member local unions. Organized business, however—especially
the San Francisco Employers Council—proved to be the "major, most powerful" opponent of fair employment legislation and the accompanying watchdog
agencies.[27]

Six years after Cole won his victory against Local 518, his wife, Josephine
Cole, became the city's first African American high school teacher; in 1949, she
served on the Mayor's Committee on Human Relations that urged the Board of
Supervisors to pass an ordinance establishing a city Fair Employment Practices
Commission. The CCU and the civil rights organizations gave the measure
unqualified support, just as they had done with Proposition 11, an unsuccessful
initiative on fair employment practices that appeared on the state ballot in
November 1946. The San Francisco Employers Council, Chamber of Commerce, and other business groups opposed both the measure and the proposed
city ordinance. The CIO and AFL Labor Councils joined the civil rights coalition in supporting the statewide ballot proposition, as did the Association of
Catholic Trade Unionists (ACTU). John F. Shelley, who was one of the founders of the Catholic organization and was close to its chaplain, Father Hugh A.
Donohoe, joined Donohoe in adding a clause to the ACTU's bylaws specifying
that "the worker has a duty to enforce strict honesty within the union and a
square deal for everybody regardless of race, color or creed." The AFL Labor
Council also set up a permanent committee to combat discrimination in the
operation of its member local unions. Now, in 1949, the Labor Councils lobbied

the board to pass the city ordinance establishing a city Fair Employment Practices Commission, provided that its language specified that nothing in the commission's mandate would allow it to set aside collective-bargaining agreements or interfere with seniority rights to expand minority hiring. At the end of a year of hearings and public debate, the Board of Supervisors decided, as Supervisor James Leo Halley put it, that "the necessity for this type of legislation at the community level has not been shown." The board postponed a vote on a city fair practices measure until January 1, 1951, and called on business organizations, labor unions, and other community interest groups to explore voluntary methods to improve "inter-group relations."[28]

When the Board of Supervisors began its reconsideration of the fair employment ordinance in the spring of 1951, the Chamber of Commerce and San Francisco Employers Council reasserted their condemnation of the measure. In 1949, the Employers Council had considered the ordinance "discrimination against *majority* groups," denied that "lack of opportunity foments unrest and tension," and considered "references to discrimination . . . a libel on San Francisco," which, it insisted "is exceptionally free of discrimination." Now, on the basis of questionnaires submitted by 70 percent of its member firms, the council argued that "there is not enough deliberate discrimination by San Francisco business firms generally to justify an ordinance creating a Fair Employment Practices Commission with police powers to harass San Francisco employers at the instigation of malcontents and those who, for their own propaganda purposes, would seek to use such an official body unjustifiably." The council's president, Almon Roth, urged the Board of Supervisors to consider "permanently tabling any motions for a compulsory ordinance exercising police powers in this field of private enterprise." Adrien Falk, president of a San Francisco wholesale grocery business and head of the California State Chamber of Commerce, quoted Abraham Lincoln in defense of free enterprise at a forum on the city ordinance at USF: "We [in business] want to be free ourselves . . . this country cannot survive—as Lincoln said—half slave and half free." Falk also insisted that labor deserved half the blame for discrimination. "What must be done is to break down the existing barriers and the attitude of the employer who does not want any more problems," he said. "He must be prodded [but not made the subject of government regulation] and those workers with certain inherent dislikes or prejudices must be educated."[29]

In contrast to the San Francisco Employers Council, which denied that its members practiced discrimination, and the state and city Chambers of Commerce, which admitted that discrimination existed but could be solved only by prodding and education, the AFL Labor Council, joined by the CIO Labor Council and the now independent ILWU, admitted that they found "both in the city as a whole and in the labor movement in particular . . . a serious minority problem in San Francisco." George Johns, an AFL county council officer since 1939 who became executive secretary in November 1948 when Shelley took his seat as the city's representative in California's Fifth Congressional District, blamed "fear, ignorance, misinformation, and a misguided self-interest" for employment discrimination among workers. Johns reiterated the council's support "for fair employment legislation on a local, state, and national basis" and described how the Labor Council had developed a program of "re-education" during "The Year of Trial," which included a professionally produced film and a booklet dedicated to "improving human relations and promoting the cause of tolerance." Johns contrasted the Labor Council's "constructive job, and not a mere token demonstration" with the apparent lack of comparable activity on the part of the city government, Board of Education, state Department of Employment, and "private industry." Rabbi Alvin Fine of Temple Emanu-El, who had served with Josephine Cole on the Mayor's committee in 1949 and would become one of the charter members of the HRC when it was established in 1964, endorsed fair employment legislation for the second time in 1951 "simply because the moral principles in the issue remain the same." Fine argued, "Where glaring inequalities and the abuse of equal rights exist in any degree, the so-called 'voluntary' or 'informal' approach is inadequate." The Board of Supervisors voted six to five against establishing the ordinance at the end of a lively meeting with a standing-room-only audience; the *Sun-Reporter* alerted its readers that they could vote against two of the opponents of the measure who would be running for reelection in the fall and listed those who had voted in favor, including Supervisor George Christopher, who had been the leading advocate for the ordinance among the board members.[30]

The *Sun-Reporter* endorsed Christopher when he ran unsuccessfully for mayor in 1951 on the basis of his outspoken support for racial justice during his ten years as supervisor and again in 1956, when he won the election. Christopher was a Greek American who had grown up in a poor family in the rough-and-tumble South of Market district and worked his way through college. He bought a failing dairy business and turned it into a going concern but fell afoul of the law when he was prosecuted for a misdemeanor violation of a state anti-price fixing law. By the time he first ran for supervisor in 1945, Christopher had reclaimed his reputation, and as a board member he developed a record as a friend of the labor movement as well as a booster of the city's business community. When he ran for mayor, his campaign managers were Joseph Alioto, a Democrat in state and national politics who supported fair employment legislation, and Walter A. Haas Sr., a Republican who opposed it. The Democrats Carlton Goodlett, Thomas Fleming, and Terry Francois, leaders of the left wing and center in the African American community, and the most prominent leader on the right, Republican James Stratten, all campaigned for Christopher.

By the end of his first year as mayor, a new San Francisco Committee for Equal Job Opportunity, now including several younger reform-oriented Republicans from business and the professions (including Walter Haas Jr.) was supporting Christopher's call for fair employment legislation. In early September, the *Sun-Reporter* used its editorial column to urge readers to register to vote in the election in 1956. It alerted them that "within the near future" the Board of Supervisors would consider another fair employment ordinance, and this one would be "a Test for Mayor Christopher."[31]

In the weeks between Christopher's election to the Mayor's Office and his inauguration in January 1957, the San Francisco civil rights front launched an all-out effort to get a fair employment ordinance passed by the Board of Supervisors. The backgrounds of the co-chairmen of the new Committee for Equal Job Opportunity testified to the changes and the continuities that marked the city at the end of the 1950s. Their social origins differed, as did their economic interests, but they all agreed that "a man's [*sic*] right simply to compete for a job" [must rest only] on the basis of his ability to perform, without reference to arbitrary factors such as his race, religion, or ancestry." Reverend Hamilton T. Boswell, who had been one of the famous Wiley College "Great Debaters," had left Texas, attended the University of Southern California, and then moved to San Francisco, where he became the pastor of Jones Memorial Methodist Church. Boswell mentored Willie Brown, introduced him to Democratic Party politics, and served as his first campaign manager. The Republican Jesse C. Colman, a popular business owner and city supervisor for twenty-five years, was a native San Franciscan whose father had marched with the Committee of Vigilance in 1856; Colman's father-in-law was the senior rabbi at Temple Emanu-El for a generation. William Matson Roth grew up in the trans-Pacific Protestant social and business elite of California and Hawaii and graduated from the Cate School and Yale University. By the 1950s, he was publishing the controversial novelist Henry Miller, supporting the Democratic Party, and helping to start San Francisco's historic landmark preservation movement. Edgar de Pue Osgood, Roth's co-chair on the Committee for Equal Job Opportunity, was a former president of the California Young Republicans (he later chaired San Francisco County's Republican organization and signed on as an early supporter of Ronald Reagan for governor). Osgood owned the DePue Warehouse Company and was an importer and exporter who had grown up in a cosmopolitan trans-Atlantic multilingual social world and was schooled at the École Alsacienne in Paris. He joined U.S. Naval Intelligence before the United States entered World War II in 1940, served in the North African and Mediterranean theaters (working initially for the Royal Air Force) and later in the Pacific, and received a personal commendation from President Franklin D. Roosevelt. He settled in San Francisco after the war, committing himself to "Renaissance values" and racial justice after having participated in the successful multinational effort to "overcome Hitler and Tojo, who were trying to turn Europe and Asia into the darkness."[32]

It was Osgood—who many years later confessed, "I like action"—who took on the day-to-day work from December 1956 to July 1957 that led to the passage of the city ordinance creating the CEEO; seven years later, Shelley, a Democrat, appointed the Republican Osgood as the first chairman of the HRC. In the campaign leading to the passage of the CEEO, Osgood and his co-chairmen reached out beyond the black and white residents to recruit leaders from the growing number of Japanese, Chinese, Hispanic, and Filipino residents, including Colonel Narcisco L. Manzano, one of the commanders of the Philippine Scouts who had fought with General Douglas MacArthur. Advocates like Manzano, Masao Satow of the Japanese American Citizens League, Father Joseph Munier, and Marguerite Henning of the National Council of Catholic Women called for the fair employment legislation with an appeal that mixed moral absolutism with national patriotism and the need to maintain San Francisco's reputation. Osgood lectured the Board of Supervisors that the city's good name was endangered because, by refusing to pass a fair employment law, it was falling behind the eleven cities that had enacted such laws since Minneapolis led the way in 1947. Representatives of the New York State Chamber of Commerce and Boston Chamber of Commerce and "dozens of similar testimonials" testified that "such laws are not only effective, but do not impose a hardship on *any* segment of the population." Fair employment was a moral absolute and a patriotic necessity, he said, because "in America our concern for the protection of human rights does not depend upon the exact extent of violations at any given time." The nation could not ignore its commitment to "a man's right simply to compete for a job on the basis of his ability to perform [and] such a policy is vital to the general community welfare as well as to the minority groups who are victimized in its absence." Because "San Francisco and California are far behind the progressive areas of our country," he said, "establishment of the fair employment ordinance was necessary to restore "the true spirit of San Francisco. . . . The moral, patriotic, and even international implications of this issue cry out for attention."[33]

The debate leading up to the passage of the law laid bare differences among San Franciscans over how to define the public interest, specifically disagreements about how to interpret the meaning of liberty and freedom in relation to economic opportunity. The advocates of civil rights in business and labor who supported the proposed reforms were on a collision course with business and labor *opponents* who regarded their institutions' freedom to operate independently of government oversight as threatened by fair employment legislation. Supporters of the legislation agreed with the principle, as described by Osgood, that "human rights . . . are supposed to be vested *in each individual*" and such rights are only "clothed with reality by virtue of the fact that the individual usually has some channel of recourse open to him in the event of violation." Adrien Falk, representing a coalition of eight business organizations, and Frank Foisie, representing the Federated Employers (formerly the San Francisco Employers Council) insisted that the city should use "a positive voluntary program of education and persuasion" to combat "intolerance and inequity in employment," because legislation would produce "injustice and disturbance to business and to civic harmony." George Johns disagreed and pledged the San Francisco Labor Council to a "strong" fair employment practices ordinance, mindful at the same time that several of the council's member unions representing workers in the building trades opposed the measure. The *Sun-Reporter* agreed that some unions were dragging their feet but claimed they "could not by any stretch of imagination be deemed as representative of the general laboring class." Falk and Foisie were in no mood to excuse racial discrimination in labor unions, and they condemned what they regarded as a tendency by the public to make business "the scapegoat" when, in their view, blame should also be laid on "the closed union that bars minority workers." They criticized the civil rights front for having failed to acknowledge and attack the issue of racial discrimination by labor unions. When Falk raised the issue explicitly, he admitted that it was a delicate matter because employers could not "expose such unions," given the reality that "they must live with these unions daily and the successful conduct of their businesses is dependent on maintaining harmonious relations with them." However, it was time for civil rights reformers to "promote remedial labor legislation with the same fervor with which they [were] backing this ordinance. Surely, employers have no monopoly on 'passing the buck.'"[34]

On May 20, 1957, the Board of Supervisors passed the fair employment ordinance after an impassioned speech by Supervisor J. Eugene McAteer. Like Congressman Jack Shelley, Bishop Hugh Donohoe, and Father Joseph Munier, the forty-one-year-old McAteer was a native son of San Francisco's Catholic Mission District. After graduating from Mission High School, he attended UC Berkeley and was an "All American" captain of its football team. After rising to the rank of lieutenant-commander in the wartime Navy, McAteer and a partner opened a popular restaurant on Fisherman's Wharf, and McAteer won election to the Board of Supervisors in November 1953. His bravery during the war had earned him decorations from the U.S. Navy, and his prowess as a handball player at the Olympic Club brought tournament trophies to the club. His speech mixed patriotism with civic pride and a blunt reference to his faith-based decision, arrived at after "wrestling with my conscience." He explained that "in the eyes of the Lord," the Filipino Scout, the black infantryman, and the Ute Indian who died for their country were all "of equal quality and dignity."

"We should now provide our peacetime citizens an equal chance to get a 'shot' at employment without reference to his skin pigmentation!" The ordinance passed in a seven-to-four vote, but Osgood and other proponents then found themselves facing the prospect of a business-led grassroots movement to repeal it via a referendum vote in the November election. To forestall the possibility of an expensive and potentially divisive and polarizing campaign, Osgood and Foisie petitioned the supervisors to delay a final vote and revised the ordinance to reflect Foisie's and Falk's criticisms. The Board of Supervisors passed the revised ordinance on July 10, to become effective on August 9, 1957. During the two years that it operated before the state agency subsumed its work in late 1959, eighty complaints were filed with the city's CEEO, and all but five complained about racial discrimination. Seventy-two of the eighty complaints were against employers, six were against unions, and the balance were against employment agencies. Of the workers who brought complaints, 43 percent held sales and clerical positions; 37.5 percent held skilled, semi-skilled, or unskilled jobs; and almost 10 percent were taxi drivers. Refusal to hire and unlawful discharge were the cause of action in sixty-seven of the cases, and seven were based on denial of union membership. Of the seventy-two complaints against employers, thirty-six were dismissed, and twenty-six were adjusted satisfactorily, compared with ten complaints against labor unions, eight of which were dismissed and the remaining two settled in a satisfactory way. In its final report in September 1960, the commission described how in one of those cases it had succeeded in working with a local union to admit the first African American member. At the same time, behind the scenes, to establish "a personal relationship based on mutual friendship, trust and understanding that could prove most helpful and constructive in the future," George Johns had begun meeting privately at his home with Carleton Goodlett of the *Sun-Reporter*; Joseph Kennedy, who had become the president of the NAACP branch; Art Bradford of the National Urban League; and Richard Bancroft, who chaired the NAACP's labor committee.[35]

By 1959, when George Johns began his efforts to develop "trust and understanding" through personal relationships with leaders of the African American civil rights front, the Labor Council was a joint AFL-CIO organization. The dockworkers and warehouse workers and the teamsters were independent of the Labor Council but frequently cooperated in community affairs. This was the case with the sponsoring of the Town Meeting by Earl Raab's Bay Area Human Relations Clearing House on December 10, 1959, at the Nourse Auditorium, with Mayor George Christopher serving as honorary chairman. Similarly, the Labor Council and the independent organizations contributed to a rally for Martin Luther King Jr. on August 8, 1961, organized by Reverend Hamilton Boswell of Jones Memorial Methodist Church. The NAACP and the National

Urban League welcomed such efforts, but they eventually concluded that more aggressive tactics—similar to the ones being used in the Southern campaigns—might yield more "progress in substance." Some progress was evident, to be sure, with black applicants beginning to be hired, and becoming union members, in various hotel jobs; in restaurants; as milk, bread, and soft-drink delivery drivers; and as bartenders at prestigious hotels and the San Francisco airport. But the Yellow Cab Company agreed to hire African American drivers only after a two-year boycott by the NAACP; attempts by the Urban League to place black applicants in apprenticeship programs had yielded "negligible" results. And despite what the NAACP described as its "relentless campaign," the seamen's union was still segregated, as were several unions in the building trades. Thomas Fleming singled out the city's Chamber of Commerce for particular scorn because of its claim that "San Francisco is the most tolerant of all American cities." In fact, Fleming asserted, "Jim Crow is as bad here as in any of the large American cities."[36]

Fleming often used exaggeration to make a point in his columns, and while this particular comparison went wide of the mark, it demonstrated the existence of a particular tactical use of rhetoric that would become more prevalent in the debate over fair employment in San Francisco during the years of the Kennedy and Johnson presidencies. Fleming was not alone in criticizing the Chamber of Commerce, singling out its alleged myth-making while refusing to make substantive contributions to racial justice. By mid-1963, George Johns was smarting from a growing litany of complaints from the civil rights front and from the press and employers about unions in the Labor Council's membership who were still balking at opening their membership to non-white applicants. In his official capacity as head of the Labor Council, Johns defended labor by accusing the Chamber of Commerce of deliberately increasing "Negro Unemployment" by orchestrating the elimination of "half of our production jobs." "We've seen two hundred warehouses close each year. These were places where workers with limited skills or training could be dispatched for jobs. The powers that be decided San Francisco should change its characteristics. It should be a city of business, distribution, finances, entertainment and conventions. And in this planned change, spearheaded by our Chamber of Commerce, a great number of simple production jobs went down the drain."[37]

Johns noted that the civil rights leadership had "recently been using the term 'power structure.' This is something to think about." In the summer of 1963, the repressive actions of Public Safety Commissioner Bull Connor in Birmingham and their reverberations in San Francisco were influencing the debate over employment discrimination much in the same way that they had influenced the debate over racial equality in the public schools, but with a twist. The long historical conflict of interest and struggle for power between organized business and organized labor was kept simmering by the fight over the Taft-Hartley bill in 1947 and the Proposition 18 battle in 1958. The conflict was now revived again, with business demanding that racist labor unions share the blame for discrimination in employment and labor responding that a greed-driven conspiracy by business had destroyed tens of thousands of job opportunities for non-whites. Mayor Christopher's call for a new brace of committees to meet, study, and report on human relations was interpreted by both the Labor Council and the new United San Francisco Freedom Movement as an affront to their dignity. The Labor Council refused to be shunted into a committee with civil rights and religious leaders, while business and professional leaders met in a separate group, and government leaders met in another. Johns reported to his membership that "neither personally nor on behalf of the labor movement, do we intend to be segregated by any politician." Wilfred Ussery told the *Sun-Reporter* that Christopher's proposal was "paternalistic" and refused to participate. The polarization that would increasingly mark employment discrimination politics was foreshadowed when Thomas N. Burbridge, chairman of the USFFM, asked to meet with the Labor Council and the West Coast Conference of Teamsters. He was issued an invitation and then declined to show up for the meeting.[38]

Eleven months after Burbridge failed to show up for his meeting with the labor organizations, Judge David French sentenced him to ninety days in the San Francisco County Jail for sitting in at the Cadillac showroom on Van Ness Avenue on April 11, 1964. Burbridge was one of more than 500 people who were arrested during the series of CORE, NAACP, and USFFM demonstrations that created a "climate of conflict" in the city in the winter and spring of 1963–1964. The marches and sit-ins took place despite the communitywide discussions organized by Mayor Christopher's human relations coordinator, James P. Mitchell. Now senior vice-president of San Francisco's Crown-Zellerbach Corporation, Mitchell had served seven years as President Eisenhower's secretary of labor. He had endeared himself to civil rights advocates by scolding Governor Orval Faubus for trying to stop the racial integration of Central High School in Little Rock, Arkansas, in 1957 and was known as "the social conscience of the Republican Party." On January 4, 1964, Mitchell presented outgoing Mayor Christopher with a "Human Relations Program," which was needed because "San Francisco, like all American cities, is caught up in the resolution of Negroes to achieve their legitimate and undeniable goals of integration and equality in American life." Four days later, John F. Shelley became the mayor of San Francisco, and Mitchell worked with the Interim Committee on Human Relations, appointed by Shelley, to implement the recommendations of his report. The committee, with Earl Raab effectively in charge, defined its task as deciding "what affirmative actions can be taken cooperatively by the various sectors of our community to provide realistic opportunities for the full-scale economic integration of minorities."[39]

On July 13, the same day that Burbridge received his jail sentence for trespassing, failure to disperse, and unlawful assembly at the Cadillac showroom, the Board of Supervisors unanimously voted to establish the San Francisco HRC recommended by Shelley's interim committee. Clothed with powers beyond that of the CEEO to monitor discrimination in housing as well as employment, the new fifteen-member commission wielded the power to subpoena witnesses and their records. The HRC began operation with Edgar Osgood as chairman and a membership that included leading veterans from the civil rights campaigns, including Earl Raab and Rabbi Alvin Fine, Sister Maureen Kelly, and Zuretti Goosby of the NAACP. Mayor Shelley, who in 1942 had urged labor unions in San Francisco to rid themselves of racial discrimination, received a forthright "recommendation" from his new agency:

> We recommend that all unions in our city examine their entrance requirements and apprenticeship programs to bring them in line with the AFL-CIO objective of non-discrimination. Unions hold the key to open the doors to many jobs. Some have done an acceptable and others an excellent job of holding the doors open to all. Others have a long history of discrimination and today find themselves trapped in this situation: with a limited number of jobs available, the white members of a predominantly white union will fight tenaciously to preserve their seniority rights to jobs by keeping the door closed to non-whites. For their own health and that of the community, this situation must be changed.

As the HRC began its work in late 1964, it opened a new chapter in San Francisco's long history of contests over how to define the public interest, partly because "affirmative action" as Earl Raab later recalled, "was in our consciousness from the beginning" and partly because, as he wrote in a report to Mayor Shelly in 1964, the commission's attention would be "drawn mainly to the problems of Negroes, [but] it is mindful that the other two large minority groups must also be included in affirmative programs."[40]

10

"Land Values, Human Values, and the City's Treasured Appearance"

The Freeway Revolt

I n January 1959, neighborhood preservationists and land use reformers convinced the San Francisco Board of Supervisors to rescind its approval of seven of nine freeways scheduled for construction by the state highway department.[1] Extensive consultation then took place involving the supervisors, city planners, design consultants, landscape architects, and state engineers. In 1966, after having rejected a plan to run a new freeway through the so-called Panhandle part of Golden Gate Park two years earlier, the board met again, this time to consider both a second revised Panhandle freeway and a redesigned Golden Gate Freeway. The Panhandle Freeway would have run through part of Golden Gate Park; it would also have displaced hundreds of residents, many of them African American, in the city's Western Addition. The Golden Gate Freeway would have cut through part of the Fisherman's Wharf area and run alongside the city yacht harbor in the Marina District. The new plans included major changes in design and landscaping meant to reduce housing displacement, improve aesthetic quality, and lessen environmental damage. The Board of Supervisors rejected both of the new plans, leading the U.S. Bureau of Public Roads to withdraw funding for any additional interstate highways in the city and county of San Francisco.[2]

The vote in 1966 dismayed Mayor John F. Shelley, as well as Governor Edmund G. Brown, who had both urged supervisors to approve the new plans. Brown and Shelley regarded the redesigned crosstown freeways as necessary for the future progress of the city in the region and fully compatible with their city's special peninsular character (both were native San Franciscans). The mayor maintained his sense of humor, remarking, "There will be a freeway on the moon before we get one in San Francisco." Governor Brown, however, made no secret of his disappointment and declared, "I can't think of anything that's happened in San Francisco or California that I regret more than the failure of the Board of Supervisors to come up with a plan to move traffic in and out of San Francisco."[3]

Two years later, the city had a new mayor. Joseph L. Alioto, a former member of San Francisco Redevelopment Agency who, like Shelley and Brown, was a city native and shared with them their enthusiasm for downtown development and economic growth. At the same time, the new mayor regarded freeways as a desecration of San Francisco's landscape, and he was on record as having demanded the demolition of the Embarcadero Freeway. In May 1968, he declared victory in another freeway fight. The city had won its five-year battle with the state over the routing of a four-mile section of the Junipero Serra Freeway (Interstate Highway 280) that ran through city-owned watershed land in San Mateo County. The engineers insisted on putting the freeway on the shoreline of Crystal Springs Reservoir. The city wanted to avoid water pollution and preserve the shoreline area for recreational use, and it enlisted federal assistance on its behalf and forced the state to move the highway one mile east along a ridge overlooking the reservoir.[4]

By end of the 1960s, journalists routinely characterized the city's refusal to cooperate with state highway engineers as "the San Francisco freeway revolt." In addition to its hills and views and reputation as "the city that knows how," San Francisco now could boast of having won the first victory in what *Business Week* magazine in 1967 called "The War over Urban Expressways."[5] For twenty-five years, freeway building occupied an important place in urban policy considerations in San Francisco. In their debates over how to accommodate the automobile age and preserve the city's amenities, San Franciscans expressed their determination to exert local control over air and water quality, neighborhood integrity, safe and healthy housing, the physical beauty of the landscape, and unique and historic features of the built environment, as well as land use decisions that affected property values, the local tax base, and business opportunities. On August 26, 1963, the Board of Supervisors passed a resolution declaring that all future transportation plans had to be compatible with the preservation of "land values, human values, and the preservation of the city's treasured appearance."[6] A genuine grassroots movement played a key role in the success of the freeway revolt, as did well-placed individuals of the social, political, and economic elite and both private and public policymaking institutions. Opponents of the freeway revolt played a role in the story, as did the reformers themselves, and so did individual activists inside and outside government, existing and newly formed interest groups, partisan politics, and intergovernmental relations.[7] This chapter begins with an account of events in the 1940s that prefigured later freeway politics. It then describes the events that led to the vote in 1956 against the Western Freeway that began the "freeway revolt," the rejection of the seven proposed routes in 1959, the final dismissal of the redesigned Panhandle and Golden Gate freeway plans, and the successful campaign to relocate the Junipero Serra freeway.

A sense of urgency concerning transportation planning developed during the late 1930s, when the opening of the Golden Gate and San Francisco–Oakland Bay bridges in 1936–1937 created new highway connections between the city and Marin and Alameda counties. In addition, the gradual increase in population and industry on the peninsula stimulated increased highway traffic between the city and San Mateo County. State highway engineers worked on plans for new highway connections. City supervisors and bureaucrats in the city's public works and public utilities departments vied with one another over whose office should exercise how much authority over the new routes, and activists from the city's nongovernmental planning agencies offered advice to both city and state officials.[8]

World War II produced an economic boom and a population influx that, in turn, generated a crisis atmosphere surrounding discussion of transportation. The war created increased pressures on the city's already troubled Market Street and Municipal Railway (MUNI) transit systems (the two were merged under MUNI's auspices in 1944). The war also intensified the commitment among private and public activists to improve streets and boulevards within the city, build better highway connections between the city and the region, and create an efficient balance between highway building and transit modernization and expansion.[9]

A controversy in 1942 over highway planning foreshadowed the conflicts that became evident as a regular feature of freeway politics after the war. Disagreements among members of the Board of Supervisors led to the cancellation of transportation consulting contracts with the state highway engineer Charles H. Purcell and with the firm of Madigan-Hyland. The Chamber of Commerce originally suggested that the board hire Purcell, a nationally eminent transportation planner, but when board members expressed concerns about possible conflict of interest, the proposal was rejected. Mayor Angelo Rossi then met with Robert Moses in New York City to seek his advice about who should be hired instead of Purcell, and Moses recommended the New York firm of Madigan-Hyland. However, criticism of bringing in an "outside" firm led the divided Board of Supervisors to reject that contract, as well, leading to a stalemate.[10]

Several months later, another private organization, the San Francisco Planning and Housing Association, its work supported by the Junior Chamber of Commerce and private philanthropists, called for action on transportation when it published the pamphlet "Now Is the Time to Plan: First Steps to a

Master Plan for San Francisco." The widely distributed pamphlet asked residents, "Why Must San Francisco Plan?" answering, "Land values are wrong . . . people are moving to the suburbs" and "Areas in the city which lose to the suburbs decay and go to seed—these are the *blighted areas* which must be replanned and rebuilt and bring the suburbs back to the city." Transportation planning occupied a central place in the association's analysis: "The automobile has created problems which force us to re-shape our city," the pamphlet stated, and citizens were advised to "increase the value of SAN FRANCISCO and your section of it, by a comprehensive MASTER PLAN."[11]

In November 1943, Roger Dearborn Lapham, a Yale graduate who had led the waterfront employers during the strike of 1934, won election to the Mayor's Office. A business-sponsored candidate who promised to assume active leadership of a program of infrastructure and public works planning, Lapham appointed the Citizens Postwar Planning Committee in April 1945. This voluntary organization functioned as a quasi-public body and in October it presented a prioritized list of public works projects, including highways, as well as a plan for financing their implementation. Lapham also presided over the preparation of San Francisco's first formal planning document, a project that was part of the program of his fellow Republican, Governor Earl Warren, who used his office to facilitate the creation of local planning agencies throughout California.[12]

Lapham's predecessor, Angelo Rossi, hired San Francisco's first planning director, L. Deming Tilton, in 1942. Tilton set to work preparing the city's first master plan. The plan appeared in December 1945, and it included recommendations for crosstown freeways that originated with State of California's highway engineers.[13] The director of planning and the state highway engineers disagreed almost immediately over how to implement several key elements in plans for the city's first freeway. Commenting on the state's proposed extension of the Bayshore Freeway in April 1945, Tilton put into play a point of view that would recur throughout the debates during the twenty years to come. A freeway, he warned, "is a device which can make or break the city. It can liberate or contribute to congestion. It can cut the city into unrelated parts, or bind it together. It can destroy values, or create new ones. The State cannot soundly develop its urban freeway plans without attention to the planning problems of the city itself." Tilton criticized the state for a narrow approach that considered merely "the assembly and interpretation of traffic data" and the "engineering problem of designing bridges and tunnels" and practice of making plans "without adequate consideration of local problems and without reference to local planning bodies." Tilton emphasized the need "to plan future improvements which will bring maximum benefits to the business interests *and* people" and insisted that "this first freeway ought . . . to be definitely related to the city's plans for *mass transportation* as well as for the movement of private vehicles. Failure to provide for transit service on the Freeway will result in an unmanageable deluge of private automobiles in the already congested areas of the city."[14]

Tilton underscored three broad issues in his statement and in an article published in *American City* in 1946. First, he insisted on local input in state planning. Second, he stressed the importance of serving business interests in a fashion that would jeopardize neither the property values of neighborhood residents nor the aesthetic values of the community. Third, he urged the city to face squarely the challenge of combining freeway building with transit expansion. "Freeways," he said, "must be designed and built to carry transit vehicles." Tilton's personal influence was limited by his brief tenure as the city's planner (he left in 1946), but the issues he identified soon generated debate beyond the confines of planners and politicians. The policymaking process became more complex after 1945, as the state moved to implement freeway plans contained in the master plan and the more detailed transportation plan of 1948, which both the city and the state adopted as the "Trafficways Plan" in 1951. New plans, the product of reappraisal and redesign prompted by testimony at public hearings, media criticism, and discussions within and among the branches of city government, were produced in 1955, 1960, 1964, and 1966. The Bayshore Freeway, the Southern Freeway, and parts of the Central and Embarcadero freeways were constructed. The Western Freeway and six others were never built.[15]

The complex character of the policy implementation process derived from divisions over several sets of issues that developed as the city, the state, and the federal government moved beyond planning into selecting and constructing routes. During the late 1940s and early 1950s, divisions appeared over the basic question of the extent to which automobiles and trucks constituted a promise to San Francisco and to what extent they posed a threat. Questions developed about the extent to which freeways might address the transportation needs of intercity travelers to and from other Bay Area communities while at the same time worsening the problems of city residents. Discussions that began in 1945 over the optimal mix of freeway and modes of mass transit intensified in the following decade as planning for the Bay Area Rapid Transit, or BART, system proceeded. Disagreements developed between the city and the state about where freeways should be located on city land and about the nature and extent of the city's participation in and control over such decisions. Differences about freeway planning policy based on disciplinary perspectives and professional career practice manifested themselves among the planners and engineers on the city payroll and between city and state personnel. In addition, alignments among city interest groups multiplied as competing and potentially polarizing sets of priorities became apparent that were based on aesthetic and preservationist considerations, questions of neighborhood integrity, a desire to preserve residential property values, and a determination to enhance commercial and retail income-generating potential.[16]

San Francisco's city planner during the mid-1950s, Paul Oppermann, urged business to "take leadership, that City Hall will follow."[17] Business and labor leaders stressed the need for the city to maintain as much of its traditional domination of commercial and retailing activities in the Bay Area as possible. They regarded freeway construction as a source of livelihood for unionized workers and completed freeways as a vital means for the kind of intercity auto and truck movement that would allow San Francisco to compete more effectively with regional rivals in an increasingly dispersed metropolitan economy. Citywide business organizations and the labor movement displayed considerable solidarity with state highway engineers. They urged city officials to move ahead with construction of the system of freeways planned by the State of California and approved by the Board of Supervisors in 1944 and codified in the master plan of 1945 and the Trafficways Plan of 1951. The AFL-CIO County Labor Council, the San Francisco Chamber of Commerce, and the Downtown Association asked its members to speak with a single voice in support of the planned freeways.[18]

When differences did develop among business and labor interests during the 1950s, they reflected the tensions that existed as the regional economy shifted toward the service-oriented economy of the future and away from the city's commercial and manufacturing past. Those who emphasized the future growth of tourism regarded massive freeways as incompatible with the preservation of the kind of old-fashioned ambience that would attract the maximum number of convention-goers and recreational tourists to San Francisco. A telling instance of this point of view occurred when Charles Blyth, one of the founders of a nongovernmental planning agency called the Blyth-Zellerbach Committee, telephoned his friend George Christopher a few days after he had taken office as mayor in January 1956. Blyth asked Mayor Christopher to find a way to limit the damage that the Embarcadero Freeway—particularly the section that ran in front of the Ferry Building—might do to the future growth of tourism and to office development along the waterfront. The mayor met with Blyth, other business leaders, and the editor of the *San Francisco Chronicle* and agreed to seek an alternative to the two-level concrete structure. Christopher insisted at the time, and has insisted since, that he would rather have seen the proposed Ferry Building Park at the foot of Market Street than the freeway, but he eventually abandoned the effort. He could not put together a financial plan to pay the additional construction costs needed to replace the state's elevated highway with an underground boulevard below the surface.[19]

Organized business and the labor movement cooperated in endorsing the importance of completing the state's system of freeways as incorporated in the city's master plan. However, the freeway revolt was more than a simple two-sided conflict, with downtown business leaders, joined by labor bureaucrats and government officials, on one side arrayed against a coalition of neighborhood people and environmentalists on the other.[20] Newspapers in San Francisco also played an important role in the freeway revolt, for as the state's plans moved to the implementation stage, articles and editorials on the subject increased in volume, and the nature of coverage changed markedly. Prior to the mid-1950s, a note of technological triumph pervaded media coverage. From then on, however, the press, television, and radio began to air doubts about the high social and cultural costs of crosstown freeways and raised questions about the wisdom and judgment of the state highway engineers and their allies in the city.

The *San Francisco Chronicle* played a particularly important role in the freeway revolt after its executive editor, Scott Newhall, decided that any additional freeways would add to the already considerable damage to the Bay Area's unique character caused by demographic and social changes since World War II. Newhall, a maverick descendant of one of the state's wealthiest nineteenth-century land developers, operated according to the philosophy: "The editorial page was my particular interest and baby."[21] Thirty years after the freeway revolt, he explained: "I didn't want to be Democratic or progressive or communist or anything else. I just wanted to be independent and speak our minds, no matter what."[22] Newhall's friend and sailing companion Karl Kortum directed the Maritime Museum on the northern waterfront, and in the late 1940s he and his father organized local residents and forced state highway engineers to move a planned section of Highway 101 near their Petaluma ranch in Sonoma County. Now Kortum shocked Newhall with photographs he had taken showing the damage done to the city of Seattle by the intrusive character of its recently completed waterfront freeway.[23]

The *Chronicle*'s anti-freeway position had the extra benefit of allowing Newhall to claim moral superiority over the rival morning paper, the Hearst family's *San Francisco Examiner.* The Hearst paper presented itself as the voice of reason on the subject of freeways, arguing that the automobile was here to stay; freeways were necessary; and the city ought to be choosing the best design rather than calling for a stop to their construction. One of Newhall's goals as executive editor, he later explained, was "to supplant the *Examiner* as the basic Number One influence on the political life, social life of San Francisco."[24] Newhall succeeded in winning the circulation war, expanding his paper's circulation beyond his fondest hopes, and the two papers eventually signed a joint operating agreement, with the *Examiner* publishing an afternoon paper.[25]

In the early 1950s, before Newhall realized that what happened in Seattle could occur in San Francisco, the *Chronicle* had endorsed the state's freeway plans. The paper went as far as to provide front-page space above the fold on

August 9, 1954, for an article written by the engineering staff of the California Division of Highways. Headlined "S.F. Skyways to Ease Traffic, Open Up Vistas," the article praised the new "system of Skyways" because "the beauty which has long been San Francisco's fame will . . . be unfolded to the public entering from all directions." On December 8, 1955, however, the paper used its lead editorial to announce: "Planners Sound Freeway Warning." Readers learned that the urban planner Francis Violich and the architect William Wurster condemned "a headlong rush to concrete" and that even Oppermann, San Francisco's city planner, urged restraint. San Franciscans, the *Chronicle* said, should regard "a blind rush for a freeway, any kind of freeway, right now [as] an expensive, unsightly, and very durable civic blunder for future generations to mourn over." One cartoon typical of the paper's increasingly critical point of view appeared above the caption, "Hold it! Not so fast!" The cartoon showed a determined police officer halting a truck filled with construction workers with picks and shovels and containers of "instant freeway." The truck bore the label, "Willy-Nilly Construction Company," and the Ferry Building stood in the background behind a "Danger—Men at Work" sign.[26]

News stories appeared about divisions within the business community over the details of freeway planning. The columnist Herb Caen condemned freeways because they destroyed the special ambience of his "Baghdad by the Bay." The *Chronicle*'s feature writer Harold Gilliam, who served an extended term as the official "writer in residence" at the U.S. Department of the Interior in 1961, analyzed the potential impact of freeway construction in detailed articles.[27] The paper also took full advantage of the possibilities for caricature presented by the new governor, the Democrat Pat Brown, whom voters sent to Sacramento in early 1959. Brown campaigned on a platform of public works construction that included completion of the state's interstate highway system. To the *Chronicle*, Brown's determination to push expressways through San Francisco made him a traitor to his city. He was lampooned in cartoons as an unfeeling "Sun King," accumulating a reputation as a master builder while allowing his "highwaymen" in the California Highway Commission (CHC) and the Division of Highways to destroy the people's environment.[28]

By the late 1950s, the *Chronicle* was providing detailed reporting on city planning personnel who questioned aspects of the state's highway plans. The paper also covered the activities of several neighborhood organizations that mobilized to protect homes, businesses, and parks as the highway department moved to begin construction of the planned freeways. In its reporting and its editorializing, the *Chronicle* sided with the growing grassroots mass movement, which it characterized favorably as a righteous crusade to defend the city from the depredations of soulless pencil-pushing state bureaucrats.[29]

At about the same time that Newhall joined the cause, media coverage of freeway issues increased generally because of the newsworthy activities of neighborhood associations in the Glen Park, Sunset, Telegraph Hill, and Marina districts. These areas, slated for freeways according to the master plan, now mobilized to exercise more effective control over future land use decisions in the city. The city planner L. Deming Tilton had enunciated this principle eleven years earlier, and a variety of neighborhood associations, individual homeowners, and small-business owners had complained against freeway-related displacement in the late 1940s. Their objections were typically voiced in letters to the editor to local newspapers or to the mayor and the city planners, or they were presented at public hearings convened by the state's highway department. The city's media provided little coverage, and the few editorials that did appear typically sided with the highway builders. Opportunities for widespread opposition to the freeways in the late 1940s were also limited because much of the highway building in those years took place on land previously used for rights of way by the Southern Pacific Railroad. In addition, the number of homes and businesses to be displaced was substantially smaller than would later be the case, and the individuals and organizations in the largely blue-collar districts affected in the late 1940s lacked resources and effective leadership.[30]

The prospects for successful resistance improved between 1955 and 1959. California's legislature revised the Streets and Highways Code to require the Division of Highways to solicit public response to new freeway plans, and in San Francisco, the highway engineers' proposals affected well-to-do parts of the city where hundreds of homes and businesses faced displacement and relocation. Neighborhood organizations and influential business owners and politicians from the Glen Park and Sunset districts generated the interest and resources necessary to create successful grassroots movements at a time that the press and media was becoming more receptive to their cause. The Sunset District campaign involved tens of thousands of residents opposed to the Western Freeway. A property developer and a politician proved particularly influential at this stage of the freeway revolt. The property developer, Christopher McKeon, was a resident of the Sunset District, which would have been bisected by the state's planned Western Freeway. In 1956, he employed direct mailing and house-to-house canvassing to put together the Property Owners' Association of San Francisco, a neighborhood-based anti-freeway organization. He also enlisted the support of Father Harold Collins, a Roman Catholic priest whose parishioners at St. Cecilia's would see their quality of life adversely affected if the Western Freeway were built. McKeon and Collins filled neighborhood auditoriums to standing-room-only conditions for several public meetings in the spring of 1956 to protest the construction of a freeway through the Sunset District.[31]

McKeon and Collins successfully mobilized Sunset District residents determined to protect the city's aesthetic character (and the value of their investments), while the politician, William Blake, went on to provide leadership in the citywide freeway revolt from a position inside city government for a decade. Blake was a millionaire who had originally been appointed to the Board of Supervisors by Mayor Elmer Robinson. As the chairman of the board's Committee on Streets, Blake became an outspoken critic of freeways, and in June 1956 he joined McKeon and Collins and leaders representing other neighborhood organizations in pressuring the board to pass a resolution protesting the construction of the Western Freeway. Mayor Christopher vetoed the resolution, but the board's action encouraged the grassroots anti-freeway sentiment and strengthened the opposition to crosstown freeway construction.[32]

The views of the attorney Joseph L. Alioto, chairman of the San Francisco Redevelopment Agency in October 1956, typified the emerging consensus on behalf of the anti-freeway cause: "For my part, I see no justification for freeways in the center of San Francisco. Any freeways needed should be built near the city's borders."[33] On January 23, 1959, the Board of Supervisors voted unanimously to reject the Western Freeway, along with the six other freeways in the master plan. Adopting the rhetorical style of Patrick Henry defending American virtue against imperial oppression, Blake endorsed the environmentalist position at a meeting packed with spectators who cheered their approval. Board members who had previously supported the state's proposed freeways joined opponents to send a unanimous message of non-cooperation to the freeway builders.[34] Later, in 1967, Blake admitted having taken on the leadership role in the freeway revolt partly because he surmised that "it's good politics to oppose the freeway."[35]

After the board's action in rejecting the seven freeways, Mayor Christopher—drawing on the model provided by Mayor Lapham's Citizens Postwar Planning Committee of 1945—appointed a Citizens Freeway Committee to develop recommendations for future freeway policy. Christopher appointed McKeon to chair the committee. The group met for ten months, then the mayor abruptly ordered them to submit a report describing their progress and to disband.[36] This destroyed the chances that a "blue ribbon" citizens' group might put the freeway program back on track. The committee, bitterly divided, came up with two separate reports. The mayor's dismissal of the committee was a response to an article in the *San Francisco News-Call Bulletin* that accused McKeon of a conflict of interest that called into question his ability to discharge his duties ethically. The article suggested that McKeon would benefit financially by the delays caused by the freeway revolt and by the adoption of a routing plan that he supported for connecting the San Francisco and San Mateo sections of the proposed freeways.[37] If the state could be delayed long enough for McKeon to rezone a piece of land owned by his family's firm (the Zita Corporation) that stood in the path of the Junipero Serra Freeway, he stood to make a substantial profit. McKeon did buy a 375 acre trace in St. Francis Heights for $1 million at about the same time that he organized the Property Owners' Association. Five years later, he completed the rezoning and sold 18.5 acres (the portion required for the interstate highway) to the state for $950,000, a price that reflected the higher valuation.[38]

McKeon was outraged at the accusation that he intended "to maneuver freeway routes for his own business purposes." He flatly denied the charges and filed a $100,000 libel and slander suit against the three members of the committee who, he claimed, had informed the reporter that he had been "dishonest in his duties as chairman and member of the freeway committee." The committee members denied having intended to defame McKeon and hired attorneys to defend themselves, but the case never went to trial. Five years later, McKeon quietly withdrew his suit and paid his court costs and attorney fees, as well as those of the defendants. McKeon went on to serve as a member of the California State Contractors License Board and became a director of the Golden Gate Bridge and Highway District Board, but he never provided further information about the incident. When he died in 1967, he left an estate valued at $6.2 million, including stock in the Zita Corporation amounting to $3.7 million dollars.[39]

McKeon's absence from the leadership of the freeway revolt after the middle of 1960 had little effect on the grassroots movement. The campaign against the Western Freeway in the Sunset District developed a momentum that carried it beyond McKeon's personal inspiration or influence. He could not have generated the high levels of public opposition to the Western Freeway, or turned out the large numbers at public meetings, had it not been for the growing influence and increased militancy of the neighborhood associations. As the city planners and state engineers worked with consultants and the Board of Supervisors on revised plans for interstate expressways in San Francisco, the freeway revolt intensified.[40] The thousands of city residents who signed petitions against freeways, and the hundreds who packed the meetings of the Board of Supervisors, refused to accept even minimal incursion of freeways into the city's Golden Gate Park or additional freeway construction along the waterfront.

The leaders and the grassroots supporters of the movement regarded freeways as absolutely incompatible with the city's geographic, social, cultural, and historic character, and they called for the demolition of those freeways that had already been constructed. In August 1963, the Board of Supervisors established its policy declaring that all future transportation plans in San Francisco had to be compatible with of "land values, human values, and the preservation of the city's treasured appearance."[41] Between 1963 and 1966, using tactics that were also proving successful in the civil rights movement, new leaders emerged who joined William Blake in his campaign, conducted from his position as the chairman of the Streets Committee of the Board of Supervisors, to keep "the concrete monstrosities" out of the city altogether.

In 1964, Sue Bierman, a resident of the neighborhood adjacent to the Panhandle section of Golden Gate Park, mobilized a district association called the Haight-Ashbury Neighborhood Council to convince the supervisors to reject the first revised plans for the Panhandle Freeway. Five years earlier, her husband, Arthur K. Bierman, had organized a group called San Franciscans for Academic Freedom and Education, which had succeeded in mobilizing public opinion to protest against the local hearings of the House Committee on Un-American Activities. Sue Bierman originally became active in environmentalist causes when her neighbor, Dianne Feinstein, recruited her to join a campaign to protect the city's Sutro Forest from future development.[42] Jean Kortum (whose husband, Karl, had convinced Newhall to support the freeway revolt) organized the Freeway Crisis Committee. Using the slogan "Save Our City," Jean Kortum brought all of the separate neighborhood defense groups together in a citywide coalition. The result was the successful campaign in 1966 that stopped the Panhandle and Golden Gate freeways.[43]

Bierman and Kortum were leading figures in the reform faction of the county Democratic Party headed by Phillip Burton, a member of the California State Assembly, who would later become one of the leading voices in the U.S. House of Representatives for using public policy to expand the nation's national parks. John Burton, Phillip's younger brother, worked alongside Kortum on the Freeway Crisis Committee.[44] The campaign against the Panhandle Freeway plan of 1964 operated out of the campaign office of Willie Brown, a protégé of Burton's who had won his first term in the State Assembly during the election of 1964. Brown played an active part in the freeway revolt, pointing out that housing displacement by the Panhandle Freeway would have an especially deleterious effect on the large numbers of African American residents of the Fillmore District.[45]

The anti-freeway leaders and the reform faction in the Democratic Party generated enough grassroots support to cancel out the influence of the city's and the state's Democratic leaders, Mayor Shelly and Governor Brown. The board responded by rejecting state plans for the Panhandle and Golden Gate projects by a narrow six-to-five vote. The board even rejected new studies for alternative routes within the city limits that had been proposed by Supervisor Jack Morrison and by a coalition of business and labor organizations.[46] By the middle of 1966, Mayor Shelley and an angry Governor Brown had resigned themselves to the cancellation of federal funds for interstate highways through San Francisco.

A few months earlier, on January 3, 1966, Mayor Shelley had written to President Lyndon Johnson and to Undersecretary of Commerce for Transportation Alan S. Boyd. He expressed his desire to avoid "becoming pitted against [the State of California] in expensive acrimonious litigation" over the location of a section of a new federal interstate highway linking San Francisco and San Jose. The controversy had arisen because the city and the state preferred different routes for a 4.2 mile section of the Junipero Serra Freeway (I-280) in San Mateo County. Determined to "exhaust this last chance for agreement," Shelley requested federal assistance in settling a dispute over whether to build the freeway along the shore of the Crystal Springs Reservoir or along a ridge one mile east overlooking the reservoir. Either of the proposed routes would have constituted a small portion of a total of fourteen miles of watershed land owned by the City and County of San Francisco that would be granted to the state for highway building. However, the state preferred the shoreline route, while the city wanted the ridge route. Although Mayor Shelley imagined his letter to represent the last chance for settling a dispute that had begun in 1957, in fact he set in motion the last three years of a freeway controversy that was finally concluded by his successor, Joseph Alioto, with a compromise agreement in March 1969.[47]

When President Dwight D. Eisenhower signed the Federal Aid Highway Act on June 29, 1956, the legislation gave responsibility for route selection to state highway departments; cities and towns were expected to cooperate with their state highway engineers. The California Division of Highways received federal aid funds for I-280 in subsequent months and then announced route options and began public hearings on the alternatives in April 1957. Large numbers of residents from the well-to-do communities in the path of the proposed new freeway turned out for the hearings. The engineers presented two proposed routes, requiring the demolition of 500 and 100 homes and businesses, respectively. Both options met overwhelming resistance, and local government officials demanded another location.[48]

One month later, B. W. Booker, the state highway engineer, offered another possible route. This one avoided the built-up parts of San Mateo County (and the need for housing displacement) by running through fourteen miles of watershed land owned by the City and County of San Francisco. James H. Turner, manager of the city's Water Department, immediately criticized the new proposal. Turner objected because part of the route, a 4.2 mile stretch of the freeway running alongside the city's Crystal Springs Reservoir, created a "problem of turbidity (muddy water runoff) and contamination of the San Francisco water supply."[49]

The California Division of Highways compiled engineering data showing that the purity of the water could be protected even if the freeway were built on the edge of the reservoir. Don Fazackerley, a member of the San Francisco

Public Utilities Commission, noted, however, that the highway engineers were "not impressed with our sacred watershed." The Public Utilities Commission did, however, give the state permission to use the fourteen miles of watershed land, but only with the understanding that the city preferred the most easterly route possible above the reservoir in the Crystal Springs section. In January 1958, the Public Utilities Commission formally adopted Resolution 17-825, stating that "as a policy of the Commission to protect the public water supply the proposed Junipero Serra Freeway through the City's watershed property adjacent to San Andreas and Crystal Springs reservoirs in San Mateo County should follow the most easterly route possible on watershed lands."[50] In April 1958, the Board of Supervisors backed the Public Utilities Commission's resolution with a similar policy declaration. Then, three months later, the Public Utilities Commission adopted a revised state route plan for the fourteen miles in the city's watershed, including a four-mile section alongside the Crystal Springs Reservoir. This series of decisions by San Francisco bedeviled the intergovernmental relations important to the I-280 project throughout the next ten years, because the state and the city interpreted them differently. As federal officials discovered nearly a decade later, the CHC and state highway engineers interpreted the revised Public Utilities Commission document to mean they had been given a green light to proceed without further revisions to their route plans. The city officials, however, interpreted the agreement as subject to future revision, and they expected in the course of events to exchange the undesirable shoreline route for the preferred ridge route.[51]

The potential for conflict implicit in the fact that city and state officials interpreted the agreements differently was magnified by the escalation of mutual distrust associated with crosstown freeways within San Francisco. An institutionalized pattern of suspicion and intransigence developed between the city and the state, aggravated at times by partisan rivalry between Democrats and Republicans and by intraparty bickering between representatives of rival Democratic Party factions.

The change of regimes in the San Francisco municipal government that took place after Shelley became mayor in January 1964 also made resolving the differences implicit in the agreements of 1957–1958 more difficult. Shelley was a liberal Democrat who had been a prominent local and state labor leader before becoming a state senator and eight-term congressman. Like his Republican predecessor, George Christopher (served 1956–1963), Shelley was determined to make his mark as a pro-development mayor, but at the same time, he appointed one of the nation's leading conservationists, former Undersecretary of the Interior James K. Carr, as his director of public utilities.[52] While serving under Stewart L. Udall in the U.S. Interior Department, Carr became friends with Harold Gilliam, the *San Francisco Chronicle* writer. Gilliam went to Washington in 1961 at the request of his friend Wallace Stegner, the writer and Stanford University professor. Gilliam helped Udall write the first draft of his book *The Quiet Crisis,* which had been suggested to him by Stegner while Stegner served briefly as an adviser to Udall.[53]

In August 1964, Carr, in his capacity as the city's new general manager of the San Francisco Public Utilities Commission, and his counterpart in San Mateo County met with engineers of the Division of Highways to discuss the Junipero Serra Freeway. The I-280 construction project, which had been proceeding from south to north, was nearing the last phase, from the town of Woodside north to Daly City. Carr requested that the CHC approve the city's long-established, but also long-ignored, policy declaration that the city's water supply would be endangered unless the state used the ridge route for the Crystal Springs Reservoir section of the freeway.[54]

Neither Carr's predecessor in the Public Utilities Commission nor the general manager of the Water Department who served before Shelley's administration had adopted a proactive stance on this dormant issue during the years of Mayor Christopher's administration after the watershed route agreement in 1957. To make matters worse, the staffs of the Public Utilities Commission and the Water Department, lacking instructions or leadership to the contrary, had created their own cooperative working relationships with the state highway engineers for some five years on the assumption that the shoreline route would be constructed. Consequently, and somewhat understandably, the highway department and the CHC reacted to Carr's initiative with a combination of astonished disbelief and extreme annoyance.[55]

Carr's proposal initiated a year-long series of maneuvers by the City of San Francisco, other municipalities on the peninsula, state officials, and consultants hired by the parties to the dispute. The CHC initially rejected the request to reopen the route-selection process, but it did agree to reconsider the provisions for maintaining water purity, given the Public Utilities Commission's newly announced concerns. San Francisco and San Mateo counties persisted in calling for new hearings on the routes on the grounds that the hearings and studies in 1957 and 1958 required updating. However, the governments of Woodside and Daly City reaffirmed their support for the shoreline route. The Peninsula Highway Design Committee, a voluntary association formed during the first hearings process and made up of representatives from Santa Clara County, as well as from San Francisco and San Mateo counties—along with other peninsula cities and Stanford University—also renewed its support for the shoreline route. Leeds, Hill, and Jewett, an engineering consulting firm hired by the Division of Highways, insisted that complete water-purity-protection systems could be built for either route, but that the cost for such a system would be a half-million dollars more for the ridge route. San Francisco's consultant, Professor Rolf

Eliassen of Stanford and of the firm Hall and Metcalf, argued that a comparative analysis of the two systems showed that pollution could only be avoided if the ridge route were chosen. After reviewing the new studies and listening to testimony on water-quality control, the CHC voted five to two in favor of reaffirming the shoreline route. Chairman Thomas F. Stack of the San Francisco Public Utilities Commission reacted to the negative decision by announcing the city's determination to "go to the ridge or go to court."[56]

As it happened, the city went to the White House and to the federal bureaucrats rather than to court, for it was at this point that Mayor Shelley requested mediation from the White House and from the Office of Transportation in the U.S. Department of Commerce. His request generated an invitation to a meeting at the White House on January 13, 1966, with Director of Transportation Alan Boyd.[57] Mayor Shelley, James Carr, and Thomas Stack traveled to Washington, D.C., in the first of what the city's critics on the CHC would later characterize as "airborne caravans."[58] One week after the meeting, Boyd instructed Deputy Undersecretary for Transportation Lowell K. Bridwell to order a thorough study of the central issues in the dispute. In an informal handwritten note to Bridwell, Boyd indicated his sympathy for San Francisco's point of view. Provided that the city would "equalize the cost of construction through agreement on [right-of-way] cost," Boyd wrote, "what valid reasons do Highway people have for objecting to ridge routing?"[59]

Boyd and Bridwell had their answer within two weeks, following a trip to San Francisco by Edward Swick, the director of locations and rights of way at the Bureau of Public Roads. After meeting with all of the state and city representatives who were parties to the dispute and touring the proposed sites, Swick reported that the state was correct in arguing that the shoreline route would be more direct, safer, and cheaper to build. The city, however, was correct in its argument that the ridge route posed less danger to water purity. "There seems little question that the ridge route will give less possibility of contamination to the Crystal Springs Reservoir," he stated, "although the degree of the importance of this element is questioned [by the state highway engineers]." Given the state's questions, Swick examined data maintained by the manager of the Public Utilities Commission's Peninsula Division and concluded that the complex system of ditches and pipes designed by the highway engineers to handle water runoff during and after the construction of the shoreline route "probably have an adequate theoretical design but . . . are so extensive and elaborate that adequate maintenance is not practical." The city took the position that "failure in times of storm is almost certain." Such a storm in fact occurred during Swick's visit, giving him an opportunity for personal evaluation. He agreed with the Public Utilities Peninsula Division manager's evaluation and reported to Bridwell and Boyd that "experience to date in the maintenance of the system at the San Andreas site indicates that he may well be correct."[60]

Swick took care in his report to recommend that the federal Bureau of Public Roads provide neither "assistance [n]or interference" in the resolution of the dispute and urged that "this problem should be worked out between the Division of Highways and the [San Francisco] Public Utilities Commission." If the state and city remained stalemated, then the Bureau of Public Roads, in Swick's estimation, ought to concur with the California Division of Highways and allow the shoreline route to proceed. However, Swick's recommendation posed a dilemma for the federal government, which he outlined explicitly: "Public Roads would be subject properly to criticism if we approve a Division of Highways line and serious pollution does occur which can be related even remotely to the highway location."[61]

Undeterred by Swick's suggestion that they were improperly involving the federal government in a dispute that should be settled by state and city officials, Boyd and Bridwell moved quickly on two fronts. First, they asked the Division of Highways to make an official estimate of the added costs involved in relocating the disputed section of the freeway from the shoreline to the ridge route. Second, they expressed their dissatisfaction that the Public Utilities Commission "was less than fully communicative on the possibilities of offsetting additional costs." Even though they realized that "this may very well be a temporary bargaining position on the part of the [Public Utilities Commission]. . . it is quite important that Jim Carr be made to understand that we cannot be of any assistance in developing the ridge route unless he is willing to give us assistance through free right-of-way."[62]

The Division of Highways took less than a month to prepare a comparative cost analysis that yielded an estimate of a net increase of $6.2 million should the ridge route be chosen. The Public Utilities Commission, however, did not respond favorably to the federal government's insistence on monetary concessions to offset the (now official) cost increases, even though, according to Bridwell, "If we get such assurance, I believe that both the California Highway Department and the Bureau of Public Roads will approve the Ridge Route."[63] Instead, the city attorney announced that a new report by the Federal Water Pollution Control Administration corroborated the city's estimate of the damage that the shoreline route would cause to water quality. Also, the Public Utilities Commission's engineers and the Office of the City Attorney had examined the state highway engineer's cost figures and "reached the contrary conclusion that, if all costs are considered, moving the freeway to the high alternate route would actually result in an overall savings of some $2,190,000 to the Federal Government and to the State."[64]

While it is true that the federal proposal for compromise in March 1966 did not yet have the final approval of state officials, the city attorney's rejection of the proposal on April 26 increased the intransigence of the state highway engineers and the CHC and tested the patience of the federal officials. Matters were made worse by the fact that the city attorney's introduction of the new bargaining position was announced only four weeks after the Board of Supervisors had rejected the joint federal and state proposals to build the Golden Gate and Panhandle freeways through San Francisco.[65]

San Francisco tested the patience of state and federal officials even further when it enlisted the support of the California Department of Public Works, whose Bureau of Sanitary Engineering now announced its preference for the ridge route, and when Mayor Shelley asked Governor Brown to put pressure on the CHC to reconsider its earlier vote rejecting a change in routes.[66] At the governor's behest, the CHC met and agreed to restudy the feasibility of the ridge route. By the beginning of August, however, Bridwell had already given the general manager of the Public Utilities Commission "another ten days" three times. Now he decided that either the city had to back down from its refusal to offset the cost increases for the ridge route or he would instruct the Bureau of Public Roads that it was "free to go ahead in any manner it deems advisable."[67]

During the next several months, events took place outside the circumscribed arena of highway politics that changed the character of the Junipero Serra Freeway fight, shaped the evolution of a settlement between the state and the city during 1967–1968, and led to a victory by the city in early 1969.

The first of those events occurred on October 15, 1966, when the U. S. Congress passed Public Law 89-670 creating the U.S. Department of Transportation. The declaration of policy that accompanied the legislation contained language that was seized on by the San Francisco side in the Junipero Serra Freeway dispute to strengthen the city's position that only the ridge route was acceptable. In a letter to Boyd in his new position as secretary of transportation, Mayor Shelley pointedly referred to two specific provisions of the law—namely, "special effort should be made to preserve the natural beauty" and "public park, recreation area, wildlife and water fowl refuge, or historic sites" were off-limits unless there were no feasible and prudent alternatives."[68]

The advantage that San Francisco hoped to gain from the language of the Department of Transportation Act was compounded by a requirement in the legislative mandate that the secretary of the new department "cooperate and consult with the Secretaries of the Interior, Housing and Urban Development, and Agriculture . . . to maintain or enhance the natural beauty of the lands traversed."[69] During the next several months, Boyd and Bridwell, who had moved up to become the federal highway administrator, heard from all three cabinet officials. While Orville Freeman of the Department of Agriculture excused himself by reason of lack of expertise on the subject of the Junipero Serra Freeway, Stewart Udall of the Department of the Interior strongly supported the San Francisco side and condemned the state officials for taking a "very limited view of costs." Robert Weaver, secretary of the Department of Housing and Urban Development, also supported the San Francisco side, and he urged Boyd to follow his department's example in resolving a similar controversy in Philadelphia by using his offices to firmly move the disputants toward compromise. Boyd soon did exactly that when he called all of the parties to the controversy to a meeting in San Francisco with the federal highway administrator on August 24.[70]

If the establishment of the new federal Department of Transportation raised the hopes of San Francisco and strengthened its resolve not to accept the shoreline route, the election of Governor Ronald Reagan in November 1966 and his appointment of a new state secretary of business and transportation and four new members of the CHC led to the hardening of the state's position in favor of the shoreline route. Although the commission agreed to Boyd's request for another—third, study of alternative routes, Gordon C. Luce, the new state secretary of business and transportation, reminded Boyd that "sole authority" over where to locate the freeway belonged to the CHC "at a regularly called meeting." Luce also made clear his dislike of interference or favoritism by the federal government and declared his and the commission's determination to resist federal pressure when it came time to vote on the final routes.[71]

Although partisan differences aggravated the dispute during 1967–1968, Boyd and Bridwell continued to use their control over federal funds as a reminder to both the state and the city that some compromise was necessary or the money would be withdrawn from California.[72] By the end of 1967, the City of Redwood City, the Sierra Club, the California Society of Professional Engineers, and newspapers and television stations from San Francisco and the peninsula were backing the ridge route. The CHC's third study ended in a mixed conclusion: the shoreline route was superior in highway operation and engineering; the ridge route was a better choice if recreation was considered a high priority. In all other respects, either route would be satisfactory.[73]

In October, the city finally acquiesced to the demand that Boyd had made nearly two years earlier and agreed to grant the entire watershed right of way, including the ridge section, to the state at approximately two-thirds of the previously announced cost. This action led the federal officials to anticipate the signing of a formal agreement between the state and the city in the near future. The CHC took another view, diminished the value of the city's concession, and adopted a new hardline strategy. In its meeting in December 1967, the commission received a new consultant's report that concluded that neither the ridge route nor the shoreline route provided the best access for recreational activities in the watershed lands and recommended consideration of an entirely new route approximately midway between the two. Relations between the state and the city parties, never amicable, now worsened dramatically.[74] When the city's new mayor, Joseph Alioto, took office in January, he immediately demanded that the U.S. Department of Transportation take two actions: require the California Division of Highways to demolish the Embarcadero Freeway in San Francisco and inform the state that the federal share of funds for building I-280 (90%) would be granted to California only if the ridge route was chosen.[75] Demolition of the Embarcadero Freeway had to wait until 1991, after damage caused by the Loma Prieta earthquake of October 17, 1989, rendered the structure unsafe. Resolution of the Junipero Serra Freeway dispute required more than another year. The CHC stalled; diehard members of the commission postured; and the director of the state's Department of Public Works, Samuel B. Nelson, recommended that action be delayed until after the election in November 1968 on the assumption that Boyd and Bridwell would be replaced with Republicans appointed by Richard M. Nixon.[76] On September 12, 1968, Bridwell announced that the State of California would have to return federal funds for the entire I-280 freeway unless the ridge route in the Crystal Springs section was accepted. Predictably, the state side denounced Bridwell's decision as "an unwarranted intervention by Federal officials in a local freeway dispute."[77] Then, in March 1969, the CHC formally voted to accept the ridge route, but only after approving a statement that "the commission . . . is not surrendering, but is agreeing to a compromise." Construction began almost immediately, and the completed stretch of the freeway opened to traffic in September 1973.[78]

The Junipero Serra and San Francisco crosstown freeway controversies, like the disputes over redevelopment, education, and employment, contributed to changing the terms of the debate over how to define the public interest and moved San Francisco in the direction of its post-1960s political culture. Once again, determined citizens' groups insisted on exercising greater control in shaping public policy, and this time they focused on protecting the purity of air and water, preserving natural beauty, and expanding urban outdoor recreational space. The freeway revolt involved differences in opinion among officials of the local, state, and federal governments and a variety of expert consultants and organized interest groups; partisan politics complicated the proceedings and hindered compromise. The freeway revolts that occurred elsewhere in the nation after the actions of the Board of Supervisors in 1959 proceeded according to patterns that, in many respects, were similar to San Francisco's experience. However, in contrast to many other controversies over route location and displacement—particularly those in Baltimore, Boston, Philadelphia, Miami, Birmingham, and New Orleans—issues of race and ethnicity played a relatively minor role in the San Francisco freeway revolt.[79]

The San Francisco freeway revolt also demonstrated the evolution of the political process by which citizens' groups forced elected and appointed public officials to build a new set of values into the content of public policy.[80] In the crosstown freeway revolt, grassroots citizens' groups developed a new and powerful ability to shape the exercise of federal and state power. Grassroots activism sparked the Junipero Serra dispute, but its resolution demonstrated the power of the experts and the officials who decided what weight should be assigned to competing location criteria. In the controversy over relocating the Junipero Serra Freeway, federal officials used administrative and legislative authority to force a compromise between state and local government officials. In both cases, individuals and groups inside and outside government successfully used politics to build what today would be called environmentalist values into the substance of public policy decisions affecting the everyday lives of millions of Americans.

11

"I Came Out of the New Deal"

Redefining the Public Interest,
1967–1980

When Joseph Alioto took the oath of office to become San Francisco's thirty-sixth mayor on January 8, 1968, nearly twenty years had passed since the San Francisco Communist Party urged its members to take the Catholic threat to their cause more seriously. In the spring of 1948, frustrated by its inability to limit Catholic political power in local elections and in the labor movement, the party's county committee commissioned the research report "Catholicism in San Francisco." The eight-page, single-spaced report went out to all party members, along with a recommendation for "our people [to] read LENIN ON RELIGION." It stated, "We Communists have been negligent in taking this factor into consideration, and while there has been a token recognition of the importance of Catholicism in our community, we have not given it the attention it merits." Party activists discussed the report at neighborhood branch meetings and then at a day-long conference in September. As they prepared for the elections in 1948, San Francisco communists did so with the understanding that "Catholicism has a broad mass appeal which has been carefully fostered over the centuries"; that "Catholic Action is a world wide movement"; and that "the Church through Catholic Action is out to reclaim its lost worlds."[1]

By the end of the 1960s, communism appealed to few San Franciscans, but the laying of the cornerstone for the new Cathedral of St. Mary of the Assumption on December 13, 1967, suggested that Catholicism was thriving. The veterans of the Catholic Action crusade of the 1930s and 1940s could be forgiven for imagining that the election of Joseph Alioto the previous month signaled a San Francisco expression of the renewal of Catholic vitality that many associated with the Vatican II reforms in Rome. The young seminarians who urged the city's churches and synagogues to intensify their efforts on behalf of racial equality expressed confidence that "the actions of our newly-elected mayor, Joseph Alioto, are reason to hope for a vigorous and intelligent leadership."[2] In fact, neither the former crusaders nor the future priests anticipated the force of the social and cultural changes that were under way and that would continue to challenge Catholic San Francisco through the 1970s. During his eight years as mayor, Alioto drew on the Catholic-influenced liberalism that had informed his public life since the 1930s, only to meet resistance from critics dedicated to the robust secularism and radical individualism of irreligious liberals, New Left activists, counterculture celebrants, and Black Power and Third World Liberation ethnic/racial nationalists.

A native son who grew up in the Italian American North Beach neighborhood of San Francisco, Alioto was the only boy of four children in the family of Giuseppe Alioto, a fish wholesaler and proprietor of the International Fish Company, and Domenica Lazio Alioto, a homemaker. Joseph and his sisters, Angelina, Stephanie, and Antoinette, learned Italian as their first language, speaking it at home before they started school. Alioto began his education at the neighborhood public school, then transferred to Saints Peter and Paul Elementary School, a Catholic private school operated by the Salesians, an Italian order of Catholic priests. He graduated from Sacred Heart High School in 1933 and received his bachelor's degree magna cum laude from Saint Mary's College in Moraga, California, in 1937. A leader in school affairs in high school and college and valedictorian of his class at Saint Mary's, Alioto excelled in debate and public speaking. A scholarship to the School of Law at Catholic University of America took him to Washington, D.C., where he received his bachelor of laws degree in 1940.[3]

After working as an intern at the prestigious Brobeck, Pfleger, and Harrison law firm in San Francisco, Alioto served in Washington, D.C., as a special assistant in the Antitrust Division of the U.S. Department of Justice. He and Angelina Genaro, the daughter of a wholesaler and distributor in Dallas, were married on June 2, 1941. During World War II, Alioto went to work for the Board of Economic Warfare. He returned to San Francisco after the war, started a family that eventually comprised five boys and one girl, and opened a law practice specializing in private antitrust suits. In 1948, he represented the Society of Independent Motion Picture Producers, an organization established by Walt Disney, David O. Selznick, and Samuel Goldwyn, in a suit against United Detroit Theatres Corporation, a firm controlled by Paramount Pictures. In 1951, he represented Samuel Goldwyn separately in a suit against the West Coast operation of Twentieth Century Fox. The case was settled in Goldwyn's favor, with $1.9 million in damages awarded to him in 1961. Alioto's successes in defending the Hollywood moguls in antitrust actions brought against their studios and in other cases during the late 1940s and 1950s brought him financial security, professional respect, and national recognition. In 1959, he became general manager of the California Rice Growers Association, moving to the presidency of the organization in 1964. He successfully expanded its sales, particularly across the Pacific, and modernized production methods and transportation techniques.

When asked to describe his philosophy of government several years after he retired from public office, Alioto replied, "I came out of the New Deal." Indeed, a review of the highlights of his political career from the 1940s to 1967 reads like a textbook sidebar illustrating the pursuit of the "Vital Center" Democratic Party liberalism that attracted Catholic and non-Catholic activists in American big-city politics during the postwar period. From 1948 to 1954, Alioto served as a member and as president of the Board of Education; he then he chaired the San Francisco Redevelopment Agency from 1955 to 1959. During his term with the Redevelopment Agency, Alioto, a Democrat, embroiled himself in highly publicized differences over the details of land use policy with the Republican Mayor George Christopher. Yet Christopher and Alioto agreed on the basics of urban renewal and redevelopment. When Christopher ran for a second term in 1959, Alioto served as his campaign co-chairman along with the Republican stalwart Walter A. Haas Sr., and when Christopher's dairy business faced complaints of unfair practices in 1961, Alioto successfully represented him in court.[4]

When Alioto referred to the New Deal as the source of his inspiration in 1989, he also explicitly referred to the Catholic character of his New Deal philosophy. He explained that his public philosophy derived from his service as an administrative assistant to Monsignor Francis J. Haas when Haas served in the U.S. Department of Labor and then the Fair Employment Practices Commission. The influence of Catholic social justice theory is therefore evident in Alioto's own testimony concerning the principles that guided his public career, and his testimony takes on greater significance when considered in the context of San Francisco Catholicism. Alioto developed the moral agenda that energized his political career in San Francisco's Catholic Action campaign, beginning with his "Catholic Internationale" speech to the Young Men's Institute on 1936. Four years later, he wrote to James Hagerty, his former philosophy professor, about the *Moraga Quarterly* article "Catholic Action and the Lawyer," pointing out that although he was living in Washington, D.C., he kept informed about San Francisco Catholic Action by reading the official Catholic newspaper *The Monitor*. Later that year, Alioto became an associate in the San Francisco law offices of Brobeck, Phleger, and Harrison. A partner in the firm, Maurice Harrison, an activist in the California Democratic Party, helped organize the Catholic Action group called the St. Thomas More Society. Harrison believed that the exemplary public stand of the recently canonized Saint Thomas More provided "to Catholics in general, and to Catholic laymen particularly, the true answer to the problems which confront the world today." After a brief association, Alioto left Brobeck, Phleger, and Harrison for a position with the federal government's Board of Economic Warfare. In 1942, Archbishop John J. Mitty invited Alioto to address the First Regional Catholic Congress on the "The American Catholic Tradition." The event was organized by the archbishop in connection with the wartime Bishop's Committee to Unite the Catholic Youth of America.[5]

By the late 1940s, Alioto was backing causes similar to those supported by centrist liberals elsewhere, such as promoting school bonds and higher salaries for teachers and removing a ban by the Board of Education on teachers' participating in political campaigns after school. Like other Catholic anticommunists, Alioto critiqued the textbook selection process, arguing that too much material sympathetic to communism was allowed to find its way to students in the city's public schools, and he warned against several members of the faculty at San Francisco State College who, he charged, were sympathetic to communism. Like his friend and fellow businessman Benjamin H. Swig, owner of the Fairmont Hotel, Alioto raised funds and organized election campaigns for moderate liberal Democratic Party candidates for state office during the 1950s. During his tenure with the city's Redevelopment Agency, he drew on Catholic moral philosophy to argue, first, that land use policy necessitated careful balancing of the interests and needs of all residents, and second, that government officials represented the popular will. Therefore, third, when conflicts over particular projects arose, as they inevitably would, government officials had a moral duty to place the common good of the city as a whole—as they defined it in relation to the will of their constituents—above the property rights and self-interested claims of particular individuals, interest groups, or neighborhood associations.[6]

Alioto took the oath of office in January 1968, but when the mayoral campaign got under way in the spring of 1967, neither he nor any San Franciscans imagined that he would be a candidate in the nonpartisan election. The mayoral campaign of 1967 coincided with the intensification of the contests over redevelopment, education, employment, and freeway construction. Mayor John F. Shelley's administration came under intense criticism for having failed to respond effectively to these controversies. Critics from the left demanded more controls on business and "power to the people." Critics from the right demanded more free enterprise and "colorblind" policies. The Chamber of Commerce and business leaders critical of Shelley's pro-labor brand of Catholic centrist liberalism backed the Republican restaurant owner and attorney Harold Dobbs, a former city supervisor. The liberal Democratic strategists Ben Swig and Joseph Alioto backed State Senator Eugene McAteer; they had been his main supporters when he ran successfully for the California State Senate in 1958. Like Shelley and Alioto, McAteer was a product of San Francisco's liberal, pro-labor, Catholic political culture, but he was younger and more vigorous than Shelley and seemed a better bet to win against Dobbs. Then, on May 16, 1967, McAteer dropped dead of a heart attack while playing handball at the Olympic Club. His campaign organization remained intact, withholding support from others and assessing the dramatically altered race to decide whether to support another candidate. Meanwhile, to fill the Senate seat vacated by McAteer's death, the city faced a special election that August. To the surprise of Democratic activists, the moderate Republican Milton Marks defeated a left-liberal Democrat, John Burton, brother of Phillip Burton, the leader of the party's left-liberal faction.[7]

John Burton campaigned on a left-liberal issue-oriented platform. He warned Democratic voters that if Marks won the election, the State Senate would be split twenty to twenty between Democrats and Republicans. If that happened, California's conservative governor, Ronald Reagan, would win control of the State Senate. Still, San Francisco's voters—approximately two-to-one registered Democrats—elected Marks. The support Marks received from moderate, middle-income Democrats was an indicator of the changing temper and changing concerns of a large portion of San Francisco's voters that proved vital for the municipal elections in November. The outcome for Democrats, who controlled all four of the city's State Assembly seats, was dismaying, making all the more significant a decrease in Democratic voter registration. Because of their involvement in the State Senate race, the Burtons had not made an endorsement in the mayor's race, making Shelley's chances seem all the more tenuous, and the former McAteer supporters became all the more intent on putting forward a centrist Democrat who could appeal to moderate Republicans. They increasingly turned to the charismatic Alioto as a possible candidate.[8]

Shelley had been the first Democratic mayor of San Francisco in the twentieth century, but even after McAteer's death, polls showed Shelley lagging far behind his Republican rival. On July 2, a *San Francisco Chronicle* poll showed Shelley trailing Dobbs by more than 20 percent, and even among Democrats, Shelley led Dobbs by fewer than 3 percentage points. With McAteer stalwarts still considering whom to support, Shelley, amid rumors of ill health, continued to trail Dobbs by significant margins in voter polls, and in September he withdrew from the race. In the statement announcing his withdrawal, Shelley emphasized medical rather than political reasons: "[My doctors] don't make political decisions, only medical ones, [so I] decided—in no uncertain terms—that I must withdraw from a rigorous race for re-election."[9]

On September 8, Alioto formally announced his candidacy for mayor. Immediately, critics charged that a "deal" had been engineered by influential financial backers in which Shelley, who seemingly had no chance to win in a two-man race against Dobbs, would withdraw from the race to make room for Alioto. Thus, the *Chronicle*'s front-page story on September 8 reporting on Shelley's anticipated withdrawal from the race captioned a photograph of Alioto with the words "heir apparent." In an opinion column, Dick Nolan of the *San Francisco Examiner* also voiced this notion: "Alioto stepped in, like a tag team rassler [*sic*]." The promotion of this idea in the press enabled Dobbs to appropriate it for his campaign rhetoric against Alioto. Thus, when Shelley announced his formal endorsement of Alioto in early October, Dobbs opined: "The transfer of all the assets and liabilities of Mayor Shelley's administration to his heir apparent is now complete."[10]

Charges of a Shelley–Alioto backroom deal came most forcefully from the left wing of San Francisco's Democratic Party. Congressman Phillip Burton and his brother, State Assemblyman John Burton, both expressed their suspicions of Shelley's withdrawal and Alioto's entry into the race. Phillip Burton alleged that "murky circumstances" surrounded the decision, asserting in a press conference on September 8 that "it looks a lot more like a deal of some kind." At a press conference of his own, John Burton echoed his older brother's suspicions and went further to condemn the "deal" as antidemocratic.[11]

Supervisor Jack Morrison announced his decision to enter the race on September 12, and he immediately seized on the allegations of a Shelley–Alioto deal as a campaign issue. Like his political allies Phillip and John Burton, Morrison equated the alleged Shelley–Alioto deal with an attempt by large financial interests to manipulate the election. "In the minds of a few fat cats, Shelley could not win," Morrison stated at a press conference announcing his candidacy on September 12. Shelley flatly denied the charges of a deal. He maintained that his decision to withdraw was strictly medical, and he formally responded to charges of a deal on September 25, when he returned to office for the first time since being hospitalized earlier in the month. "There was no deal, no understanding, no arrangement," he said. "Mr. Alioto was in to see me on Tuesday before I withdrew, but he only wanted to say he supported me and to ask how he could help me in the campaign."[12]

Alioto turned the charges of a deal into a positive campaign theme. He denied the charges during a press conference on September 8 announcing his candidacy: "I want to make clear that I am completely independent. I have made no deals of any kind with anyone nor will I." This aggressive declaration of independence proved to be one of Alioto's more effective campaign themes. Throughout the race, he promoted himself as a "new face" who was "independent" and who could claim detachment from the partisan struggles and problems linked to the current city administration. Alioto repeatedly stressed the need for a new type of leadership in San Francisco, arguing that "we need a new look at City Hall . . . there is a need for new faces, new ideas." In so doing, he aimed to appeal to voters in the large center of the electorate, including both Democrats and Republicans, who had grown frustrated with the city's seeming inability to contain its highly publicized discontents. Alioto elaborated on the need for a fresh and imaginative approach to the city's problems. "Up to now there has been an absolute failure to discuss the basic issues and problems of our city in an imaginative way," he said. "The problems that beset San Francisco and other American cities cannot be solved by the same old faces in the same old places going through the same old paces."[13]

Voters elected Alioto to the Mayor's Office in a three-way race, giving him 110,405 (43.4%) votes to 94,504 (37.2%) votes for Dobbs and 40,436 (16%) votes for Morrison. In a postmortem on the campaign, the *Chronicle* called it "the liveliest election in years—after giving signs of being the dullest." Alioto's "new faces" campaign and his personal style were judged a significant factor in his victory. Having successfully appealed to both liberals and moderates, he declared on election night: "This victory is not mine personally. It is that of a great coalition of San Franciscans representing a broad cross-section of the entire community." He reiterated the more effective elements of his platform when he addressed his supporters on election night, repeating his pledge to seek tax relief for owners of residential property by exploring ways to shift more of the burden to owners of business property, a liberal measure that Dobbs had forcefully opposed. Alioto repeated his opposition to a plan for redevelopment in the Mission District that residents of the area had rejected, stating that before proceeding with any plan in that area, he wanted to "talk to the people out there." He reminded the city that he would insist on enforcing law and order while at the same time assuring minority groups that police brutality would not be condoned or allowed to persist. Alioto stressed his friendship with labor, and in what may have been a show of good faith and appreciation to organized labor, he made an additional promise on election night that had not been part of his campaign: "I will seek an amendment so that no non-union goods will be supplied to the San Francisco government's purchasing department under the competitive bid system."[14]

The *Chronicle* and the *Examiner* concluded that the election of Alioto marked a significant setback for what the press and the media had begun calling "the Burton Machine." Alioto's campaign offered a platform liberal enough to win the support of the majority of the city's Democrats that at the same time stopped short of several left-liberal planks that were less attractive to the city's more moderate voters. In addition, for those who blamed the Shelley administration for the city's problems, Alioto, the New Deal Democrat running as a self-proclaimed independent, was able to offer voters a non-Republican alternative. Two days after the election, the *Chronicle,* which had endorsed Dobbs,

provided the following assessment of the election: "By this election, San Francisco is presented with a new man and a new style of leadership in City Hall,
coming at a time when the city is in the midst of a number of disruptive controversies and uncertainties that must be resolved."[15] In many respects, this
appraisal aptly summarized Alioto's campaign in 1967. As a late entry into the
field and as someone who had never held an elected office, Alioto promoted
himself as a "new face" who would bring a new and energetic approach to solving the city's problems. San Francisco in 1967, like most big cities, was pressed
with concerns for civil rights, public education, law and order, tax relief, downtown redevelopment, neighborhood renewal, and the quality of the environment. When Alioto addressed these issues in the campaign, his claim of detachment from the current city administration proved to be an advantage. He
successfully campaigned as an independent, nonpartisan candidate for a nonpartisan office, building a winning electoral base. His base of support included
Democrats and Republicans among the white voters who had dominated the
pre-1960s city, as well as sizeable numbers of the African American, Chinese,
Latino, and other non-white newcomers to the city. His two administrations,
from January 1968 through December 1975, would be filled with dramatic
events that would test his and the city's ability to satisfy the rising expectations
of an increasingly diverse, increasingly impatient, and increasingly politicized
San Francisco.

As mayor, Alioto drew explicitly on Catholic social teaching when he
argued—as he did in his second inaugural address—that "what our City needs,
what every big city needs, is a 'Declaration of Independence' from unwieldy
state control. What we need is more local autonomy, more local sovereignty, if
you will, to meet our problems head on and seek our own unique answers
to them." This principle that public matters, whenever possible, ought to be
decided at the level of government closest to the people—or "subsidiarity," in
Catholic political philosophy—also appeared in Alioto's call for charter reform.
His support for "expanding the City's grant of power" to insure that "the State
Legislature [is] forbidden to mandate programs of any kind unless it provides
the money to cover the cost of those programs" proved unsuccessful. However,
he did manage, with support from the Chamber of Commerce and the Labor
Council, to convince the State of California to transfer ownership of the port
from the state to the city.[16]

Alioto's strategy during the student and faculty strike at San Francisco State
College from November 6, 1968, to March 21, 1969, demonstrated both his
Catholic perspective and the influence of the church. During the strike, Alioto
rebuffed Governor Ronald Reagan's offers of assistance, insisting that the city
could mind its own affairs. He affirmed the right of dissenting students to
express their grievances and supported their call to recruit more non-white

students and make the college curriculum more relevant to their needs. But he also authorized a sizeable police presence on campus and strongly condemned the intimidation of non-striking students and acts of violence, arguing that events such as the firebombing in the business building damaged the social contract and would not be tolerated. Alioto was vilified in left and left-liberal publications for authorizing the police and for criticizing the far-left Progressive Labor Party's role in the strike leadership, especially its argument that there should be "no sell-out and no compromise with the ruling class." The Black Students Union and the Third World Liberation Front insisted that their demands were "non-negotiable," but George Johns of the Labor Council convinced Mayor Alioto to appoint a citizens' committee to work behind the scenes to end the strike. The students then agreed to meet with Auxiliary Bishop Mark J. Hurley, who chaired the committee, provided that the word "negotiation" was not used to describe the process and the talks were not made public. Bishop Hurley worked independently of the Mayor's Office, with the mayor's approval, seeking "reconciliation within the community based upon justice for all." After weeks of personal diplomacy, Hurley hammered out a settlement between the college administration and the strike's leaders. He correctly predicted that his committee's work was "predestined to be unsung in the public media and virtually unknown to the public it would serve."[17]

The strike at San Francisco State College provided a dramatic illustration of the impact of the demographic, social, and cultural changes that had brought new voices into San Francisco's debates about how to define and implement the public interest since Alioto began his public career. Black residents moved beyond the Fillmore and Bayview–Hunters Point districts into the Oceanview, Merced Heights, and Ingleside (OMI) neighborhoods. Irish Catholics and other white residents moved out of the Fillmore and Mission districts to suburbs or to new neighborhoods in the Parkside and Sunset districts west of Twin Peaks. Hispanics from Central America and Mexico replaced the Irish and Germans as the largest ethnic/racial populations in the Mission District. Following the liberalization of federal law in 1965, immigration from Asia resumed in the late 1960s. Chinatown burst its traditional boundaries and spilled over into North Beach, replacing Italian Americans who had moved to the Marina District or to suburban enclaves such as Burlingame. Clement Street in the Richmond District and Irving Street in the Sunset District became main streets of new Chinatowns. By the time the federal census of 1970 was taken, the city had become 14 percent Asian (Chinese, Filipino, Japanese, and Korean and, later, Vietnamese), 12 percent Hispanic, and 13 percent black. By the mid-1970s, the formerly Irish and German Catholic Haight-Ashbury and Eureka Valley neighborhoods had attracted such large enough numbers of lesbian, gay, bisexual and transgender (LGBT) residents that Eureka Valley became known as "the Castro" and pundits began referring to San Francisco's "gay ghetto."[18]

Increasing social diversity complicated the politics of defining the common good and debating the public interest in accordance with the city's commitment in 1943 to provide "all residents of the city an equal opportunity to participate in the community life and to enjoy its benefits." Catholic influence waned as large numbers of priests and laymen and laywomen left the church or moved out of San Francisco, and Vatican II's reforms in doctrine, liturgy, and cultural style split Catholics into warring factions as never before. Liberal and conservative Catholics alike took to heart the popular phrase "We Are the Church," with liberals opting out of Vatican policies regarding divorce and birth control and conservatives deciding they could ignore the church's teachings on social justice. Liberal priests questioned the adage that "a superior may err in commanding, but you can never err in obeying" and insisted on being "open to the truth, whether we find it on the lips of the Pope, a communist, an old conservative or a young liberal."[19]

And young homophile, New Left, and counterculture newcomers had no patience for what they regarded as the moral absolutism, political authoritarianism, and cultural conservatism of the church and challenged Catholic influence in the city's politics and policymaking. New political alignments developed along lines of class, neighborhood, ethnic/racial, and sexual preference solidarity. Changes in the city's political culture also reflected cultural changes associated with the Cold War. The demonstration against the hearings of the House Committee on Un-American Activities at City Hall earned national attention. San Francisco's anti–Vietnam War protest demonstrations brought tens of thousands into the streets, further enhancing the city's postwar reputation as a haven for writers and artists who had been conscientious objectors against World War II. One of these pacifists, Lewis Hill, founded a listener-supported FM radio station in Berkeley, KPFA, which gave San Franciscans a forum for criticizing the "military-industrial complex" from the early 1960s. During the height of U.S. involvement in the Vietnam War, from the mid-1960s to the mid-1970s, the city became a leading center of antiwar organizing and protest demonstrations.[20]

From the late 1950s through the 1970s, San Francisco developed an international reputation as the Mecca of the Beat and hippie countercultures and as the Gay Capital of the United States. San Francisco was not the only place where critics of "the American Way of Life" sought harmony with nature, sexual freedom, spiritual experimentation, poetic revelry, rock music, and psychedelic drugs, but it did play a leading role in shaping the expression of these aspects of the American "counterculture." A distinctive style of San Francisco music and several local bands—notably, the Grateful Dead and the Jefferson Airplane—played an influential role in the development of the rock music scene nationally. The civil rights movement, like the labor movement and the women's rights campaigns, had demanded equal rights to participate in the center of public life rather than being relegated to the fringes. The counterculture movements, including homophile activists, demanded the freedom to choose to live either beyond the mainstream but with full citizenship rights or more securely within the mainstream with public acceptance of what made them different. Homophile activists founded the Daughters of Bilitis, the nation's first lesbian political organization, in 1955, and the Society for Individual Rights, founded in 1964, established the first gay community center in 1966. In North Beach, Haight-Ashbury, and the Castro, dissenters who rejected the sexual and political norms of Main Street USA created lifestyles meant to provide models for American everywhere who felt limited by convention and demanded liberation from tradition and authority.[21]

The saloons, coffeehouses, restaurants, and clubs of North Beach attracted poets and writers who scorned what they saw as the materialism and militarism of capitalist corporate America. The neighborhood of narrow streets, low rents, and continental restaurants was reminiscent of the Left Bank in Paris but still within (yet on the edge of) the United States. The San Francisco Art Institute and San Francisco State College offered spaces for creating the distinctive San Francisco and Bay Area style of abstract expressionism in painting developed during this period, and a "renaissance" in poetry, both centered in local art schools and colleges, attracted national attention. Several offshoots of that "scene" continue to thrive today, including City Lights Bookstore, founded in 1953; City Lights Publishing Company, founded in 1955; and the San Francisco State University Poetry Center, founded in 1954. Media attention gave San Francisco's Beat writers, hippie entrepreneurs, and gay and lesbian community builders a national audience. *Life* magazine reported the "not guilty" verdict in the trial of Lawrence Ferlinghetti and Shigeyoshi Murao for selling Allen Ginsberg's allegedly obscene poem "Howl" in 1957. Several years later, *Life* dubbed the city the "Gay Capital" of the nation. In 1967, the television networks chronicled the thousands of hippies who listened to the Buddhist chants and Zen prayers of the Beat luminaries Gary Snyder and Allen Ginsberg at the Human Be-In at the Polo Field in Golden Gate Park in 1967.[22]

The Beat movement, hippie counterculture, and homophile LGBT community used media and the arts to claim space in the public life of San Francisco. Some projects drew on classic European roots, such as the San Francisco Mime Troupe, founded in 1959 by R. G. Davis in the *commedia dell'arte* tradition. Others, like Gay Freedom Day, commemorating the Stonewall uprising of 1969, drew on the model of antiwar marches and demonstrations of the 1960s. An extensive independent press and media dedicated to investigative reporting provided an information infrastructure for the city's progressive politics beginning in the mid-1960s. Numerous weekly newspapers, magazines, and independent publishers flourished and attracted newcomers to the city and the Bay Area, several operating in a deliberately irreverent spirit. One example is *Ramparts* magazine (1962–1975), which began as a moderate liberal Catholic review but by 1967 had become an outlet for the writing of what its editor, Warren Hinckle, described as "Left Wing Catholics," whose emergence, he said, was "the best thing that has happened to the Catholic Church since probably Jesus Christ." Bay Area readers could also turn to, among others, Bruce Brugmann's weekly newspaper the *Bay Guardian,* founded in 1966; *Rolling Stone,* founded in 1967; *Gay Sunshine,* founded in 1970; the *Bay Area Reporter,* founded in 1971; and *Common Sense,* founded in 1973.[23]

The mayoral election of 1967 reflected the robust pluralism, unknown before the World War II years, that had become a feature of San Francisco's political culture by the late 1960s, altered as it was by social diversity, cultural changes, and new partisan alignments related to Cold War state and national congressional and presidential politics. Alioto more successfully appealed to this electorate than did Harold Dobbs and Jack Morrison; future candidates for office would also need to assemble coalitions made up of identifiable, although sometimes overlapping, blocs of voters: blacks, Chinese, Hispanics, gays, environmentalists, labor supporters, business supporters, several varieties of liberal, moderate, and conservative residents, and others. Many were organized into political clubs for the purposes of endorsement, fundraising, and mobilization. By the 1970s, winning the mayor's race required collecting endorsements from the city's fast-growing political organizations, including the Black Leadership Forum, the Mexican-American Political Alliance, the Labor Council's Committee on Political Education, the Chamber of Commerce, the Republican County Central Committees, and as many of the Democratic clubs—such as the Feminist Democrats, the Chinese-American Democratic Club, the Alice B. Toklas Lesbian/Gay Democratic Club, and the Harvey Milk Gay and Lesbian Democratic Club—as possible.

In his inaugural address in January 1968, Mayor Alioto urged San Franciscans to construct a just society and a moral economy. In doing so he explicitly drew on the Catholic moral tradition when he urged city residents to reject "the standard of Jeremy Bentham," the English philosopher (1748–1832) who touted the greatest good for the greatest number, which Alioto regarded as "no longer acceptable as a criterion of government. Closer to the mark is the more ancient philosophy which views government as an ordinance of reason for the 'common good.'" By invoking Bentham only to dethrone him, the new mayor gave notice that he defined the public interest not in secular utilitarian terms but, rather, in terms of a faith-based civic moral order. This approach was in keeping with the mayor's Catholic moral tradition, but it clashed with the secularism, irreligious individualism, and moral relativism of large numbers of city residents who, regardless of whether they had studied philosophy, would have celebrated Bentham's "hedonistic calculus," cheered his embrace of women's rights, and praised his early call to decriminalize homosexuality.[24]

Alioto's uncompromising Catholic moral absolutism, centrist philosophy of government, and brash self-confidence—expressed in a forceful, sometimes theatrical, personal style—guaranteed him a continual barrage of criticism from the city's determinedly secular New Left and left-liberal activists. When demonstrators with Marxist banners crashed the grand opening of the Mission District station of the new Bay Area Rapid Transit (BART) system and tried to shout down the mayor, charging that he put profits before people, the former college debater shouted back, saying that their "socialist" critique rang hollow in the face of his fostering of job creation for minority applicants, upgraded urban planning guidelines, and strong measures to preserve the city's aesthetic beauty and environmental quality. Condemning, as he had done since his student days in the 1930s, the socialist left as well as the laissez-faire capitalist right, Alioto governed as a centrist, supporting both downtown commercial redevelopment and redevelopment in the Western Addition and the Mission District. To critics who decried the "Manhattanization" of San Francisco, he replied that he supported such investments to insure the future well-being of the city; he made the Transamerica Pyramid in the financial district a pet project, and he championed the completion of the Embarcadero Center complex of offices and apartments that replaced the aging wholesale produce market adjacent to the waterfront and the Yerba Buena Center project in the South of Market District.[25]

Like the Chamber of Commerce, which had opposed his election in 1967, and the city's labor movement, which had for the most part backed his candidacy, Alioto had supported regional rapid transit and redevelopment since the late 1940s. Like his predecessors John F. Shelley and George Christopher, he backed the business, labor, and government growth coalition based on the vision of San Francisco as the "hub city" for Bay Area metropolitan coordination, financial headquarters for the Pacific, cultural center for the region, and tourist Mecca for the world. During Alioto's term as chairman of the Redevelopment Agency, the newly formed Blyth-Zellerbach Committee, a nongovernmental agency headed by two prominent city business leaders, endorsed the redevelopment of the wholesale produce market adjacent to the financial district. They wanted to make the produce market area harmonize with the more comprehensive plans of the San Francisco Bay Area Council, and in 1959 they created the San Francisco Planning and Urban Renewal Association to increase public support for redevelopment. The association joined with another new organization, the San Francisco Convention and Visitors Bureau, to promote redevelopment and tourism and to revitalize the city's downtown retail shopping district.[26]

The BART system was also intended to benefit San Francisco. Alioto backed the project long before his impromptu debate with critics of his brand of liberal growth policy at the Mission District station. BART began in the Bay Area Council's conviction that postwar growth had created a pressing need for coordinated regional transportation services. The labor movement regarded the project as a prime opportunity for construction jobs and, once the system was operational, union jobs for operations and maintenance personnel. The city's growth coalition agreed that the city's downtown retail, financial, and theater district should be the hub of a fixed rail transit system designed to link the parts of the Bay region together. The Bay Area Council then worked with the California legislature to create a Bay Area Rapid Transit Commission in 1951, and then the Bay Area Rapid Transit District in 1957. In 1962, members of the Blyth-Zellerbach Committee and the Chamber of Commerce formed Citizens for Rapid Transit to campaign for passage of a bond issue in November to finance the system. Their massive advertising campaign stressed that BART would relieve traffic congestion, reduce air pollution, and improve the quality of life. San Mateo and Marin counties dropped out of the Rapid Transit District before the election, but voters in San Francisco, Alameda, and Contra Costa counties approved the $792 million bond issue. Another $180 million came from Bay Bridge tolls, from a special state tax on retail sales to area residents, and from the U.S. Department of Housing and Urban Development. Trans-bay BART service began in 1974, with some seventy-five miles of track, thirty-four stations, and the longest underwater rapid transit tube in the world.[27]

By the time commuters began riding BART from their homes in Alameda and Contra Costa counties to their offices in San Francisco's financial district, the Alioto administration had become embroiled in a highly publicized contest over redevelopment in the South of Market neighborhood. This project, like BART, originated in the early 1950s when the Board of Supervisors designated an area of hotels for transients, small manufacturing companies, and low-income residences as a redevelopment site. Then Alioto invited his fellow Democratic Party activist Ben Swig to formally submit his "San Francisco Prosperity Plan" for approval by the Redevelopment Agency; the plan would have covered six blocks in the designated site with a convention center, sports stadium, office buildings, transportation terminal, auditorium, theater, and shopping center. Despite endorsement by the Redevelopment Agency and support from the city's business and labor organizations, major daily newspapers, and television stations, the project faced considerable opposition for more than a decade before becoming one of the Alioto administration's longest-running headaches.[28]

Resistance initially came from elderly, mostly male, residents who lived in the single-room occupancy hotels that filled the area. They were led by the retirees George Woolf and Peter Mendelsohn, feisty left-wing veterans of the waterfront strike of 1934. Woolf and Mendelsohn, in contrast to their former comrade Harry Bridges, had never converted from Marxist radicalism to liberal gradualism; they proudly announced their principled opposition to compromise of any kind in their refusal to be displaced and relocated. In 1969, Woolf, Mendelsohn, other hotel residents, and proprietors of small businesses in the area formed Tenants and Owners Opposed to Redevelopment (TOOR). With assistance from non-resident sympathizers and volunteer public interest attorneys, TOOR used a variety of techniques that included verbal abuse of officials at public meetings of the Redevelopment Agency, noisy protest marches and demonstrations, and insulting portrayals of the proponents of redevelopment in agitprop performances derived from the Cultural Front work of the 1930s—all of which alienated, and sometimes bewildered, city officials.

Alioto defended the Yerba Buena Center project in testimony to Congress when he requested additional federal funding for the project, which he promised would "revitalize, restore and rehabilitate an entire downtown area—to energize business, to expand a tax base dramatically, and to provide new urban spaces and buildings to satisfy both the eye and the soul." To San Franciscans, the mayor complained that TOOR and its supporters should be discounted because some were too incapacitated by old age, or too ill, to recognize that their best interests would be served by agreeing to be displaced, and others were misguided, naïve romantics. "It is a controversial project, because some 2,500 pensioners and alcoholics must be rehoused (even though in better circumstances) and another Mayor might have walked away from abuse from largely Radical Chic quarters," he said. Alioto also emphasized the importance of the project for the population of the city as a whole and for the future:

1. Our sagging Number One industry—tourism—must have the vital boost of a new exhibit hall and convention center.
2. The 30,000 construction and permanent jobs Yerba Center will provide are equally vital, especially when so many San Franciscans are out of work, particularly minorities, and on the streets during a recession.
3. This commercial development will support and help pay for much of San Francisco's subsidized housing—and without Yerba Buena Center such housing could not be funded. Many have felt that low-to-moderate income housing should be built there instead, but the Mayor has called for a balanced program of both development and housing, throughout the entire City.[29]

Despite Alioto's cheerleading on behalf of the project and his condemnation of its critics, TOOR's efforts slowed down and modified the Yerba Buena Project, partly because Alioto's planning director, Allan Jacobs, resisted comprehensive planning for the South of Market District. Jacobs "feared that residents would be forced out of the area faster as a result of a concentrated planning effort than if there were none" and believed that there "were too few governmental resources and programs, local or national, that could be directed toward solving the problems of the people in that kind of area" In addition to Jacobs's "benign neglect," to use a phrase from the time, the outcome of the controversy was shaped by a tactic that complemented TOOR's noisy confrontations, protest demonstrations, and agitprop: a lawsuit against the San Francisco Redevelopment Agency and the U.S. Department of Housing and Urban Development Department. After a highly publicized period of legal wrangling that lasted into 1973, with Mayor Alioto serving as counsel for the Redevelopment Agency and former Governor Pat Brown offering advice, federal courts eventually forced the Redevelopment Agency to provide the residential housing that Alioto had rejected. Members of TOOR were unhappy with the terms of settlement and with the young public interest attorneys whose expertise had made the settlement possible, but in the end the project was scaled down, redesigned, and modified to include provision for low-income residents displaced from the demolished hotels. Alioto's successor, Mayor George Moscone, appointed a citizens' committee in 1976 that drew up the compromise plans that would guide future construction of the Yerba Buena Center project, including Woolf House, with 112 apartments for low-income seniors, which was named after TOOR's co-founder, who died in 1971.[30]

The adversarial political process and recourse to litigation that shaped the outcome of South of Market redevelopment also slowed the progress of redevelopment in the Fillmore District. In December 1968, Federal Judge William T. Sweigert issued an injunction that stopped redevelopment in the Western Addition until the Department of Housing and Urban Department provided residents with a relocation plan more in keeping with the priorities of the Western Addition Community Organization (WACO). Sweigert's ruling was only a partial victory by WACO's standards, but it encouraged WACO and other grassroots organizations in the Fillmore District to move from protest to political bargaining and construction of new housing. By the fall of 1971, as he began his campaign for reelection, Mayor Alioto was boasting that his administration had succeeded in moving the redevelopment process beyond "dissension, obstruction and WACO picket lines" to construct, or begin construction of, a series of new housing complexes, some of them named in honor of African American historical figures—for instance, Martin Luther King Square, Banneker Homes,

Prince Hall Apartments, Marcus Garvey Square, Malcolm X Square, and Frederick Douglass Haynes Gardens.[31]

During his reelection campaign in 1971, when his two major opponents were Dianne Feinstein and Harold Dobbs, Alioto appealed to potential black voters in Bayview–Hunters Point, as well as those in the Fillmore District: "At Hunters Point, the building of a complete new city within the City is now well underway on a steep hillside where there has only been despair and worn-out barracks housing condemned as unlivable as long ago as 1948." He pointed to the Jackie Robinson Garden Apartments and the Ridgepoint Methodist Church, then under construction, and his success in insuring that "at least 50 percent of the workers—under an Affirmative Action program—have been residents of the community." Alioto's appointments of the first blacks, Hispanics, and Asians to positions on the Police Commission, Public Utilities Commission, Board of Education, and Board of Supervisors earned him praise for creating "a true urban coalition [that] has been forged to conquer the crisis afflicting and killing other cities." Richard Hongisto, who successfully ran for the office of County Sheriff in 1971, attributed the mayor's popularity to the fact that he "delivered on certain promises [to black and Hispanic residents]. I talked with many people in the Mission and they were solidly behind Alioto because he delivered Model Cities, he got them jobs, and they felt money was being pumped into the Spanish speaking community. That's real. That's what counts. I'm not saying having one black on the police commission is an earth-shaking reform, but any fool will tell you it's never been done before in this city."[32]

Alioto deliberately pursued a strategy of inclusion because he believed in the principle of social equality and because he was determined to attract black, Latino, and Asian voters who had supported Morrison in 1967 and might endorse Feinstein in 1971. The process by which black labor leaders allied with Alioto and built a new power bloc in the African American community foreshadowed the way that future candidates would need to operate to assemble winning coalitions in the city's fractious, heterogeneous electorate. Shortly after he decided to run in 1967, Alioto had reached out to William Chester, LeRoy King, and several other black (and white) ILWU leaders. He solicited their aid, promising "to appoint a trade unionist to every city commission and blacks to every commission," and he appointed Revels Cayton as deputy of social services. The success of this strategy was evident in Alioto's impressive margin of victory in the 20th Assembly District in 1967, which included Bayview–Hunters Point, and in the number of influential community leaders who backed his reelection campaign. In 1971, both Eloise Westbrook and Reverend G. L. Bedford supported Alioto. Westbrook chaired the Bayview–Hunters Point Joint Housing Committee and was considered "perhaps the most respected leader in

Hunters Point." Bedford was president of the Baptist Ministers Union, which claimed a membership of some 40,000 black church members in the Western Addition, Bayview–Hunters Point, and OMI neighborhoods. Bedford especially pointed to Alioto's success in creating jobs for unemployed black youths as reason for considering him "a good friend of the Blacks."[33]

The black ministers who supported Alioto worked closely with the black ILWU officials, who were so omnipresent during his administration that one reporter claimed, "Alioto makes no decisions at all about San Francisco's black communities without consulting with someone connected with the longshoremen's union." William Chester was vice-president of the ILWU and president of the Labor Assembly for Community Action, a black political action group formed in 1963 and made up of union members dedicated to building bridges between labor and other community groups in the black community. Chester credited "the bulldog aggressiveness of Joe Alioto," who had "relentlessly pushed affirmative action programs," for making it "now mandatory that a fair break in job openings on redevelopment and other building projects involving the City government be given to Black breadwinners of thousands of San Francisco families."[34]

LeRoy King was a member and sometime president of the ILWU's political arm called the Northern California District Council; he began his political work in the late 1940s when he joined the Frontiersmen Club, a caucus of black longshoremen dedicated to electing African Americans to positions in the union leadership. During the 1950s and early 1960s, the Frontiersmen Club built bridges with the leaders and members of the city's black churches to overcome the "guilt by association" they experienced as ILWU members. "They called us Reds and Communists because of [Harry] Bridges," King recalled, but "we finally got an alliance with these churches." By the time the election was held in 1967, King and other black ILWU officials had established working relationships with leading black ministers, including Reverend Frederick Douglass Haynes, Hamilton T. Boswell, and G. L. Bedford. They, in turn, mobilized black voters for Alioto in the Fillmore, Bayview–Hunters Point, and OMI neighborhoods. Years later, King recalled standing with William Chester and Revels Cayton in the basement of City Hall watching the final vote count in 1967 on television, when Carlton Goodlett and Thomas Fleming walked over: "[Goodlett] screamed, 'You got the black community and now anytime anything goes wrong in the black community you guys are going to be responsible for it. You got that God damn guy in there. He's not our guy. You got him in there, so you guys are going to be responsible. We're [at the *Sun Reporter*] going to put every heat on you three.' We were taking the political action. He used to be the spokesman, so we had taken it all away from them. He used to attack us all the time in the paper."[35]

Goodlett and Fleming kept their word and attacked the Alioto administration consistently, as when the columnist Emory Curtis of *Sun Reporter* rhetorically asked, "Why deliver us to the Man without the Man delivering, or even promising, a damn thing of benefit to the Black residents of this city?" During the campaign in 1971, Goodlett endorsed Alioto's main competitor for black votes, Dianne Feinstein, as did Arthur Coleman, who had helped establish the Bayview–Hunters Point Community Health Service and chaired the Economic Opportunity Council for two years during the Shelley administration. Feinstein also won the endorsement of a newly formed Black Leadership Forum by a vote of twenty-five to twenty-two, after a raucous meeting filled with charges of "power politics" against Alioto's supporters and countercharges of violation of protocol against Feinstein's supporters. William Chester rebuked the Black Leadership Forum, saying that the "political strength of the Black community of San Francisco lies in the labor movement with its thousands of skilled and unskilled jobs and decent living wages. It does not rest in any suddenly-formed handful of Black professionals and executives who feel they have 'made it' and can speak for their less fortunate brothers."[36]

Alioto himself questioned the right of "the well-to-do black, bourgeois professionals" to speak on behalf of the entire African American community. In addition to reaching out to black unionists, he sought support among young residents, many of them jobless, who were seeking opportunities for leadership in the city's black districts. Marvin Robinson, who managed the mayor's Hunters Point campaign office, typified these young political activists. A licensed radio engineer in his early twenties, Robinson was a lifelong resident of San Francisco who had lived in Bayview–Hunters Point for sixteen years. His youth and determination earned him recognition as "somewhat of a political phenomenon in San Francisco." He served as the chairman of the Bayview–Hunters Point Model Cities Commission and was a co-founder of the Hunters Point Security Guards, a program used by the Redevelopment Agency to protect its properties in the area. Robinson campaigned for Alioto in 1971 (he later became a critic of the mayor) because he believed the mayor could do more for Hunters Point than either Feinstein or Dobbs. The same was true for Alex Pitcher Jr., Adam Rogers, and Sylvester Brown, whose positions in the city's poverty program reflected the philosophy of "put the tough guys on payrolls." Their work as liaisons between Hunters Point and the Mayor's Office contributed to cooling tensions between the community and police on a number of occasions.[37]

Alioto's campaign in black neighborhoods in 1971 received a boost in mid-September when he received a letter of endorsement from Mayor Carl B. Stokes of Cleveland, the first African American mayor of a major American city. A controversial figure whose political style exacerbated Cleveland's political divisions, Stokes had decided not to run for reelection in 1971; the Alioto campaign, by its own admission, released Stokes's letter with a degree of trepidation. "The voters of San Francisco don't really need any help from outside of the City in making up their minds on the Mayor's race," Alioto stated. "But Carl Stokes is regarded nationally as one of the remarkable Mayors of our day, and for that reason perhaps his thoughts are worth sharing with the people of San Francisco."[38]

Mindful of the controversy surrounding Stokes, Alioto's campaign decided nonetheless that the endorsement could aid their campaign, both in the black community and among supporters of civil rights beyond it. Stokes commended Alioto's strong leadership and courage as an advocate of America's big cities and credited him especially for his steadfast commitment to civil rights. "Your personal courage and commitment to the needs of oppressed people may well be equaled by others—but not surpassed," Stokes wrote. "There are specific things on which you and I have differed but never on the fundamental of doing whatever is necessary to help those who because of age, race, sex, skin-color or physical affirmity [*sic*] could not easily help themselves." In his correspondence with Stokes, Alioto anticipated that the letter would appeal to "all segments of our community" and "not just [to] one group." The Alioto campaign reproduced the letter in a flyer with a picture of the smiling Stokes on the cover accompanied by the caption, "Mayor Carl Stokes Calls Mayor Joe Alioto the Best." The flyer opened to reveal excerpts of the letter alongside photos of a beaming Alioto surrounded by black children.[39]

Stokes's endorsement accurately described Mayor Alioto's civil rights record as an expression of personal commitment to the principle of racial equality; it was also an effective strategy for building a winning electoral coalition. In the campaign in 1971, Alioto highlighted his appointments of black, Latino, and Asian American officials to city government posts, and he reminded voters that his administration had worked with city agencies, private employers, and labor unions to begin recruitment programs for minority workers. He earned praise from unions affiliated with the AFL-CIO Labor Council by supporting the right of public employees to strike and by personally facilitating settlement of the newspaper strike of 1968 and the student and faculty strikes at San Francisco State College. (Later, he would similarly intervene to help settle police and firefighters' strikes in 1975.) Alioto's appeal to labor went beyond the moderate and conservative members of unions affiliated with the Labor Council. Besides the African American ILWU activists who helped his campaign and took positions in his administration, the mayor counted on support from white, former left-wing leaders of waterfront unions. He appointed Harry Bridges to a seat on the Charter Revision Committee and to the position of port commissioner of the City of San Francisco. David Jenkins, an ILWU activist and former

Communist Party recruiter, recalled in 1989 that former Communist Party comrades had shunned him because in their eyes he compounded the disgrace of leaving the party by campaigning for Alioto and then accepting a position in his administration. Catholic veterans of the battles with Communist Party unionists during the 1930s and 1940s appreciated the combination of magnanimity and Machiavelli demonstrated in this aspect of Alioto's practice of urban liberalism.[40]

Mayor Alioto's strategy of winning elections and governing San Francisco at a time marked by increasing social and cultural diversity and rising expectations by building "a great coalition" was especially evident in the Mission District. The Mission was home to not one but several Spanish-speaking communities, including Mexican nationals, Mexican Americans, Puerto Ricans, Nicaraguans, Cubans, and Salvadorans. "People talk about the 'Spanish speaking community' as if that's some big unified community. There's no such thing," noted a resident interviewed for a profile in the *Examiner*. "About the only thing they have in common is that they do speak Spanish, unless someone coalesces them." Hispanic, or Latino, residents made up some 30–40 percent of the greater Mission District and about 60 percent of the smaller "Inner Mission" neighborhood that would soon contain two new BART stations. And the Mission housed still sizeable numbers of whites of several generations derived from Irish, German, Italian, Russian, and Scandinavian backgrounds. Addressing an excited crowd at the opening of his Mission District headquarters on October 2, Alioto was "at his campaign trail best, pressing flesh with the outstretched hands, grabbing a fiddle to accompany a mariachi band—he was right on key—and grinning with the assurance of a man who knew he was among his supporters." The mayor thanked his supporters and stressed the grassroots character of his campaign, saying, "With all that phony stuff that is being talked about around town [about the Alioto administration being a front for corporate interests] let us not forget this election will be won in the neighborhoods." A mariachi band was on hand again when Alioto spent two hours touring the Mission District on October 30, but beneath the flair that characterized both of his campaigns, Alioto's Mission District strategy in 1971 was different from his strategy in 1967, and the differences reflected the continuing changes in the city's political culture.[41]

In 1967, Alioto had benefited from the strong presence of organized labor in the Mission, and with even firmer labor backing in 1971 he could again expect the unions to provide campaign organizers and precinct workers in the district. But the second Mission campaign was complicated by the existence of what the press was calling a "powerful and well-organized Spanish speaking political movement"—the Mission Coalition Organization (MCO). The MCO was organized in 1968; its influence peaked in 1971; and it its history reflected both the changing political culture of the city and Mayor Alioto's strategy of moderately liberal coalition-based governance. What the press and the media did not know, or chose not to report, was the extent to which MCO owed its existence to the mayor. The MCO was a successor to an earlier group, the Mission Council on Redevelopment (MCOR), organized in the spring of 1966 by residents who demanded that the city allow them to participate in the plans for urban renewal in their neighborhood. The organizers believed that opponents of redevelopment in the Fillmore and South of Market areas would have been more successful if they had pushed harder for a voice in the planning earlier in the process; they were determined to avoid becoming unwitting victims of the Redevelopment Agency's bulldozers. Mike Miller—a young white city native who had done civil rights work in the South, organized for the Student Non-violent Coordinating Committee (SNCC), and trained with the nation's pre-eminent community organizer, Saul Alinsky—facilitated the first meeting.[42]

The organization that grew out of these efforts included Catholic priests and Catholic lay activists, Protestant ministers, and Mission District poverty program personnel, as well as leaders from the Laborers Union Local 261, Centro Social Obrero (a community center and Latino caucus in Local 261), and the newly formed Organization of Business, Education and Community Advancement (OBECA). Herman Gallegos of OBECA became the temporary chairman. A Catholic lay activist, Gallegos had worked with Fred Ross in the Community Services Organization, the group inspired by Alinsky that had recruited Cesar Chavez and Dolores Huerta into labor and civil rights work. During six months of hearings that lasted into 1967, MCOR lobbied members of the Board of Supervisors and filled the supervisors' chambers with opponents of the "Inner Mission Redevelopment Project." Eduardo Lopez, director of the archdiocesan Catholic Council for the Spanish Speaking (known as Concilio), helped turn out several hundred people for community meetings and Board of Supervisors deliberations. Monsignor John Murray, pastor of St. John's Church, where Mayor Shelley was a parishioner, tried without success to enlist the mayor's support in the cause of stopping the Mission project, but he was competing with representatives of building trades unions who pressured Shelley to support the proposal. Herman Gonzales, the chairman of MCOR, then made a personal appeal to Archbishop Joseph McGucken, hoping that McGucken would submit a letter on behalf of MCOR's position to the board. McGucken surprised Gonzales by instead telephoning Supervisor William Blake and asking him to vote "no." Blake agreed. Blake's action so disturbed M. Justin Herman, director of the San Francisco Redevelopment Agency, who was observing the proceedings from the audience, that he leaped from his chair and shouted at Blake, "But you promised me your vote!" The board turned down the Redevelopment Agency's proposal by a vote of six to five, thus stopping further work on urban renewal in the Mission District.[43]

Having succeeded in its goal of blocking the city's plans for redevelopment of the Mission District endorsed by Mayor Shelly, MCOR disbanded; its successor, the MCO, came to life as the result of an invitation from Shelley's successor, Joseph Alioto. In his campaign in 1967, Alioto made two promises rooted in liberal Catholic social justice theory: he would work to foster self-government and local autonomy while using federal funds to create opportunities to improve the health, education, and welfare of city residents. In February 1968, one month after his inauguration, Alioto presented the keynote address at the Spanish Speaking Issues Conference sponsored by the Mission Area Community Action Board, a poverty-program in the Mission District. He promised to apply for a federal Model Cities grant for the Mission District, but only if the request came from a neighborhood organization that encompassed all of the various elements of the community. This was in line with Alioto's principle that a grassroots deliberative body, with the authority to represent the Mission's interests, should be responsible for the operation of the federal program.[44]

Several leaders from MCOR, including Gallegos, Abel Gonzalez, Father Jim Casey of St. Peter's Church, and the Presbyterian minister Dave Knotts—plus a newcomer, Ben Martinez, a recent graduate of San Francisco State College who worked for OBECA—took up Alioto's challenge. The temporary group, with the community organizer Mike Miller serving as the full-time staff director, held a founding convention in October. The conference nearly broke up when delegates from the far-left Progressive Labor Party and others who were associated with the Mission Rebels organization, representing together about 10 percent of the attendees, tried to derail the project. Reverend Jesse James, director of the Mission Rebels, and a cadre of his young associates occupied the stage, seized the microphone, and lectured the delegates that the proposed new group was a "phony organization" that was merely "fronting for Mayor Alioto" and that if it was allowed to operate, it would merely "rip the neighborhood off." But a pre-planned keynote speech from Cesar Chavez broadcast via a telephone hookup, plus an appeal by Gallegos to James that played on Chavez's remarks about the importance of brotherhood, kept the meeting from falling apart. After a second convention a month later, the MCO was officially under way, with the blessing of the mayor and a membership of some one hundred organizations that ranged from St. Peter's (Catholic) Church Council to the Mission Merchants Association and the Mission Rebels. By the time of Alioto's reelection campaign got under way in 1971, the MCO represented a "new guard" in the Mission, working in pursuit of goals already defined by its various member organizations and with the Mayor's Office in connection with its role as the neighborhood organization with responsibility for the city's Mission Model Cities program.[45]

Contests over redevelopment reflected San Francisco's changing political culture during the 1970s. So did contests over environmental issues, the rights of LGBT residents, and district elections of supervisors. In his "state of the city" report in 1971, Mayor Alioto declared: "Our most recent efforts to improve the quality of San Francisco's environment clearly show that we are paying more than lip service to ecology." Proud to be considered the mayor who celebrated the nation's first Earth Day on the first day of spring in 1970, Alioto also pointed to his leadership in the fight against freeways, as well as the opening of nineteen mini-parks, landscaping of 250 acres of city-owned land, planting of 13,000 street trees, improvements in Golden Gate Park, and pre-serving of 23,000 acres of city watershed property from "commercial develop-ment and exploitation." State Senator George Moscone praised Alioto as "a man who hasn't talked much about conservation but has done a great deal." Assemblyman John F. Foran, author of the Pure Air Act of 1968, agreed: "A cold analysis of exactly what has been accomplished during Joe Alioto's first term in office for the conservation and enhancement of our City's natural beau-ties is extremely impressive."[46]

Alioto defined environmental quality and economic growth as mutually desirable common goods and believed that government had a duty to insure that both received a high place in the priorities that defined the public interest. "The challenge is to strike a proper urban ecological balance between jobs and beauty, environment and education, housing and highrises," he explained at the dedication of three new mini-parks on October 19. Addressing an issue that would continue to divide the city beyond the 1970s, Alioto criticized the assumption that "labor unions are on one side, and the environment and ecol-ogy and beauty are on the other side." That he said, is "simply not true." This message attained heightened importance in the campaign of 1971 because Ali-oto, along with most other leading public figures in and out of government, urged voters to vote "no" on Proposition T—a controversial ballot measure that sought to impose a citywide height limit on new buildings in San Francisco.[47]

Fueled by a grassroots effort of environmental activists and written by the businessman and conservationist Alvin Duskin, Proposition T was designed to curb what its proponents derisively called the Manhattanization of San Fran-cisco. If passed, the measure would bypass the city's Urban Design Plan by requiring any proposed building that exceeded six stories or seventy-two feet to be approved by a "majority of voters on the question in a general or special election." Duskin and his supporters believed that the Urban Design Plan had proved "inadequate to defend the city against the ravages of mindless develop-ment." Proposition T had the potential to cause fundamental change in the city's urban planning process; it reflected the growing conviction that San Franciscans had a right to resist any perceived threat to their city's natural beauty and to oppose any change to the built environment that they did not specifically endorse. The ballot measure was the first of its kind in the city, and in the nation, and it received national press coverage. If passed, one reporter predicted, it would "probably launch a full-scale national movement to give a new meaning to 'power of the people' in city planning."[48]

Harold Dobbs and Diane Feinstein joined Alioto in opposing Proposition T, as did a formidable list of city officials, labor unions, community organizations, minority group leaders, real estate associations, construction firms, banks, and large corporations. Besides decrying the measure because it would "[kill] jobs and maim the economy," Alioto counterattacked the measure's backers by arguing that they were unwitting dupes of a cockeyed notion of urban aesthetics. If San Francisco went along with the proposal, he argued, it might end up with "masses of six-story, all-alike monotonous bulky buildings with no open space," and he reminded voters that "mile after mile of low-rise sameness—the kind one finds in Jersey City—isn't at all beautiful." Proposition T took a thumping, gaining only 37 percent of the vote, and a follow-up measure on the ballot in 1972—Proposition P, which advocated a 160 foot height limit—garnered only 43 percent. But the support for limits to downtown development would continue to grow in the future, with the *San Francisco Bay Guardian* publishing investigative reports and proponents lobbying the Board of Supervisors and filing (unsuccessful) lawsuits claiming that corporations such as Pacific Gas and Electric were illegally financing the opposition to limits on high-rises.[49]

The fight over Proposition T signaled the coming of age of a robust environmentalist constituency in San Francisco, the members of which sometimes, but not always, overlapped with the increasingly politicized LGBT residents of the city. In the mayoral election of 1971, for the first time in the city's history, LGBT activists called for a "political awakening," and candidates competed for the support of LGBT organizations. Most of these organizations endorsed Alioto's rival Dianne Feinstein, a liberal on cultural issues who had grown up in an upper-middle-class Jewish family and was a graduate of the Catholic Convent of the Sacred Heart High School and Stanford University. The *Chronicle* reporter Jerry Carroll noted this "dramatic departure from the past" and described the "sustained and determined effort [that] is under way to raise money and political consciousness, organize precinct workers, distribute campaign literature and pursue all other avenues classically associated with the development of political muscle."[50]

To a certain extent, Mayor Alioto was responsible for this new militancy because he had vetoed a local ordinance that would have legalized all sexual acts between consenting adults in private. Feinstein had voted in favor of the legislation and proclaimed, "I'm all for people to have the opportunity to live their individual life styles without undue harassment." The issue created tension within the Alioto camp because, as the campaign aide Wes Willoughby explained, "We just don't go far enough for them," but "Mrs. Feinstein does, or gives the impression that she does." However, the LGBT electorate was not a political machine, did not vote as a unified bloc, and was far from united in its preference for Feinstein. One member of the Daughters of Bilitis complained that Feinstein was receptive to only certain segments of the LGBT community: "Many of us quite frankly don't trust her. She's talked out of several sides of her mouth. She is more responsible to [the Society for Individual Rights] than to women and that bothers me." Another group that claimed to represent "outcast" gay men, the Gay Activist Alliance, first endorsed Feinstein and then withdrew its endorsement, announcing, "We just don't trust Dianne."[51]

Alioto fared better in attracting endorsements from the various other neighborhood and political clubs, beyond organized labor, and from several Democratic Party activists who had opposed him in 1967, including Agar Jaicks, chairman of the party's Central Committee. California State Senator George Moscone, Secretary of State Jerry Brown, and Assemblymen John F. Foran and Leo T. McCarthy all endorsed Alioto. Assemblymen John Burton and Willie Brown, who had campaigned for Jack Morrison in 1967, stayed neutral four years later. Brown remarked that Feinstein was "a female Joe Alioto. If you have two Aliotos, why not pick Joe? I just don't think she's offered the breath of fresh air to move away from the incumbent." Moscone, who had joined Brown and Burton in supporting Morrison in 1967 rallied voters for Alioto at several campaign events in 1971; in late October, he issued a statement urging Democrats to back Alioto rather than Feinstein in the nonpartisan election to keep the Republican Dobbs from receiving a plurality large enough to win the election. In the end, Alioto received 38 percent to Dobbs's 27 percent and Feinstein's 21 percent, increasing his margin of victory over his closest opponent to 18,000 in 1971 from 15,000 in 1967. He won all four of the city's assembly districts and scored best in the Bayview–Hunters Point and Western Addition areas, the Mission, and the precincts in North Beach that still housed large numbers of Italian American voters. The city's most liberal neighborhoods provided Alioto with his largest margin of victory, and it was residents of these neighborhoods, along with organized labor, who would plan and lead the campaign to make a fundamental change in the city's political culture by establishing district election of city supervisors.[52]

The campaign for district elections began in 1970 and continued during Alioto's second term when a new organization, Citizens for Representative Government, challenged the city's seventy-five-year-old system of electing supervisors at large. The Citizens for Representative Government's campaign in 1973 attracted gay men from the Castro determined to elect one of their own as their supervisor—someone who was not Catholic, straight, and middle aged; Mission District Latinos, including "community control" advocates who were convinced that a Spanish-speaking supervisor would best represent their area; and white New Left socialists from Haight-Ashbury and elsewhere who were convinced that working men and women would have more opportunities to be elected supervisor because it would cost less to campaign in a district than citywide and that this would advance the worldwide struggle for "peoples' needs v[ersus] corporate profits." The Citizens for Representative Government's campaign for district elections, Proposition K on the ballot, included many other backers, with various interests and ideologies, who were united only by their conviction that the current system favored the Chamber of Commerce, Redevelopment Agency, Labor Council, and other "downtown" interests. The measure was defeated by two to one, with opponents arguing that district elections would bring a return to the allegedly boss-ridden politics of the nineteenth century, narrow parochialism, and the neglect of citywide public needs.[53]

One year later, George Moscone, who had become the majority leader in the State Senate, decided to run for mayor of San Francisco instead of governor of California. Moscone, also a native son, was a left-liberal Catholic who had attended St. Brigid parochial school and St. Ignatius High School before moving on to University of the Pacific and Hastings College of the Law. In the campaign of 1975, Moscone promised a more inclusive administration than his fellow Democratic predecessors Shelley and Alioto at a moment when the city was particularly sensitive to questions of ethnic/racial justice and public security. When the campaign got under way, the city was still coming to terms with a "law and order" crisis that had divided it during the so-called Zebra murders, when four African American men influenced by Black Muslim teachings conducted a 179 day reign of terror in the city. They assaulted twenty-three white men and women in late 1973 and 1974; fifteen died of their wounds and eight survived, included Art Agnos, a social worker who would become San Francisco's thirty-ninth mayor (1989–1993). Mayor Alioto came under severe criticism when he ordered officers to stop and interrogate all young black men who fit a profile of the "Zebra" killers based on a witness's testimony. (The name was derived from the "Z for Zebra" radio channel the police used in the case.) In the end, it was an informant, not the San Francisco Police Department dragnet, that led to the apprehension, arrest, and conviction of the four men after a 376 day trial, the longest criminal trial in California's history. Moscone promised the city he would make the streets of San Francisco safe without endangering the civil liberties of the city's non-white residents. He also promised to be more effective than Shelley and Alioto in staffing his administration with representatives of all of the city's diverse populace, including LGBT residents; more responsive to environmental concerns; more active in providing services to job seekers and renters; and more vigilant in regulating and monitoring downtown development and uptown redevelopment. He took office in 1976, winning an election that sharply divided the city. Unions joined blacks and Latinos, environmentalists, moderate and leftist liberals (including liberal Catholics), and the LGBT community to give Moscone a narrow victory over John Barbagelata. An archconservative Republican real estate broker, Barbagelata received enthusiastic support from conservative Catholics and others who mourned the passing of the old order and who believed that "San Francisco's problems were caused by all the 'new people,' the gays, and the immigrants, and the excessive power of the public sector and craft unions."[54]

Moscone won by only 4,400 votes out of a total of about 200,000, but his victory was taken to heart by advocates of district elections, and shortly after his election, a new organization, San Franciscans for District Elections (SFDE), resumed the campaign. Stressing their conviction that "the people of San Francisco know better how to manage their affairs than the present aloof and special interest domination majority of the present board," the SFDE enlisted the robust New Left socialist community as well as the moderate to conservative liberal Labor Council. The socialist Northern California Alliance turned out large numbers of canvassers and publicized the campaign in its newspaper *Common Sense*; the Labor Council, for the first time making common cause with the LGBT organizations and the socialists, held a series of community conferences in support of district elections. (Labor was incensed with the incumbent supervisors, who sided with city business associations and passed a series of punitive measures against city employees following strikes in 1974, 1975, and 1976.) The district election proposition passed by a narrow margin, with voters aligning themselves almost exactly as they had in the Moscone–Barbagelata contest the year before. The election of a new Board of Supervisors in 1977, closely following Moscone's election in 1975 and the victory of district elections in 1976, provided a dramatic conclusion to a decade of change in the city's political culture, especially since one of the new supervisors was Harvey Milk, the first openly gay public official in the nation. The close vote on district elections, and the chagrin over the election of Milk and several left-liberal men and women, led partisans of the ancien régime to carry out a political counter-reformation. Led by disgruntled members of the old at-large Board of Supervisors supported by the Chamber of Commerce, the counter-reform coalition drew heavy support from the well-to-do western districts of the city that still housed significant numbers of Catholic cultural conservatives. In a special mid-summer election in 1980, voters directed a return to at-large elections.[55]

The restoration passed by only 1.15 percent of the ballots cast, with only 35 percent of the city's eligible voters participating. Some local journalists and columnists argued that citywide elections to the board would help restore civic unity in the aftermath of two violent episodes in November 1978 and May 1979. The first of these events took place in Guyana. Congressman Leo Ryan, staff members, and journalists had arrived to gather information about the community established by the former San Francisco revivalist Jim Jones, who had become a minor figure in city politics when Moscone appointed him chairman of the Housing Authority as a reward for turning out his People's Temple congregation members to work on the election campaign of 1975. After coming under criticism in San Francisco, Jones had moved with hundreds of followers to Jonestown in Guyana. Some of his staff murdered Ryan and members of his party, and then 900 residents of Jonestown—and Jones himself—committed mass suicide.[56]

Ten days after the first gruesome news arrived from Guyana, Dan White, a former police officer, firefighter, and supervisor who had resigned his seat on the board, snuck his police-issue handgun into City Hall through a basement window and murdered Mayor George Moscone and Supervisor Harvey Milk. White, a conservative Catholic, was embittered by Moscone's refusal to reappoint him to the board after he changed his mind about resigning. He was also scornful of Milk and angered by the LGBT movement's growing power in city affairs. White had been elected as a "law and order" conservative and had promised his heavily blue-collar, white-ethnic district voters that he would hold the line against "the new people" of San Francisco. His campaign slogan was "Stand and Fight with Dan White." On May 21, 1979, a jury found White guilty of voluntary manslaughter, not murder. That night, thousands of demonstrators burned police cars and smashed doors and windows at City Hall in an expression of their outrage at justice denied. Later the same night, a number of police officers retaliated by trashing a gay saloon in the Castro and harassing its customers.[57]

Dianne Feinstein, who as the president of the Board of Supervisors become mayor upon Moscone's death, pleaded for civic unity in the aftermath of the murders; she called on residents to demonstrate to the world that the voice of reason could prevail in San Francisco. One newspaper columnist regarded the repeal of district elections as a shining example of political good sense and communal reason: "Perhaps the city has at last decided to put behind itself its recent passion for self-destructive special interest politics, and to behave once again in a manner befitting its stature as one of the great cities of the world." Others disagreed, one claiming to find "the basic issue being whether only well heeled, well financed candidates can run for supervisor." For the vice-president of the Chamber of Commerce and the secretary-treasurer of the Labor Council, the basic issue appeared to be which method of electing supervisors best insured policy outcomes marked by fairness, not favoritism. John Crowley of the Labor Council preferred the district approach because "we have entrée to the board," but Gregory P. Hurst of the Chamber of Commerce opposed election by district because its "actions are clearly contrary to a healthy business climate." The SFDE, the coalition that had unsuccessfully defended the three-year old reform, immediately collected some 40,000 signatures in only twelve days and placed the measure before voters again on the ballot in November 1980.[58]

The at-large system of electing supervisors was upheld on November 4, prompting one observer to describe the city's political culture as "pluralism run amok."[59] But despite worried critics' warnings about the dire consequences of pluralism, a politics of inclusion has continued to thrive in the competition produced by ethnic/racial and economic-class interest groups, LGBT residents, and many others, including those representing poor elderly residents, the homeless, and the disabled. This chapter has focused on several contests during the Alioto years and the tragically brief period between the elections of Mayor George Moscone and Supervisor Harvey Milk in 1975 and 1977, their murders in 1978, and the passage, then repeal, of district election of supervisors. The period marked the end of an era in which widespread agreement existed among San Franciscans that the common good required residents to conform to a civic moral order derived from religious traditions of any kind. Increasingly— although not without resistance from those still committed to the old order— San Franciscans would make politics and policy according to a vision of the common good premised on unlimited individual rights, unbounded individual freedom of choice, and government activism on behalf of rights, not duties; entitlements, not obligations; diversity, not unity.

In the 1980s and 1990s, debates about how to define the public interest became ever more complex, with more mainstream businesses and homeowners (including many black, Latino, and Asian voters) often squaring off against a fractious progressive reform movement divided within and splitting into factions that emphasized primarily environmental issues, social issues, or radical populist issues.[60] The Catholic Church and Catholic lay activists continued to participate in this new political order, typically adopting a strongly liberal orientation on issues of economic justice and questions of war and peace, side by side with an equally strongly conservative stance on cultural issues. A case in point is the history of San Francisco's adoption of the nation's first municipal law that extended to "domestic partners" of city employees benefits that historically have been available only to married spouses. Archbishop John R. Quinn (served 1977–1995) wrote to Mayor Feinstein urging her to veto the city's pioneering domestic partners legislation passed by the Board of Supervisors in 1982; Quinn's letter was generally acknowledged to have convinced the mayor to issue the veto, which the board did not overturn. And when the Board of Supervisors unanimously passed a second version seven years later, it was the church and Catholic activists who led a successful referendum vote that rendered the legislation null and void. Then, in 1990, city voters reestablished domestic partners legislation by initiative, and this time the Catholic-supported repeal measure went down to a solid defeat.[61] Much had changed in the turbulent years between the inauguration of Joseph Alioto in 1968 and the reestablishment of at-large elections of supervisors in 1980, but Archbishop Quinn's reply to critics of his support for the nuclear freeze movement suggested that the church's determination to shape public opinion remained firm: "Sometimes, powerful people do not want to be contradicted with opposing views that show the moral weakness of their position. They want the church to be silent unless it agrees with them. [But] it's my right and obligation to speak on the moral dimensions of these public issues."[62]

CONCLUSION

Beyond the New Deal

S an Francisco in the 1980s was significantly different from the "Pacific Coast metropolis" of ninety years earlier. The Spanish–American War, two world wars, and a global Cold War had brought permanent new additions to the built environment and new residents by the thousands. International economic growth and development made the city a node in a globalization process that both enhanced its opportunities and increased its dependence on business decisions beyond the control of city residents. Federal government monies helped build the bridges, interstate highways, and international airport that connected the city to nearby communities and overseas destinations. African American residents were a sizeable presence in several neighborhoods; they and newcomers from Mexico, Central America, Asia, and the Pacific Islands, pushed by revolutions and wars and pulled by the lure of a better life, together made up half of San Francisco's population.

The developments narrated in this book were less visible than, but in many ways as significant as, the more dramatic markers of change because they shaped the character of the debate over how to define the common good, influenced the outcome of the politics of inclusion, and contributed to the evolution and development of San Francisco's political culture. From the early 1890s through the 1970s, a Catholic faith-based enterprise, fostered by the city's archbishops and involving both lay activists and diocesan priests, constituted a dynamic element in San Francisco's political culture. In the years before the Great Depression, in the context of Vatican teachings, natural disaster, and the nation's first red scare, Catholics challenged the presumptions of organized capital to unilaterally define the public interest. The contests involving organized business, organized labor, and the Catholic Church were then complicated by transnational rivalries, including the Communist Party's entry into politics and its competition with Catholic Action. The city's Catholic business, labor, and civic leaders, in complex relations with the political left and the business right, contributed to the shaping of a local New Deal liberal regime that favored expanded rights for organized labor.[1] Organized business, Catholics, and the left, including the Communist Party, also played key roles in redefining the city's priorities around the importance of fostering future economic growth and human rights.

San Francisco did not undergo a wholesale "transformation" as a consequence of World War II.[2] But during the war and the subsequent Cold War, the city did experience dramatic population changes, and the newcomers influenced the character and the outcome of contests over how to define the public interest. Important continuities linked post-1945 San Francisco with its prewar history, even as business reoriented its approach to economic development; the labor movement coped with regional, national, and international economic restructuring; the Catholic population dispersed into the metropolitan Bay Area and became a smaller proportion of San Francisco residents; and the Communist Party shrank in numbers and influence. Rivalry between the city's Catholic Action movement and the Communist Party also contributed to shaping the city's Cold War political culture. Both men and women participated in the debate over how to define the common good, as illustrated in the work of women in Catholic Action and in the Communist Party, and in the career of Julia Gorman Porter, whose political and policy activism began in the Progressive era and continued to the 1970s.

As they debated urban redevelopment, public education, equality in employment, and freeway construction from the late 1930s through the 1960s, San Franciscans were motivated by ideas and ideologies and moved by the impact of demographic changes; local, national, and international economic dynamics; and dramatic and unanticipated national and international events. In the 1960s and 1970s, debates in San Francisco about how to define the common good took place in the context of a national conversation about the constitutional rights of individuals and the duties of government toward groups that historically had been excluded from participation in policymaking. As one leader in redevelopment politics put it, "[The people are] saying to their government: 'We want a hand in the activities of the Government when we are directly affected.'"[3] Joseph L. Alioto's campaign promise in 1967 that he would assemble a "grand urban coalition" that would succeed in representing all of the city's diverse interests won him the Mayor's Office; his administrations demonstrated the continued influence of the Catholic public philosophy that inspired him, as well as growing impatience with the old order that he represented. Alioto may have come out of the New Deal, but his accommodations to new demands dramatized how the city had already moved beyond the New Deal, a process accelerated by Mayor George Moscone and Supervisor Harvey Milk and continued by Mayor Dianne Feinstein, Planning Commissioner and Supervisor Sue Bierman, and many others since the 1980s.

San Francisco was not exceptional in being a city marked by the faith-based activism of Catholic bishops, priests, and laymen and laywomen, but its history demonstrates a distinctive expression of the American encounter between religion and politics. Many causes contributed to the city's history of successful Catholic activism on behalf of defining the public interest. San Francisco may have been unique in the coincidence of two features: the absence of a Protestant establishment and the presence of Catholic residents determined to exercise their "right to the city." San Franciscans also constructed their political culture in the context of dynamics similar to those that played out in other cities in other regions: the timing of the Vatican's social justice encyclicals in relation to the rise of the American labor movement; the leadership of the city's archbishops; the impact of the international Catholic–communist rivalry, two world wars, and the Cold War; the social and political networks in which Catholic men and women created the public space where they translated church teachings, mediated through American values, into political agendas; and the promulgation of liberal, then conservative, Vatican reforms in relation to the American "civil wars" of the 1960s and "culture wars" of the 1970s.[4]

By 1980, the city's public arena, which in 1890 was open only to white men—and privileged the "better sort" of white men—was officially committed to equality, and a municipal Human Rights Commission monitored the behavior of its residents and business firms. The undeniable progress in human rights signified by these reforms has not silenced concern about their limited practical consequences. As David Harvey, Michael J. Sandel, and David Hollinger have shown for the United States generally, in San Francisco formal political inclusion has not guaranteed economic security, perfected civic morality, or generated the social solidarity necessary for "us and them" to become "we the people."[5] The role that religious tradition and faith-based activism should play in urban politics has continued to be a subject of debate, and the very concept of *the public interest* has been criticized as an elitist and exclusionary social construction. For some, creating a "just city" will require "reimagining political space" and mobilizing a secular popular struggle to overcome the deleterious effects of neoliberal globalization. Others advocate a "comprehensive pluralism" to counter the dangers inherent in the post-1980s "de-privatization" of religion by those who argue that meaningful and lasting civic political participation requires increasing "the power of religion in the public sphere."[6] San Franciscans have debated these matters since the 1890s, and this book has presented a reconsideration of the city's history that takes into account the influence of those debates. Their reverberations have persisted beyond the events recounted in this book. After Monsignor Bernard Cronin stepped down as director of the archdiocesan refugee resettlement program in 1958, he served for twenty years as the pastor of St. Matthew's Church in San Mateo, a suburb of San Francisco. He continued to preach after his retirement in 1979, and in a homily delivered the Sunday before Election Day in 1984, Cronin announced that "the separation of church and state is not absolute." The church, he argued, "has the right to express moral judgments about public policy, to add moral dimensions to public debate and form right conscience of its believers. In short, the government may encourage religion without establishing it."[7]

Since the 1980s, Catholics and other San Franciscans who believe that the common good derives from a foundation of faith-based morality, that individual rights have God-given limits, and that government has a duty to require citizens to learn and practice a religiously based civic creed have not ceased their attempts to influence public policy. But their success has been limited by city residents who demand that the public sphere be open to all and who insist that public policy recognize, honor, and encourage multiple conceptions of the common good, not enshrine a single tradition-based vision of the public interest.[8] And while San Francisco remains distinctive in many ways, its residents continue to partake in a venerable American tradition as they participate in the national debate about the role that religious tradition and faith-based activism should play in defining the public good and shaping the city's public policies.

NOTES

INTRODUCTION

1. Among the numerous works that have informed my thinking about American political culture, I have been especially influenced by Michael J. Sandel, *Democracy's Discontent: America in Search of a Public Philosophy* (Cambridge, Mass.: Harvard University Press, 1996); Michael J. Sandel, *Liberalism and the Limits of Justice,* 2d ed. (New York: Cambridge University Press, 1998); John Rawls, *Political Liberalism,* exp. ed. (New York: Columbia University Press, 2005); John Rawls, *The Law of Peoples* (Cambridge, Mass.: Harvard University Press, 1999); Rogers M. Smith, *Civic Ideals: Conflicting Visions of Citizenship in American History* (New Haven, Conn.: Yale University Press, 1997); Michael Walzer, *Thinking Politically: Essays in Political Theory,* 2d ed., ed. David Miller (New Haven, Conn.: Yale University Press, 2007); Barry Bozeman, *Public Values and Public Interest: Counterbalancing Economic Individualism* (Washington, D.C.: Georgetown University Press, 2007); Louis Dupré, "The Common Good and the Open Society," in *Catholicism and Liberalism: Contributions to American Public Philosophy,"* ed. R. Bruce Douglass and David Hollenbach (New York: Cambridge University Press, 1994), 172–195; Jean Bethke Elshtain, "Catholic Social Thought, the City, and Liberal America," in *Catholicism, Liberalism, and Communitarianism: The Catholic Intellectual Tradition and the Moral Foundations of Democracy,* ed. Kenneth L. Grasso, Gerard V. Bradley, and Robert P. Hunt (Lanham, Md.: Rowman and Littlefield, 1995), 97–114; Gary D. Glenn and John Stack, "Is American Democracy Safe for Catholicism," *Review of Politics* 62, no. 1 (Winter 2000), 5–29; Judith N. Shklar, *American Citizenship: The Quest for Inclusion* (Cambridge, Mass.: Harvard University Press, 1991); Mary Ann Glendon, *Rights Talk: The Impoverishment of Political Discourse* (New York: Free Press, 1991); Akhil Reed Amar, *The Bill of Rights: Creation and Reconstruction* (New Haven, Conn.: Yale University Press, 1998); Mark Hulliung, *The Social Contract in America from the Revolution to the Present Age* (Lawrence: University Press of Kansas, 2007). For an impressive synthesis that places in the forefront theories about and the practice of "collective action for the public good" in the American city from the eighteenth century to the present, see John D. Fairfield, *The Public and Its*

Possibilities: Triumphs and Tragedies in the American City (Philadelphia: Temple University Press, 2010). For a useful online forum with material regarding the concept of the public sphere, see Social Science Research Council, "Public Sphere Guide," available online at http://publicsphere.ssrc.org/guide.

2. The excellent existing scholarship on San Francisco's political culture is referenced throughout this book, but see esp. Richard Edward DeLeon, *Left Coast City: Progressive Politics in San Francisco, 1975–1991* (Lawrence: University Press of Kansas, 1992); Robert W. Cherny, "Patterns of Toleration and Discrimination in San Francisco: The Civil War to World War I," *California History* 73 (Summer 1994): 130–141; Philip J. Ethington, *The Public City: The Political Construction of Urban Life in San Francisco, 1850–1900* (New York: Cambridge University Press, 1994); Glenna Matthews, "Forging a Cosmopolitan Civic Culture: The Regional Identity of San Francisco and Northern California," in *Many Wests: Place, Culture, and Regional Identity*, ed. David M. Wrobel and Michael C. Steiner (Lawrence: University Press of Kansas, 1997), 211–234; Gray Brechin, *Imperial San Francisco: Urban Power, Earthly Ruin* (Berkeley: University of California Press, 1999); Barbara Berglund, *Making San Francisco American: Cultural Frontiers in the Urban West, 1846–1906* (Lawrence: University Press of Kansas, 2007); Rebecca Solnit, *Infinite City: A San Francisco Atlas* (Berkeley: University of California Press, 2010).

3. The importance of studying both the distinctive character of individual cities and the dynamic nature of their histories is addressed in several excellent "state of the field" essays by Robert O. Self, "City Lights: Urban History in the West," in *A Companion to the American West*, ed. William Deverell (Malden, Mass.: Blackwell, 2004), 412–441; Philip J. Ethington and David P. Levitus, "Placing American Political Development: Cities, Regions, and Regimes, 1789–2008," in *The City in American Political Development*, ed. Richardson Dilworth (New York: Routledge, 2009), 154–176; Clarence N. Stone, "Urban Politics Then and Now," in *Power in the City: Clarence Stone and the Politics of Inequality*, ed. Marion Orr and Valerie C. Johnson (Lawrence: University Press of Kansas, 2008), 267–316.

4. The literature on the history of constitutional interpretation and the politics of policymaking in relation to the development of American political culture is extensive: see, e.g., Sandel, *Democracy's Discontent*, and other works cited in n. 1 in this chapter.

5. Thomas C. Cochran and William Miller, *The Age of Enterprise: A Social History of Industrial America*, rev. ed. (New York: Harper and Row, 1961), 153. See also Sarah S. Elkind, *How Local Politics Shape Federal Policy: Business, Power, and the Environment in Twentieth Century Los Angeles* (Chapel Hill: University of North Carolina Press, 2011).

6. For existing accounts that examine the influence of business, see Jeffrey Haydu, *Citizen Employers: Business Communities and Labor in Cincinnati and San Francisco, 1879–1916* (Ithaca, N.Y.: Cornell University Press, 2008); Brechin, *Imperial San Francisco*; John H. Mollenkopf, *The Contested City* (Princeton, N.J.: Princeton University Press, 1983); Chester Hartman, *City for Sale: The Transformation of San Francisco*, rev. ed. (Berkeley: University of California Press, 2002).

7. As Charles Lippy writes, "The First Amendment aside, American religious life and American political life were never divorced from each other, but intertwined": Charles H. Lippy, *Pluralism Comes of Age: American Religious Culture in the Twentieth Century* (Armonk, N.Y.: M. E. Sharpe, 2000), 124. Among the best of a recent outpouring of books on this topic are Donald L. Drakeman, *Church, State, and Original Intent* (New York: Cambridge University Press, 2010); John Witte Jr. and Joel A. Nichols, *Religion and the American Constitutional Experiment*, 3d ed. (Boulder, Colo.: Westview Press, 2011); Paul Horwitz, *The Agnostic Age: Law, Religion, and the Constitution* (New York: Oxford Uni-

versity Press, 2011). See also John T. Noonan Jr., *The Lustre of Our Country: The American Experience of Religious Freedom* (Berkeley: University of California Press, 1998); Christopher L. Eisgruber and Lawrence G. Sager, *Religious Freedom and the Constitution* (Cambridge, Mass.: Harvard University Press, 2007); Steven K. Green, *The Second Disestablishment: Church and State in Nineteenth-Century America* (New York: Oxford University Press, 2010).

8. Exceptions to the general neglect of Catholicism in San Francisco history include Jeffrey M. Burns, ed., *Catholic San Francisco: Sesquicentennial Essays* (Menlo Park, Calif.: Archives of the Archdiocese of San Francisco, 2005); Richard Gribble, *Catholicism and the San Francisco Labor Movement, 1896–1921* (San Francisco: Mellen Research University Press, 1993); William Issel, *"For Both Cross and Flag": Catholic Action, Anti-Catholicism, and National Security Politics in World War II San Francisco* (Philadelphia: Temple University Press, 2010).

9. See Kathleen Neils Conzen, "The Place of Religion in Urban and Community Studies," *Religion and American Culture* 6 (Summer 1996): 108–114; Philip Goff, "Religion and the American West," *A Companion to the American West,* ed. William Deverell (Malden, Mass.: Blackwell, 2004), 286–303; Paula Kane, "Review Essay: American Catholic Studies at a Crossroads," *Religion and American Culture* 16 (Summer 2006), 263–271.

10. Robert W. Cherny is at work on a history of the Communist Party in California: see Robert W. Cherny, "Prelude to the Popular Front: The Communist Party in California, 1931–35," *American Communist History* 1 (June 2002), 11, 19–20; Robert W. Cherny, "The Communist Party in California, 1935–1940: From the Political Margins to the Mainstream and Back," *American Communist History* 9 (April 2010), 3–33.

CHAPTER 1

1. Minutes of the Board of Directors, Merchants Association of San Francisco, January 7, 1897, in California Historical Society Library, San Francisco (hereafter, CHS).

2. Phelan and the charter reformers aspired to make San Francisco equal to "the most Progressive cities of the United States." The quote is from Merchants Association, "New Charter Catechism, Plain Questions and Honest Answers," pamphlet, copy in CHS.

3. See Kevin E. Schmiesing, *Within the Market Strife: American Catholic Economic Thought from Rerum Novarum to Vatican II* (Lanham, Md.: Lexington Books, 2004), for a well-informed recent survey of these matters.

4. For insights into such complexities, see Jon Gjerde, *The Minds of the West: Ethnocultural Evolution in the Rural Middle West, 1830–1917* (Chapel Hill: University of North Carolina Press, 1997), esp. chaps. 4, 6; David M. Emmons, *Beyond the American Pale: The Irish in the West, 1845–1910* (Norman: University of Oklahoma Press, 2010), esp. chaps. 8–9.

5. On the women's rights movement and changing definitions of the public interest, see Robert W. Cherny, Mary Ann Irwin, and Ann Marie Wilson, eds., *California Women and Politics: From the Gold Rush to the Great Depression* (Lincoln: University of Nebraska Press, 2011). For recent studies of Chinese, Japanese, and African Americans that address the politics of defining the public interest, see Yong Chen, *Chinese San Francisco, 1850–1943: A Trans-Pacific Community* (Stanford, Calif.: Stanford University Press, 2000); Izumi Hirobe, *Japanese Pride, American Prejudice: Modifying the Exclusion Clause of the 1924 Immigration Act* (Stanford, Calif.: Stanford University Press, 2001); Albert Broussard, *Black San Francisco: The Struggle for Racial Equality in the West, 1900–1954* (Lawrence: University Press of Kansas, 1993).

6. Phelan outlined his plans for making San Francisco "the pride of the American continent" in a series of public addresses between his return from a European tour in 1883 and his election to the Mayor's Office in 1896. The quote is from "The New San Francisco," speech at the opening of the Mechanics Institute Fair, September 1, 1896, in James Duval Phelan Papers, Bancroft Collection, Bancroft Library, University of California, Berkeley (hereafter, BC), carton 2. See also James P. Walsh and Timothy J. O'Keefe, *Legacy of a Native Son: James Duval Phelan and Villa Montalvo* (Los Gatos, Calif.: Forbes Mill Press, 1993), 55–66.

7. The Koster quote is from *The Valley Road: A History of the Traffic Association of California, the League of Progress, the North American Navigation Company, the Merchants Shipping Association, and the San Francisco and San Joaquin Valley Railroad* (San Francisco: Wheeler, 1896), 13–16, 42–45, quote on 45.

8. For detailed descriptions of aspects of the city's economic, political, and social history referred to here, see William Issel and Robert W. Cherny, *San Francisco, 1865–1932: Politics, Power, and Urban Development* (Berkeley: University of California Press, 1986). See also Haydu, *Citizen Employers,* chaps. 2, 4, 6.

9. The Koster quote is from *San Francisco Chamber of Commerce Activities* 3 (June 1, 1916): 3.

10. For details, see *Objects and Some Activities of the California Development Board,* California State Chamber of Commerce, 1916, pamphlet, copy in Doe Library, UC Berkeley. On competition with other cities and military-related urban development, see Roger W. Lotchin, "The City and the Sword: San Francisco and the Rise of the Metropolitan-Military Complex, 1919–1941," *Journal of American History* 65 (March 1979), 996–1020; Roger W. Lotchin, "The Metropolitan-Military Complex in Comparative Perspective: San Francisco, Los Angeles, and San Diego, 1919–1941," in *The Urban West,* ed. Gerald D. Nash (Manhattan, Kans.: Sunflower University Press, 1979), 19–30; Roger W. Lotchin, "The City and the Sword in Metropolitan California, 1919–1941," *Urbanism, Past and Present* 7 (Summer–Fall 1982), 133–137.

11. Minutes of the Board of Directors, San Francisco Chamber of Commerce (hereafter, Minutes BD), September 19, 1916, January 31, 1922, in CHS. The statement of purpose is from *The City,* the monthly publication of the Bureau of Governmental Research; the Chamber of Commerce's role in maintaining these organizations is discussed in Minutes BD, September 19, 1916, March 9, 1920, March 23, 1920, May 3, 1921, November 12, 1924, in CHS.

12. Issel and Cherny, *San Francisco, 1865–1932,* 35–52.

13. Minutes BD, various dates, in CHS.

14. A revealing confirmation of the scope of the chamber's publicity work can be seen in the details of its contract with *Sunset* magazine: Chamber of Commerce Records, CHS, box 4, folder 63c. For additional documentation of these activities, see William Issel, "Business Power and Political Culture in San Francisco, 1900–1940," *Journal of Urban History* 16 (November 1989): 52–77.

15. The Yorke quote is from *The Monitor,* November 7, 1896. On Phelan's strategy and tactics in building the successful charter campaign, see Issel and Cherny, *San Francisco, 1865–1932,* 149–152; Terrence J. McDonald, *The Parameters of Urban Fiscal Policy: Socioeconomic Change and Political Culture in San Francisco, 1860–1906* (Berkeley: University of California Press, 1986), 257–261.

16. Issel and Cherny, *San Francisco, 1865–1932,* 143–146. See also Ethington, *The Public City,* 387–398.

17. Cherny, "Patterns of Toleration and Discrimination in San Francisco." See also James P. Walsh, "Peter Yorke and Progressivism in California, 1908," *Eire-Ireland* 10 (1975): 73–81; E. Digby Baltzell, *The Protestant Establishment: Aristocracy and Caste in America* (New York: Vintage, 1964); Thomas A. Guglielmo, *White on Arrival: Italians, Race, Color, and Power in Chicago, 1890–1945* (New York: Oxford University Press, 2003).

18. Issel, "Business Power and Political Culture in San Francisco," 57.

19. Irena Narrell, *Our City: The Jews of San Francisco* (San Diego: Howell-North, 1981); Fred Rosenbaum, *Cosmopolitans: A Social and Cultural History of the Jews of the San Francisco Bay Area* (Berkeley: University of California Press, 2009).

20. Moses Rischin, "Sunny Jim Rolph: The First 'Mayor of All the People,'" *California Historical Quarterly* 53 (Summer 1974): 165–172; *San Francisco Chronicle,* June 5, 1934.

21. *The Monitor,* June 17, 1891.

22. Board of Manufacturers and Employers, quoted in Ira B. Cross, *A History of the Labor Movement in California* (Berkeley: University of California Press, 1935), 210.

23. The best treatment of the 1901 strike is Jules Tygiel, *Workingmen in San Francisco, 1880–1901* (New York: Garland, 1992), 294–348. See also John Elrick, "Social Conflict and the Politics of Reform: Mayor James D. Phelan and the San Francisco Waterfront Strike of 1901," *California History* 88, no. 2 (2011): 4–23.

24. David Emmons accurately describes Phelan's political talents, stating "that he managed to stay on the right side of the Irish, the church, and labor while simultaneously socializing with Anglo-American Protestant high society was a tribute to his political agility and/or exceptional Irish luck": Emmons, *Beyond the American Pale,* 274.

25. *San Francisco Municipal Reports, 1896–1897* (San Francisco: City and County of San Francisco, Board of Supervisors, 1897), app. 8.

26. *The Monitor,* August 24, 1901; *San Francisco Chronicle,* August 30, 1901.

27. *Merchants Association Review,* October 1901, 8.

28. *San Francisco Chronicle,* August 13, 1901.

29. *Organized Labor,* August 3, 1901; *The Monitor,* August 3, 1901; *San Francisco Chronicle,* August 9, 1901; Bernard Cornelius Cronin, *Father Yorke and the Labor Movement in San Francisco, 1900–1910* (Washington, D.C.: Catholic University of America Press, 1943), 74; James P. Gaffey, *Citizen of No Mean City: Archbishop Patrick Riordan of San Francisco (1841–1914)* (Wilmington, N.C.: Consortium Books, 1976), 375–376.

30. *The Monitor,* August 10, 1901. See also Timothy J. Sarbaugh, "Father Yorke and the San Francisco Waterfront, 1901–1916," *Pacific Historian* 25 (Fall 1981): 29–35.

31. *The Star,* September 14, 1901; *San Francisco Chronicle,* September 14, September 20, 1901.

32. *San Francisco Chronicle,* September 20, 1901; *The Monitor,* September 14, 1901.

33. The quote is from *The Monitor,* September 28, 1901. Robert Knight, *Industrial Relations in the San Francisco Bay Area, 1900–1918* (Berkeley: University of California Press, 1960), 82; Tygiel, *Workingmen in San Francisco,* 321.

34. The Yorke quote is from *San Francisco Examiner,* September 22, 1901.

35. Tygiel, *Workingmen in San Francisco,* 335–340; Elrick, "Social Conflict and the Politics of Reform," 18–23.

36. The Schmitz quote is from *Merchants Association Review,* December 1901, 2. For the Union Labor Party, see Issel and Cherny, *San Francisco, 1865–1932,* 154–161.

37. Issel and Cherny, *San Francisco, 1865–1932,* 156–157. See also Michael Kazin, *Barons of Labor: The San Francisco Building Trades and Union Power in the Progressive Era* (Urbana: University of Illinois Press, 1987), 82–107.

38. *The Monitor,* September 3, September 10, 1910; Issel and Cherny, *San Francisco, 1865-1932,* 91, 161-199.

39. The Koster quote is from *San Francisco Chronicle,* July 11, 1916. Issel and Cherny, *San Francisco, 1865-1932,* 177-180.

40. *San Francisco Chronicle,* July 26, 1916; *Town Talk,* July 22, 29, 1916; *Organized Labor,* September 9, 1916.

41. *The Bulletin,* July 21, 29, 1916; *The Leader,* August 12, 1916; *Organized Labor,* September 9, 1916. Rabbi Nieto's speeches were reprinted in *The Bulletin,* July 21, 1916, and copies of his columns in the same newspaper are in the Nieto Scrapbooks, Western Jewish History Center, Judah Magnes Museum, Berkeley, Calif. (The records are now held in the BC). The Hanna quote is from *Organized Labor,* September 9, 1916. See also Richard Gribble, *An Archbishop for the People: The Life of Edward J. Hanna* (New York: Paulist Press, 2006), 120-121.

42. The Hanna quote is from an interview with Frederick W. Ely, editor of *Organized Labor,* in *Organized Labor,* June 9, 1923. See also Edward J. Hanna to Charles A. McGrath, January 19, 1922, in Archbishop Edward Hanna Collection, Chancery Archives of the Archdiocese of San Francisco, Menlo Park, Calif. (hereafter, CAASF), Labor file. See also Issel and Cherny, *San Francisco, 1865-1932,* 92-100; Kazin, *Barons of Labor,* 234-276.

43. Issel and Cherny, *San Francisco, 1865-1932,* chap. 8; David G. Dalin, "Public Affairs and the Jewish Community: The Changing Political World of San Francisco Jews," Ph.D. diss., Brandeis University, Waltham, Mass., 1977, chaps. 2-3; David G. Dalin, "Jewish and Non-Partisan Republicanism in San Francisco, 1911-1963," *American Jewish Historical Quarterly* 68 (June 1979): 492-516; Susan Englander, *Class Conflict and Coalition in the California Woman Suffrage Movement, 1907-1912: The San Francisco Wage Earners' Suffrage League* (Lewiston, N.Y.: Edwin Mellen, 1992); Mark Hopkins, "No Undue Familiarity: Gender, Vice, and the Campaign to Regulate Dance Halls, 1911-1921," in Cherny, Irwin, and Wilson, *California Women and Politics,* 289-307; Sister Helena Sanfilippo, "Sisters of Mercy," in Burns, *Catholic San Francisco,* 101-107; Lisa Anne Goodrich-Boyd, "Charity Redefined: Katherine Felton and the Associated Charities of San Francisco," master's thesis, San Francisco State University, 1995; Glenna Matthews, "There is No Sex in Citizenship: The Career of Congresswoman Florence Prag Kahn," in *We Have Come to Stay: American Women and Political Parties, 1880-1960,* ed. Melanie Gustafson, Kristie Miller, and Elisabeth I. Perry (Albuquerque: University of New Mexico Press, 1999), 131-140; Jessica Ellen Sewell, *Women and the Everyday City: Public Space in San Francisco, 1890-1915* (Minneapolis: University of Minnesota Press, 2011).

44. Issel and Cherny, *San Francisco, 1865-1932,* 206-207; Victor Low, *The Unimpressible Race: A Century of Educational Struggle by the Chinese in San Francisco* (San Francisco: East/West, 1982), chaps. 4-6; Yuji Ichioka, *The Issei: The World of the First Generation Japanese Immigrants, 1885-1924* (New York: Free Press, 1988), chaps. 6-7.

45. Douglas Henry Daniels, *Pioneer Urbanites: A Social and Cultural History of Black San Francisco* (Philadelphia: Temple University Press, 1980), 108.

46. Minutes of the Sunset Transportation and Development Association, December 12, 1925, in Sunset Transportation and Development Association Records, CHS.

47. Broussard, *Black San Francisco,* 32.

48. Phelan's quotes about white supremacy are from Robert E. Hennings, *James D. Phelan and the Wilson Progressives of California* (New York: Garland, 1985), 41, 136-137, 152, 194. The comment about renting Heaven and living in California is from James D. Phelan to Gertrude Atherton, letter, June 13, 1915, quoted in Walsh and O'Keefe, *Legacy of a Native Son,* 1.

CHAPTER 2

1. On Furuseth, Lundeberg, and the competition between communists and anticommunists in the sailors' unions, see Bruce Nelson, *Workers on the Waterfront: Seamen, Longshoremen, and Unionism in the 1930s* (Urbana: University of Illinois Press, 1988), 40–48, chaps. 8–9. A photograph of the dedication of the Furuseth memorial, from the *San Francisco Call Bulletin*, September 1, 1941, can be viewed in the San Francisco Historical Photograph Collection, San Francisco Public Library, available online at http://sfpl .org/index.php?pg=0200000301.

2. For a perceptive examination of the continuity between programs of the Hoover administration and subsequent New Deal innovations, see Jason Scott Smith, *Building New Deal Liberalism: The Political Economy of Public Works, 1933–1956* (New York: Cambridge University Press, 2006). Historians have been slow to document how in specific U.S. cities postwar urban growth liberalism was the product of decades-long contests over how to define the public interest. For an exception to this neglect, see Joel Schwartz, *The New York Approach: Robert Moses, Urban Liberalism, and Redevelopment of the Inner City* (Columbus: Ohio State University Press, 1993), 295–305. John Mollenkopf critiques business leaders and politicians who allied themselves with business values in his study of growth politics in Boston and San Francisco, in Mollenkopf, *The Contested City*. On the politics of growth generally, see Alan Wolfe, *America's Impasse: The Rise and Fall of the Politics of Growth* (New York: Pantheon Books, 1981); Robert M. Collins, *The Business Response to Keynes, 1929–1964* (New York: Columbia University Press, 1981); Robert M. Collins, *More: The Politics of Economic Growth in Postwar America* (New York: Oxford University Press, 2000).

3. Issel and Cherny, *San Francisco, 1865–1932*, 52.

4. Ibid.; D. V. Nicholson to A. P. Giannini, letter, May 25, 1932, in Bank of America Archives, San Francisco.

5. *San Francisco Chronicle*, March 7, 1930; William H. Mullins, *The Depression and the Urban West Coast, 1929–1933: Los Angeles, San Francisco, Seattle, and Portland* (Bloomington: Indiana University Press, 1991), 36–38, 103–104.

6. Morton Keller, *Regulating a New Economy: Public Policy and Economic Change in America, 1900–1933* (Cambridge, Mass.: Harvard University Press, 1990), 37–38; *Twenty-First Annual Report of the California Development Board* (1910), n.p.

7. "Your State Organization: The California Development Association," *California Journal of Development* (July 1923): 47; Frederick J. Koster, "The Obligation of Leadership," *California Journal of Development* (February 1927): 10.

8. "Iron, Steel, and Allied Industries of California: Proceedings of the Second Annual Conference" (Hotel Del Monte, Del Monte, Calif., January 22–23, 1926), *California Journal of Development* (February 1926): 20–27; R. Earl Fisher, "The Responsibility of Organized Business," *California Journal of Development* (June 1930): 29, 45–46; Koster, "The Obligation of Leadership," 29.

9. Issel and Cherny, *San Francisco, 1865–1932*, 194–198; Preston Devine, "The Adoption of the 1932 Charter of San Francisco," master's thesis, University of California, Berkeley, 1933; San Francisco Chamber of Commerce, Municipal Affairs Committee, "History of General Obligation Bond Issues, City and County of San Francisco, 1928 through 1948," November 5, 1948, copy in Greater San Francisco Chamber of Commerce Records, CHS, box 4, folder 56.

10. Information regarding Koster's Catholicism is from my interview with the family's spiritual adviser, Father John J. Reilly, St. Patrick's Seminary, Menlo Park, Calif.,

September 13, 1997. The Koster quotes are from "Organization of Business," *California Journal of Development* (September 1933): 6; "National Industrial Recovery Act," *California Journal of Development* (June 1933): 4–5, 14, 24–25.

11. "National Industrial Recovery Act," 24. Koster was more successful in developing support for his cooperative vision in San Francisco than in California generally: see Jason Sjoberg, "The National Industrial Recovery Act: Business and Organized Labor in California 1933–1935," honors thesis in history, San Francisco State University, 1996. Mayor Rossi's gradual acceptance of New Deal policies is demonstrated in Ronald R. Rossi, "Trickle-Down Paternalism: Mayor Angelo Rossi's Embrace of the New Deal State," master's thesis, San Jose State University, 2009. See also Colin Gordon, *New Deals: Business, Labor, and Politics in America, 1920–1935* (New York: Cambridge University Press, 1994); Kim Phillips-Fein, *Invisible Hands: The Business Crusade against the New Deal* (New York: W. W. Norton, 2009).

12. The organization of regional councils is described in "National Industrial Recovery Act," 24; A. E. Goddard, "The Whole State Speaks through the Regional Councils," *California Journal of Development* (June 1935): 4.

13. Alexander Heron announced the formation of the Bay Area Council in the *San Francisco Chronicle,* September 1, 1944. See also Richard A. Sundeen Jr., "The San Francisco Bay Area Council: An Analysis of a Non-Governmental Metropolitan Organization," master's thesis, University of California, Berkeley, 1963, 68–71; *San Francisco Chronicle,* November 17, 1943, and obituary of Alexander Heron, *San Francisco Chronicle,* February 8, 1965.

14. Sundeen, "The San Francisco Bay Area Council," 73. On corporatism, see Gordon, *New Deals*; Donald R. Brand, *Corporatism and the Rule of Law: A Study of the National Recovery Administration* (Ithaca, N.Y.: Cornell University Press, 1988); Ellis W. Hawley, "The Corporate Ideal as Liberal Philosophy in the New Deal," in *The Roosevelt New Deal: A Program Assessment Fifty Years After,* ed. Wilbur J. Cohen (Austin: University of Texas Press, 1986), 85–103; Ellis W. Hawley, "A Partnership Formed, Dissolved, and in Renegotiation: Business and Government in the Franklin D. Roosevelt Era," in *Business and Government: Essays in Twentieth Century Cooperation and Confrontation,* ed. Joseph R. Frese and Jacob Judd (Tarrytown, N.Y.: Sleepy Hollow Press and Rockefeller Archive Center, 1985), 187–219.

15. Mel Scott, *The San Francisco Bay Area: A Metropolis in Perspective* (Berkeley: University of California Press, 1959), 261–263. On labor participation, see F. N. Belgrano to George Wilson, November 20, 1944, in San Francisco CIO Records, BC (hereafter, SFCIO), carton 1, Committees of San Francisco CIO Council folder; Frank N. Belgrano Jr. to members of the San Francisco Bay Area Council, memorandum, August 3, 1945, in SFCIO, carton 3, General Correspondence folder.

16. The Thomas G. Plant quote is from Plant to Frances Perkins, telegram, June 23, 1934, in Papers of Secretary of Labor Frances Perkins, National Archives and Records Administration, record group 174 (hereafter, Perkins Papers), box 35, Conciliation-Strikes-Longshoremen-1934 file.

17. "New Deal Slate of Officials," *Voice of the Federation,* January 28, 1937, 9. The founding and activities of the Maritime Federation of the Pacific are documented in the organization's records at the Northern California Labor Archives and Research Center, San Francisco State University (hereafter, LARC).

18. Frank J. Taylor, "All Quiet on the Waterfront," *California: Magazine of Pacific Business* (April 1937), 18–21, 36, 38–39; Frank J. Taylor, "A Program for Labor Peace,"

California: Magazine of Pacific Business (June 1937), 34–35; Minutes BD, June 24, 1937, in CHS.

19. *San Francisco Chronicle,* November 3, 1937; Minutes BD, January 13, February 3, 1938, in CHS; "Laboratory of Labor Relations," *California: Magazine of the Pacific* (January 1939), 10–11, 23.

20. For evidence of Harry Bridges's Communist Party membership, see Harvey Klehr, John Earl Haynes, and Fridrikh Igorevich Firsov, *The Secret World of American Communism* (New Haven, Conn.: Yale University Press, 1995), 104; *San Francisco News,* June 4, 1938, 3, 6; *San Francisco Chronicle,* June 4, 1938, 1.

21. "The Town Meeting," editorial, *Labor Clarion,* June 10, 1938, 4; "The San Francisco Labor Council and the Committee of 43 Hereby Announce the Establishment of the Joint Labor Committee," memorandum, in San Francisco Labor Council Records, BC (hereafter, SFLCR), carton 117, Committee of 43 file; "Laboratory of Labor Relations," 23.

22. Ira B. Cross, "Why a Dictatorship?" *Organized Labor,* May 5, 1934, 1.

23. Minutes of the meeting of the California State Industrial Union Council, December 14, 1941, in SFCIO, carton 1, Protest Letters and Replies (National) folder; mimeographed transcript of the proceedings of the California Conference on Labor and the War, June 6–7, 1942, 75, 24, copy in SFCIO, carton 18, CIO Report on the War folder.

24. "Resist Trimming Labor Gains," San Francisco Labor Council resolution, attached to J. A. O'Connell to Franklin D. Roosevelt, June 17, 1940, in SFLCR, box 37, U.S. President folder. The events of the hotel and department store strikes can be followed in the extensive newspaper clipping files at the San Francisco History Center, San Francisco Main Public Library (hereafter, SFHC). See also *San Francisco Chronicle,* March 12, June 5, 1942; *San Francisco Board of Supervisors Journal of Proceedings* (hereafter, *Journal of Proceedings*), February 2, 1942, 225–226; *Journal of Proceedings,* February 11, 1942, 264–269; *Journal of Proceedings,* February 16, 1942, 278–280. The streetcar controversy is described by Mayor Lapham in "Mayor's Message" (reviewing events of 1944), *Journal of Proceedings.* January 2, 1945, 8–11, and discussed by the Board of Supervisors in *Journal of Proceedings,* October 9, 1944, 2128–2129. The machinists' dispute is analyzed in Richard P. Boyden, "The San Francisco Machinists and the National War Labor Board," in *American Labor in the Era of World War II,* ed. Sally M. Miller and Daniel A. Cornford (Westport, Conn.: Praeger, 1995), 105–119.

25. Howard Kimeldorf, *Reds or Rackets: The Making of Radical and Conservative Unions on the Waterfront* (Berkeley: University of California Press, 1988), 148–149, 208, and Charles P. Larrowe, *Harry Bridges: The Rise and Fall of Radical Labor in the United States,* rev. ed. (Westport, Conn.: Lawrence Hill, 1972), 293–297, provide a generally pro-labor analysis of the strikes in 1946 and 1948. For the employers' point of view, see "White Paper: West Coast Maritime Strike," October 11, 1948, Pacific American Shipowners Association and Waterfront Employers of California, copy in SFHC, Vertical File Collection, San Francisco Strikes Maritime 1946 folder.

26. Leland W. Cutler, *America Is Good to a Country Boy* (Stanford, Calif.: Stanford University Press, 1954), 182–194.

27. Ibid.

28. Ibid., 184–185.

29. The Chamber of Commerce described its program in *San Francisco: Hub of Western Industry* (1939), copy in BC. See also Chamber of Commerce, "Annual Report 1939 and Work Program for 1940," mimeograph copy in Chamber of Commerce Records, CHS; *San Francisco Examiner,* November 6–7, 1939. The evolution of this policy process

can be followed in Wm. L. Montgomery to R. R. Cooley, memorandum, June 8, 1943, in SFCIO, carton 2, Postwar Plan folder; *Journal of Proceedings,* March 29, 1943, 718–719, April 5, 1943, 758, June 21, 1943, 1661–1662, August 21, 1943, 1812–1813, September 18, 1944, 2019–2020; San Francisco League for Municipal Research, vol. 1 (April 1943). For the committee's report, see "Mayor's Message" (events of 1945), *Journal of Proceedings,* January 14, 1946, 58–59; "Report of the Citizen's Postwar Planning Committee," August 20, 1945, app. E, "Mayor's Annual Report to the Board of Supervisors" (1946), 40–76, copy in SFLCR, carton 52, Mayor's Office 1946 folder.

30. Theresa Selfa, "Revenue and Expenditure in San Francisco: A Study of the Controller's Annual Reports, 1933–1987," independent study paper, San Francisco State University, 1989, 4–9; San Francisco Chamber of Commerce, Municipal Affairs Committee, "History of General Obligation Bond Issues," 4, 6–7. For details of these campaigns, see "Mayor's Message," *Journal of Proceedings,* January 2, 1945, 9; "Report of the San Francisco Juvenile Court," *Journal of Proceedings,* January 2, 1945, 83–86; *San Francisco Examiner,* November 11, 1944; Citizen's Committee for Sewer Bonds to "Dear Friends," September 15, 1944, in SFLCR, box 50, Law and Legislative Committee 1944–1946 folder; "United Labor Says Do Your Part for Jobs and Security" campaign flyer, in SFLCR, box 50, Charter Amendment 1945 folder; *San Francisco Examiner,* November 5, 1945.

31. While serving on the War Labor Board, Lapham wrote a lengthy treatise describing his thinking titled, "Thinking Aloud; or, The Present Thoughts of One Employer," March 18, 1942. The paper was intended, he wrote, "to provoke discussion among employer members of the War Labor Board," and he sent copies to business and labor leaders all over the country. A copy of the document, along with replies from a wide variety of correspondents, is in Roger Dearborn Lapham Papers, BC, carton 1, Thinking Aloud folder. See also Andrew A. Workman, "Creating the Center: Liberal Intellectuals, the National War Labor Board, and the Stabilization of American Industrial Relations," Ph.D. diss., University of North Carolina, Chapel Hill, 1993, 41, 135–149, 158–161; Nelson Lichtenstein, *Labor's War at Home: The CIO in World War II* (New York: Cambridge University Press, 1982), 216–222.

32. Royce Deems Delmatier, "The Rebirth of the Democratic Party in California, 1928–1938," Ph.D. diss., University of California, Berkeley, 1955, 236, 239; *San Francisco Chronicle,* September 18, 22, 1934.

33. See Herman Phleger, "Sixty Years in Law, Public Service, and International Affairs," oral history interview by Miriam Feingold Stein, 1979, in Regional Oral History Office, Bancroft Library, University of California, Berkeley (hereafter, ROHO-UCB), 65, 75, 87–99; Roger Lapham, "An Interview on Shipping, Labor, City Government, and American Foreign Aid," oral history interview by C. L. Gilb, 1957, in ROHO-UCB, 140–141.

34. Maurice E. Harrison, *St. Thomas More: An Address before the St. Thomas More Society,* October 8, 1941 (privately printed), copy in BC, 7, 9.

35. Elinor Raas Heller, "A Volunteer Career in Politics, in Higher Education, and on Governing Boards," two-volume oral history by Malca Chall, 1974–1980, ROHO-UCB, 1984, 182, 185, 187, 202; *Brobeck, Phleger, and Harrison: The Earlier Years,* privately printed booklet, 1973, 59, copy in Herman Phleger Papers, BC, carton 2.

36. William Malone, oral history interview conducted by Malca Chall, 1978, ROHO-UCB, 33, 48, 91, 115; Heller, "A Volunteer Career in Politics," 252.

37. The fifty-fifty rule is described in Heller, "A Volunteer Career in Politics," 206. "Julia Gorman Porter: Biographical Information," Julia Gorman Porter Papers, BC, box 1, folder 1, 49; Franck Roberts Havenner, "Reminiscences," oral history interview by Corinne L. Gilb, 1953, ROHO-UCB, 1953, 91, 93.

38. Havenner, "Reminiscences," 95; Malone interview, 116.

39. Nelson, *Workers on the Waterfront*, 226–266; Harvey Klehr and John Earl Haynes, *The American Communist Movement: Storming Heaven Itself* (New York: Twayne, 1992), 92–95.

40. Havenner, "Reminiscences," 97; Malone interview, 117–119; *San Francisco Examiner*, November 8, 1939.

41. Havenner, "Reminiscences," 99–102; *San Francisco Examiner*, November 6, 1940.

42. Ethington, *The Public City*, 55–58.

43. Norman Elkington, "From Adversary to Appointee: Fifty Years of Friendship with Pat Brown," oral history interview by Julie Shearer, 1978–1979, ROHO-UCB, 1982, 8–10, 21; Harold Clinton Brown, "A Lifelong Republican for Edmund G. Brown," oral history interview by Julie Shearer, 1978, ROHO-UCB, 1982, 15–28; *San Francisco Examiner*, November 5, 1941, November 3, 1943; *Journal of Proceedings*, January 8, 1942, 21–23.

44. Malone interview, 121.

45. Ibid., 151–155.

46. Ibid., 24; Julia Porter to Helen Gahagan, July 2, 1943, in Julia Gorman Porter Papers, BC, box 1, folder 1, 1; Lapham, "An Interview on Shipping," 140–141; Phleger, "Sixty Years in Law," 75–76.

47. Roosevelt's letter of commendation is described in Phleger, "Sixty Years in Law," 75–76. During the campaign, Lapham urged voters to support him because "I know my way around Washington." The quote was used in a campaign speech on the radio station KFRC by Julia Porter. A copy of the speech is in Julia Gorham Porter Papers, BC, box 1, folder 1, 48.

48. Richard Lynden and David Hedley to "Dear Brothers and Sisters," October 8, 1943, and CIO Political Action Committee to "Dear Fellow Union Member," October 29, 1943, both in SFCIO, carton 17, Municipal Elections folder; *Labor Herald*, October 15, 1943; Malone interview, 154; Workman, "Creating the Center."

49. *San Francisco Examiner*, November 3, 1943.

50. "Factors Contributing to the Victory of Lapham in the San Francisco Elections," n.d. (but after the November 1943 election), in SFCIO, carton 17, Election Campaign Summaries folder. Someone wrote in the top margin of the typewritten report, "Lapham is still bad."

51. "United Labor's Legislative Committee, Executive Board Report on 16 May 1944 Primary Election," in SFLCR, box 48, Miscellaneous 1944 folder; "Report of the Political Action Committee of the SF CIO Council," July 21, 1944, in SFCIO, carton 16, PAC 1945–1944 folder; David Jenkins, "The Union Movement, the California Labor School, and San Francisco Politics," oral history interview by Lisa Rubens, 1987–1988, ROHO-UCB, 1993, 68, 113, 141; Estolv Ethan Ward, "Organizing and Reporting in the East Bay, California, and the West, 1925–1987," oral history interview by Lisa Rubens, 1987, ROHO-UCB, 1989, 59, 100, 152–154; Klehr and Haynes, *The American Communist Movement*, 98, 100, 103.

52. "Can S.F. Endure Two Years More of Lapham and His Downtown Pals?" editorial, *San Francisco Progress*, Richmond district ed., February 14–15, 1946; Recall Lapham Committee of 1100, Inc., to CIO Community Services Committee, n.d., in SFCIO, carton 6, Roger D. Lapham Mayor folder.

53. Lapham, "An Interview on Shipping," 166–175; "Blind-Date Proposal," editorial, *San Francisco Chronicle*, June 14, 1946; Paul Schnur, quoted in "CIO Steps Up Interest in City," *Christian Science Monitor*, February 16, 1946; CIO-PAC Minutes, April 2, 1946, in SFCIO, carton 5; CIO-PAC Minutes, July 19, 1946, in SFCIO, carton 6, June–December folder; CIO Council recall election statement, June 21, 1946, in SFCIO, carton 6, Roger D.

Lapham Mayor folder. The election data results were compiled from the San Francisco City and County Registrar of Voters' official statement of votes cast, San Francisco History Room, San Francisco Main Public Library. See also Dennis P. Kelly, "Mayor Roger D. Lapham, the Recall Election of 1946, and Neighborhood Voting in San Francisco, 1938–1952," *California History* 76 (Winter 1997–1998), 122–135, 152–155.

54. Norman Leonard, "Life of a Leftist Labor Lawyer," interview by Estolv Ethan Ward, 1985, ROHO-UCB, 1986, 84–89; Ward, "Organizing and Reporting in the East Bay," 162; *San Francisco Chronicle,* January 22, April 26, 1949; See also Kimeldorf, *Reds or Rackets,* 162–169.

55. *San Francisco Call-Bulletin,* September 29, 1947.

CHAPTER 3

1. Joseph L. Alioto, "The Catholic Internationale," *Moraga Quarterly* 7, no. 2 (Winter 1936): 68–72.

2. For demographic and social history, see Issel and Cherny, *San Francisco, 1865–1932*; Robert W. Cherny and William Issel, *San Francisco: Presidio, Port, and Pacific Metropolis* (San Francisco: Boyd and Fraser, 1981). Jeffrey Burns has written a three-volume history of San Francisco Catholic life: Jeffrey M. Burns, *San Francisco: A History of the Archdiocese of San Francisco* (Strasbourg: Editions du Signe, 1999–2001). Volume 1 is titled *1776–1884, From Mission to Golden Frontier*; volume 2 is titled *1885–1945, Glory, Ruin, and Resurrection,* and volume 3 is titled *A Journey of Hope, 1945–2000*.

3. Generalizations about attendance at mass and similar indicators of participation in parish and archdiocesan life are based on data available in census and financial files of the CAASF.

4. The English text of *Rerum Novarum* is available online at http://www.vatican.va/holy _father/leo_xiii/encyclicals/documents/hf_l-xiii_enc_15051891_rerum-novarum_en.html.

5. The English text of *Il Fermo Proposito* is available online at http://www.vatican.va/ holy_father/pius_x/encyclicals/documents/hf_p-x_enc_11061905_il-fermo-proposito_en .html. See also http://www.vatican.va/holy_father/pius_xi/encyclicals/documents/hf_p -xi_enc_23121922_ubi-arcano-dei-consilio_en.html; http://www.vatican.va/holy_father/ pius_xi/encyclicals/documents/hf_p-xi_enc_11121925_quas-primas_en.html.

6. Jeffrey M. Burns, "Mitty, John Joseph," in *The Encyclopedia of American Catholic History,* ed. Michael Glazier and Thomas J. Shelley (Collegeville, Minn.: Liturgical Press, 1997), 967–968; "Life Summary of Archbishop Mitty," *The Monitor,* August 31, 1935, 2.

7. See http://www.vatican.va/holy_father/pius_xi/encyclicals/documents/hf_p-xi _enc_29061931_non-abbiamo-bisogno_en.html; http://www.vatican.va/holy_father/pius _xi/encyclicals/documents/hf_p-xi_enc_19310515_quadragesimo-anno_en.html.

8. Sermon by Coadjutor Archbishop John J. Mitty to the Council of Catholic Women, May 7, 1932, in Mitty Sermon Collection, CAASF.

9. The role of the NCWC in encouraging and monitoring diocesan implementation of papal Catholic Action theory is described in a personal handwritten letter from Reverend John J. Burke, general-secretary of the NCWC, to Archbishop John J. Mitty, June 1, 1932, in CAASF, NCWC 1932–1935 Correspondence file, folder 1 of 2. See also excerpt from the minutes of the NCCW, November 16, 1933, quoted in "Department of Catholic Action Study, National Catholic Welfare Conference," in CAASF, NCWC Catholic Action Study file, folder 3 of 3.

10. "Catholic League for Social Justice in the Archdiocese of San Francisco," pamphlet, in CAASF; "Report of Progress in the Crusade for Social Justice, Bulletin no. 6, June

16, 1933," mimeographed newsletter, in CAASF, Crusade for Social Justice file, PR118 folder; Amleto Giovanni Cicognani to Edward J. Hanna, date illegible, in CAASF, NCWC Correspondence 1933 file, folder 1 of 2. "Program for the Year," August 11, 1933, and Roy A. Bronson to John J. Mitty, September 28, 1933, both in CAASF, Catholic League for Social Justice file, A46.9 folder.

11. Details concerning the strike events of 1934, unless indicated otherwise, are from David F. Selvin, *A Terrible Anger: The 1934 Waterfront and General Strikes in San Francisco* (Detroit: Wayne State University Press, 1996).

12. Cherny, "Prelude to the Popular Front," 11, 19–20.

13. Documentary evidence of Harry Bridges's membership in the Communist Party has been discovered in the archives of the former Soviet Union by Robert Cherny, who describes the complicated relationship between Bridges and the Communist Party in Robert W. Cherny, "Constructing a Radical Identity: History, Memory, and the Seafaring Stories of Harry Bridges," *Pacific Historical Review* 70 (2001): 571–599; Robert W. Cherny, "Harry Bridges and the Communist Party: New Evidence, Old Questions; Old Evidence, New Questions," paper presented at the Annual Meeting of the Organization of American Historians, April 4, 1998 (copy in my possession). See also Harvey Klehr and John E. Haynes, "Communists and the CIO: From the Soviet Archives," *Labor History* 35 (1994): 444–446; Klehr, Haynes, and Firsov, *The Secret World of American Communism,* 104; *The Monitor,* June 9, 1934, 1; *The Leader,* July 28, 1934.

14. *The Monitor,* June 9, 1934, 1.

15. *San Francisco Chronicle,* June 21, 27, 1934. Biographical information about Sylvester Andriano, when not indicated otherwise, is from the fifteen-page, single-spaced, typewritten autobiography contained in Sylvester Andriano to James L. Hagerty, letter, March 10, 1943 (hereafter, Andriano autobiography), and from biographical data in letters from Andriano to Hagerty, all in James L. Hagerty Papers, Archives of St. Mary's College of California, Moraga, box 237.

16. *The Leader,* July 28, 1934; Andriano autobiography.

17. Transcript of Archbishop Edward J. Hanna's radio broadcast of July 13, 1934, is available online at http://www.sfmuseum.org/hist4/maritime9.html.

18. Thomas G. Plant to Frances Perkins, telegram, July 23, 1934, Perkins Papers, box 35, Conciliation-Strikes-Longshoremen-1934 file.

19. Andriano autobiography; memorandum of a telephone conversation of July 15, 1934, between Roger Lapham and Frances Perkins, July 18, 1934, Perkins Papers, box 42, Conciliation-Strikes-Longshoremen-1934 file; *The Leader,* July 28, 1934.

20. *The Leader,* July 21, 1934.

21. Ibid., July 28, 1934; *The Monitor,* July 28, 1934.

22. *San Francisco News,* July 23, 1934; Cherny, "Prelude to the Popular Front," 41.

23. Generalizations about the Communist Party's strategy and tactics, unless indicated otherwise, are based on Cherny, "Prelude to the Popular Front"; Cherny, "The Communist Party in California."

24. "Concise Summary on Communism by Fr. Feely, S.J.," *The Monitor,* May 4, 1935; Cherny, "The Communist Party in California."

25. "Mayor Rossi's Letter to Governor Merriam, Requesting Additional National Guardsmen for San Francisco," July 14, 1934, available online at http://www.sfmuseum .org/hist4/maritime13.html (accessed July 19, 2008). Rossi's statement on driving communists out of San Francisco is quoted in Mike Quin (pseudonym of Paul William Ryan), *The Big Strike* (Olema, Calif.: Olema, 1949), 163. Robert Cherny describes a variety of anticommunist offensives in California (but not those of the Catholic Church): see

Robert W. Cherny, "Anticommunist Networks and Labor: The Pacific Coast in the 1930s," in *Labor's Cold War: Local Politics in Global Context,* ed. Shelton Stromquist (Urbana: University of Illinois Press, 2008), 17–48.

26. Chief Quinn's testimony was given to the state Peace Officers Association, an anticommunist organization chaired by William F. Hynes, the head of the Los Angeles Police Department's "Red Squad." Quinn served as second vice-president: quoted in Larrowe, *Harry Bridges,* 34. See also *The Communist Situation in California: Report of Sub-Committee on Subversive Activities of the Crime Prevention Committee* (Oakland, Calif.: Peace Officers Association, 1937), 48–49.

27. Hugh Gallagher to Your Excellency, handwritten letter, n.d., and attached report dated November 2, 1936, in CAASF, Correspondence Files, Communism 1936–1937 folder; Joseph S. Connelly ("Anti-Subversive Committee, American Legion, Dept. Cal.") to Reverend Dr. Thomas A. Connolly, August 31, 1936, and Thomas A. Connolly (Chancellor-Secretary) to Joseph S. Connelly, September 2, 1936, both in CAASF, Correspondence Files, Communism 1936–1937 folder.

28. Birth certificate of Oleta O'Connor, filed May 6, 1910, San Francisco Department of Public Health; Gallagher to Your Excellency; Connelly to Connolly; Connolly to Connelly.

29. "In re: Olita [*sic*] O'Conner [*sic*]," typed report attached to Gallagher to Your Excellency; Oleta O'Connor Yates, June 26 testimony in transcript of 1952 trial in Federal District Court for violation of the Smith Act (hereafter, Yates Transcript), reprinted in "What a Communist Told the Court: The Testimony of Oletta O'Connor Yates," *People's Daily World Extra,* August 1, 1952, 5.

30. Yates Transcript, 9. American Legion investigator, quoted in *San Francisco Examiner,* August 5, 1935. Memorandum from Wooster Taylor, August 6, 1935, and memorandum to Mr. Chase, February 20, 1935, both in SFHC, Associations, Communism File (Yates) (hereafter, Yates File). "Biographies Provided by Department of Justice on Seven San Francisco Communists Arrested Today by FBI," telegram from Joshua Eppinger to *Examiner,* San Francisco, July 26, 1951, copy in Yates File.

31. "Address at St. Vincent De Paul Golden Jubilee Dinner Condemning Idea of Totalitarian State," January 5, 1936. *The Monitor,* February 22, 1936. *Quod Apostolici Muneris* (On Socialism) is available online at http://www.vatican.va/holy_father/leo_xiii/encyclicals/documents/hf_l-xiii_enc_28121878_quod-apostolici-muneris_en.html.

32. "Inaugural address at the World Catholic Press Exposition," May 12, 1936, *The Monitor,* May 16, 1936.

33. *Western Worker,* November 21, November 25, December 2, 1935, January 16, January 30, February 10, October 26, 1936, all quoted in Cherny, "The Communist Party in California," 11–13.

34. Hugh Gallagher to Archbishop John J. Mitty, June 5, August 3, 1936; "Special Memorandum in re. Harry Bridges"; Carmel Gannon to Monsignor Thomas A. Connolly, September 28, 1936, and attached two-page handwritten list of individuals under surveillance; George Maisak to Archbishop John J. Mitty, September 15, 1936; Harry M. Connelly III to Fellow American, September 12, 1936, all in CAASF, Correspondence Files, Communism 1936–1937 folder.

35. "Arbitration Urged by Archbishop Mitty in S[an] F[rancisco] Waterfront Dispute," copy in CAASF, Correspondence Files, Labor 1934–1939 folder.

36. Larrowe, *Harry Bridges,* 98–100, 112–114; Paul C. Smith, *Personal File, an Autobiography* (New York: Appleton-Century, 1964), 156–157.

37. Attendance figures are from newspaper articles and attendance numbers included in notes on photographs: *Western Worker,* August 17, 1936; *San Francisco Chronicle,*

October 25, 1936; photograph of the Feast of Christ the King Celebration (AAC-5340) and of the Eucharistic Congress, 1941 (AAC-5217), in digital photograph collection, SFHC. The encyclical *Quas Primas* (On the Feast of Christ the King) is available online at http://www.vatican.va/holy_father/pius_xi/encyclicals/documents/hf_p-xi_enc_11121925_quas-primas_en.html.

38. *San Francisco News,* October 19, 1936; *San Francisco Chronicle,* October 25, 1936.

39. "An Appeal to Catholic People, a Reply to Archbishop Mitty," in CAASF, Correspondence Files, Communism 1936–1937 folder.

40. Election data are from http://www.joincalifornia.com/candidate/6219.

41. Transcript of radio address by Vernon Healy, delivered over KGO Radio, October 24, 1936, in CAASF, Correspondence Files, Communism 1936–1937 folder.

42. Voter registration and election results are from Cherny, "The Communist Party in California," tables 1–2, 7–8. J. A. Hall to Archbishop John J. Mitty, March 19, 1937; Archbishop John J. Mitty to Reverend Bryan J. McEntegart, March 20, 1937; Reverend Bryan J. McEntegart to Archbishop Mitty, March 30, 1937; Archbishop John J. Mitty to Reverend James J. McHugh, April 14, 1937; Archbishop John J. Mitty to Reverend Bryan J. McEntegart, April 14, 1937, all in CAASF, Correspondence Files, Communism 1936–1937 folder.

CHAPTER 4

1. *Divini Redemptoris* (On Atheistic Communism) is available online at http://www.vatican.va/holy_father/pius_xi/encyclicals/documents/hf_p-xi_enc_19031937_divini-redemptoris_en.html.

2. *The Monitor,* May 1, 1937; *San Francisco News,* April 29, 1937.

3. "Report on April 28, 1937, Dreamland Auditorium Meeting under Auspices of American Friends of the Soviet Union," in CAASF, Correspondence Files, Communism 1936–1937 folder.

4. *New York Times,* July 26, 1938; *People's World,* January 3, 1938; Clyde H. Ashen to State Officers, Deputies, Grand Knights, Officers, and Members of the Knights of Columbus, California State Council Jurisdiction, July 30, 1937, in CAASF, Correspondence Files, Knights of Columbus 1937 folder; Archbishop John J. Mitty to Hugh Gallagher, June 13, 1938, in CAASF, Correspondence Files, Communism 1938–1939 folder; Martin H. Carmody to Archbishop John J. Mitty, date illegible but 1938, in CAASF, Correspondence Files, Knights of Columbus 1938 folder.

5. Carmody to Mitty; Louis Kenedy to Reverend Wilfred G. Hurley, C.S.F., February 25, 1939; Archbishop John J. Mitty to Louis Kenedy, March 25, 1939; Edward J. Heffron to Archbishop John J. Mitty, March 30, 1939, all in CAASF, Correspondence Files, National Council of Catholic Men/National Council of Catholic Women 1938–1939 folder 2 of 2; José M. Sánchez, *The Spanish Civil War as a Religious Tragedy* (Notre Dame, Ind.: Notre Dame University Press, 1987), 172–198; J. David Valaik, "Catholics, Neutrality, and the Spanish Embargo," *Journal of American History* 54 (June 1967), 73–85.

6. The quote on the breakdown of public order is from Stanley G. Payne, *The Collapse of the Spanish Republic, 1933–1936: Origins of the Civil War* (New Haven, Conn.: Yale University Press, 2006), 362; J. David Valaik, "American Catholics and the Second Spanish Republic, 1911–1936," *Journal of Church and State* 10 (Winter 1968): 13–28; Donald F. Crosby, "Boston's Catholics and the Spanish Civil War," *New England Quarterly* 44 (March 1971): 82–100; "Memorandum on Communism" prepared for Archbishop John J. Mitty by Father Hugh A. Donohoe (hereafter, Donohoe memorandum), attached to a

letter from Donohoe to Mitty, September 2, 1937, in CAASF, Correspondence Files, Communism 1936–1937 folder, 3.

7. Sánchez, *The Spanish Civil War as a Religious Tragedy,* 9. The quote "the greatest anticlerical bloodletting Europe has ever seen" is from Mary Vincent, "'The Keys of the Kingdom': Religious Violence in the Spanish Civil War, July–August 1936," in *The Splintering of Spain: Cultural History and the Spanish Civil War, 1936–1939,* ed. Chris Ealham and Michael Richards (New York: Cambridge University Press, 2005), 68. See also Paul Preston, *The Spanish Holocaust: Inquisition and Extermination in Twentieth Century Spain* (New York: W. W. Norton, 2012), 107–108, 233–236.

8. Donohoe memorandum, 3; J. David Valaik, "American Catholic Dissenters and the Spanish Civil War," *Catholic Historical Review* 53, no. 4 (January 1968): 537–555.

9. The biographical information for Charles A. Ramm is from the University of California's website at http://sunsite.berkeley.edu. On Tobin, see Lewis Francis Byington, *History of San Francisco,* vol. 3 (Chicago: S. J. Clarke, 1931), 74–78.

10. "Text of Address of William F. Montavon," October 27, 1936, in CAASF, Correspondence Files, Communism 1936–1937 folder.

11. Aurelio M. Espinosa, *The Spanish Republic and the Causes of the Counter-Revolution* (San Francisco: Spanish Relief Committee, 1937), 19. Umberto Olivieri became an ordained Catholic priest in 1958, at seventy-four, and spent the last fifteen years of his life ministering to the Otomi tribe in Mexico: see Sister Josephine Olivieri Targuini, "My Favorite Priest," at http://avemaria.bravepages.com.

12. Umberto Olivieri, *Democracy! Which Brand, Stalin's or Jefferson's?* (San Francisco: Spanish Relief Committee, 1937), preface, 15.

13. The quote "The great scandal of silence" is from Sánchez, *The Spanish Civil War as a Religious Tragedy,* 116; F. R. Fuller to Archbishop John J. Mitty, April 22, 1937, in CAASF, Correspondence Files, Communism 1936–1937 folder; F. R. Fuller to Father Raymond J. Feely, February 1, 1938, in CAASF, Correspondence Files, Communism 1938–1939 folder.

14. *People's World,* January 21, October 26, 1938.

15. The encyclical *Mit Brennender Sorge* is available online at http://www.vatican.va. Maria Mazzenga "Condemning the Nazis: Father Charles Coughlin, Father Maurice Sheehy, the National Catholic Welfare Conference, and Kristallnacht," paper presented at the American Catholic Historical Association, Washington, D.C., January 6, 2008 (copy in my possession).

16. *Mit Brennender Sorge.* The German ambassador is quoted in Anthony Rhodes, *The Vatican in the Age of the Dictators (1922–1945)* (New York: Holt, Rinehart, and Winston, 1973), 206.

17. Gribble, *An Archbishop for the People,* 113–114; Reverend M. J. Ahern to Archbishop John J. Mitty, March 13, July 24, 1936, and Mitty to Ahern, April 14, 1936, in CAASF, Correspondence Files, "A" 1936–1937 folder.

18. *The Monitor,* January 1, 1938. The text of Mitty's radio address is reprinted in *The Monitor,* November 19, 1938; the transcript of the entire broadcast and an audio clip is at http://libraries.cua.edu/archrcua/packets.html.

19. *The Monitor,* November 19, 1938.

20. *People's World,* January 21, February 3–4, March 8, March 11, 1938.

21. Ibid., May 2, May 4, July 30, October 1, October 5, October 24–26, 1938.

22. William Schneiderman, *Dissent on Trial: Memoirs of a Political Life* (Minneapolis: MEP Publications, 1983), quoted in Cherny, "The Communist Party in California," 23; Al Richmond, *A Long View from the Left* (Boston: Houghton Mifflin, 1972), 174.

23. *San Francisco Chronicle,* October 28, 1938; *San Francisco Call-Bulletin,* October 27, 1938; "Address on Catholic Action," October 29, 1938, in Mitty Sermon Collection, CAASF.

24. Hugh A. Donohoe, "Communism: Anti-Religious and Anti-American," *The Argonaut,* 117, November 11, 1938, 7–8. The editor of *The Argonaut,* W. W. Chapin, had originally asked Archbishop Mitty to write the article on communism, but Mitty delegated the job to Father Donohoe, warning him, "You had better be prepared, however, for some comeback to your article": Archbishop John J. Mitty to Reverend Hugh A. Donohoe, September 2, 1938, in CAASF, Correspondence files, Communism 1938–1939 folder.

25. Havenner, "Reminiscences," 91–93; Malone interview, 116, 254; *San Francisco Examiner,* November 8, 1939.

26. Jack Henning, "The Catholic College Graduate and Labor," *Moraga Quarterly* 9 (Spring 1939): 165–70.

CHAPTER 5

1. This chapter focuses on the work of Catholic men in the church's Catholic Action program. Given the gender separation that was characteristic of the church's practice during the period, women's work in Catholic Action developed parallel to that of the men and will be discussed in Chapter 6. For more detail on Alioto, see Chapter 11. The quote is from Harold E. Fey, "Can Catholicism Win America?—A Series of Eight Articles Reprinted from *The Christian Century*" (Chicago: Christian Century, 1945), 2.

2. *The Monitor,* May 8, 1943.

3. CAASF, Personal Record of Hugh A. Donohoe folder.

4. *The Monitor,* November 14, 1942.

5. CAASF, Personal Record of Hugh A. Donohoe folder. The dissertation is titled "Collective Bargaining under the NIRA" (Ph.D. diss., Catholic University of America, Washington, D.C., 1935).

6. *San Francisco Chronicle,* February 7, 1948, August 12, 1958, August 18, 1987; CAASF, Personal Record of Hugh A. Donohoe folder.

7. Sister Patrice Donohoe, interview by Michael Kelly, April 28, 1999, Belmont, Calif., quoted in Michael Kelly, "Reverend Hugh A. Donohoe," seminar paper, Department of History, San Francisco State University, 1999 (copy in my possession).

8. Correspondence relating to these duties is in Hugh A. Donohoe Papers, CAASF, box 4; Bishop Edwin O'Hara to John J. Mitty, April 8, 1937, in CAASF, Correspondence Files, Social Action School for Priests folder; *The Monitor,* June 26, 1937.

9. Donohoe, "Collective Bargaining under the NIRA," 91.

10. Ibid., 93.

11. Ibid., 100.

12. Hugh A. Donohoe, "As the Editor Sees It," *The Monitor,* December 19, 1942.

13. See the discussion of this point in the review essay Ronald W. Schatz, "American Labor and the Catholic Church," *International Labor and Working Class History* 20 (Fall 1981), 49–50. A revealing exchange of letters in 1948 between Harry Bridges and Reverend Charles Owen Rice of Pittsburgh is reprinted in Charles J. McCollester, *Fighter with a Heart: Writings of Charles Owen Rice, Pittsburgh Labor Priest* (Pittsburgh: University of Pittsburgh Press, 1996), 68–70. Cherny, "Harry Bridges and the Communist Party." The importance of distinguishing between "responsible" anticommunism and "extremist" red-baiting is a theme of Richard Gid Powers, *Not without Honor: The History of American Anticommunism* (New York: Free Press, 1995).

14. *The Monitor,* September 12, 1936, February 13, May 1, September 11, 1937, September 10, 1938, April 20, September 7, 1940, April 12, 1941; Reverend Harold E. Collins, Secretary to the Archbishop, to Monsignor William McGough, August 20, 1946, in CAASF, Labor/Miscellaneous 1946 file.

15. Monsignor George G. Higgins with William Bole, *Organized Labor and the Church: Reflections of a "Labor Priest"* (New York: Paulist Press, 1993), 58–62; Dennis A. Deslippe, "'A Revolution of Its Own': The Social Doctrine of the Association of Catholic Trade Unionists in Detroit, 1939–50," *Records of the American Catholic Historical Society of Philadelphia* 102 (Winter 1991): 19–36.

16. Laura Smith to Monsignor Thomas A. Connolly, enclosing a copy of a mimeographed pamphlet "It's Our City Too," September 26, 1938, and Gus Gaynor, Brotherhood of Railway Clerks, press release dated October 18, 1938, in CAASF, Labor 1934–1939 file; Constitution of the ACTU of San Francisco, reprinted in *The Monitor,* January 28, 1939.

17. J. J. McDonough to John J. Mitty, n.d. but during October 1938, in CAASF, Labor 1934–1939 file. John J. Mitty to Hugh A. Donohoe, January 14, 1939, in Donohoe Papers, CAASF, Assorted Correspondence folder 8; *The Monitor,* September 9, 1939, May 10, 1941, August 28, 1943, November 18, 1944, April 26, 1947, March 5, 1948. John J. Mitty to Hugh Gallagher, March 20, 1941, in CAASF, Labor 1939–1943 file.

18. *The Monitor,* January 15, 1944. Data on the ACTU are from the organization's membership and dues ledgers, checking account statements, attendance lists at meetings, and correspondence in Labor Management School Records/ACTU, Archives of the University of San Francisco.

19. At the point of its greatest activity, the organization had 599 dues-paying members. I have been able to identify the union membership of all but sixty-four. The longshoremen's unions dominated the organization, with the 274 members from the ILWU divided as follows: 191 from Local 10; 67 from Local 34; and 16 from Local 6. Fifty teamsters from Local 85 belonged to the ACTU, as did forty retail clerks from Local 1100. Membership in the ACTU appears to have been concentrated in the one San Francisco union in which the Communist Party influence posed a realistic threat to rank-and-file control. The building trades, for instance, were poorly represented.

20. Cherny, "Harry Bridges and the Communist Party." Data on Kearney's and Bradley's electoral successes in Local 10 are from the subject card files and from various issues of the union's newspaper, *The Dispatcher,* in the Anne Rand Research Library, ILWU, San Francisco. For a typical treatment of the opposition to the leftist officers and members, see Kimeldorf, *Reds or Rackets?,* 138, 150. Kearney's Catholicism is ignored by Kimeldorf, as are the ILWU members who paid dues to the ACTU, as well as to the ILWU. Kearney merits a mention as a popular officer of Local 10 and one of many Catholic officers in various CIO unions in Vincent Silverman, *Imagining Internationalism in American and British Labor, 1939–49* (Urbana: University of Illinois Press, 2000). Silverman, however, does not take the religious character of the ACTU seriously, characterizing it wholly negatively as an anticommunist outfit. He appears to have ignored the ACTU's records altogether and mistakenly dismisses the importance of Kearney's Catholicism and the ACTU work in San Francisco on the basis of oral history testimony by a single informant. To his credit, Silverman is forthright about his point of view, writing, "I grew up almost instinctively hating such nefarious figures as Walter Reuther, James Carey, and Joe Curran": Silverman, *Imagining Internationalism in American and British Labor,* xi, 130, 242. Handwritten notes taken at ACTU meetings are in the Paul Pinsky Collection, LARC. That the leftist officers of the ILWU's international organization took the ACTU considerably more seri-

ously than have subsequent historians is evident from the research director's careful monitoring of its activities during the late 1940s.

21. Hugh A. Donohoe, "As the Editor Sees It," *The Monitor,* February 16, 1946, 63, February 22, 1947, 15. Congress passed the Taft-Hartley Act in June 1947 over President Truman's veto, and while it did not repeal the Wagner Act, it fundamentally changed the character of the federal government's regulation of labor relations by establishing a variety of controls on the actual substance of collective-bargaining agreements and unions' internal procedural matters. The closed shop, prohibiting the hiring of non-union employees, was made illegal, and the government could obtain injunctions requiring a "cooling-off" period of eighty days during a strike considered dangerous to health or safety. The Taft-Hartley Act also included a clause that allowed states to prohibit union shops. Anti-labor coalitions in eleven states immediately succeeded in lobbying for such "Right to Work" (anti-union shop) legislation at the state level.

22. Hugh A. Donohoe, "As the Editor Sees It," *The Monitor,* December 8, 1945.

23. Hugh A. Donohoe, "Invocation at CIO Conference, 1945," in Donohoe Papers, CAASF, box 4.

24. "S.F. Labor Honors Bishop Donohoe," *The Monitor,* October 24, 1947, 1–2.

25. *Who's Who in Labor* (New York: Dryden Press, 1946), 323–324; *San Francisco Chronicle,* October 2, 1974; *San Francisco Examiner, California Living,* April 30, 1967; *San Francisco Examiner,* September 23, 1963.

26. *San Francisco Chronicle,* October 2, 1974.

27. A copy of the election flyer with the quotation is at http://www.sfmuseum.org/hist1/shelley.html. See also http://bioguide.congress.gov/scripts/biodisplay.pl?index=S000327 for the official congressional biography.

28. This and the next paragraph are based on material in Chapters 2–3 in this volume.

29. "Catholicism in San Francisco," mimeographed typewritten report given at the Communist Party County Convention, July 10–11, 1948, 2–3, copy in Southern California Library for Social Studies and Research, Los Angeles, Subject File, Communist Party 1948 folder.

30. Quoted in James W. Kelly Jr., "USF Labor-Management School, 1972," *Western Jesuit* (Fall 1972): 22.

31. The role of the Communist Party in the California Labor School is described by one of its founders, David Jenkins, in Jenkins, "The Union Movement." See also Joseph M. McShane, "A Survey of the History of the Jesuit Labor Schools in New York: An American Social Gospel in Action," *Records of the American Catholic Historical Society of Philadelphia* 102 (Winter 1991): 37–64.

32. USF-Labor Management School Course Schedules, various years, Labor Management School Collection, Archives of the University of San Francisco.

33. Ibid. Summary Enrollment Statistics, Records Department, University of San Francisco.

34. *San Francisco Chronicle,* October 13, 1957. See also "Discrimination in Employment"; "The Employment Problems of the Negro Worker in San Francisco," *Labor Management Panel* 7 (January 1956): 1–4.

35. *The Monitor,* May 17, June 27, October 10, 1947; *San Francisco Chronicle,* October 28, October 30, 1958.

36. Right Reverend Leo T. Maher, Chancellor-Secretary, to J. Francis Cardinal McIntyre, July 11, 1958, and Joseph T. McGucken to Right Reverend Monsignor Leo T. Maher, July 14, 1958, in CAASF, Labor/Miscellaneous 1946–1974 file; *The Monitor,* April

26, 1947; *San Francisco Chronicle,* October 24, October 30–31, November 3, 1958, May 12, 1970; Maurice Harrison to My Dear Archbishop Mitty, November 2, 1942, in CAASF, Correspondence HA-HD 1942 folder; Leonard, "Life of a Leftist Labor Leader"; Clark Kerr and Lloyd Fisher, "Conflict on the Waterfront," *Atlantic Monthly,* vol. 184, September 1949, 17–23; Thomas L. Pitts, President, California State Federation of Labor, to Most Reverend John J. Mitty, November 26, 1958, and Most Reverend Hugh A. Donohoe to Reverend F. C. Falque, November 28, 1958, in CAASF, Labor/Miscellaneous 1946–1974 file.

37. Joseph D. Munier, "Organized Cooperation of Labor and Management for the Establishment of a Moral Economic Order," in Joseph D. Munier, *From Pulpit to Platform: Collected Homilies* (San Francisco: Ignatius Press, 1984), 240; CAASF, Personal Record of Joseph D. Munier folder; *Redwood City Tribune,* March 19, 1977; *The Monitor,* February 1, 1979.

38. Joseph D. Munier to John J. Mitty, August 17, 1957, and Personal Record of Joseph D. Munier, both in CAASF; Joseph D. Munier, "Some American Approximations to Pius XI's 'Industries and Professions,'" Ph.D. diss., Catholic University of America, Washington, D.C., 1943.

39. Munier, "Organized Cooperation of Labor and Management," 241; Joseph D. Munier, "Keynote Address, 10th Annual Convention of the Christian Family Movement," in Munier, *From Pulpit to Platform,* 193–205. See also Jeffrey M. Burns, *Disturbing the Peace: A History of the Christian Family Movement, 1949–1974* (Notre Dame, Ind.: University of Notre Dame Press, 1999).

40. Joseph D. Munier to John J. Mitty, May 30, 1950; John J. Mitty to Bishop Aloysius J. Muench, June 1, 1950; Muench to Mitty, June 6, 1950; Joseph D. Munier to John J. Mitty, June 22, 1950, all in CAASF, Joseph D. Munier Personal Record folder. On Muench, see Suzanne Browne-Flemming, *The Holocaust and Catholic Conscience: Cardinal Aloisius Muench and the Guilt Question in Germany* (Notre Dame, Ind.: University of Notre Dame Press, 2005).

41. Joseph D. Munier, "Christian Worker Education Programs: Report and Recommendations," Bad Nauheim, Germany, September 10, 1950, 2, mimeograph copy in CAASF, Joseph D. Munier Personal Record folder.

42. Wilhelm Damberg, "'Radikal Katholische Laien an die Front!' Beobachtungen zur Idee und Wirkungsgeschichte der Katholischen Aktion," in Joachim Köhler and Damian van Melis, *Siegerin in Trümmern: Die Rolle der katholischen Kirche in der deutschen Nachkriegsgesellschaft* (Stuttgart: Verlag W. Kohlhammer, 1998), 151 (my translation). I am grateful to Professor Damberg for sending me a copy of his article. Munier, "Christian Worker Education Programs," 5–6.

43. Munier, "Christian Worker Education Programs," 30. Munier's report seems to have been filed and forgotten, which is not surprising, since by the time he submitted it to the USHCG, Bishop Muench had been sidelined by General Lucius Clay, the head of the military government, who went as far as to try (unsuccessfully) to force him to remain in the United States after a visit home in 1947: see Frederic Spotts, *The Churches and Politics in Germany* (Middletown, Conn.: Wesleyan University Press, 1973), 75–76, 87–88.

44. The quote is from a sermon preached by Monsignor Joseph D. Munier at the investiture of Father Bernard Cronin as a monsignor, at St. Matthew's Church in Redwood City, Calif., November 19, 1972, in Bernard C. Cronin Papers, CAASF, Education/Career folder; Cronin, *Father Yorke and the Labor Movement in San Francisco.*

45. Details of Cronin's biography in this paragraph and the next are from CAASF, Personal Record of Bernard D. Cronin folder.

46. "Father Cronin at the ACTU Meeting April 9," in Bernard C. Cronin Papers, CAASF, Homilies/Papers folder.

47. Truman's address at the opening session of the General Assembly of the United Nations, October 23, 1946, is available online at http://trumanlibrary.org. Truman's acceptance speech at the Democratic National Convention, July 15, 1948, is available online at http://millercenter.virginia.edu.

48. (Monsignor) Howard J. Carroll to John J. Mitty, January 24, 1947; Father James M. Murray to John J. Mitty, January 10, 1947; John J. Mitty to Caroline MacChesney, February 6, 1947; John J. Mitty to Eric Cullenward, February 12, 1947; "Proposed News Release," February 12, 1947, all in CAASF, Correspondence Files, Displaced Persons folder 2 of 2.

49. "Jewish Refugees: 488 Leave for N.Y. by Chartered Train—Thence to Europe, Israel," *San Francisco Chronicle,* February 23, 1949; "DP Twins Baptized," *The Monitor,* October 28, 1949.

CHAPTER 6

Note: The women whose stories are the subjects of this chapter were white residents of San Francisco of European origin, and thus they were representative of the vast majority of the city's population. The absence of non-white women in this chapter mirrors their absence in the public sphere for the first two-thirds of the city's history in the twentieth century and should not be regarded as a lack of appreciation for the importance of the lived experience and the social history of non-white women in the city. The ways that non-white women used the limited options that were available to them deserve more attention from historians, but two excellent studies are suggestive: see Judy Yung, *Unbound Feet: A Social History of Chinese Women in San Francisco* (Berkeley: University of California Press, 1995); Judy Tzu-Chun Wu, *Doctor Mom Chung of the Fair-Haired Bastards: The Life of a Wartime Celebrity* (Berkeley: University of California Press, 2005).

1. Sylvester Andriano, "The Program of Catholic Action in the Archdiocese of San Francisco" (paper presented at the Diocesan Theological Conference, September 13, 1938), *Moraga Quarterly* 9 (Fall 1938): 3–6.

2. See the following sources in History of Catholic Action Collection, Christian Brothers Archives, Mont La Salle, Napa, Calif.: Cardinal Giuseppe Pizzardo, "Catholic Action Aims," pamphlet; Sylvester Andriano to Brother S. Edward, December 30, 1938; *Student Catholic Action,* vol. 1, no. 5 (November 1941): 2; *Catholic Action for You,* box 170; *Student's Handbook of Catholic Action,* vol. 27, box 346.02.

3. Josephine J. Molloy to Archbishop John J. Mitty, July 10, 1936, and Genevieve E. Manning to Archbishop John J. Mitty, July 2, 1937, both in CAASF, Correspondence Files, YMI/YLI 1936–1937 folder; "Y.L.I. Grand Institute," July 18, 1937, in Mitty Sermon Collection, CAASF.

4. For more about Agnes G. Regan, see Dorothy A. Mohler, "Agnes Regan as Organizer of the National Council of Catholic Women and the National Catholic School of Social Service," in *Pioneering Women at the Catholic University of America,* ed. E. Catherine Dunn and Dorothy A. Mohler (Washington, D.C.: Catholic University of America Press, 1988), 21–35.

5. Eugene J. Shea to Archbishop John J. Mitty, August 9, 1939, and Margaret McGuire to Reverend and Dear Father, March 3, 1937, both in CAASF, Correspondence files, Youth Programs 1937–1941 folder; Agnes G. Regan to Archbishop John J. Mitty, January 6, 1937, CAASF, Correspondence Files, NCCW/M 1938–1939 folder 2 of 2.

6. Margaret McGuire to Right Reverend Thomas A. Connolly, October 4, 1936, and "Catholic Action," memorandum, both in CAASF, Correspondence files, NCCW/NCCM 1938–1939 folder 2 of 2; "NCCW Archdiocesan Council Hold Annual Meet in San Francisco," May 29, 1937, in Mitty Sermon Collection, CAASF.

7. Memorandum from Monsignor Thomas A. Connolly to Archbishop John J. Mitty, March 9, 1938, and Maude Fay Symington to Archbishop John J. Mitty, January 14, 1939, both in CAASF, Correspondence Files, NCCW/NCCM 1938–1939 folder 2 of 2; "N.C.C.W. Fifteenth Conference Ends with Luncheon at City Club—Archbishop Mitty," *The Monitor,* May 27, 1939.

8. Pizzardo, "Catholic Action Aims"; "Address of His Holiness, Pope Pius XII, to the Congress of the International Union of Catholic Women's Leagues, Rome, April, 1939"; Agnes G. Regan to Most Reverend Thomas A. Connolly, November 4, 1939; "Memorandum from Representatives of N.C.W.C. to Congress, I.U.C.W.L. Rome—1939," all in CAASF, Correspondence Files, NCCW/NCCM 1938–1939 folder 1 of 2.

9. Pizzardo, "Catholic Action Aims"; "Proposed Project for San Francisco Archdiocesan Council: Clean Reading Campaign"; "Motions Relative to Magazine Rack Clean-Up Campaign," n.d. but sometime in February 1938, all in CAASF, Correspondence Files, NCCW/NCCM 1938–1939 folder 1 of 2.

10. "Report of the Committee on Indecent Literature," May 5, 1938, and James L. Hagerty to Archbishop John J. Mitty, May 18, 1938, in CAASF, Correspondence Files, Catholic Men of San Francisco 1938–1941 folder 1 of 2; Margaret McGuire to Archbishop John J. Mitty, June 11, 1938, in CAASF, Correspondence Files, NCCW/NCCM 1938–1939 folder 1 of 2.

11. Archbishop John J. Mitty to Reverend and Dear Father, June 10, 1938, letter marked "Official," in Mitty Sermon Collection, CAASF.

12. Florentine Schage to Reverend Harold E. Collins, February 28, 1939, in CAASF, Correspondence Files, NCCW/NCCM 1938–1939 folder 2 of 2; John Francis Noll, *Catechism Dealing with Lewd Literature* (Huntington, Ind.: Our Sunday Visitor Press, 1939), 8; "Magazines Banned by the National Organization for Decent Literature," October 12, 1939, in CAASF, Correspondence Files, National Catholic Welfare Conference Catholic Action Study 1939 folder.

13. James L. Hagerty to Joseph Breen, Esq., November 18, 1938; James L. Hagerty to Archbishop John J. Mitty, November 18, 1938; Right Reverend Thomas A. Connolly to James L. Hagerty, November 19, 1938, all in CAASF, Correspondence Files, Catholic Men of San Francisco 1938–1941 folder 1 of 2. For more on the Production Code and Breen's role, see Thomas Doherty, *Hollywood's Censor: Joseph I. Breen and The Production Code Administration* (New York: Columbia University Press, 2007); Gregory D. Black, *Hollywood Censored: Morality Codes, Catholics, and the Movies* (New York: Cambridge University Press, 1994).

14. Archbishop John J. Mitty to Most Reverend Amleto G. Cicognani, D.D., March 30, 1939, and Amleto G. Cicognani to Your Excellency, March 19, 1939, both in National Catholic Welfare Conference, CAASF, Catholic Action Study 1939 folder.

15. The text of the Atherton Report was reprinted in the *San Francisco News,* March 16, 1937. For more on the investigation and its outcome, see Cherny and Issel, *San Francisco,* 61–62.

16. Joseph J. Truxaw to Most Reverend Thomas A. Connolly, January 13, 1940; Reverend Edwin J. Kennedy to Honorable William J. Quinn, January 26, 1940; Reverend Edwin J. Kennedy to Reverend Joseph J. Truxaw, January 31, 1940; Charles W. Dullea to Reverend Edwin J. Kennedy, April 2, 1940, all in National Catholic Welfare Conference,

CAASF, Catholic Action Study 1940 folder; Anna E. McCaughey to Archbishop John J. Mitty, June 5, 1941, in CAASF, National Council of Catholic Women/National Council of Catholic Men 1940–1941 folder.

17. Margaret Sanger, quoted in Sue Barry, "News and Views," *People's World,* May 22, 1939; Anthony B. Diepenbrock to Board of Directors, Golden Gate International Exposition, March 4, 1939, in CAASF, Correspondence Files, Golden Gate Exposition 1939–1940 folder.

18. Vivian McGucikin Raineri, *The Red Angel: The Life and Times of Elaine Black Yoneda, 1906–1988* (New York: International, 1991), 1, 36, 103–105.

19. A photograph of the lynch rope is in the Elaine Black Yoneda Papers, LARC; Raineri, *The Red Angel,* 132–133.

20. Correspondence describing the family's experience in Manzanar is in the Yoneda Papers, LARC; Raineri, *The Red Angel,* 255–260.

21. "Strike a Blow" pamphlet, copy in Yates File, Niebyl Proctor Marxist Library, Berkeley, Calif. (hereafter, NPML).

22. Richard Lynden, typescript, KYA radio broadcast, November 1, 1943, and John Pittman, typescript, KGO radio broadcast, October 25, 1943, both in NPML.

23. Oleta O'Connor Yates, typescript, KYA radio broadcast, October 11, 1947, in NPML. The quote "women as active agents" is from Deborah A. Gerson, "'Is Family Devotion Now Subversive?': Familism against McCarthyism," in *Not June Cleaver: Women and Gender in Postwar America, 1945–1960,* ed. Joanne Meyerowitz (Philadelphia: Temple University Press, 1994), 155.

24. Yates typescript (October 11, 1947).

25. Oleta O'Connor Yates, typescript, KSFO radio broadcast, October 21, 1941, in NPML; "FBI Fails in Yates Ballot Ban," *People's Daily World,* August 1, 1951.

26. "Communists Double Activities in State through New Fronts, Probers Charge," *San Francisco Examiner,* November 5, 1943.

27. Yates's travails occurred during the height of the postwar Red Scare, aptly characterized by Klehr and Haynes as a time when anticommunists busied themselves with "Attacks on an Already Defeated Foe." See Klehr and Haynes, *The American Communist Movement,* 125–142; *San Francisco Examiner,* August 1, 1951; Oleta O'Connor Yates, testimony in transcript of the trial in federal District Court for violation of the Smith Act, June 26, 1952, reprinted in "What a Communist Told the Court: The Testimony of Oletta [*sic*] O'Connor Yates," *People's Daily World Extra,* August 1, 1952. The Dorothy Healey quote is in Dorothy Ray Healey and Maurice Isserman, *California Red: A Life in the American Communist Party* (Urbana: University of Illinois Press, 1993), 143.

28. Oleta O'Connor Yates, "Would YOU Be An Informer? A Letter from the County Jail," July 1952, in Oleta O'Connor Vertical File, SFHC; U.S. Supreme Court [*Yates v. United States,* Syllabus] 354 U.S. 298, decided June 17, 1957, copy in the Norman Leonard Collection, LARC, accession no. 1985/006, box 341.

29. The letter signed by Yates is reprinted in Healey and Isserman, *California Red,* 162; "We Quit Red Party—Yates," *San Francisco Examiner,* March 3, 1964.

30. For a recent study of the role of women in urban planning in Redlands, Santa Barbara, and Oakland, see Lee M. A. Simpson, *Selling the City: Gender, Class, and the California Growth Machine, 1880–1940* (Stanford, Calif.: Stanford University Press, 2004). Jacqueline Braitman is researching the activities of California women in partisan politics during this period: see Jacqueline R. Braitman, "Elizabeth Snyder and the Role of Women in the Postwar Resurgence of California's Democratic Party," *Pacific Historical Review* 62 (May 1993): 197–220; Jacqueline R. Braitman, "Partisans and Policy Makers: Women

Activists and Women's Issues During the Pat Brown Years," *California Politics and Policy* (1997): 25–36. For "growth politics" generally, see Collins, *More.*

31. Julia Gorman Porter, "Dedicated Democrat and City Planner, 1941–1975," interview by Gabrielle Morris, 1975, ROHO-UCB, 1977, 7–19.

32. Ibid. See also Mary Ellen Leary, "A Journalist's Perspective on Government and Politics in California and the San Francisco Bay Area," interview by Harriet Nathan, 1979, ROHO-UCB, 1981, 123–127.

33. John F. Baranski, "Alice Griffith and the San Francisco Housing Authority," seminar paper, Department of History, San Francisco State University, 1994.

34. Charles A. Hogan, "An Interview by Amelia Fry," Helen Gahagan Douglas Project, vol. 2, Women in Politics Oral History Project, ROHO-UCB, 1981, 365–368. David A. Diepenbrock, "Florence Wyckoff, Helen Hosmer, and San Francisco's Liberal Network in the 1930s," seminar paper, Department of History, San Francisco State University, 1993.

35. Dorothy W. Erskine, "Environmental Quality and Planning: Continuity of Volunteer Leadership," interview by John R. Jacobs, 1971, ROHO-UCB, 1976, 121a, 122–129; Leary, "A Journalist's Perspective," 125.

36. Brief biography and various materials in carton 26, Catherine (Bauer) Wurster Correspondence and Papers, 1931–1964, Bancroft Library, University of California, Berkeley (hereafter, CBWC). T. J. Kent Jr., "Statewide and Regional Land-Use Planning in California, 1950-1980," interview by Malca Chall, 1981, ROHO-UCB, 1984, 11–26.

37. Issel, "Business Power and Political Culture in San Francisco," 52–55.

38. Kent, "Statewide and Regional Land-Use Planning in California," 26–30.

39. Porter, "Dedicated Democrat," 48.

40. Julia Porter, KFRC Radio speech for Roger Lapham, in Julia Gorman Porter Papers, BC, box 1, folder 1:48; Kent, "Statewide and Regional Land-Use Planning in California," 33.

41. Julia Porter described "the great wave of idealism" in "Dedicated Democrat," 100. Tilton's career prior to accepting the San Francisco position is described in Gabriele Gonder Carey, "From Hinterland to Metropolis: Land-Use Planning in Orange County, California, 1925–1950," Ph.D. diss., University of California, Riverside, 1997, 26–79.

42. Tilton's philosophy is contained in the speech "State Planning in California" from 1936, quoted in ibid., 72. The difficulties between Tilton and Lapham are described in Kent, "Statewide and Regional Land-Use Planning in California," 31–40.

43. See Chapter 3. For a political scientist's analysis, see Frederick M. Wirt, *Power in the City: Decision-Making in San Francisco* (Berkeley: University of California Press, 1974), 114–130, 217–239).

44. Porter, "Dedicated Democrat," 175.

45. Kent, "Statewide and Regional Land-Use Planning in California," 33–45, 85–95.

46. The controversy over the Transamerica pyramid is described in Wirt, *Power in the City,* 193–197, and is discussed in connection with a waterfront development proposal by U.S. Steel that Porter supported in Barbara Ferman, *Governing the Ungovernable City: Political Skill, Leadership, and the Modern Mayor* (Philadelphia: Temple University Press, 1985), 190–195.

47. Porter, "Dedicated Democrat," 163–173.

48. See DeLeon, *Left Coast City*; Stephen J. McGovern, "The Politics of Downtown Development: Dynamic Political Cultures in San Francisco and Washington, D.C. (Lexington: The University Press of Kentucky, 1998). See Chapter 10 for the freeway revolt.

49. Supervisor Sue Bierman, interview by the author, October 18, 1998, San Francisco. See also John Jacobs, *A Rage for Justice: The Passion and Politics of Phillip Burton* (Berkeley: University of California Press, 1995), 39–58; James Richardson, *Willie Brown: A Biography* (Berkeley: University of California Press, 1996), 45–102; Jerry Roberts, *Dianne Feinstein: Never Let Them See You Cry* (New York: Harper Collins West, 37–79); Bruce Brugmann and Greggar Sletteland, *The Ultimate Highrise: San Francisco's Mad Rush toward the Sky* (San Francisco: San Francisco Bay Guardian Books, 1971).

CHAPTER 7

1. *San Francisco Chronicle,* October 13, 1957. The city of Richmond established the first fair employment ordinance. Bakersfield followed just weeks before San Francisco: Milton A. Senn, "The Politics and Policies of Civil Liberties," in *California Politics and Policies: Original Essays,* ed. Eugene P. Dvorin and Arthur J. Misner (Reading, Mass.: Addison-Wesley, 1966), 310–312.

2. This chapter centers on Jewish and Catholic participation in the Civil Rights Movement in San Francisco, but it should be stressed that, like their counterparts in Los Angeles, the white San Franciscans worked in a coalition alongside non-white racial reformers: see Broussard, *Black San Francisco.* Several recent studies have documented the multiethnic/racial character of civil rights reform beyond San Francisco: see Shana Bernstein, *Bridges of Reform: Interracial Civil Rights Activism in Twentieth Century Los Angeles* (New York: Oxford University Press, 2011); Shana Bernstein, "Interracial Activism in the Los Angeles Community Service Organization: Linking the World War II and Civil Rights Eras," *Pacific Historical Review* 80, no. 2 (May 2011): 231–267; Mark Brilliant, *The Color of America Has Changed: How Racial Diversity Shaped Civil Rights Reform in California, 1941–1978* (New York: Oxford University Press, 2010); Charlotte Brooks, *Alien Neighbors, Foreign Friends: Asian Americans, Housing, and the Transformation of Urban California* (Chicago: University of Chicago Press, 2009); Scott Kurashige, *The Shifting Grounds of Race: Black and Japanese Americans in the Making of Multiethnic Los Angeles* (Princeton, N.J.: Princeton University Press, 2008); Kevin Allen Leonard, *The Battle for Los Angeles: Racial Ideology in World War II* (Albuquerque: University of New Mexico Press, 2006); Scott Harvey Tang, "Pushing at the Golden Gate: Race Relations and Racial Politics in San Francisco, 1940–1955," Ph.D. diss., University of California, Berkeley, 2002. Important earlier work includes Quintard Taylor, *In Search of the Racial Frontier: African Americans in the American West, 1528–1990* (New York: Oxford University Press, 1998); Ronald Takaki, *Strangers from a Different Shore: A History of Asian Americans* (New York: Penguin, 1989); Matt S. Meier and Feliciano Ribera, *Mexican Americans/American Mexicans: From Conquistadors to Chicanos* (New York: Hill and Wang, 1993); Kenneth C. Burt, "Latino Empowerment in Los Angeles: Postwar Dreams and Cold War Fears, 1948–1952," *Labor's Heritage* 8 (Summer 1996): 4–25; Raymond A. Mohl, *South of the South: Jewish Activists and the Civil Rights Movement in Miami, 1945–1960* (Gainesville: University Press of Florida, 2004). Jewish and Catholic activists did not participate in racial reform work because as Jews and Catholics, they were bound to express some identifiable transhistorical "Jewish" or "Catholic" essences. For a cogent critique of such "essentialism," see David A. Hollinger, *Science, Jews, and Secular Culture: Studies in Mid-Twentieth-Century American Intellectual History* (Princeton, N.J.: Princeton University Press, 1996), 10–15. See also Marc Dollinger, *Quest for Inclusion: Jews and Liberalism in Modern America* (Princeton, N.J.: Princeton University Press, 2000).

3. San Francisco Jews and Catholics were not alone in responding to these events by developing a new appreciation for civil rights at home: see Stuart Svonkin, *Jews against Prejudice: American Jews and the Fight for Civil Liberties* (New York: Oxford University Press, 1997). When the American Jewish Congress met in Chicago in May 1942, it called for the Roosevelt administration to end racial discrimination in the U.S. Army: see Gulie Ne'eman Arad, *America, Its Jews, and the Rise of Nazism* (Bloomington: Indiana University Press, 2000), 111.

4. Lucy McWilliams, a Catholic lay person active in local civil rights work, served as the first chairperson of the Council against Discrimination: "Minutes of the Third Meeting of the Bay Area Council against Discrimination," March 19, 1942, in C. L. Dellums Papers, BC, carton 23, Bay Area Council against Discrimination folder.

5. Hilda Taba, Elizabeth Hall Brady, and John T. Robinson, *Intergroup Education in Public Schools* (Washington, D.C.: American Council on Education, 1952), 15. Detroit and Chicago, according to Stuart Svonkin, established civic unity councils in 1943, the year after the Bay Area Council against Discrimination began its work and the year before the San Francisco Civic Unity Council organized: Svonkin, *Jews against Prejudice,* 27. The men and women who staffed the most active organizations, including those whose work persisted into the 1960s in Chicago, Philadelphia, Detroit, San Francisco, and Los Angeles shared information and communicated by means of the National Association of Intergroup Relations Officials, which currently goes by the name National Association of Human Rights Workers: Edward W. Howden, former executive secretary of the Council for Civic Unity, telephone interview by the author, December 4, 1999.

6. William Issel, "Liberalism and Urban Policy in San Francisco from the 1930s to the 1960s," *Western Historical Quarterly,* 22 (November 1991), 431–450; Broussard, *Black San Francisco.* See also Eric Fure-Slocum, "Emerging Urban Redevelopment Policies: Post–World War II Contests in San Francisco and Los Angeles," master's thesis, San Francisco State University, 1990; Max Silverman, "Urban Redevelopment and Community Response: African Americans in San Francisco's Western Addition," master's thesis, San Francisco State University, 1994; Bruce Melendy, "The Entering Wedge: African Americans and Civil Rights in San Francisco, 1933–1946," master's thesis, San Francisco State University, 1999.

7. Broussard credits the interracial liberal coalition for making the city "far more open and integrated on the eve of the historic decision in *Brown v. Board of Education of Topeka* in 1954 than at any previous time in the city's history." He concludes that while full equality had not been achieved by the end of the 1950s, "San Francisco went further [in achieving civil rights reforms] than other American cities": Broussard, *Black San Francisco,* 204–205.

8. James F. Findlay Jr., *Church People in the Struggle: The National Council of Churches and the Black Freedom Movement, 1950–1970* (New York: Oxford University Press, 1993); Cheryl Greenberg, "Negotiating Coalition: Black and Jewish Civil Rights Agencies in the Twentieth Century," in *Struggles in the Promised Land: Toward a History of Black–Jewish Relations in the United States,* ed. Jack Salzman and Cornel West (New York: Oxford University Press, 1997), 153–175.

9. Howard S. Becker and Irving Louis Horowitz, "The Culture of Civility," in *Culture and Civility in San Francisco,* ed. Howard S. Becker (Chicago: Aldine, 1971), 5–6.

10. Cherny, "Patterns of Toleration and Discrimination in San Francisco."

11. At the ceremony in New York City at which Hanna received his award, Judge Joseph M. Proskauer of New York, who later served as president of the American Jewish Committee, praised the archbishop for his efforts to eradicate the "vicious disease—racial

prejudice": *The Monitor,* November 7, 28, 1931. Earl Raab, "From the American Scene: 'There's No City Like San Francisco': Profile of a Jewish Community," *Commentary* 10 (October 1950): 369.

12. See Moses Rischin and John Livingston, eds., *Jews of the American West* (Detroit: Wayne State University Press, 1991); Moses Rischin, ed., *The Jews of the West: The Metropolitan Years* (Waltham, Mass.: American Jewish Historical Society, 1979); Edward S. Shapiro, *A Time for Healing: American Jewry since World War II* (Baltimore: Johns Hopkins University Press, 1992), 133–136; Issel and Cherny, *San Francisco, 1865–1932.*

13. The population data for San Francisco in this and the following paragraph are from Issel and Cherny, *San Francisco, 1865–1932,* table 5, 56; Issel and Cherny, *San Francisco,* 71–73; Brian J. Godfrey, *Neighborhoods in Transition: The Making of San Francisco's Ethnic and Nonconformist Communities* (Berkeley: University of California Press, 1988), 94–127.

14. Thomas C. Fleming, "In the Black World: A Memoir," unpublished ms. (in my possession), 207. See Mark Wild, *Street Meeting: Multiethnic Neighborhoods in Early Twentieth-Century Los Angeles* (Berkeley: University of California Press, 2005), for a study of the impact of social diversity in the everyday life in Los Angeles.

15. Edward W. Howden, interview by the author, San Francisco, September 17, 1999, December 4, 1999; Daniel E. Koshland Sr., "The Principle of Sharing," oral history interview by Harriet Nathan, 1968, ROHO-UCB, 1971, 159, 256–257; David F. Selvin, former executive secretary of the Bay Area Council against Discrimination, interview by the author, Berkeley, Calif., February 3, 1993; David F. Selvin, interview by Bruce Melendy, Berkeley, Calif., May 27, 1994; Melendy, "The Entering Wedge."

16. "The Essentials of a Good Peace," statement issued by the NCWC Administrative Board in the name of the bishops of the United States, November 14, 1942.

17. Ibid., November 11, 1943.

18. The centrist character of the racial reform coalition was also a feature of the campaign in Los Angeles: see Bernstein, *Bridges of Reform.* A copy of the Council for Civic Unity's proposal to the Columbia Foundation is included as appendix B in Josephine Whitney Duveneck, "Working for a Real Democracy for Children and Other Minority Groups," oral history interview by Gabrielle Morris, 1975, ROHO-UCB, 1976; Howden interview (September 17, 1999); Koshland, "The Principle of Sharing," 159, 256–257; William Matson Roth to Alvin Fine, February 21, 1952, in Alvin Fine Collection, Western Jewish History Center (hereafter, WJHC), General Files 1948–1958, Civil Rights, Civil Liberties 1950–1953 folder.

19. Issel, "Liberalism and Urban Policy in San Francisco," 432–434; Dorothy Ross, "Liberalism," *A Companion to American Thought,* ed. Richard Wightman Fox and James T. Kloppenberg (Cambridge, Mass.: Blackwell, 1995), 397–400; Edward A. Purcell Jr., "Consensus," in *A Companion to American Thought,* 140–141.

20. Several oral history sources corroborate on the degree to which the Bay Area Council against Discrimination and the Council for Civic Unity (CCU) evolved out of the Survey Committee. Other institutions played a role, as well. The federal government's War Manpower Commission stimulated the organization of the Bay Area Council against Discrimination, and the American Council on Race Relations and the National Conference of Christians and Jews influenced the CCU: Selvin interview (February 3, 1993); Selvin interview (May 27, 1994); Howden interview (September 17, 1999); Samuel A. Ladar, "A Reflection on the Early Years of the San Francisco Jewish Community," interview by Eleanor K. Glaser, 1990, ROHO-UCB, 1990, iv, 7–8; Eugene Block, interview by Jill Lerner Halinan, 1976–1977, WJHC, 1979, 43–44, 63. Raymond A. Mohl, "Cultural Pluralism in

Immigrant Education: The International Institutes of Boston, Philadelphia, and San Francisco, 1920–1940," *Journal of American Ethnic History* 1 (Spring 1982): 35–58.

21. Koshland, "The Principle of Sharing," 176.

22. Harold J. Boyd to Senator John Shelley, April 23, 1943, in SFLCR, box 47, Citizens Committee for Democratic Freedom in North Africa folder; Frank Peterson to Most Reverend John J. Mitty, August 23, 1944, in CAASF, "J "1944–1945 folder; *San Francisco Chronicle,* October 21–22, 1945, October 19, 1946.

23. Frederick J. Koster to Archbishop John J. Mitty, October 30, 1943, in CAASF, "J" 1943 folder; Reilly interview (September 13, 1997); Frederick J. Koster, "National Industrial Recovery Act," *California Journal of Development* (June 1935), 4–5, 14, 24–25; Knight, *Industrial Relations in the San Francisco Bay Area,* 311–312; *San Francisco Chronicle,* November 20, 1958.

24. Benjamin H. Swig, interview by Amelia Fry, September 11, 1978, copy in BC, 4. According to Bernice Scharlach, the author of a biography of Benjamin Swig, his empathy for African Americans derived from his experience in a partnership with a black businessman in Boston during the Great Depression: Bernice Scharlach, telephone interview by author, October 1, 1999.

25. Walter A. Haas Sr., "Civic, Philanthropic and Business Leadership," interview by Harriet Nathan, 1971–1972, ROHO-UCB, 1975, 37.

26. Robert McWilliams, "The Catholic and Intercreedal Cooperation," pamphlet reprinted from *The Monitor,* July 20, July 27, 1946, copy in SFCIO, carton 8, National Conference of Christians and Jews folder; *San Francisco Chronicle,* March 5, 1935, April 4, 1944, October 25, 1955.

27. *San Francisco Chronicle,* April 13, 1935, November 25, 1936, February 20, 1953; *People's World,* May 10, 1943; Minutes, Board of Directors, CCU, November 16, 1944, copy in Stewart-Flippin Papers, Moorland-Spingarn Research Center, Howard University, Washington, D.C., box 97-19, folder 378.

28. Howden interview (September 17, 1999). Earl Raab belonged to the Socialist Workers Party: Earl Raab, "Executive of the San Francisco Community Relations Council, 1951–1987; Advocate of Minority Rights and Democratic Pluralism," interview by Eleanor K. Glaser, 1996, ROHO-UCB, 1998, 7–12.

29. Arthur M. Schlesinger Jr., *The Vital Center* (Boston: Houghton Mifflin, 1962 [1949]).

30. See the sources in nn. 15, 23, in this chapter. See also Earl Raab, *American Race Relations Today* (New York: Doubleday, 1962); Earl Raab and Seymour Martin Lipset, *The Politics of Unreason: Right Wing Extremism in America, 1790–1970* (New York: Harper and Row, 1970).

31. See the sources in nn. 15, 23 in this chapter. See also Harry L. Kingman, "Citizenship in a Democracy," interview by Rosemary Levenson, 1971–1972, ROHO-UCB, 1973; Carol F. Cini, "Harry Kingman and the Fair Employment Practice Committee in the World War II West," paper presented at the Annual Meeting of the American Historical Association, Pacific Coast Branch, August 15, 1992, Corvallis, Ore.; Yori Wada, "Working for Youth and Social Justice: The YMCA, the University of California, and the Stulsaft Foundation," interviews by Frances Linday, 1983, and Gabrielle Morris, 1990, ROHO-UCB, 1991; Dante Gutierrez, "An Unlikely Equation: The Story of Yori Wada," seminar paper, Department of History, San Francisco State University, 1993; Harry L. Kingman to Herbert Blumer, February 15, 1961, copy in SFLCR, box 99, "C" 1961 folder.

32. Howden interview (September 17, 1999); Selvin interview (February 3, 1993); Selvin interview (May 27, 1994); Jennifer Jo Miller, "Oleta O'Connor Yates and the Communist Party in San Francisco, 1931–1958," seminar paper, Department of History, San Fran-

cisco State University, 1999). The breadth of participation in Mayor Lapham's San Francisco Civic Unity Committee and the Council for Civic Unity during its first year is apparent in the minutes of both organizations, in Stewart-Flippin Papers, Moorland-Spingarn Research Center, Howard University, Washington, D.C., box 97-19, folders 373–383. See also Robert Cook, *Sweet Land of Liberty? The African-American Struggle for Civil Rights in the Twentieth Century* (New York: Addison Wesley Longman, 1998), 57–58, 73–74.

33. "Municipal Platform of the Communist Party of San Francisco," 1945, in SFCIO, carton 18, San Francisco Municipal Election 1945 folder; Joseph James to Roy Wilkins, June 13, 1946, in Library of Congress, NAACP Records, Group II (hereafter, NAACP), box C20, 1946 folder; Paul Robeson and Revels Cayton to Dear Friend, October 1, 1946, in SFCIO, carton 8, National Negro Congress folder; Buell G. Gallagher to Roy Wilkins, May 18, 1947, in NAACP, box C20, 1947 folder; Adrien J. Falk, "Statement Opposing the Adoption of an FEPC Ordinance," February 13, 1957, copy in SFLCR, carton 143, FEP California folder.

34. See Fred Rosenbaum, "Zionism versus Anti-Zionism: The State of Israel Comes to San Francisco," in Rischin and Livingston, *Jews of the American West,* 116–135; Raab, "From the American Scene."

35. Howard Thurman, *With Head and Heart: The Autobiography of Howard Thurman* (New York: Harcourt Brace Jovanovich, 1979), 139–162; "The Church for the Fellowship of All Peoples, 20th Anniversary Dinner Program," September 17, 1964, and NAACP, San Jose Branch, Sixth Annual Banquet program, January 14, 1961, both in Saul White Collection, WJHC, folder 3; Congregation Beth Sholom, "Bulletin" 16 (July–August 1970), in Saul White Collection, WJHC, Biography/Obituaries folder; *San Francisco Chronicle,* March 17, November 4, 1983. Elliot M. Burstein, "We Can't Remain Silent," *Emanu-El,* undated clipping from 1943, in Saul White Collection, WJHC, folder 14.

36. Elliot M. Burstein, "Slavery in Modern Times" and "What Is Americanism?" in Elliot Burstein Collection, WJHC, Radio and Television Talks and Lectures folder.

37. Elliot M. Burstein, "Christian–Jewish Answer to the World's Crisis," in ibid.

38. Elliot M. Burstein, "Religion and Democracy," in ibid.

39. Ibid.

40. See David A. Hollinger, "Cultural Pluralism and Multiculturalism," in Fox and Kloppenberg, *A Companion to American Thought,* 162–166; David A. Hollinger, *Postethnic America: Beyond Multiculturalism* (New York: Basic, 1995), 79–104.

41. *The Monitor,* December 4, 1937. Biographical information about Thomas F. and John J. Burke is available online at http://www.paulist.org/archives/PERSON1.HTM.

42. Raab, "Executive of the San Francisco Community Relations Council," 26.

43. Him Mark Lai to the author, letter, October 26, 1999; Howden interviews (September 17, December 4, 1999); Thomas W. Chinn, *Bridging the Pacific: San Francisco Chinatown and Its People* (San Francisco: Chinese Historical Society of America, 1989), 244, 258–260; Minutes of the Area Advisory Committee on Minority Group Problems, April 10, 1950, copy in California Federation for Civic Unity Records, BC, carton 2, FEPC folder; Seaton W. Manning to Lester B. Granger, June 15, 1950, National Urban League Records, Series I.D., Library of Congress (hereafter, Urban League Records), box 127, San Francisco Urban League 1950 folder; San Francisco Labor Council, "Official Bulletin" 1 (June 21, 1950); "Defeating Discrimination: Fact Sheet, Council for Civic Unity of San Francisco," 1951, nine-page, mimeographed pamphlet (in the author's possession); Jefferson Beaver, "President's Report: San Francisco Branch, NAACP," January 16, 1955, all in NAACP, box C20, 1951–55 folder; Seaton W. Manning to Lester B. Granger, August 21, 1959, Urban League Records, box 127, San Francisco Urban League 1959 folder.

44. "Discrimination and Christian Conscience," statement issued by the Catholic Bishops of the United States, November 14, 1958, copy in CAASF, Eugene J. Boyle file.

45. Francois presided over the local NAACP branch from 1959 to 1963 and served on the Board of Supervisors from 1964 to 1978. Terry A. Francois to Dear Friend, November 17, 1959, in NAACP West Coast Region Records, BC (hereafter, NAACPWCR), carton 17, San Francisco branch correspondence folder; "Francois, Terry A.," in Shirelle Phelps, ed., *Who's Who among African Americans,* 11th edition (Detroit: Gale Research, 1998), 437; Rita Semel, interview by the author, San Francisco, October 26, 1999; Howden interviews (September 17, December 4, 1999).

46. Peter E. Haas, "President, Jewish Community Federation of San Francisco, the Peninsula, Marin and Sonoma Counties, 1977–78," interview by Eleanor K. Glaser, 1992, ROHO-UCB, 1994, 74–75.

47. Richard L. Sloss, "Out of the Depths," typewritten sermon, in Richard L. Sloss Collection, WJHC, box 2, Sermons and Meditations 1948–1957 folder.

48. Fred Rosenbaum, *Architects of Reform: Congregational and Community Leadership, Emanu-El of San Francisco, 1849–1980* (Berkeley: Western Jewish History Center, Judah L. Magnes Memorial Museum, 1980), 147–173. Biographical information is in "Guide to the Rabbi Alvin I. Fine Collection," WJHC.

49. The archbishop received numerous requests that the archdiocese increase its official public support for interfaith cooperation and civil rights reforms during this period: see, e.g., Ulyss Stanford Mitchell to Most Reverend John J. Mitty, April 4, 1944, and Joseph M. Proskauer to Most Reverend John J. Mitty, October 23, 1944, both in CAASF, "J" 1944–1945 folder; J. Joseph Sullivan to Most Reverend John J. Mitty, May 29, 1950, and Karl Bennet Justus to Archbishop John J. Mitty, August 12, 1953, both in CAASF, Jews–Christians and Jews Conference 1950–1961 folder.

50. Reverend James N. Brown to Most Reverend John J. Mitty, January 14, 1952, in CAASF, Jews–Christians and Jews Conference 1950–1961 folder. See also Lerond Curry, *Protestant–Catholic Relations in America: World War I through Vatican II* (Lexington: University Press of Kentucky, 1972), 52–60; Gregg Ivers, *To Build a Wall: American Jews and the Separation of Church and State* (Charlottesville: University Press of Virginia, 1995), 10–33, 66–69.

51. Howden interview (December 4, 1999); Burns, "Mitty, John Joseph"; Clay O'Dell, "From Pioneer Mission to Interracialism: The Catholic Church and African Americans in San Francisco, 1928–1960," paper presented at the History of Bay Area Catholicism XIV conference, San Francisco, 1999. Mitty's response exemplified the tensions among Protestants, Catholics, and Jews that existed nationwide: see Benny Kraut, "A Wary Collaboration: Jews, Catholics, and the Protestant Goodwill Movement," in *Between the Times: The Travail of the Protestant Establishment in America, 1900–1960,* ed. William R. Hutchinson (Cambridge: Cambridge University Press, 1989), 193–230; Martin E. Marty, *Modern American Religion, Volume 3: Under God, Indivisible, 1941–1960* (Chicago: University of Chicago Press, 1996), 162–172; Charles R. Morris, *American Catholic: The Saints and Sinners Who Built America's Most Powerful Church* (New York: Times Books/Random House, 1997), 250–254.

52. John J. Mitty to Reverend Francis J. Connell, July 8, 1941, in CAASF, Inter-Faith Movement folder.

53. Ibid.

54. Rosenbaum, "Zionism versus Anti-Zionism"; Benjamin Ginsberg, *The Fatal Embrace: Jews and the State* (Chicago: University of Chicago Press, 1993); Joseph E.

O'Neill, ed., *A Catholic Case against Segregation* (New York: Macmillan, 1961); David W. Southern, *John LaFarge and the Limits of Catholic Interracialism, 1911–1963* (Baton Rouge: Louisiana State University Press, 1996); John T. McGreevy, *Parish Boundaries: The Catholic Encounter with Race in the Twentieth Century Urban North* (Chicago: University of Chicago Press, 1996); John T. McGreevy, "Thinking on One's Own: Catholicism in the American Intellectual Imagination, 1928–1960," *Journal of American History* 84 (June 1997): 97–131.

55. William Issel and James Collins, "The Catholic Church and Organized Labor in San Francisco, 1932–1958," *Records of the American Catholic Historical Society of Philadelphia* 109 (Spring/Summer 1999), 81–112; Raab, "Executive of the San Francisco Community Relations Council," 7–8.

56. D. Donald Glover, "The Employment Problems of the Negro Worker in San Francisco," *Labor Management Panel* 7 (January 1956): 1–4.

57. "Institute on Minority Group Employment," *Labor Management Panel* 1 (April 1951): 1–2.

58. "Discrimination in Employment" (verbatim transcription of radio broadcast), *Labor Management Panel* 4 (January 1954): 1–4.

59. Kenneth C. Burt and Fred Glass, "FEPC's 40th Birthday," *California Labor News* 42 (April 1999), 1.

60. "Defeating Discrimination"; Howden interview (September 17, 1999).

61. See the discussion of Vatican II in Maurice Isserman and Michael Kazin, *America Divided: The Civil War of the 1960s,* 2d ed. (New York: Oxford University Press, 2004), 256–260.

62. Philip Gleason, "Catholicism and Cultural Change in the 1960s," *Review of Politics* 34 (October 1972): 98.

63. Raymond Sontag quote from "Negroes not Treated as Persons," *Monitor,* April 17, 1963, 1.

64. James P. Gaffey, "The Anatomy of Transition: Cathedral Building and Social Justice in San Francisco, 1962–1971," *Catholic Historical Review* 70 (January 1984): 45–73. Jeffrey Burns has analyzed several aspects of the changes that took place during the 1960s: Jeffrey M. Burns, "Postconciliar Church as Unfamiliar Sky: The Episcopal Styles of Cardinal James F. McIntyre and Archbishop Joseph T. McGucken," *U.S. Catholic Historian* 17 (1999): 64–82; Jeffrey M. Burns, "Eugene Boyle, the Black Panther Party and the New Clerical Activism," *U.S. Catholic Historian* 13 (1995): 137–158; Jeffrey M. Burns, "No Longer Emerging: *Ramparts* Magazine and the Catholic Laity, 1962–1968," *U.S. Catholic Historian* 9 (1990): 321–333.

65. "Resume: Reverend Eugene J. Boyle," copy in CAASF, Eugene J. Boyle file; Eugene Boyle, "Social Justice in the Archdiocese of San Francisco, 1962–1972: A Personal Reflection," (unpublished paper delivered at the Conference on the History of Bay Area Catholicism, 1991), CAASF.

66. Burns, "Eugene Boyle," 145; Semel interview.

67. Issel, "Liberalism and Urban Policy in San Francisco," 44; Frank A. Quinn (former director, San Francisco Human Rights Commission), interview by John Dobbs, April 2, 1996, San Francisco, audiotape transcript in my possession.

68. For the Market Street protest marchers who charged that Senator Barry Goldwater was "the anti-civil rights candidate," see the UPI story and photograph in the digital photograph collection, SFHC, available online at http://sflib1.sfpl.org:82/search~/a?search type=X&searcharg=%22civil%22+rights+march+market+street&SORT=D&x=0&y=0. See

also Robert O. Self, *American Babylon: Race and the Struggle for Postwar Oakland* (Princeton, N.J.: Princeton University Press, 2003), 260–268, for the role of the California Real Estate Association and the fight over Proposition 14 in Oakland. Goldwater's speech is available online at http://www.americanrhetoric.com.

69. William Byron Rumford, "Legislator for Fair Employment, Fair Housing, and Public Health," interview by Joyce A. Henderson, Amelia Fry, and Edward France, 1971, ROHO-UCB, 1973, 112–133.

70. Ibid. "Two Views of Fair Housing Bill," *Monitor* April 26, 1963, 9; Donovan Bess, "Behind Rumford Struggle," *San Francisco Chronicle,* March 13, 1964, 1, 9. Marshall Kaplan, "Discrimination in California Housing: The Need for Additional Legislation," *California Law Review* 50 (October 1962), 635–649.

71. "Two Views of Fair Housing Bill."

72. Ibid.

73. "On Racial Harmony," statement approved by the Administrative Board, National Catholic Welfare Conference, August 23, 1963, CAASF, Correspondence Files, Rumford Fair Housing Act 1963–1964 folder.

74. "Statement and Resolution," adopted by Council Delegates in Convention, November 17, 1963, in CAASF, National Council Conference for Interracial Justice file.

75. Materials concerning the newspaper ad are in CAASF, Correspondence Files, Rumford Fair Housing Act 1963–1964 folder; "Repeal of Rumford Act could 'Enthrone Injustice,'" *The Monitor,* January 31, 1964, 20.

76. For Governor Brown's role, see Martin Schiesl, "The Struggle for Equality: Racial Reform and Party Politics in California," in *Responsible Liberalism: Edmund G. "Pat" Brown and Reform Government in California, 1958–1967,* ed. Martin Schiesl (Los Angeles: Edmund G. "Pat" Brown Institute for Public Affairs, 2003), 107–117; "Rumford Vote Confirmed," *San Francisco Chronicle,* February 25, 1964, 3; "Squeeze on Rumford," *San Francisco Chronicle,* March 16, 1964, 14; *Justice* (newsletter of the CIC of San Francisco), March 1964, copy in CAASF.

77. Burns, "Postconciliar Church as Unfamiliar Sky," 71–74, 76–77; "Cardinal Stays Out of Politics," *San Francisco Chronicle,* July 29, 1964, 9; Francis J. Weber, "The California Bishops and Proposition 14," in *Past Is Prologue: Some Historical Reflections, 1961–1991* (Mission Hills, Calif.: St. Francis Historical Society, 1992), 119–126.

78. Bishop (previously Monsignor) Francis A. Quinn to Mary Anne Wold, November 29, 1993, copy in possession of Mary Anne Wold. Quinn edited *The Monitor* in 1963 and 1964 and served on the Archdiocesan Social Justice Commission.

79. Archbishop Joseph T. McGucken to John Delury, December 12, December 17, 1963, in CAASF, Correspondence Files, Rumford Fair Housing Act 1963–1964 folder.

80. Eleanor K. Glaser to Joseph T. McGucken, letter, May 13, 1964; McGucken to Glaser, letter, May 15, 1964; Archbishop Joseph T. McGucken to Father Eugene J. Boyle, May 13, 1964. Archbishop McGucken sent a $100 contribution. See the following exchange of letters: Benjamin H. Swig to Most Reverend Joseph T. McGucken, August 28, 1964; McGucken to Swig, August 28, 1964, all in CAASF, Correspondence Files, Rumford Fair Housing Act 1963–1964 folder.

81. Eugene T. Boyle, "Introduction of Dr. King," May 26, 1964, in CAASF, Civil Rights file.

82. "McGucken Calls Rumford Repeal Immoral," *San Francisco Examiner,* May 27, 1964, 1.

83. "McGucken Assailed over Fair Housing Initiative," *San Francisco Chronicle,* June 11, 1964, 2.

84. Boyle, "Personal Reflections," 15 in CAASF, Eugene J. Boyle Collection; "Archdiocese Sets Up Social Justice Body," *The Monitor,* July 31, 1964, 1, 5.

85. "Parish Social Justice Committees to Form," *The Monitor,* August 14, 1964, 1; survey material in CAASF, Sermons on Civil Rights/Race file.

86. *The Monitor,* October 22, 1964, 1.

87. "McGucken Denounces Prop[osition] 14," *San Francisco Chronicle,* October 23, 1964, 1. The archbishop received commendation as well as criticism for his public letter: see especially Benjamin H. Swig to Joseph T. McGucken, November 12, 1964, and John F. Moran to Joseph T. McGucken, November 6, 1964, in CAASF, Correspondence Files, Rumford Fair Housing Act 1963–1964 folder.

88. *Justice,* vol. 4, no. 10, September 1963, in CAASF; *The Monitor,* September 27, 1963, 20.

89. *The Monitor,* December 13, 1963, 14.

90. Reverend Joseph Farraher, "Immorality of Racial Bias Explained by Theologian," *The Monitor,* September 3, 1964, 7; "Are We Obliged to Vote 'No' on Prop. 14," *The Monitor,* October 15, 1963, 9.

91. Letters to the editor, *The Monitor,* September 19, 1964, 22.

92. "Brother versus Brother," *The Monitor,* October 18, 1963; "Fair Housing Law," *The Monitor,* December 6, 1963, 22.

93. Editorial cartoon, *The Monitor,* December 27, 1963, 18.

94. "A 'Catholic' Vote?" *The Monitor,* January 10, 1964, 20.

95. "Church and Race," *The Monitor,* August 27, 1964, 16.

96. Monsignor Bernard Cummins, "Church and Prop. 14," *The Monitor,* October 1, 1964, 16.

97. "Need for Understanding," *The Monitor,* October 22, 1964, 22.

98. Boyle, "Personal Reflections," 11.

99. "Interracial Group Hits Anti-Fair Housing Initiative," *The Monitor,* June 12, 1964, 5.

100. CAASF, Civil Rights: Letters Received File.

101. "Statement of President," n.d., in CAASF, CIC-General File.

102. "Realtor Forms 'Yes on 14' Group for Catholics," *The Monitor,* September 24, 1964, 5.

103. "Churchmen Stand Firm on Prop. 14," *San Francisco Chronicle,* September 5, 1964, 9; *The Monitor,* November 8, 1963; "Rumford Support," *San Francisco Chronicle,* May 25, 1964, 19; "USF Theology Dep[artmen]t Condemns Prop[osition] 14," *The Monitor,* October 8, 1964, 1; "Archdiocesan Council of Catholic Women Says Vigorous 'No' to Prop[osition] 14," *The Monitor,* October 8, 1964, 1.

104. Howden interviews (September 17, December 4, 1999); Boyle, "Personal Reflections," 15. See also Raab, "Executive of the San Francisco Community Relations Council."

105. "Readers Speak Out on Race," *The Monitor,* October 15, 1964, 7; Letters to the editor, *The Monitor,* May 8, 1964.

106. Father George Kennard, interview by Mary Anne Wold, November 18, 1993.

107. Boyle, "Personal Reflections," 17.

108. John Delury, interview by Jeffrey M. Burns, October 3, 1987, in CAASF.

109. Clay Mansfield O'Dell, "On Stony Ground: The Catholic Interracial Council in the Archdiocese of San Francisco," Ph.D. diss., University of Virginia, Charlottesville, 2005, 174, 205–206.

110. See Thomas J. Sugrue, "Shanker Blows Up the World," *The Nation,* November 12, 2007, available online at http://www.thenation.com.

CHAPTER 8

1. Diana Walsh, "Sam Jordan—Popular Bayview Tavern Owner," *San Francisco Chronicle,* July 1, 2003; Jackie Wright, "The Late Sam Jordan 'Singing Sam' Mayor of Butchertown to be Honored," available online at http://www.wrightnow.biz. This chapter benefits from the research of Eric Fure-Slocum, Bruce Melendy, and Max Silverman, used with permission: Fure-Slocum, "Emerging Urban Redevelopment Policies"; Silverman, "Urban Redevelopment and Community Response"; Melendy, "The Entering Wedge."

2. Carleton Goodlett, interview by the author, September 21, 1987, San Francisco. See also Gloria La Riva, "Dr. Carleton Goodlett, African American Pioneer," available online at http://www.workers.org. Mel Scott, "Western Addition District Redevelopment Study," San Francisco City Planning Commission, November 26, 1947 (hereafter Scott Report), 6. See also Godfrey, *Neighborhoods in Transition,* 94–127.

3. City and County of San Francisco, "Public Hearing on Redevelopment of the Western Addition" (transcript of the public hearing held by the Board of Supervisors), June 3, 1948, index to speakers; *San Francisco Chronicle,* June 4, 1948. For a detailed analysis of redevelopment in San Francisco in relation to national urban planning history and local social history, see Theresa J. Mah, "Buying into the Middle Class: Residential Segregation and Racial Formation in the United States, 1920–1964," Ph.D. diss., University of Chicago, 1999.

4. San Francisco Housing Association, *Annual Report,* 1911, Doe Library, UC Berkeley; John F. Baranski, "Making Public Housing in San Francisco: Liberalism, Social Prejudice, and Social Activism, 1906–1976," Ph.D. diss., University of California, Santa Barbara, 2004, 57, 62; minutes of the San Francisco Housing Authority, April 22, 1938, quoted in Baranski, "Making Public Housing in San Francisco," 63.

5. Erskine, "Environmental Quality and Planning," 123. See also Florence Richardson Wyckoff, "A Volunteer Career from the Arts and Education to Public Health Issues," oral history interview by Gabrielle Morris, 1971, ROHO-UCB, 1976, 169–179; "San Francisco's Chinatown Housing," October 1939, copy in CBWC; City and County of San Francisco, *1939 Real Property Survey, San Francisco California,* vol. 1 (San Francisco: San Francisco Junior Chamber of Commerce, 1941). See also Angelo Rossi to John A. O'Connell, August 28, 1941, and Angelo Rossi to Walter A. Haas, August 13, 1941, both in SFLCR, carton 41, Mayor of San Francisco 1942 folder; California Housing and Planning Association, "Program for 1941," in SFLCR, carton 41, Miscellaneous folder 2; "Report of Activities of the San Francisco Planning and Housing Association," October 1941–May 1942, in CBWC, carton 26, San Francisco Planning and Housing Association folder; San Francisco Housing and Planning Association, "Now Is the Time to Plan: First Steps to a Master Plan for San Francisco," 1941, in CBWC, carton 26, San Francisco Planning and Housing Association folder. The "blighted districts" quote is from "We Need Redevelopment Legislation," San Francisco Planning Administration to Supervisor Chester MacPhee, memorandum, June 5, 1944, Institute of Governmental Studies Library, University of California, Berkeley (hereafter, IGSL).

6. Federal redevelopment money was only one of the many types of state and national government funding that became an important source of the city's income from the New Deal years to the 1970s. Such state and federal funds increased as a percentage of the city's and county's budget from 9.5 percent (state) in 1933 to 34 percent (combined state and federal) in 1973 in constant dollars, as calculated from data in San Francisco city and county *Controller's Annual Reports* for 1933–1983. On redevelopment generally, see Alex-

ander von Hoffman, "The Lost History of Urban Renewal," *Journal of Urbanism* 1 (November 2008): 281–301; Roger Biles, *The Fate of Cities: Urban America and the Federal Government, 1945–2000* (Lawrence: University Press of Kansas, 2011), chaps. 1–2.

7. "What Do We Want?" editorial, *Sun-Reporter,* June 9, 1951. Thomas Fleming, interview by the author, September 21, 1987, San Francisco; Scott Report, 6. The description of the crowds on Fillmore Street on Friday nights is based on my experience as a resident of the Fillmore District from 1945 to 1952.

8. Scott Report, 4. Biographical information on Scott is from Skip Lowney and John D. Landis, eds., *Fifty Years of City and Regional Planning at UC Berkeley: A Celebratory Anthology of Faculty Essays* (Berkeley, Calif.: NSQ Press, 1998), 401.

9. Scott Report, 12. On social control, see Paul Boyer, *Urban Masses and Moral Order in America, 1820–1920* (Cambridge, Mass.: Harvard University Press, 1978).

10. Scott Report, 36–37, 64–66. The description of the working relationship between the Chamber of Commerce and the new Bay Area Council is from Angelo Siracusa, Executive Director, Bay Area Council, interview by the author, September 24, 1987, San Francisco.

11. Scott Report, 70.

12. "Minutes of the San Francisco CIO Council Executive Board," March 15, 1946, in SFCIO, carton 5, Executive Board folder; Harry Steingart, "Report of the San Francisco CIO Council Housing Committee," n.d. but after August 9, 1945, in SFCIO, carton 3, Housing folder; Paul Schnur, "Statement to the San Francisco Board of Supervisors," n.d., 1946, in SFCIO, carton 5, Housing folder.

13. Booklet of the CIO Legislative Conference, January 28, 1945, 5, in SFCIO, carton 16, Legislative Program and State Legislation folder.

14. Goodlett interview; Communist Party of San Francisco, "Municipal Platform," 1945, 4, in SFCIO, carton 18, San Francisco Municipal Elections 1945 folder; San Francisco Baptist Bay City Union, "Annual Report of the 29th Year, May 1, 1947–April 30, 1948, presented May 14, 1948," 65, and "Third Baptist Church, Souvenir Program, Ninety-Fifth Anniversary, 1852–1947," August 18–24, 1947, 6, both in Archives of the American Baptist Seminary of the West, Berkeley, Calif.

15. F. D. Haynes for Supervisor Committee, "Fundraising letter," Fall 1947, in SFCIO, carton 19, CIO Council Endorsements Supervisors folder; "Haynes Script—KYA," Fall 1947, 3, in SFCIO, carton 20, PAC SF Municipal Election Haynes for Supervisor Publicity folder.

16. Fleming interview; Thomas Fleming, interview by Eric Fure-Slocum, May 1, 1989, San Francisco; Daniel Collins, telephone interview by Eric Fure-Slocum, May 9, 1989, San Francisco; *San Francisco Chronicle,* June 4, 1948.

17. City and County of San Francisco, "Public Hearing on Redevelopment of the Western Addition," 7–8.

18. Ibid., 13–16.

19. Ibid., 19, 23–24. The residential and ethnic/racial data are from city directories and from my clipping files and personal acquaintance with the individuals.

20. City and County of San Francisco, "Public Hearing on Redevelopment of the Western Addition," 26–28.

21. Ibid., 60.

22. Ibid., 40–41. Poole served as an assistant district attorney in San Francisco under Edmund G. "Pat" Brown; as special assistant to Brown when he became the governor of California; and, from 1976 to 1996, as a judge for the U.S. District Court and then the Ninth

Circuit Court of Appeals: see Ninth Judicial Circuit Historical Society, Judge Cecil F. Poole Project, available online at http://www.njchs.org; *New York Times,* November 16, 1997.

23. *San Francisco Chronicle,* July 20, 1948; Goodlett interview; Fleming interview. The quote is from Lloyd Dickey, interview by Eva Jefferson Paterson, San Francisco, November 12, 1980.

24. Reverend William Turner and Reverend E. C. Washington to Board of Supervisors, July 9, 1948; Yukio Wada to San Francisco Board of Supervisors, July 24, 1948, copies of letters included in the appendix to City and County of San Francisco, "Public Hearing on Redevelopment of the Western Addition," 67, 69. Seven community organizations sent formal written testimony to the Board.

25. Council for Civic Unity of San Francisco, "Memorandum on Redevelopment Nondiscrimination Ordinance," October 11, 1948, 1, and CCU, "Background Notes on Recent Redevelopment History," n.d. 1948, both in San Francisco Board of Supervisors files, folio 3623.

26. Senator Gerald O'Gara to Chester MacPhee, November 24, 1948, in San Francisco Board of Supervisors files, folio 3623.

27. *San Francisco Chronicle,* May 2, 1949.

28. The coalition included the American Civil Liberties Union of Northern California, American Jewish Congress, American Friends Service Committee, Communist Party of San Francisco, American Veteran's Committee, Booker T. Washington Community Center, Chinese American Citizens Alliance, Japanese American Citizens League, Filipino Community Inc., Filipino Methodist Church, Ministerial Alliance, Fillmore Republican Club, San Francisco NAACP, San Francisco Urban League, CIO County Council, and AFL County Council. Letters from these organizations describing their arguments are in San Francisco Board of Supervisors, files, folios 3623, 3900. The description of the public meeting is from *San Francisco News,* May 13, 1949. Resolution 8660 is in San Francisco Board of Supervisors files, folio 3623. On the public housing resolution, see *San Francisco Chronicle,* November 22, 1949. On "interest group liberalism," see Theodore Lowi, *The End of Liberalism: The Second Republic of the United States,* 2d ed. (New York: W. W. Norton, 1979), 42–63.

29. San Francisco Redevelopment Agency, "San Francisco's Redevelopment Program: Summary of Project Data and Key Elements, San Francisco Redevelopment Agency (hereafter, SFRA), Executive Office Files, carton 43; San Francisco Redevelopment Agency, "Western Addition A-2 Project Summary," in SFRA, Gene Suttle's Files, PA-28 folder. See also "Relocation in San Francisco Housing," in NAACPWCR, carton 30, 1961 folder.

30. The quotes from the San Francisco Redevelopment Agency's reports of 1963 and 1976 are from "Western Addition A-1" and "Western Addition A-2," available online at http://www.sfredevelopment.org. See Hartman, *City for Sale,* 63–64, 411, for additional evidence about displacement based on data from 1960–1961.

31. Revels Cayton, interview by Max Silverman, June 27, 1992; Thomas Fleming, interview by Max Silverman, April 27, 1992; Broussard, *Black San Francisco,* 208, 227–230; NAACPWCR Monthly Reports 1946 folder; NAACPWCR, carton 25, Regional Secretary Reports folder; NAACPWCR, box 25, Correspondence National Membership Director 1957–1962 folder; Anthony Hart to Roger Wilkins, May 14, 1947, NAACP, box C20, 1947 folder; Gallagher to Wilkins (May 18, 1947); N. W. Griffin to Roger Wilkins, November 21, 1949, NAACP, 1948–1949 folder; *Sun-Reporter,* July 7, 1956.

32. *Sun-Reporter,* March 1, March 8, 1958, March 25, April 1, 1961; Revels Cayton interview by Max Silverman, July 24, 1991; see also Broussard, *Black San Francisco,* 209, 222, 236.

33. *Sun-Reporter,* April 7, December 8, December 15, December 22, 1951, October 4, October 18, 1952, March 21, 1953; *San Francisco Chronicle,* October 15, 1952; Cayton interview (July 24, 1991).

34. Revels Cayton. interview by Max Silverman, May 4, 1992, San Francisco; "Minutes of a Special Meeting of the San Francisco Redevelopment Agency," July 19, 1960, Anne Rand Research Library, ILWU, San Francisco, ILWU History Files, St. Francis folder.

35. The description of Mayor George Christopher's thinking is from George Christopher, interview by the author, August 14, 1997, San Francisco. M. Justin Herman became notorious as "the last of the Robert Moses autocrats": *National Journal,* September 18, 1973, 1939. He may have been his own worst enemy, but he was acutely aware of the need to attend to issues of social justice, if perhaps only for purely instrumentalist reasons. In a letter dated February 24, 1961, to Robert C. Weaver, administrator of the Housing and Home Finance Agency (and later, first secretary of the new cabinet-level Department of Housing and Urban Development), he warned that urban redevelopment programs could come "to a dead stop" because of "the adverse treatment that it gives to the economically, socially, or racially disadvantaged": M. Justin Herman to Robert C. Weaver, February 24, 1961, in National Archives and Records Administration, College Park, Md., record group 207, Robert C. Weaver Subject Correspondence Files, box 62, General Correspondence 1961 A–F folder. For an extensive critique of M. Justin Herman and redevelopment in San Francisco, see Clement Kai-Men Lai, "Between 'Blight' and a New World: Urban Renewal, Political Mobilization, and the Production of Spatial Scale in San Francisco, 1940–1980," Ph.D. diss., University of California, Berkeley, 2006. On Japantown, see Meredith Akemi Oda, "Remaking the 'Gateway to the Pacific': Urban, Economic, and Racial Redevelopment in San Francisco, 1945–1970," Ph.D. diss., University of Chicago, 2010, 74–94, 130, 156, 205–218; "History of the Nihonmachi in the Western Addition area A-2," June 1976, in Gene Suttle's Files, SFRA, PA-31 folder.

36. Oda, "Remaking the 'Gateway to the Pacific,'" 156; *Sun-Reporter,* March 5, 1960, May 23, 1961; *The Dispatcher,* May 31, 1963. On November 11, 1963, KRON television broadcast "Integration, Western Style," which contains footage of the protest on May 26, 1963: see https://diva.sfsu.edu/collections/sfbatv/bundles/191511. For the James Baldwin interview, see: http://www.pbs.org/kqed/fillmore/learning/qt/baldwin.html.

37. The Congress on Racial Equality (CORE) and Goodlett picketed, but the regional NAACP office convinced the San Francisco branch members to refrain: Carlton Goodlett, "An Open Letter to My Son," *Sun-Reporter,* January 5, 1963; *Sun-Reporter,* January 12, 1963.

38. *Sun-Reporter,* July 27, 1963; Ralph Goodwin to Joseph Kennedy and Tarea Hall Pittman to Gloster Current, July 24, 1963, NAACP (Group III), Branch Files, SF 1962–1963 folder. See also Richardson, *Willie Brown,* 81–84; Richard Young, "The Impact of Protest Leadership on Negro Politicians in San Francisco," in *Black Liberation Politics: A Reader,* ed. Edward Greer (Boston: Allyn and Bacon, 1971), 281–304.

39. "Freedom Rally Program, Monday, July 29, 1963," NAACP (Group III), San Francisco Branch Files, SF 1962–1963 folder; *Sun-Reporter,* June 29, August 3, August 10, 1963; *The Dispatcher,* August 10, 1963; NAACPWCR, carton 25, Annual Report 1963 folder; August Meier and Elliott Rudwick, *CORE: A Study in the Civil Rights Movement* (Urbana: University of Illinois Press, 1975), 203; Daniel Crowe, *Prophets of Rage: The Black Freedom Struggle in San Francisco* (New York: Garland, 2000), 125.

40. Charles Turner to A. Phillip Burton, April 2, 1959, in NAACPWCR, box 38, Housing 1958–1959 folder; *Sun-Reporter,* March 28, 1959; Tarea Hall Pittman to Executive Board Members of SFNAACP, memorandum, December 1960, in NAACPWCR,

carton 38, Housing 1960 folder; "Redevelopment—For Human Welfare, or Financial Gain," *Sun-Reporter,* May 4, 1961. The USFFM statement is quoted from Justin Herman, "Western Addition Area 2," speech before SPUR, November 19, 1963, in SFRA, Gene Suttle's Files, PA 31 folder.

41. *San Francisco News-Call Bulletin,* April 16, 1964; "ILWU Statement on Dislocation of Residents of Area #2," Housing—Anne Rand Research Library, ILWU, San Francisco, ILWU History Files, St. Francis folder; *The Dispatcher,* February 21, 1964; Crowe, *Prophets of Rage,* 125; see also Carol Cuenod (ILWU librarian and archivist), "Redevelopment A-1 and the Origin of St. Francis Square" and "The ILWU and Western Addition Redevelopment A-2," FoundSF, available online at http://foundsf.org. New residents of the St. Francis Square housing are interviewed in the KRON television's "Integration, Western Style."

42. San Francisco Civic Unity Council newsletter, March 1964, Anne Rand Research Library, ILWU, San Francisco, ILWU History Files, Housing St. Francis folder; Robert B. Marquis, Richard Adams, Louis Goldblatt and Richard Ernst, "Relocation in Redevelopment Area A-2," n.d. but 1964, Anne Rand Research Library, ILWU, San Francisco, ILWU History Files, Housing St. Francis folder; Richard Ernst and Louis Goldblatt to Morris Watson, memorandum, May 4, 1964, Anne Rand Research Library, ILWU, San Francisco, ILWU History Files, St. Francis folder; Jerry Mandel, Reid Strieby, Carl Werthman, "A Critical Assessment of the Plan Prepared by the San Francisco Redevelopment Agency for Western Addition Area II," prepared for the United San Francisco Freedom Movement, April, 1964, in SFRA, Gene Suttle's Files, PA-31 folder. The description of the production of the USFFM critique is from a biographical statement by Jerry Mandel, available online at http://sociology.berkeley.edu.

43. The material in this and the following paragraphs is from San Francisco Redevelopment Agency, "Hearing Transcript, 14 April 1964–16 April 1964," in SFRA, Executive Office Files, CR-36 folder. The agency prepared a detailed forty-eight page reply to eighty statements of criticism offered by participants at the hearings in "Review of Western Addition Area 2 Redevelopment Plan Resulting from the Redevelopment Agency's Public Hearing Held April 14, 15 and 16, 1964," May 15, 1964, in ibid.

44. "Hearing Transcript."

45. Office of the Mayor, San Francisco, "A Housing Program for San Francisco," April 27, 1964, copy in CBWC, Incoming Correspondence, M. J. Herman folder.

46. Justin Herman was skeptical about the possible success of any plan that would come from City Hall, and he explained the reasons for his skepticism in a letter to his friend and fellow housing reformer Catherine Bauer Wurster. Herman recounted that the SFRA and the NAACP "were working together harmoniously on Western Addition Area 2 until the Birmingham experience generated a new, aggressive NAACP and United Freedom protest movement." (Herman is referring to the events in Birmingham, Alabama, of April–May 1963 that involved 2,500 arrests, attacks on demonstrators by police dogs and water cannons, and the bombing of the motel at which Martin Luther King Jr. was staying, as well as of King's brother's house.) "Cooperation with 'the establishment' became in the view of the civil rights and minority leadership impossible for the time being." In his view, "The protest groups must have their time of protest before they are willing to go to work": M. Justin Herman to Catherine B. Wurster, April 29, 1964, letter marked "PERSONAL AND CONFIDENTIAL," in CBWC, Incoming Correspondence Files, M. J. Herman folder. The Bradley quotes are from Meier and Rudwick, *CORE,* 214, 252, 304, 363, 387. William Bradley (now Oba T'Shaka) provides his personal narrative of these events on his website at http://www.obatshaka.com/biography.

CHAPTER 9

1. The quote is from *San Francisco Call-Bulletin,* September 4, 1957. For details on the educational philosophy of Harold Spears, including material derived from personal interviews, see Larry Cuban, *Urban School Chiefs under Fire* (Chicago: University of Chicago Press, 1976), 57–80, 157–164. Doris Fine provides a detailed account from the standpoint of a former fourth-grade teacher in the schools who resigned, moved to academe, and became a participant in the city's school desegregation process: Doris R. Fine, *When Leadership Fails: Desegregation and Demoralization in the San Francisco Schools* (New Brunswick, N.J.: Transaction, 1986). See also John Kaplan, "San Francisco," in *Affirmative School Integration: Efforts to Overcome De Facto Segregation in Urban Schools,* ed. Roscoe Hill and Malcolm Feeley (Beverly Hills, Calif.: Sage, 1967), 64–79; Robert L. Crain, *The Politics of School Desegregation: Comparative Case Studies of Community Structure and Policy Making* (Chicago: Aldine, 1968), 81–94; David L. Kirp, "Multitudes in the Valley of Indecision: The Desegregation of San Francisco's Schools," in *Limits of Justice: The Court's Role in School Desegregation* (Cambridge: Ballinger, 1978), 411–492; David L. Kirp, *Just Schools: The Idea of Racial Equality in American Education* (Berkeley: University of California Press, 1982), 82–116. For the early institutional history of public schooling in the city, see Issel and Cherny, *San Francisco, 1865–1932,* 102–105, 147; Vincent L. Shradar, "Ethnicity, Religion, and Class: Progressive School Reform in San Francisco," *History of Education Quarterly* 20 (Winter 1980): 385–401; Low, *The Unimpressible Race.* This chapter benefits from the research assistance of Stuart McElderry and John J. Rosen.

2. San Francisco Unified School District, Minutes of the Board of Education, January 23, 1962, in SFHC (hereafter, SFUSD Minutes). The new strategy was enunciated at the fifty-second annual convention of the NAACP during the summer of 1961 "to ensure the end of all segregated public education in fact or by law by all means available": quoted from June Shagaloff to West Coast Regional Office, San Francisco, memorandum, March 25, 1962, in NAACPWCR. Tarea Hall Pitman to June Shagaloff, January 16, 1962, in NAACPWCR. The biographical information on Spears is from the Harold Spears Manuscripts Collection, available online at http://www.indiana.edu; the biographical information on Axelrod is from Roz Payne, Axelrod obituary, available online at http://lists.village .virginia.edu/lists_archive/sixties-l/4272.html.

3. June Shagaloff and Robert L. Carter to California State Board of Education, April 12, 1962, in NAACPWCR; *San Francisco Chronicle,* May 11–12, 1962.

4. SFUSD Minutes, March 6, 1962; *San Francisco Chronicle,* March 7, 1962.

5. West of Twin Peaks Central Council to Superintendent Harold Spears, March 28, 1962, SFUSD Minutes, May 1, 1962, app.; *San Francisco Chronicle,* May 2, 1962.

6. In the early to mid-1960s, the argument that white privilege needed to be offset by affirmative action to achieve equality was deployed by African American and white civil rights advocates in San Francisco. Soon thereafter, the expansion of the national civil rights campaign into a human rights movement more generally, plus the city's increasing population diversity, with growing numbers of Hispanic and Asia-Pacific Islands residents whose children attended public schools, expanded the discussion in San Francisco of who deserved affirmative action to include many more ethnic/racial groups (and other, non-ethnic/racial groups). These changes and their consequences for the debate about the public interest are beyond the scope of this book, The Spears quote is from *San Francisco Chronicle,* May 14, 1962. Three years later, President Lyndon B. Johnson made this definition of the public interest a national goal, in his commencement address at Howard

University on June 4, 1965: Lyndon B. Johnson, "To Fulfill These Rights," available online at http://www.lbjlib.utexas.edu.

7. SFUSD Minutes, January 9, April 3, April 24, 1962; *San Francisco Chronicle*, May 16, 1962.

8. Crain, *The Politics of School Desegregation*, 84, 89; U.S. Bureau of the Census, *U.S. Census of Population and Housing: 1960 Census Tracts*, Final Report PHC (1)–132 (Washington: U.S. Government Printing Office, 1961).

9. Report by Roy E. Simpson, State Superintendent to California State Board of Education, May 29, 1962, in NAACPWCR; California State Board of Education, "Declaration of Policy with Reference to De Facto Racial Segregation in Public Schools," June 14, 1962, NAACPWCR; statement of Robert W. Formhals, executive secretary, California School Boards Association, "Concerning the Proposed Regulations of the California State Board of Education to Implement Their Statement of Policy Regarding Racial Segregation in Public Schools," presented to the State Board of Education, Los Angeles, June 15, 1962, in NAACPWCR.

10. Harold Spears, "The Proper Recognition of a Pupil's Racial Background in the San Francisco Unified School District," SFUSD Minutes, June 19, 1962, app.

11. Ibid., 17, 24–25.

12. *San Francisco Chronicle*, August 1, August 7, 1962.

13. SFUSD Minutes, August 7, 1962; *San Francisco Chronicle*, August 8–9, 1962.

14. *San Francisco Chronicle*, August 9, August 11–12, August 14, 1962.

15. Ibid., August 14–16, 1962.

16. Ibid., August 14, 17–18, 1962; Crain, *The Politics of School Desegregation*, 85.

17. *San Francisco Chronicle*, August 17–18, 1962; Crain, *The Politics of School Desegregation*, 86. The biographical information for Markel is from Ron Culver, *The History of the California Republican Assembly*, available online at http://www.pa-ra.org.

18. SFUSD Minutes, August 21, 1962; *San Francisco Chronicle*, August 22, August 24, 1962; Fine, *When Leadership Fails*, 29; Crain, *The Politics of School Desegregation*, 81. The school enrollment data are from San Francisco Unified School District, "Racial Estimates of Pupils Attending San Francisco Public Schools, October 1964," released August 1965; San Francisco Unified School District, "Change in Racial Makeup of Pupils in the San Francisco Public Schools, 1964–1965," released November 1965; San Francisco Unified School District, "Pupil Enrollment in the San Francisco Public Schools, September 1966," released November 1966, all in box 93, Records of the San Francisco Unified School District, SFHC.

19. Jeanne Bogard, letter to the editor, *San Francisco Chronicle*, August 22, 1962; SFUSD Minutes, September 18, 1962; *San Francisco Chronicle*, September 20, 1962; *San Francisco Examiner*, September 28, 1962; Tarea Hall Pittman to Gloster B. Current, December 8, 1962, in Annual Report Summary, NAACPWCR, 1962 folder, 7–8.

20. *Report of the Ad Hoc Committee of the Board of Education to Study Ethnic Factors in the San Francisco Public Schools*, April 2, 1963, in Records of the San Francisco Unified School District, SFHC, 7–8, 14; *San Francisco Chronicle*, April 3–4, April 17, 1963.

21. The leading professional journal devoted to African American education policy asked Spears and his director of school-community improvement programs to contribute an article to the special issue "Educational Planning for Socially Disadvantaged Children and Youth," *Journal of Negro Education* 33 (Summer 1964): 245–253. The article was titled "How an Urban School System Identifies Its Disadvantaged" and was published during the summer of 1964, the very time that the superintendent came under renewed attack in San Francisco. The quote about the Civil Rights Movement and the Spears quote are from

Crain, *The Politics of School Desegregation,* 88. The quote about the unanticipated consequences of Spears's decision over the school bond issue is from Kirp, *Just Schools,* 88. The polling data are from "Human Rights Commission of the City and County of San Francisco and Ad Hoc Committee of the San Francisco Board of Education, Joint Conferences on Racial and Ethnic Distribution in San Francisco Schools," August 23, August 26, 1965, in Records of the San Francisco Unified School District, SFHC.

22. Harold Spears and William L. Cobb, "Selected Data for Study in the Challenge to Effect Better Racial Balance in the San Francisco Public Schools," unpublished ms., San Francisco Unified School District, November 1965, Records of the San Francisco Unified District, SFHC.

23. The quote from Willie L. Brown is from *San Francisco Chronicle,* August 6, 1965. Cuban, *Urban School Chiefs under Fire,* 79–80; Kirp, "Multitudes in the Valley of Indecision," 424; Crain, *The Politics of School Desegregation,* 88.

24. "Joint Conferences," 55.

25. The racism quote is from "To All Affiliated Unions Greetings!" from John F. Shelley and John A. O'Connell, March 31, 1942, in SFLCR, carton 42, Cooks Union Local 44 folder. The Rossi quote is from *San Francisco Chronicle,* March 7, 1942. See also Broussard, *Black San Francisco,* 153–154. Arthur Caylor wrote, "The firemen point out the problem of living quarters should this 'test case' open further civil service jobs to negroes. Policemen recall that recently there was a charter amendment making promotions dependent on written examinations alone [and] all types of civil service workers might eventually be affected": Arthur Caylor, "Behind the News," *San Francisco News,* January 10, 1942. For conflicting accounts by two insiders about the racism and the preference for those with Irish ethnic backgrounds in the Police Department's hiring and promotion, see the autobiography by (white) former Deputy Chief of Police Kevin J. Mullen, *The Egg Man's Son: A San Francisco Irish Life* (College Station, Tex.: Virtualbookworm.com, 2009); the memoir by the city's first African American police chief, Prentice Earl Sanders with Bennett Cohen, *The Zebra Murders: A Season of Killing, Racial Madness, and Civil Rights: A True Story* (New York: Arcade, 2011); Kevin J. Mullen, review of *The Zebra Murders,* available online at http://www.sanfranciscohomicide.com.

26. "To All Affiliated Unions Greetings!"; San Francisco Labor Council, "Resolution on Audley Cole," March 21, 1942," in SFLCR, carton 41, Resolutions folder; Audley L. Cole Jr. to Fair Employment Practice Commission, February 18, 1942, NAACP, box A-251, FEPC 1941–1943 folder; Bay Area Council against Discrimination, "First Progress Report of the Bay Area Council against Discrimination," August 1942, Institute of Governmental Studies, University of California, Berkeley; *Labor Herald,* March 13, 1942; *People's World,* March 16, 1942; *San Francisco Chronicle,* March 28, 1942. The practical effects of local union worker control principles of autonomy of the local union, sanctity of collective-bargaining agreements between the union and the employer, majority rule within the local union, and respect for seniority rights in limiting the success of reforms aimed at racial equality advocated by Harry Bridges and other officers of the dockworkers' and warehouse workers' union is the subject of Bruce Nelson, "The 'Lords of the Docks' Reconsidered: Race Relations among West Coast Longshoremen, 1933–61," in *Waterfront Workers: New Perspectives on Race and Class,* ed. Calvin Winslow (Urbana: University of Illinois Press, 1998), 155–192. Andrew Wender Cohen describes the impact of worker control principles (including the use of violent tactics) by unionized craft workers and tradesmen in the city of Chicago and speculates on its significance for the development of the nation's modern industrial economy: Andrew Wender Cohen, *The Racketeer's Progress: Chicago and the Struggle for the Modern American Economy, 1900–1940* (Cambridge:

Cambridge University Press, 2004). Francine Moccio describes the ways in which worker control theory shaped the practices of male workers in the electrical trade: Francine A. Moccio. *Live Wire: Women and Brotherhood in the Electrical Industry* (Philadelphia: Temple University Press, 2009).

27. Howden interviews (September 17, December 4, 1999). For a recent study of the fair employment practice reform movement nationwide that supports Howden's assessment of the California case, see Anthony S. Chen, *The Fifth Freedom: Jobs, Politics, and Civil Rights in the United States, 1941–1972* (Princeton, N.J.: Princeton University Press, 2009).

28. Association of Catholic Trade Unionists Resolution Supporting Proposition 11, October 19, 1946, in SFCIO, carton 7, FEPC folder; Association of Catholic Trade Unionists, "Proposed Changes, Additions, and Correction in the By-Laws," July 8, 1948, ACTU Records, Labor Management School Records/ACTU, Archives of the University of San Francisco; USF; Seaton W. Manning to John F. Shelley, January 10, 1946, in SFLCR, carton 52, Urban League folder; National Urban League, San Francisco Branch, Annual Report 1948, Urban League Records, box 127, San Francisco Urban League 1948 folder; "Statement of Louis Bloch before Mayor's Committee on Human Relations," May 17, 1949, California Federation for Civic Unity Papers, BC, carton 2, Census folder; SFUSD Minutes, Conference on Fair Employment Legislation, August 13, 1949, California Federation for Civic Unity Papers, BC; transcript of statement of Almon E. Roth, San Francisco Employers Council, SFUSD Minutes, Mayor's Committee on Human Relations, August 22, 1949, in Alvin Fine Collection, WJHC, box 19, folder 4; Jack Shelley to George Johns, October 5, 1949, and "Report on F.E.P.C. Ordinance," November 1949, both in SFLCR, box 58, FEPC Ordinance file; Board Committee on County, State, and National Affairs to San Francisco Board of Supervisors, memorandum, January 6, 1950; Jack Goldberger to Board of Supervisors, telegraph, January 21, 1950; James Leo Halley to Jack Goldberger, January 27, 1950, all in ibid., carton 62, Board of Supervisors file.

29. Transcript of statement of Almon E. Roth; Almon E. Roth to Board of Supervisors, April 13, 1951, in ibid., box 65, San Francisco Employers Council folder. The Falk quote is from *San Francisco Chronicle,* April 16, 1951.

30. *Official Bulletin,* San Francisco Labor Council, May 16, 1951; statement of Alvin Fine, FEPC Hearing, May 14, 1951, in Alvin Fine Collection, WJHC, box 11, folder 6; *Sun-Reporter,* June 6, 1951; George Christopher to Jack Goldberger, January 27, 1950, in SFLCR, carton 62, Board of Supervisors file.

31. George Dorsey, *Christopher of San Francisco* (New York: Macmillan, 1962), 49–60, provides a sympathetic account of the dairy business scandal. The journalist Burton H. Wolfe wrote a scathing exposé of the Christopher case in his magazine *The Californian* in 1960, and a revised version is in "Born to Raise Hell: Memoirs of an Unrepentant Shit-Disturber—Part 2," *San Francisco Frontlines,* July 1998, 13–15. Edgar D. Osgood to John J. Ferdon, December 15, 1956, Alvin Fine Collection, WJHC, box 11, folder 6; *Sun-Reporter,* September 8, 1956.

32. Biographical information on the co-chairmen of the committee is from Real Great Debaters blog, available online at http://realgreatdebaters.blogspot.com (Hamilton T. Boswell); Lewis Francis Byington, *History of San Francisco,* vol. 3 (Chicago: S. J. Clarke, 1931), 420–422; Cate School website, available online at http://www.cate.org (William Matson Roth); Richard M. Nixon Presidential Library, White House Special Files Collection, box 54, folder 29, available online at http://www.nixonlibrary.gov (Edgar D. Osgood).

33. The Osgood quote is from his speech at the ceremony at which he was named Chevalier de la Légion d'Honneur by the French Ambassador to the United States: French

Consulate in San Francisco website, available online at http://www.consulfrance-sanfran cisco.org/spip.php?article1316. The description of the new campaign for the ordinance is Edgar T. Osgood to John J. Ferdon, December 15, 1956, in SFLCR, carton 143, FEP California file; *Sun-Reporter,* December 22, 1956, January 19, February 2, 1957.

34. Adrien J. Falk, "Statement to the County, State, and National Affairs Committee, San Francisco Board of Supervisors," February 13, 1957, Alvin Fine Collection, WJHC, box 27, folder 8, esp. 10; Frank Foisie, "The Case for Voluntary Action in Providing Equal Job Opportunity," February 13, 1957, in SFLCR, box 84, Board of Supervisors 1957 folder; *Sun-Reporter,* January 19, March 23, 1957. At the time, I was an apprentice electrician and a member of Local 6 of the International Brotherhood of Electrical Workers. My father, Charles H. Issel, served as the president of the local union. The local union officially supported the proposed equal employment opportunity act, but members of the union worried about the possible adverse impact of the ordinance on three craft-guild traditions: controlling access to apprenticeship programs to maintain high standards of workmanship; giving preference in union membership to the sons, nephews, and other relatives of existing members; and assigning work according to seniority. For the national context of such debates, see Dennis Deslippe, *Protesting Affirmative Action: The Struggle over Equality after the Civil Rights Revolution* (Baltimore: Johns Hopkins University Press, 2012).

35. J. Eugene McAteer, "Statement on Pending Fair Employment Ordinance," May 20, 1957, in Alvin Fine Collection, WJHC, box 11, FEPC 1949–1957 folder 6; Edgar D. Osgood to Dear Friends of FEPC, June 14, 1957, and attached statement, in SFLCR, carton 143, FEP California Commission folder; "Final Report of the Commission on Equal Employment Opportunity of the City and County of San Francisco," 1960, 10–15, 17, 21; George W. Johns to Richard A. Bancroft, n.d. 1959, in SFLCR, carton 89, "B" 1959 folder.

36. Eugene Block to George W. Johns, October 15, 1959, and William Becker to Reverend Hamilton Boswell, August 8, 1961, both in SFLCR, carton 89, "B" 1959 folder; Raab, "Executive of the San Francisco Community Relations Council," 66; "Your Local Branch," May 1, 1962, NAACP (Group III), San Francisco Branch 1962–1963 folder; "Program Activity Report," September 30, 1962, Box 70, San Francisco 1962 folder, Part 2, series 4, Urban League Records; *Sun-Reporter,* January 20, 1962.

37. "Negro Unemployment," *Official Bulletin,* San Francisco Labor Council, July 24, 1963, 2.

38. Ibid.; *Sun-Reporter,* June 22, 1963; memorandum regarding United San Francisco Freedom Movement, August 27, 1963, in SFLCR, box 109, "U" 1963 folder.

39. *San Francisco Chronicle,* July 14, 1964; Henry P. Guzda, "James P. Mitchell: Social Conscience of the Cabinet," *Monthly Labor Review* (August 1991): 23–29; "A Human Relations Program for San Francisco," report to Mayor Christopher by James P. Mitchell, January 2, 1964, Institute of Governmental Studies, University of California, Berkeley; "Report to Mayor Shelley by Mayor's Interim Committee on Human Relations," October 8, 1964, in Alvin Fine Collection, WJHC, Mayor's Committee folder.

40. Sister Bernadette Giles, "The San Francisco Human Rights Commission," paper presented at the History of Bay Area Catholicism VII Conference, September 28, 1991 (copy in my possession). Sister Bernadette Giles replaced Sister Maureen Kelly on the HRC in 1965. "Report to Mayor Shelley by Mayor's Interim Committee on Human Relations"; Raab, "Executive of the San Francisco Community Relations Council," 34. For a detailed account of the Philadelphia case of this aspect of the Civil Rights Movement outside the South, see Thomas J. Sugrue, "Affirmative Action from Below: Civil Rights, the Building Trades, and the Politics of Racial Equality in the Urban North, 1945–1969," *Journal of American History* 91 (June 2004): 145–173.

CHAPTER 10

1. San Francisco Board of Supervisors, Resolution 45-59 (adopted January 23, 1959).

2. San Francisco Board of Supervisors, Resolution 634-64 adopted (adopted October 13, 1964), Resolution 391-65-3 (adopted March 21, 1966), Resolution 391-65-4 (adopted March 21, 1966), Resolution 391-65-5 (adopted March 21, 1966).

3. *San Francisco Chronicle,* March 24, 1966; *San Francisco Examiner,* March 22, 1966.

4. Joseph L. Alioto, quoted in *San Francisco Chronicle,* October 10, 1956. Ibid., May 22, June 6, June 26, July 3, 1968.

5. "The War over Urban Expressways," *Business Week,* March 11, 1967, 4–5. See also Richard A. Miller, "Expressway Blight," *Architectural Forum* 111 (October 1959): 159–163; "The Revolt against Big-City Freeways," *U.S. News and World Report,* January 1, 1962, 48–51; Lewis Mumford, *The Highway and the City* (New York: Harcourt, Brace, and World, 1963). Jane Holtz Kay, *Asphalt Nation: How the Automobile Took over America and How We Can Take It Back* (New York: Crown, 1997), is a critique in the tradition of Helen Leavitt, *Super Highway–Super Hoax* (New York: Doubleday, 1970), and Ben Kelley, *The Pavers and the Paved* (New York: Donald W. Brown, 1971). See also Tom Lewis, *Divided Highways: Building the Interstate Highways, Transforming American Life* (New York: Viking, 1997). For a sample of the extensive scholarly literature, see Raymond A. Mohl, "The Interstates and the Cities: The U.S. Department of Transportation and the Freeway Revolt, 1966–1973," *Journal of Policy History* 20, no. 2 (2008): 193–226; Raymond A. Mohl, "Stop the Road: Freeway Revolts in American Cities," *Journal of Urban History* 30 (July 2004): 674–706; Raymond A. Mohl, "Planned Destruction: The Interstates and Central City Housing," in *From the Tenement to the Robert Taylor Homes: American Housing Policy, 1895–1990,* ed. John Bauman (University Park: Pennsylvania State University Press, 2000); Carl Abbott, *The Metropolitan Frontier: Cities in the Modern American West* (Tucson: University of Arizona Press, 1993), 154–155; Mark H. Rose and Bruce E. Seely, "Getting the Interstate System Built: Road Engineers and the Implementation of Public Policy, 1955–1985," *Journal of Policy History* 2, no. 1 (1990): 23–55; Mark H. Rose, *Interstate: Express Highway Politics, 1939–1989,* rev. ed. (Knoxville: University of Tennessee Press, 1990); Bruce E. Seely, *Building the American Highway System: Engineers as Policy Makers* (Philadelphia: Temple University Press, 1987); Samuel P. Hays, *Beauty, Health, and Permanence: Environmental Politics in the United States, 1955–1985* (Cambridge: Cambridge University Press, 1987); Robert Fishman, "The Anti-Planners: The Contemporary Revolt against Planning and Its Significance for Planning History," in *Shaping an Urban World,* ed. Gordon E. Cherry (New York: St. Martin's Press, 1980); Mark Foster, "City Planners and Urban Transportation: The American Response, 1900–1940," *Journal of Urban History* 5, no. 3 (May 1979): 365–396; John B. Rae, "The Car and the Road: Highway Technology and Highway Policy" and "Commentary on the Paper of John Rae," in *Perspectives in the History of Science and Technology,* ed. Duane H. D. Roller (Norman: University of Oklahoma Press, 1971), 99–122.

6. San Francisco Board of Supervisors, Resolution 496-63 (adopted August 26, 1963). William H. Lathrop Jr. described the freeway revolt shortly after the crucial vote in 1966: See William H. Lathrop Jr., "San Francisco Freeway Revolt," *Transportation Engineering Journal* 97 (February 1971): 133–143. Several well-researched unpublished theses and dissertations contain thoughtful analyses of aspects of the San Francisco freeway revolt: see, e.g., Herbert H. Goodwin Jr., "California's Growing Freeway System," Ph.D. diss., University of California, Los Angeles, 1969, 417–564; Lawrence Simon Jacobson, "The Effect of Political Pressure upon Freeway Route Decisions in San Francisco," master's thesis, San

Francisco State College, 1972; Seymour Mark Adler, "The Political Economy of Transit in the San Francisco Bay Area, 1945–1963," Ph.D. diss., University of California, Berkeley, 1980, 308–316, 415–417; David W. Jones Jr., "California's Freeway Era in Historical Perspective," Ph.D. diss., University of California, Berkeley, 1989, 256–301; Clifford Donald Ellis, "Visions of Urban Freeways, 1930–1970," Ph.D. diss., University of California, Berkeley, 1990, 321–365.

7. On environmental politics generally, see Samuel P. Hays, "From Conservation to Environment: Environmental Politics in the United States Since World War II," in *Out of the Woods: Essays in Environmental History,* ed. Char Miller and Hal Rothman (Pittsburgh: University of Pittsburgh Press, 1997), 101–126; Samuel P. Hays, *Explorations in Environmental History* (Pittsburgh: University of Pittsburgh Press, 1998).

8. See William A. Proctor, "Economic Factors Pertinent to Freeway Development," Planning Monograph no. 6, San Francisco Department of City Planning, July 31, 1948, Institute of Governmental Studies (IGS), University of California, Berkeley.

9. The Chamber of Commerce, following tradition, assumed leadership in the discussion of transportation policy and enlisted the support of career professionals in city agencies, as well as the cooperation of the mayor, but this tradition was changing during the period: San Francisco Chamber of Commerce, "Streets and Highways," *Annual Report, 1939 and Work Program for 1940,* 11–12, copy in CHS. See also Chapter 2 of this book.

10. Angelo Rossi, "Mayor's Annual Message," in Board of Supervisors, *Journal of Proceedings,* January 26, 1942, 114–117; Board of Supervisors, *Journal of Proceedings,* February 16, 1942, 271–275.

11. San Francisco Housing and Planning Association, "Now Is the Time to Plan" (1942), copy in Institute of Governmental Studies Library, University of California, Berkeley.

12. Two oral history interviews by ROHO-UCB contain material on the Lapham administration: interview with Dorothy W. Erskine in *Bay Area Foundation History* 3 (1971): 125–129, and Kent, "Statewide and Regional Land Use Planning in California," 31–45.

13. "The Master Plan of the City and County of San Francisco" (adopted by the City Planning Commission on December 20, 1945), San Francisco City Planning Commission, January 1946, IGS.

14. L. Deming Tilton, "Memorandum on the Proposed Extension of the Bayshore Freeway," Administrative Report no. 32, April 26, 1945, 11, copy in Freeway Collection, SFHC, folder 2A. The ninety separate folders pertaining to San Francisco's freeways at the San Francisco History Center contain originals and copies of city and state documents pertaining to freeways from the Department of City Planning, San Francisco Public Works Department, Mayor's Office, Board of Supervisors, and Planning Commission, and from various state agencies. Also included is correspondence to and from city and state agencies and citywide and neighborhood interest groups. Extensive clipping files originally assembled by City Planning Department staff are also included in the Freeway Collection. I have also examined federal government documents pertaining to the cross-town freeway fight in the U.S. Department of Transportation Records, record group 398, National Archives and Records Administration, Washington, D.C. (hereafter, DOT-NARA), box 360, Public Roads California Part II Crosstown Freeways folder.

15. L. Deming Tilton, "Traffic Control and Facilitation: Pharmacopoeia of Traffic Control," *American City* 61, no. 10 (October 1946): 127. The plans in question were *Traffic, Transit, and Thoroughfare Improvements for San Francisco,* prepared by the Technical Committee of the Mayor's Administrative Transportation Council (March

1947); *Transportation Plan for San Francisco: November 1948* (Trafficways Plan), a report to the City Planning Commission by DeLeuw Cather and Company and Ladislas Segoe and Associates (adopted by the city and the state as an amendment to the Master Plan in 1951); *Trafficways in San Francisco: A Reappraisal,* San Francisco Department of City Planning (November 1960); "Recommendations on Alternate Panhandle Freeway Routes," July 16, 1964, copy in Freeway Collection, SFHC, folder 34; *Panhandle and Golden Gate Freeways: A Joint City-State Study* (February 1966).

16. San Francisco's particular political culture influenced the politics of freeway policy, but numerous aspects of the controversies that developed in the city involved issues that had to be addressed throughout the nation: see Rose and Seely, "Getting the Interstate System Built."

17. Paul Oppermann, quoted in "Downtown Is Everyone's Problem," *San Francisco News,* March 22, 1954.

18. The San Francisco Labor Council (AFL) endorsed state freeway proposals for the first time at its meeting of March 1, 1945: see SFLCR, Resolutions 1945 File. For a typical downtown business statement, see Down Town Association of San Francisco, "The Position of the Down Town Association on Freeways," in *The Downtowner Progress Report,* June 28, 1956, Freeway Collection, SFHC, folder 57. See also "Nine Point Policy Statement of the Down Town Association of San Francisco Relative to the Freeway Construction Problem in San Francisco," *The Downtowner,* December 2, 1959, Freeway Collection, SFHC, folder 81.

19. The cooperation between labor and business can be seen in Charles L. Conlon, chairman, Committee of South of Market Industries, to George Johns, secretary, San Francisco Labor Council, October 17, 1955, in SFLCR, carton 78; folder C; Alan K. Browne, co-chairman, San Francisco Citizens Committee for Ferry Park Bonds, to George Johns, August 27, 1959, ibid., carton 90, Municipal Elections folder 59. For the position of organized business, see San Francisco Chamber of Commerce, "Construction Projects for State Highways in City and County of San Francisco, 1954–55 Budget," August 20, 1953, copy in Freeway Collection, SFHC, folder 37. The sources for Mayor Christopher's conversation with Charles Blyth and the meeting that followed are Christopher interview; B. W. Booker, assistant state highway engineer, to Mayor George Christopher, letter, April 17, 1956, Freeway Collection, SFHC, folder 18; Scott Newhall, "A Newspaper Editor's Voyage across San Francisco Bay: *San Francisco Chronicle,* 1935–1971, and Other Adventures," oral history interview by Suzanne B. Riess, 1988–1989, ROHO-UCB, 1990, 275–277.

20. See, e.g., the interpretation in Jones, "California's Freeway Era," 300–302.

21. Newhall, "A Newspaper Editor's Voyage," 140.

22. Ibid.

23. Jean Kortum, interview by the author, October 22, 1998, San Francisco.

24. Newhall, "A Newspaper Editor's Voyage," 218.

25. The journalist Warren Hinckle, who simultaneously covered the freeway revolt as a reporter for the *San Francisco Chronicle* and organized rallies against the Panhandle Freeway, provides a wry perspective on the role of the circulation war in the freeway revolt: Warren Hinckle, *If You Have a Lemon, Make Lemonade: An Essential Memoir of a Lunatic Decade* (1993) paperback ed. (New York: W.W. Norton, 1990), 19–34. See also Judith Ann Lynch, "The San Francisco Panhandle Freeway Debate: One Year of Coverage by the *Chronicle* and the *Examiner,*" master's thesis, University of California, Berkeley, 1967.

26. *San Francisco Chronicle,* December 8, 1955.

27. Harold Gilliam, interview by the author, October 27, 1998, San Francisco.

28. *San Francisco Chronicle,* July 10, 1964.

29. One of the first of such editorials, "Speaking Up on Freeway Planning," appeared on November 2, 1956.

30. Property owners in the Silver Terrace and Excelsior neighborhoods expressed similar opposition to the Southern Freeway, but successful organized protest on the scale of the Glen Park and Sunset districts did not develop. For evidence of discontent in those southeastern neighborhoods, see James B. Smith to the Honorable George Christopher, January 16, 1956, Freeway Collection, SFHC, folder 50; *San Francisco News,* February 1, 1956.

31. The *San Francisco Chronicle* devoted an editorial on November 2, 1956, to the new law requiring the highway engineers to actively seek public response to their freeway plans. Because of space limitations, and because it involved substantially more people and had a more lasting impact on policy than the Glen Park case, only the Sunset District's campaign will receive detailed attention here. One of the mimeographed flyers, distributed door to door, announced a "great mass meeting" at Lincoln High School and read in part, "Protect YOUR home—YOUR neighborhood—YOUR community! Protect our churches and our schools. . . . Did you know that ours is the last hope of any community in California to block the arbitrary and bureaucratic Highway Commission, which is trying to jam this Freeway through our neighborhood. . . . This is YOUR fight! Stand up and be counted!": copy in Freeway Collection, SFHC, folder 57.

32. For the board's action and Christopher's veto, see *San Francisco Call Bulletin,* June 12, 1956; *San Francisco Chronicle,* June 13, June 22, 1956.

33. Joseph L. Alioto, quoted in *San Francisco Chronicle,* October 10, 1956.

34. For an account of the events during the meeting of the Board of Supervisors, see Jack Burby, "Board Kills Plans for Six Freeways: Unanimous Action," *San Francisco Chronicle,* January 27, 1959.

35. William Blake, interview by Lawrence Simon Jacobson, March 1967, San Francisco, quoted in Jacobson, "The Effect of Political Pressure," 75.

36. *San Francisco Chronicle,* March 30, 1960.

37. *San Francisco News-Call Bulletin,* March 8, 1960. For the importance of such ad hoc committees, see Carl Abbott, "Portland in the Pacific War: Planning from 1940 to 1945," *Urbanism Past and Present* 6 (Spring–Winter 1981): 12–24.

38. A detailed account of the process by which McKeon's activities became known is contained in a nine-page letter from Oscar H. Fisher, Burt Edelstein, and Lou Jolly to Mayor George Christopher, April 22, 1960, that accompanied the "Minority Report" of the Mayor's Committee to Study Freeways, copy in Freeway Collection, SFHC, folder 83. Paul Oppermann of the Department of City Planning became suspicious of McKeon's motives early on: see his memorandum to the files dated October 18, 1956, copy in Freeway Collection, SFHC, folder 57.

39. Case no. 498984, *Chris D. McKeon vs. Burt Edelstein, Oscar Fisher, Lou Jolly,* filed March 11, 1960, closed March 5, 1965, Superior Court of California, County of San Francisco.

40. The city planners and state engineers enlisted the expertise of the noted landscape architect Lawrence Halprin in an attempt to improve the designs for the Panhandle and Golden Gate freeways: see "Halprin Accepts Highway Challenge in San Francisco," *Architectural Forum* 116 (April 1962): 13. Halprin was based in San Francisco and played a national role in the development of ideas for reforming the design of highways: see Lawrence Halprin, *Cities,* rev. ed. (Cambridge, Mass.: MIT Press, 1972), 198–207; Lawrence

Halprin, "Cities Don't Have to Be Ugly," *Engineering News-Record,* vol. 181, November 7, 1968, 53–55. On the role of design considerations in freeway policy generally, see Louis Ward Kemp, "Aesthetes and Engineers: The Occupational Ideology of Highway Design," *Culture and Technology* 27 (October 1986): 759–797.

41. San Francisco Board of Supervisors, Resolution 496-63 (adopted August 26, 1963).

42. Bierman interview. See also Roberts, *Dianne Feinstein,* 46.

43. Kortum interview. The committee published an effective, expensively produced professional critique of the Golden Gate Freeway entitled "The Golden Gate Freeway: A Frightening Prospect." The large-format publication included quotes from local environmental activists, as well as from President Lyndon Johnson and Vice-President Hubert Humphrey underscoring the importance of protecting the northern waterfront from "the unworthiness of the Division of Highways proposed Golden Gate Freeway": copy in Freeway Collection, SFHC, folder 32.

44. *San Francisco Chronicle,* February 16, 1966.

45. Kortum interview. Willie L. Brown Jr. to the Honorable Robert C. Weaver, February 2, 1966, carbon copy in personal possession of Jean Kortum. Brown's biographer correctly notes that the Golden Gate Freeway was "an issue about which he had shown no previous interest" before his campaign for the State Assembly in 1964: see Richardson, *Willie Brown,* 92.

46. For a detailed account of the board's actions based on extensive interviews with the principals, as well as on newspaper reporting, see Jacobson, "The Effect of Political Pressure," 85–89, 113–117, 129–136.

47. John F. Shelley to Alan S. Boyd, January 3, 1966, in DOT-NARA, box 360, Public Roads California (Crystal Springs) folder; John F. Shelley to Alan S. Boyd, April 4, 1967, in DOT-NARA, box 309, Federal Aid Highways California Junipero Serra Freeway 1967 folder.

48. *San Francisco Chronicle,* April 14, 1957.

49. Ibid., May 9, May 17, 1957.

50. The resolution from 1958 is reiterated in San Francisco Public Utilities Commission, Resolution 67-0891(October 10, 1967), in DOT-NARA, box 309, Federal Aid Highways California Junipero Serra Freeway 1967 folder. Fazackerly's comment is quoted in *San Francisco Chronicle,* June 5, 1957.

51. E. H. Swick to Lowell K. Bridwell, February 11, 1966, in DOT-NARA, box 360, Public Roads California (Crystal Springs) folder. See also *San Francisco Chronicle,* April 11, July 23, 1958.

52. The biographical data is from my files on city commissioners and department heads, 1930–1970. The changes in the Shelley administration receive brief attention in Wirt, *Power in the City,* 77. Carr, a prominent California Democrat, was an outspoken advocate of environmentalist land use and water policy planning.

53. Gilliam interview. Stewart L. Udall, *The Quiet Crisis,* New York: Avon, 1963, 203.

54. J. C. Womack to Robert B. Bradford and the Members of the State Highway Commission, September 14, 1965, in DOT-NARA, box 360, Public Roads California (Crystal Springs) folder.

55. The city's Water Department had an engineer assigned to full-time work with the Division of Highways with instructions to monitor water quality during the early phases of construction: Swick to Bridwell.

56. "Statement of Position Regarding the Proposed Realignment of Junipero Serra Freeway between Ralston Avenue and the Town Limits of Woodside," July 27, 1965, in

DOT-NARA, box 360, Public Roads California (Crystal Springs) folder; *San Francisco Chronicle,* October 20, October 25, 1965 (editorial); *Burlingame Star,* October 22, 1965; J. C. Womack to Robert B. Bradford and Members of the State Highway Commission, February 14, 1966, and Rolf Eliassen to James K. Carr, May 11, 1966, in DOT-NARA, box 360, Public Roads California (Crystal Springs) folder.

57. The White House meeting is described in Shelley to Boyd (April 4, 1967).

58. Commissioner William Whitehurst, quoted in *San Francisco Chronicle,* July 25, 1968.

59. Handwritten note from Boyd at bottom of letter from Thomas F. Stack to Alan S. Boyd, January 18, 1966, DOT-NARA, box 360, Public Roads California (Crystal Springs) folder.

60. Swick to Bridwell; *San Francisco Chronicle,* February 2–3, 1966.

61. Swick to Bridwell.

62. Lowell K. Bridwell to Alan S. Boyd, February 18, 1966; J. C. Womack to D. J. Steele, March 1, 1966; E. H. Swick to Lowell K. Bridwell, March 10, 1966, all in DOT-NARA, box 360, Public Roads California (Crystal Springs) folder.

63. Ibid.

64. Thomas M. O'Connor to Alan S. Boyd, April 26, 1966, May 12, 1966, in DOT-NARA, box 360, Public Roads California (Crystal Springs) folder; *San Francisco Chronicle,* July 13, 1965; *San Francisco News-Call Bulletin,* July 13, 1965.

65. John F. Shelley to Alan S. Boyd, telegram, February 28, 1966; S. E. Farin to Alan S. Boyd, telegram, March 21, 1966; Alan S. Boyd to Rex M. Whitton, March 22, 1966, all in DOT-NARA), box 360, Public Roads California Part II Crosstown Freeways folder; *San Francisco Chronicle,* March 22, 1966.

66. John F. Shelley to Edmund G. Brown, June 29, 1966, in DOT-NARA, box 360, Public Roads California (Crystal Springs) folder.

67. Lowell K. Bridwell to Under Secretary Alan S. Boyd, August 1, 1966, and James J. Finn to Alan S. Boyd, July 22, 1966, in DOT-NARA, box 360, Public Roads California (Crystal Springs) folder.

68. Quoted in Shelley to Boyd (April 4, 1967).

69. Department of Transportation Act, *U.S. Statutes at Large,* 80, sec. 4 (f) 1967.

70. Stewart L. Udall to Dear Mr. Secretary [Alan S. Boyd], March 13, 1967; [U.S. Senator from California] Thomas H. Kuchel to Alan S. Boyd, April 24, 1967; Orville L. Freeman to Alan S. Boyd, May 25, 1967; Robert C. Weaver to Alan S. Boyd, July 10, 1967; Alan S. Boyd to Ronald Reagan, August 9, 1967, all in DOT-NARA, box 309, Federal Aid Highways California Junipero Serra Freeway 1967 folder. The five-hour meeting on August 24 is described in detail in Lowell K. Bridwell to Secretary Alan S. Boyd, September 5, 1967, in ibid.

71. Gordon C. Luce to Lowell K. Bridwell, August 22, August 30, 1967, in ibid.

72. Lowell K. Bridwell to John F. Shelley, September 6, 1967, in ibid.

73. Lowell K. Bridwell to Gordon C. Luce, September 8, 1967, in ibid.; *San Francisco Chronicle,* September 21, 1967.

74. John F. Shelley to Lowell K. Bridwell, October 11, 1967; Lowell K. Bridwell to John F. Shelley, October 31, 1967; [Acting San Francisco Mayor] Dorothy von Beroldinger to Members of the California Highway Commission, November 15, 1967, all in DOT-NARA, box 309, Federal Aid Highways California Junipero Serra Freeway 1967 folder; *San Francisco Chronicle,* December 13, 1967.

75. *San Francisco Chronicle,* May 22, 1968.

76. Ibid., June 6, June 26, July 3, September 13, 1968.

77. Ibid., September 13, 1968.

78. Ibid., March 20, 1969, September 3, 1973.

79. See Mohl, "Planned Destruction"; Alan Lupo, Frank Colcord, and Edmund P. Fowler, *Rites of Way: The Politics of Transportation in Boston and the U.S. City* (Boston: Little, Brown, 1971), 171–187; Richard O. Baumbach Jr. and William E. Borah, *The Second Battle of New Orleans: A History of the Vieux Carre Riverfront Expressway Controversy* (University: University of Alabama Press, 1981); Robert R. Gioielli, "Hard Asphalt and Heavy Metals: Urban Environmentalism in Postwar America," Ph.D. diss., University of Cincinnati, 2008.

80. See Jeffrey M. Berry, *The New Liberalism: The Rising Power of Citizen Groups* (Washington, D.C.: Brookings Institution Press, 1999); Samuel P. Hays, "Three Decades of Environmental Politics: The Historical Context," in Hays, *Explorations in Environmental History*, 334–378.

CHAPTER 11

1. "Catholicism in San Francisco," in Southern California Library for Social Studies and Research, Los Angeles Subject File, Communist Party 1948 folder.

2. Eugene A. Boyle, ed., "San Francisco, a City in Crisis: A Report to the Churches and Synagogues Sponsored by the San Francisco Conference on Religion, Race and Social Concerns," St. Patrick's Seminary, Menlo Park, Calif., 1968, 4.

3. Biographical information in this and the following paragraph draws on William Issel, "Joseph L. Alioto," in *Scribner Encyclopedia of American Lives*, Volume 5, 1997–1999 (New York: Charles Scribner's Sons, 2002), 10–11.

4. Joseph L. Alioto, presentation at the Labor and Politics: Who Pressures Whom? conference, February 7, 1989, San Francisco (audio transcript, side 1), in LARC. The phrase "vital center" originated with Schlesinger, *The Vital Center*. Monsignor Haas's work at the U.S. Department of Labor and as chairman of the FEPC is described in Thomas E. Blantz, *A Priest in Public Service: Francis J. Haas and the New Deal* (Notre Dame, Ind.: University of Notre Dame Press, 1982), 200–227.

5. This and the next paragraph draw on material in the clipping files and biography folders in Alioto Collection, SFHC. Joseph L. Alioto to My Dear Mr. Hagerty, n.d. (1940), in James L. Hagerty Papers, Archives of St. Mary's College of California, Moraga. Alioto's position as an associate with Brobeck, Phleger, and Harrison is listed in *Brobeck, Phleger, and Harrison: The Earlier Years*. Maurice Harrison, "St. Thomas More," *Moraga Quarterly* 12 (Fall 1941): 26; "'Youth and America's Crisis' Subject of Forum," *The Monitor*, March 21, 1942.

6. On October 26, 1955, Alioto declared that the Redevelopment Agency's designation of a six-block tract in the South of Market District was "the greatest thing that has happened to San Francisco since Golden Gate Park or Hetch Hetchy": *San Francisco News*, October 27, 1955. The Alioto clipping file, SFHC, contains extensive coverage of Alioto's term on the Redevelopment Agency, documenting how he put his political philosophy into practice.

7. This and the next three paragraphs are informed by a written communication to the author from Hadley R. Roff, who participated in the Alioto campaigns in 1967 and 1971, served as Mayor Alioto's press secretary from January 1968 through 1970, and returned to serve in the administrations of Art Agnos and Frank Jordan after working on the U.S. Senate staffs of Edward Kennedy and Edmund Muskie. On Phillip Burton and his left-liberal network, see Jacobs, *A Rage for Justice*; Jonathan Bell, "'To Strive for Economic

and Social Justice': Welfare, Sexuality, and Liberal Politics in San Francisco in the 1960s," *Journal of Policy History* 22, no. 2 (2010): 193–225; Jonathan Bell, *California Crucible: The Forging of Modern American Liberalism* (Philadelphia: University of Pennsylvania Press, 2012), 259.

8. Earl C. Behrens, "Marks Beats Burton for State Senate Seat," *San Francisco Chronicle,* August 16, 1967' Earl C. Behrens, "What Marks' Election Win Could Mean," *San Francisco Chronicle,* August 17, 1967.

9. Michael Harris, "Shelley Quits Race—Alioto Gains Support," *San Francisco Chronicle,* September 8, 1967; Jack S. McDowell, "Shelley Comes Up 2d Best," *San Francisco Chronicle,* July 2, 1967; "Text of Shelley's Announcement," *San Francisco Examiner,* September 8. 1967.

10. Harris, "Shelley Quits Race"; Dick Nolan, "Alioto's Problems," *San Francisco Sunday Examiner and Chronicle,* September 24, 1967; "Shelley Formally Endorses Alioto," *San Francisco Chronicle,* October 5, 1967. The editor of the *Chronicle,* Scott Newhall, ran against the incumbent Mayor Alioto in the 1971 campaign.

11. Jack Viets, "Burton's Remarks Serve to Obscure," *San Francisco Chronicle,* September 9, 1967; Jack Welter, "J. Burton Pops Off—Not Out," *San Francisco Examiner,* September 8, 1967.

12. Earl C. Behrens, "Morrison Jumps into Mayor Race," *San Francisco Chronicle,* September 13, 1967; Jerry Burns, "Shelley Returns—Talks Politics," *San Francisco Chronicle,* September 26, 1967.

13. Michael Harris, "Alioto Moves in as Shelley Quits," *San Francisco Chronicle,* September 9, 1967; "Dobbs, Alioto in Counter Accusations," *San Francisco Chronicle,* September 22, 1967.

14. Michael Harris, "Alioto Wins over Dobbs—Prop. P Loses Decisively," *San Francisco Chronicle,* November 8, 1967; Russ Cone, "Victor Scores Even in Dobbs Strongholds," *San Francisco Examiner,* November 8, 1967.

15. Michael Harris, "New Mayor Seeks Community Unity," *San Francisco Chronicle,* November 9, 1967; Editorial, *San Francisco Chronicle,* November 9, 1967.

16. Joseph L. Alioto, "For American Cities—A Declaration of Independence," inaugural address, January 8, 1972, in Joseph L. Alioto Papers, SFHC, box 17, folder 36. See also Christopher Wolfe, "Subsidiarity: The 'Other' Ground of Limited Government," in Grasso et al., *Catholicism, Liberalism, and Communitarianism,* 81–96.

17. The Hurley quote is from a letter from the bishop to members of the Citizens' Committee, May 16, 1969, Mark J. Hurley Papers, CAASF, San Francisco State College Correspondence folder. The criticism of Alioto is from Progressive Labor Party, "Alioto: 'Isolate the Maoists,'" flyer, copy in ibid. See also Robert Smith, Richard Axen, and DeVere Pentony, *By Any Means Necessary* (San Francisco: Jossey-Bass, 1970), 228, 308–314; William H. Orrick Jr., *College in Crisis: A Report to the National Commission on the Causes and Prevention of Violence* (Nashville: Aurora, 1970), 151–153.

18. Randy M. Shilts, "Mecca or Ghetto? Castro Street," *The Advocate,* vol. 209, February 9, 1977, 20–23; Godfrey, *Neighborhoods in Transition,* 94–130.

19. Father William Cane, quoted in Jeffrey M. Burns, "Priests in Revolt: The San Francisco Association of Priests," *U. S. Catholic Historian* 26, 3 (2008): 66. See also Jeffrey M. Burns, "'The Love Book,' the Counterculture, and the Catholic City," *Argonaut: Journal of the San Francisco Historical Society* 5, 1 (Spring 1994): 22–28; Jeffrey M. Burns, "Beyond the Immigrant Church: Gays and Lesbians and the Catholic Church in San Francisco, 1977–1987," *U.S. Catholic Historian* 19, no. 1 (Winter 2001): 79–92; Burns, "Eugene Boyle."

20. Joshua Paddison, "Summers of Worry, Summers of Defiance: San Franciscans for Academic Freedom and Education and the Bay Area Opposition to HUAC, 1959–1960," *California History* 78, no. 3 (1999): 188–201.

21. Martin Meeker, *Contacts Desired: Gay and Lesbian Communications and Community, 1940s–1970s* (Chicago: University of Chicago Press, 2006); Elizabeth A. Armstrong, *Forging Gay Identities: Organizing Sexuality in San Francisco, 1950–1994* (Chicago: University of Chicago Press, 2002); Nan Alamilla Boyd, *Wide Open Town: A History of Queer San Francisco to 1965* (Berkeley: University of California Press, 2003); Josh Sides, *Erotic City: Sexual Revolutions and the Making of Modern San Francisco* (New York: Oxford University Press, 2009); Christopher Agee, "Gayola: Police Professionalization and the Politics of San Francisco's Gay Bars, 1950–1968," *Journal of the History of Sexuality* 15 (September 2006): 462–489; Christopher Agee, "The Streets of San Francisco: Blacks, Beats, Homosexuals, and the San Francisco Police Department, 1950–1968," Ph.D. diss., University of California, Berkeley, 2005; Gayle Rubin, "Sites, Settlements, and Urban Sex: Archaeology and the Study of Gay Leathermen in San Francisco 1955–1995," in *Archaeologies of Sexuality*, ed. Robert Schmidt and Barbara Voss (London: Routledge, 2000).

22. Bill Morgan and Nancy J. Peters, eds., *Howl on Trial: The Battle for Free Expression* (San Francisco: City Light Books, 2006); Michael Davidson, *The San Francisco Renaissance: Poetics and Community at Mid-Century* (New York: Cambridge University Press, 1991); Charles Perry, *The Haight-Ashbury: A History* (New York: Random House, 1984.

23. Warren Hinckle, "Left Wing Catholics," *Ramparts* 6 (November 1967): 15–24; Burns, "No Longer Emerging"; Claudia Orenstein, *Festive Revolutions: The Politics of Popular Theater and the San Francisco Mime Troupe* (Jackson: University Press of Mississippi, 1998); Boyd, *Wide Open Town*; Bell, "To Strive for Economic and Social Justice."

24. Alioto, "For American Cities." For a strong leftist critique, see "Mayor Joe Alioto," FoundSF, available online at http://www.foundsf.org/index.php?title=Mayor_Joe_Alioto. The critique was co-written by Calvin Welch, an influential community organizer in the Haight-Ashbury District during the administrations of Alioto and George Moscone.

25. The exchange between a demonstrator and Mayor Alioto at the opening of the BART station was captured on film in the documentary *Redevelopment: A Marxist Analysis*, Resolution Films/California Newsreel, 1975. The documentary was a cooperative enterprise of five left-wing activists in the Mission District and was intended to be used as a community organizing tool; a copy of the film is in the audiovisual library of San Francisco State University, and a two-minute clip, which includes explicit critiques of the Alioto administration's approach to redevelopment, is available online at http://www .archive.org. This chapter draws on the following works, several of which analyze the intersection of ethnic/racial issues and contests over land use policy: Wirt, *Power in the City*; Mollenkopf, *The Contested City*; Rufus P. Browning, Dale Rogers Marshall, and David H. Tabb, *Protest Is Not Enough: The Struggle of Blacks and Hispanics for Equality in Urban Politics* (Berkeley: University of California Press, 1984); Ferman, *Governing the Ungovernable City*; DeLeon, *Left Coast City*; McGovern, *The Politics of Downtown Development*; Hartman, *City for Sale*; Estella Habal, *San Francisco's International Hotel: Mobilizing the Filipino American Community in the Anti-Eviction Movement* (Philadelphia: Temple University Press, 2007).

26. The term "Hub City" was widely used in the press and at public meetings of business, labor, and civic organizations during this period: see "The Bay Hub," editorial, *San Francisco Chronicle*, August 28, 1980. See also Wirt, *Power in the City*, 187–193.

27. On BART, see J. Allen Whitt, *Urban Elites and Mass Transportation: The Dialectics of Power* (Princeton, N.J.: Princeton University Press, 1982).

28. This and the next three paragraphs draw on Hartman, *City for Sale,* 65–140; William Issel, "SOMA: People, Places and Politics in a Changing Urban District," lecture presented at the California Historical Society, July 11, 1996, San Francisco; James E. Carlin, "Store Front Lawyers in San Francisco," in *Culture and Civility in San Francisco,* ed. Howard S. Becker (Chicago: Aldine, 1971), 125–151.

29. "Mayor Joseph L. Alioto and Redevelopment," statement prepared for the 1971 mayoral election, Joseph L. Alioto Papers, SFHC, box 18, folder 5.

30. Allan B. Jacobs, *Making City Planning Work* (Chicago: American Society of Planning Officials, 1978), 264. According to Jacobs, "South of Market was another place [in addition to the Haight-Ashbury District] on which I could never get a handle." See also *San Francisco Examiner and Chronicle,* April 25, 1976.

31. "Mayor Joseph L. Alioto and Redevelopment."

32. Ibid.; Joseph L. Alioto, "Solving the Urban Crisis," September 15, 1971, Joseph L. Alioto Papers, SFHC, box 18, folder 15, series 5; "The Guardian Interview: Sheriff-Election Richard Hongisto," *San Francisco Bay Guardian,* December 22, 1971.

33. Wirt, *Power in the City,* 266–268; *San Francisco Examiner,* March 29–30, 1972; G. L. Bedford, "The November Election and the Blacks of San Francisco," Joseph L. Alioto Papers, SFHC, box 18, folder 14, series 5.

34. *San Francisco Examiner,* March 29, 1972; Labor Assembly for Community Action, press release dated October 6, 1971, Joseph L. Alioto Papers, SFHC, box 18, folder 15, series 5.

35. Leroy King, interview by John J. Rosen, November 6, 2002, San Francisco; "Curtis McClain Oral History," in "Fighting for Racial Justice: Warehouse Local 6, 1947–1960," ed. Harvey Schwartz, *The Dispatcher,* February 10, 1995.

36. *Sun Reporter,* November 6, November 13, 1971; *San Francisco Chronicle,* September 28–29, 1971; Labor Assembly for Community Action, press release dated October 6, 1971.

37. *San Francisco Examiner,* March 29, 1972; "Black Youth Group Campaigns for Alioto," Joseph L. Alioto Papers, SFHC, box 18, folder 14, series 5; *San Francisco Examiner,* March 27, 1972.

38. Joseph L. Alioto, "Carl Stokes—a Great Mayor, and an Extraordinary Letter," press release dated September 21, 1971, in Joseph L. Alioto Papers, SFHC, box 18, folder 14, series 5.

39. Joseph Alioto to Carl Stokes, September 20, 1971, and Alioto campaign pamphlet, in ibid., box 18, folder 10.

40. Wirt, *Power in the City,* 175–177, 265–268; David Jenkins, presentation at the Labor and Politics: Who Pressures Whom?" conference, February 7, 1989, San Francisco (audio transcript, side 2), in LARC; Charles H. (Henry) Issel, president of Local 6, International Brotherhood of Electrical Workers, interview by the author, May 1975, San Francisco.

41. *San Francisco Examiner and Chronicle,* October 3, 1971; *San Francisco Examiner,* June 19, 1972; Michael McCone to Bernie Orsi, memorandum, n.d. but 1971, Joseph L. Alioto Papers, SFHC, box 18, folder 13, series 5; Wirt, *Power in the City,* 245–250.

42. This and the next three paragraphs draw on Mike Miller, *A Community Organizer's Tale: People and Power in San Francisco* (Berkeley, Calif.: Heyday, 2009).

43. Ibid., 19–32.

44. Ibid., 33–40.

45. Joseph L. Alioto "Latin American Community Leaders Committee Backs Alioto," press release dated October 28, 1971, in Joseph L. Alioto Papers, SFHC, box 18, folder 14; Miller, *A Community Organizer's Tale,* 68–74, 279–281.

46. Joseph L. Alioto, "Report on the State of Affairs of the City," press release dated October 4, 1971, in Joseph L. Alioto Papers, SFHC, box 17, folder 59, series 5, 1–2; Joseph L. Alioto, "Senator Moscone Endorses Mayor Alioto for Re-election," press release dated September 22, 1971, in ibid., box 18, folder 14; Joseph L. Alioto, "Alioto Conservation Actions Draw Foran Praise," press release dated October 29, 1971, in ibid. box 18, folder 14.

47. *San Francisco Chronicle,* October 20, 1971; *San Francisco Labor,* July 9, 1971; Wirt, *Power in the City,* 204–207.

48. *San Francisco Examiner and Chronicle,* October 31, 1971; *San Francisco Chronicle,* September 18, October 17, 1971.

49. *San Francisco Examiner,* October 15, 1971. The decision in *Marsili v. Pacific Gas and Electric* is available online at http://law.justia.com.

50. *San Francisco Chronicle,* October 18, 1971.

51. Ibid., October 19, 1971; "Attention San Franciscans" election flyer, in Joseph L. Alioto Papers, SFHC, box 18, folder 11, series 5; Roberts, *Dianne Feinstein,* 103–113.

52. Joseph L. Alioto to John F. Henning, September 15, 1971, and Daniel F. Del Carlo to Joseph Alioto, October 19, 1971, in Joseph L. Alioto Papers, SFHC, box 18, folder 10, series 5; "Statement by Mayor Joseph L. Alioto re COPE Endorsement," September 20, 1971, in ibid., box 18, folder 14, series 5; Roberts, *Dianne Feinstein,* 104; *San Francisco Chronicle,* October 25, 1971. The vote counts are from San Francisco Election Records, Registrar of Voters, City and County of San Francisco, 1971, and *San Francisco Examiner,* November 3, 1971.

53. The description of the CRG coalition is based on my experience as a participant in the Proposition K and subsequent district election campaigns. See also Wade Crowfoot, "District Elections in San Francisco," San Francisco Planning and Urban Research, available online at http://www.spur.org.

54. Jacobs, *A Rage for Justice,* 291–293, is the source for the quote. On the Zebra murders, see Sanders with Cohen, *The Zebra Murders*; Clark Howard, *Zebra: The True Account of the 179 Days of Terror in San Francisco* (New York: Richard Marek, 1979).

55. The Northern California Alliance was "a political action organization building for socialism in the United States": "Who We Are," *Common Sense,* April 1976, 19. Robert W. Cherny, "San Francisco's Return to District Elections: The Role of the Labor Council, 1973–1977," paper presented at the Fifth Annual Southwest Labor Studies Conference, Dominguez Hills, Calif., April 20–21, 1979 (copy in my possession); Barbara Parker and Bill Issel, "District versus At-Large Elections," *Common Sense,* April 1976, 13; Mike Davis, "SF Draws the Line," *Common Sense,* April 1976, 13.

56. Kevin Starr, "Proposition A," *San Francisco Examiner,* August 21, 1980. On Jonestown, see Tim Reiterman, *Raven: The Untold Story of the Reverend Jim Jones and His People* (New York: Penguin, 1982); Deborah Layton, *Seductive Poison: A Jonestown Survivor's Story of Life and Death in the People's Temple* (New York: Anchor, 1999).

57. See Mike Weiss, *Double Play: The Hidden Passions behind the Double Assassination of George Moscone and Harvey Milk,* 2d ed. (San Francisco: Vince Emery Productions, 2010); Mullen, *The Egg Man's Son,* 177–185.

58. Dick Nolan, "District Election Repealer," *San Francisco Examiner,* June 18, 1980; Russ Cone, "Last Salvos from Proposition A Campaigners," *San Francisco Examiner,* August 13, 1980.

59. Carol Kroot, "San Francisco: 'Pluralism Run Amok,'" *San Francisco Progress,* August 15, 1980.

60. For a lively recounting of the city's "cultural shift" that focuses on "the people who radically changed San Francisco during the 1960s and 1970s," see David Talbot,

Season of the Witch: Enchantment, Terror, and Deliverance in the City of Love (New York: Free Press, 2012), xvii. For two contrasting interpretations of San Francisco politics since 1980, compare DeLeon, *Left Coast City,* and Rich DeLeon, "Only in San Francisco: San Francisco's Political Culture in Comparative Perspective," San Francisco Planning and Urban Research newsletter, December 2002, available online at http://www.spur.org, with G. William Domhoff, "Why San Francisco Is Different: Progressive Activists and Neighborhoods Have Had a Big Impact," available online at http://www2.ucsc.edu.

61. *San Francisco Examiner,* December 9–10, December 13, 1982, January 4, 1983; *New York Times,* December 10, 1982; DeLeon, *Left Coast City,* 24, 30, 166.

62. The Archbishop Quinn quote is from Don Lattin, "The Diplomat," *San Francisco Examiner Image,* August 30, 1987, 18.

CONCLUSION

1. For a political sociology perspective on these reforms at the level of national policy. see G. William Domhoff and Michael J. Webber, *Class and Power in the New Deal: Corporate Moderates, Southern Democrats, and the Liberal-Labor Coalition* (Stanford, Calif.: Stanford University Press, 2011).

2. See Roger W. Lotchin, *The Bad City in the Good War: San Francisco, Los Angeles, Oakland, and San Diego* (Bloomington: Indiana University Press, 2003), 6; Roger W. Lotchin, "California Cities and the Hurricane of Change: World War II in the San Francisco, Los Angeles, and San Diego Metropolitan Areas," *Pacific Historical Review* 63 (August 1994): 393–420.

3. Edward P. Eichler to George Johns, July 20, 1966, in San Francisco Labor Council Records, LARC, box 20, Redevelopment folder.

4. Don Mitchell, *The Right to the City: Social Justice and the Fight for Public Space* (New York: Guilford, 2003). For a sampling of recent scholarship on Catholics in urban America, see John T. McGreevy, *Catholicism and American Freedom: A History* (New York: W.W. Norton and Company, 2003); Steven M. Avella, *This Confident Church: Catholic Leadership and Life in Chicago, 1940–1965* (Notre Dame, Ind.: University of Notre Dame Press, 1992); Michael E. Engh, *Frontier Faiths: Church, Temple, and Synagogue in Los Angeles, 1846–1888* (Albuquerque: University of New Mexico Press 1992); Thomas H. O'Connor, *Boston Catholics: A History of the Church and Its People* (Boston: Northeastern University Press, 1998); Kenneth J. Heineman, *A Catholic New Deal: Religion and Reform in Depression Pittsburgh* (University Park: Pennsylvania State University Press, 1999); Mary Lethert Wingerd, *Claiming the City: Politics, Faith, and the Power of Place in St. Paul* (Ithaca, N.Y.: Cornell University Press, 2001); Deirdre M. Moloney, *American Catholic Lay Groups and Transatlantic Social Reform in the Progressive Era* (Chapel Hill: University of North Carolina Press, 2002); Evelyn Savidge Stern, *Ballots and Bibles: Ethnic Politics and the Catholic Church in Providence* (Ithaca, N.Y.: Cornell University Press, 2004); Roberto Treviño, *Church in the Barrio: Mexican American Ethno Catholicism in Houston* (Chapel Hill: University of North Carolina Press, 2006); Steven M. Avella, *Sacramento and the Catholic Church* (Reno: University of Nevada Press, 2008); James T. Fisher, *On the Irish Waterfront: The Crusader, the Movie, and the Soul of the Port of New York* (Ithaca, N.Y.: Cornell University Press, 2009).

5. David Harvey, *Social Justice and the City,* rev. ed. (Athens: University of Georgia Press, 2008); Sandel, *Democracy's Discontent*; David A. Hollinger, *Postethnic America: Beyond Multiculturalism,* rev. ed. (New York: Basic, 2006).

6. Susan S. Fainstein, *The Just City* (Ithaca, N.Y.: Cornell University Press, 2010); Nancy Fraser, "Rethinking the Public Sphere: A Contribution to the Critique of Actually Existing Democracy," in *Habermas and the Public Sphere,* ed. Craig Calhoun (Cambridge, Mass.: MIT Press, 1992), 109–142; Nancy Fraser, *Scales of Justice: Reimagining Political Space in a Globalizing World* (New York: Columbia University Press, 2010); on "comprehensive pluralism" see Michel Rosenfeld, *Law, Justice, Democracy, and the Clash of Cultures: A Pluralist Account* (New York: Cambridge University Press, 2011); Judith Butler, Jürgen Habermas, Charles Taylor, and Cornel West, *The Power of Religion in the Public Sphere* (New York: Columbia University Press, 2011); Jürgen Habermas, *An Awareness of What Is Missing: Faith and Reason in a Post-Secular Age* (Malden, Mass.: Polity, 2011).

7. "Separation of Church and State," October 28, 1984, in Bernard C. Cronin Papers, CAASF, Homilies/Papers folder.

8. For cogent discussions of how these and related tensions have become major themes in American political culture since the 1970s, see James T. Kloppenberg, *Reading Obama: Dreams, Hope, and the American Political Tradition* (Princeton, N.J.: Princeton University Press, 2011), especially chapter 2, "From Universalism to Particularism," and Daniel T. Rodgers, *Age of Fracture* (Cambridge, Mass.: Harvard University Press, 2011), especially chapter 3, "The Search for Power."

INDEX

WILLIAM ISSEL is Professor of History Emeritus at San Francisco State University and Visiting Professor of History at Mills College. He is the author of *For Both Cross and Flag: Catholic Action, Anti-Catholicism, and National Security Politics in World War II San Francisco* (Temple) and *Social Change in the United States 1945–1983*. He is the coauthor of *San Francisco, 1865–1932: Politics, Power, and Urban Development,* and co-editor and contributor to *American Labor and the Cold War: Grassroots Politics and Postwar Political Culture.*